ARCHAEOLOGY, ANTHROPOLOGY, AND INTERSTELLAR COMMUNICATION

Edited by Douglas A. Vakoch

National Aeronautics and Space Administration
Office of Communications
Public Outreach Division
History Program Office
Washington, DC
2014

The NASA History Series
NASA SP-2013-4413

Library of Congress Cataloging-in-Publication Data

Archaeology, anthropology, and interstellar communication / edited by
Douglas A. Vakoch.
    p. cm. -- (The NASA history series)
  "SP-2013-4413."
1. Life on other planets. 2. Extraterrestrial anthropology. 3.
Interstellar communication. 4. Exobiology. 5. Archaeoastronomy. I.
Vakoch, Douglas A.
  QB54.A74 2012
  999--dc23
                                2011053528

This publication is available as a free download at
http://www.nasa.gov/ebooks.

ISBN 978-1-62683-013-4

To Chris Neller,
for her ongoing support of the
Search for Extraterrestrial Intelligence

TABLE OF CONTENTS

ACKNOWLEDGMENTS

To the authors of *Archaeology, Anthropology, and Interstellar Communication*, I especially appreciate the innovation and depth of the research they share here. They deserve special thanks for thoughtfully engaging one another's ideas, as reflected in the numerous cross-references between chapters throughout the volume. Paul Duffield captures the essential themes of this conversation in his compelling cover art, and I am grateful for his creativity in translating these ideas into images, giving readers an overview of the contents before they even open the book.

Over the past 15 years, many colleagues from the SETI Institute have shared with me their insights into the Search for Extraterrestrial Intelligence, as well as the ways we can best communicate this work to the broader public. I especially thank Molly Bentley, Anu Bhagat, James Brewster, Steve Brockbank, Edna DeVore, Frank Drake, Sophie Essen, Andrew Fraknoi, John Gertz, Gerry Harp, Jane Jordan, Ly Ly, Michelle Murray, Chris Munson, Chris Neller, Tom Pierson, Karen Randall, Jon Richards, Pierre Schwob, Seth Shostak, and Jill Tarter. I am grateful to John Billingham for his many years of friendship, generosity, and commitment to exploring the societal dimensions of astrobiology. We miss him, but his memory lives on.

I warmly acknowledge the administration, faculty, staff, and students of the California Institute of Integral Studies (CIIS), especially for support from Joseph Subbiondo, Judie Wexler, and Tanya Wilkinson. Much of the work of editing this volume was made possible through a generous sabbatical leave from my other academic responsibilities at CIIS. In addition, I thank Harry and Joyce Letaw as well as Jamie Baswell for their intellectual and financial contributions to promoting the Search for Extraterrestrial Intelligence.

Among the organizations that have fostered discussions on the topics in this volume, I especially want to recognize the International Academy of Astronautics (IAA), the American Anthropological Association (AAA), and the Society for Cross-Cultural Research (SCCR). Several of the chapters in this volume are elaborations of papers first presented at AAA annual conferences.

For their openness to considering a new topic for the NASA History Series, I thank Steve Dick and Bill Barry. I am also grateful to them and to Steve Garber for leading such a thorough and helpful review process. I appreciate Yvette Smith for moving this volume into production so steadfastly and efficiently, and I thank Nadine Andreassen for her diligence in publicizing the book.

On the production side, Kimberly Ball Smith and Mary Tonkinson carefully copyedited the manuscript, and Heidi Blough created the index. In the Communications Support Services Center at NASA Headquarters, I thank the entire team that brought this book to print. Mary Tonkinson and George Gonzalez proofread the layout, and Tun Hla handled the printing. Supervisors Christopher Yates, Barbara Bullock, Cindy Miller, and Michael Crnkovic oversaw the entire process.

To my wife, Julie Bayless, I am grateful in more ways that I can or will share here. Thank you, forever.

LIST OF FIGURES

Reconstructing Distant Civilizations and Encountering Alien Cultures

Douglas A. Vakoch

On 8 April 1960, astronomer Frank Drake inaugurated a new era in the search for civilizations beyond Earth. Pointing the 85-foot telescope of the National Radio Astronomy Observatory (NRAO) in Green Bank, West Virginia, toward two Sun-like stars in the galactic neighborhood, he sought the first direct evidence of extraterrestrial intelligence. Tuning to a frequency of 1420 megahertz, he hoped that this would be a universal meeting place, known also by astronomers on other worlds as being the emission frequency of hydrogen, the universe's most prevalent element.

Although this experiment, which Drake dubbed Project Ozma, did not confirm the existence of life beyond Earth, it did inspire the development of a new field of science: the Search for Extraterrestrial Intelligence (SETI). Since that first experiment, capable of eavesdropping on the universe at only one frequency at a time, the power and extent of SETI searches have grown dramatically. As one measure of this discipline's development and to commemorate the 50th anniversary of Project Ozma, astronomers from 15 countries on 6 continents conducted a coordinated series of observations called Project Dorothy, named after the protagonist of L. Frank Baum's book series about the enchanted world of Oz.[1]

If a radio signal is detected in a modern SETI experiment, we could well know that another intelligence exists, but not know what they are saying. Any rapid, information-rich fluctuations encoded in the radio signals might be smoothed out while collecting weak signals over extended periods of time,

---

1. Shin-ya Narusawa, et al., "Project Dorothy: The 50th Anniversary of Project OZMA, Worldwide Joint SETI Observation," paper presented at the annual meeting of the Astronomical Society of Japan, September 2011.

increasing the chances of detecting these signals, but losing the content they bear in the process.

Even if we detect a civilization circling one of our nearest stellar neighbors, its signals will have traversed trillions of miles, reaching Earth after traveling for years. Using a more sober estimate of the prevalence of life in the universe, our closest interstellar interlocutors may be so remote from Earth that their signals would take centuries or millennia to reach us. Moreover, any civilization we contact will have arisen independently of life on Earth, in the habitable zone of a star stable enough to allow its inhabitants to evolve biologically, culturally, and technologically. The evolutionary path followed by extraterrestrial intelligence will no doubt diverge in significant ways from the one traveled by humans over the course of our history.

To move beyond the mere detection of such intelligence, and to have any realistic chance of comprehending it, we can gain much from the lessons learned by researchers facing similar challenges on Earth. Like archaeologists who reconstruct temporally distant civilizations from fragmentary evidence, SETI researchers will be expected to reconstruct distant civilizations separated from us by vast expanses of space as well as time. And like anthropologists, who attempt to understand other cultures despite differences in language and social customs, as we attempt to decode and interpret extraterrestrial messages, we will be required to comprehend the mindset of a species that is radically Other.

Historically, most of the scientists involved with SETI have been astronomers and physicists. As SETI has grown as a science, scholars from the social sciences and humanities have become involved in the search, often focusing on how humans may react to the detection of extraterrestrial life. The present volume examines the contributions of archaeology and anthropology to contemporary SETI research, drawing on insights from scholars representing a range of disciplines. The remaining sections of this introduction provide a chapter-by-chapter overview of the book as a whole. As befits a volume published in the NASA History Series, this collection emphasizes the value of understanding the historical context of critical research questions being discussed within the SETI community today.

Early versions of some of the chapters in this book were first presented in symposia on SETI organized by the editor and held at three annual conferences of the American Anthropological Association (AAA). The broader significance of these AAA sessions is that they represent the major SETI research areas judged important by the established scholarly community of anthropologists and archaeologists in the United States today. Indeed, the research presented in these sessions was sufficiently important that for three consecutive years, symposia addressing SETI were selected for this profession's major annual conference after a rigorous and competitive peer-review process that rejects a sizable proportion of symposium proposals.[2]

Each of these symposia addressed topics that were related to the overarching conference themes for their respective years. The first AAA session to deal specifically with SETI was held during the 2004 annual meeting, which had as its theme "Magic, Science, and Religion." Approaching this theme through an examination of scientific knowledge, this SETI symposium was called "Anthropology, Archaeology, and Interstellar Communication: Science and the Knowledge of Distant Worlds." The next year, when attendees met in Washington, DC, to explore the conference theme "Bridging the Past into the Present," the SETI session was named "Historical Perspectives on Anthropology and the Search for Extraterrestrial Intelligence (SETI)" and was later featured as a cover story in *Anthropology Today*, a leading international journal. Finally, at the 2006 conference on the theme "Critical Intersections/Dangerous Issues," the SETI symposium emphasized the intersection of multiple disciplinary perspectives from the social sciences. That symposium, titled "Culture, Anthropology, and the Search for Extraterrestrial Intelligence (SETI)," was held in San Jose, California.[3]

Historical Perspectives on SETI

To say that astronomers have been conducting SETI experiments for over a half-century might give the unwarranted impression that the search has been continuous. On the contrary, the earliest projects were of limited scope and duration, relying on existing observatories used in novel ways, with the addition of signal processing capable of distinguishing artificial signals from the cosmic background noise. Even the most ambitious project of the 1980s and early 1990s, NASA's SETI program, came about through an incremental approach, as detailed in this volume by John Billingham in "SETI: The NASA Years." Originally trained as a physician, as the former chief of NASA's SETI program, Billingham provides an autobiographical account of the key players

---

2. As Steven J. Dick notes in his chapter in this book, "The Role of Anthropology in SETI: A Historical View," a symposium at the 1974 annual convention of the American Anthropological Association addressed topics related to extraterrestrial anthropology, although this early session was not narrowly focused on SETI, as were the 2004–2006 symposia.

3. For a more in-depth description of these SETI symposia, see Douglas A. Vakoch, "Anthropological Contributions to the Search for Extraterrestrial Intelligence," in *Bioastronomy 2007: Molecules, Microbes, and Extraterrestrial Life*, ASP Conference Series, vol. 420, ed. Karen J. Meech et al. (San Francisco: Astronomical Society of the Pacific, 2009), pp. 421–427.

and events that eventually led to an innovative program with a multimillion-dollar annual budget. Through a methodical process that moved from a small in-house feasibility study, through a clearly articulated design study, to a series of in-depth science workshops, Billingham and his colleagues built the foundation for a NASA-sponsored search that commenced on 12 October 1992, the 500th anniversary of Columbus's arrival in the New World.

But just one year into this project that was planned to continue for a decade, funding was cut and the project terminated. As historian Stephen J. Garber details in "A Political History of NASA's SETI Program," chapter 2 of this volume, the reasons were political and not scientific. NASA's SETI program had encountered political opposition earlier but had survived. In 1978, Senator William Proxmire (D-WI) had given the program a Golden Fleece Award, declaring it a waste of taxpayers' money. Ultimately, however, Proxmire was convinced by astronomer Carl Sagan that the detection of extra-terrestrial intelligence would provide evidence that civilizations can survive their technological adolescence—a conclusion that both of them deemed important at a time when humankind's own future seemed uncertain.

Senator Richard Bryan (D-NV), who targeted NASA's SETI program in the early 1990s, was less open to persuasion. And so, in the fall of 1993, the program was terminated. At a time when concerns over the federal budget deficit were paramount, SETI became a natural target, lacking lobbyists from industry to advocate for it in Congress. In the same year, NASA also faced other challenges: the Hubble Space Telescope was still suffering from faulty optics, and the multibillion-dollar International Space Station Program still needed to be funded. Despite repeated endorsements of SETI by the National Academy of Sciences and the strong consensus among scientists about how and where to search for signals from extraterrestrials, political realities prevailed and NASA's funding for the project was eliminated.

With the end of NASA's SETI program, astronomers increasingly relied on private funding for SETI experiments. As the number and variety of projects increased, those involved in the search engaged social scientists in an effort to plan for success. As historian Steven J. Dick makes clear in his chapter "The Role of Anthropology in SETI: A Historical View," this engagement started on a small scale shortly after the Project Ozma experiment took place. Beginning in the early 1960s, anthropologists sporadically debated the relevance of human evolution to understanding extraterrestrial civilizations, and they attempted to anticipate the cultural impacts of detecting extraterrestrial intelligence. Anthropologists contributed to this dialogue through a variety of meetings, including a joint Soviet-U.S. conference and NASA workshops on the evolution of intelligence and technology, as well as the societal impact of discovering life beyond Earth.

Among the outcomes of these collaborations with the SETI community, anthropologists contributed to discussions of the Drake Equation, a heuristic that estimates the number of civilizations in a galaxy currently broadcasting evidence of their existence. In particular, anthropologists attempted to quantify the likelihood that intelligence and technology would evolve on life-bearing worlds.

By Dick's analysis, if SETI scientists find the sort of artificial signal they seek, we can be sure it originated from an intelligence that has changed significantly over its lifetime. If extraterrestrial intelligence is much longer lived than human civilization—a presupposition of most SETI search strategies—then in Dick's view it will inevitably have undergone cultural evolution.

Archaeological Analogues

In standard SETI scenarios, where humans and extraterrestrials are separated by trillions of miles, even a signal traveling at the speed of light may take centuries or millennia to reach its recipients. Thus, interstellar communication may be a one-way transmission of information, rather than a back-and-forth exchange. As we search for analogies to contact at interstellar distances, archaeology provides some intriguing parallels, given that its practitioners—like successful SETI scientists—are charged with reconstructing long-lost civilizations from potentially fragmentary evidence. In "A Tale of Two Analogues: Learning at a Distance from the Ancient Greeks and Maya and the Problem of Deciphering Extraterrestrial Radio Transmissions," anthropologist Ben Finney and historian Jerry Bentley suggest that we might gain clues to decoding extraterrestrial messages by examining past attempts to decode dead languages right here on Earth. As their chapter shows, however, we need to be cautious about which examples to use for our case studies. Given the importance this analogy has played in SETI circles over the years, and the fact that the lessons highlighted in Finney and Bentley's chapter are also applicable to other translation and decryption challenges addressed elsewhere in this volume, an extended preview of their argument is in order.

Finney and Bentley begin by noting an oft-cited analogy for detecting a message-laden signal from space: the transmission of knowledge from ancient Greece to medieval Europe. During the Dark Ages, European scholars had lost vast numbers of Greek works on philosophy, literature, and science. Fortunately, however, copies of these treatises were preserved by Islamic scholars, particularly in Spain and Sicily. Thus, as Europe entered the Renaissance, Western scholars were able to recover these Greek classics from Islamic centers of learning, either directly from the original manuscripts or through Arabic translations. And over the succeeding decades and centuries, the "young" European civilization was able to learn from the older Greek civilization, even though the two were separated by long expanses of time.

The analogy is an apt one for contact between Earth and the extraterrestrial civilizations being sought by SETI, because if we do detect information-rich signals, they may come from civilizations long since dead. The impact may be even more edifying for us than the influx of classical scholarship was for early modern Europe. This reclaiming of ancient knowledge provided Renaissance Europeans with alternative ways of viewing the world, which led, in turn, to new syntheses of early modern and ancient insights. If someday we detect and decode messages from civilizations beyond Earth, we will have similar opportunities to juxtapose terrestrial and otherworldly views.

But, Finney and Bentley warn us, it may not be quite that easy. While the Greek comparison is informative, as with any analogy, it does not tell the whole story. For a more nuanced understanding, they turn to other examples of decoding ancient scripts: Egyptian and Mayan hieroglyphics. Considering here only the first case, the key to decoding ancient Egyptian hieroglyphics was found in a slab now known as the Rosetta Stone, discovered in 1799 by Napoleon's army during a French military campaign in Egypt. This stone contains the same text written in three languages. Because 19th-century European linguists could read one of these languages, they were eventually able to compare the three inscriptions and thereby decipher the writing system they had previously been unable to crack: Egyptian hieroglyphics.

To state what may be obvious, if we receive a message from extraterrestrials, we cannot count on their providing direct translations from one of their native languages to any terrestrial language. And that, say Finney and Bentley, could limit how much we can learn from extraterrestrials. We may be able to understand basic mathematics and astronomy, but once extraterrestrials begin to describe their cultures, interstellar comprehension may suffer considerably. Finney and Bentley point out that those initial successes in decoding scientific parts of an extraterrestrial message might actually stand in the way of understanding more culturally specific parts of the message. As an analogy, they note that when European scholars began decoding ancient Mayan hieroglyphs, their earliest successes were in recognizing the basic numbering system used by the Maya, as well as their calendar systems, which were based on the visible motions of the Moon and Sun. In short, math and science provided the foundation for communication, just as many SETI scientists have predicted will be the case for interstellar communication.

This apparent breakthrough in reading the Mayan glyphs reinforced a Neoplatonic idea that had circulated among European scholars for centuries and which was usually attributed to Plotinus. This Egyptian-born Roman philosopher of the 3rd century followed the Platonic tradition, in which the bedrock of reality is not in the things we can see with our eyes and feel with our hands; instead, ultimate reality consists of underlying Ideas or Forms that serve as blueprints for the material world. Plotinus applied this philosophical concept to Egyptian hieroglyphics, seeing them not as abstract representations of objects but as direct expressions of the ideal essence or divine nature of those objects. They could thus symbolize ideas without the intermediary of merely human languages. Maurice Pope summarizes Plotinus's view this way: "Each separate sign is in itself a piece of knowledge, a piece of wisdom, a piece of reality, immediately present."[4] Renaissance humanists likewise believed that Egyptian hieroglyphics offered a way to escape the messiness of spoken language by directly representing ideas.

As it turns out, Plotinus was wrong, but he was in good company. Right up to the early 19th century, most eminent Egyptologists agreed with him. They dismissed the possibility that hieroglyphs could represent something as mundane as spoken language. But in the 1820s, French linguist Jean-François Champollion used the Rosetta Stone to draw parallels between the as-yet-undeciphered Egyptian hieroglyphics and both well-understood Greek *and* a form of Egyptian script used widely in business transactions. As a result, Champollion was able to show that hieroglyphics often *do* represent sounds, much like other languages. Though Plotinus's dream was broken, so, too, was the mystery of Egyptian hieroglyphics.

SETI scientists can learn an important lesson from the history of decoding hieroglyphics. Preliminary assumptions about the nature of the message can lead us astray—especially when those assumptions help us to decode parts of the message. While it is true that some Mayan characters refer directly to numbers and months, the vast majority do not. The key then to decoding ancient hieroglyphics, and perhaps also messages from extraterrestrials, is to remain open to new possibilities, even if they seem to contradict initial successes.

Literary theorist Richard Saint-Gelais is less optimistic than Finney and Bentley that the linguistic techniques used to decode ancient texts can be successfully applied to interstellar messages. In "Beyond Linear B: The Meta-semiotic Challenge of Communication with Extraterrestrial Intelligence,"

---

4. Maurice Pope, *The Story of Decipherment: From Egyptian Hieroglyphic to Linear B* (London: Thames and Hudson, 1975), p. 21.

Saint-Gelais notes that the SETI scientists who receive a message from extra-terrestrial intelligence will face a twofold task. They must first recognize the signal as a message and must then determine what it means—all without having any prior arrangement with the sender about the acceptable ranges of formats or contents.

As a terrestrial analogy of this project, Saint-Gelais outlines the process by which ancient texts have been deciphered. Initially, the linguist needs to determine the constituent components of a language on the basis of a limited sample—its phonemes (or sounds) and words that bear semantic content. This must be done without knowing, for example, how many letters the unknown language contains and whether the variations between similar-looking characters are due to the differences that occur when writing down the same letter twice or to the fact that they represent two different letters.

The breakthrough in decoding unknown languages has usually come by finding a bilingual text in which the same passage appears in both the unknown language and a language known to the decipherer, as in the case of the Rosetta Stone. Even when only fragmentary texts are available, a transla-tor can sometimes identify proper names to use as a starting point. But in interstellar communication, we would have no bilingual texts and no proper names recognizable by both civilizations. In those rare instances when ter-restrial linguists have been able to break the code of a lost language without a bilingual text or known proper names, Saint-Gelais argues, they have used methods that would be difficult to apply to understanding interstellar mes-sages. For example, although Michael Ventris used purely formal methods in the 1950s to decipher Linear B from inscriptions on clay tablets found on the island of Crete, his success ultimately derived from his ability to recognize Linear B as a transcription of an ancient form of Greek—and that recognition required his familiarity with the Greek language.

Archaeologist and anthropologist Kathryn Denning raises similar concerns about the view often expressed by those most involved in SETI that decoding messages from extraterrestrials will be an easy task. In "Learning to Read: Interstellar Message Decipherment from Archaeological and Anthropological Perspectives," she urges caution when choosing the models we use to under-stand interstellar communication. Cryptological and other communications approaches share with SETI certain epistemological commitments, but Denning notes that these approaches also carry implicit assumptions that make them unsuitable for interpreting interstellar messages. As an example, Denning points out that Claude Shannon's information theory has been accepted in SETI circles as a useful tool for understanding communication between species. However, Denning questions its relevance as an analogy—at least as it is often used. She notes that whereas information theory can provide a quantitative measure of the complexity of a communication system, it does not tackle the challenge of determining what the communication *means*.

Likewise, the SETI community's reliance on cryptological models fails to recognize the false analogy between, on the one hand, breaking a code constructed by other humans and, on the other hand, understanding a message from an extraterrestrial. In the first, we already *know* the language, and the challenge is to find a key that will let us derive the original message from the encoded message. In interstellar communication, however, we cannot assume any shared language.

Denning, then, has significant reservations about the assertions of SETI scientists who contend that combining sufficient quantities of redundant information with select explanations, such as pictures of objects, will be enough to give extraterrestrials access to human ways of viewing the world. Instead, she maintains that the best linguistic analogies for comprehending alien minds come from cases in which the meaning of communications from other cultures remains opaque even after much study, as with the Rongorongo script or Linear A.

Archaeologist Paul Wason agrees with other contributors to this volume that there may be significant, perhaps insurmountable obstacles to interpreting the specific meaning of messages from extraterrestrials. Nevertheless, he argues in "Inferring Intelligence: Prehistoric and Extraterrestrial" that archaeology can make a significant contribution by helping to clarify when a signal is actually intended as a medium of communication. To do so, however, requires a creative combination of different lines of reasoning.

Wason observes that archaeologists sometimes use "ethnographic analogies," drawing upon an understanding of cultures to which modern-day anthropologies have access, so they can make inferences about past cultures to which we do not have as immediate and complete access. Thus, stone tools found at archaeological sites in Europe could be recognized as tools rather than naturally formed rocks only when they were seen as akin to the stone tools used by contemporary Native Americans. Similarly, Wason argues, SETI scientists may misidentify signs of extraterrestrial intelligence. The challenge, then, is to seek a wide enough array of analogies that scientists can come to recognize manifestations of extraterrestrial intelligence, even when they resemble a naturally occurring phenomenon.

Once we have those analogies, Wason argues, we will also need to have an "intellectual context" that enables us to identify signs of intelligence. Only when people took seriously the possibility that chipped rocks might be prehistoric tools were they predisposed to look for them. Until then, this core piece of evidence for reconstructing extinct civilizations was simply overlooked by archaeologists doing fieldwork in Europe. The difficulty of recognizing the unanticipated, Wason suggests, may provide a solution to the Fermi paradox, which asks, "If extraterrestrial intelligence exists, why haven't we found it?" Wason answers this question by noting that we have been unable to free ourselves sufficiently from our preconceptions of extraterrestrial intelligence to recognize its existence.

As we assemble the varieties of data from which we will judge whether we have made contact with extraterrestrial intelligence, Wason reminds us of the utility of the "cabling" method of reasoning, in which any single piece of evidence may in itself come up short, like the strands of a cable that each run only part of the cable's full length. Nevertheless, by recognizing that a solid argument—like a solid cable—may be made up of elements that are in themselves not sufficient to determine the artificiality of a signal, but that when intertwined may be strong, we may be open to recognizing intelligence where we might otherwise miss it.

While Wason recognizes many problems of interpreting symbolic systems—in which "signs" stand in an arbitrary relationship to the ideas they signify—he also maintains that we may be able to get a general sense of the intent of a message, even if we cannot divine its specific meaning. Indeed, he suggests that even our ability to detect purposive agency may be an evolved trait, which may be shared by intelligent beings on other worlds, making it plausible that even if we cannot understand *what* another civilization is trying to say, intelligent beings may have the capacity to recognize that *someone* is saying *something*.

Anthropology, Culture, and Communication

In "Anthropology at a Distance: SETI and the Production of Knowledge in the Encounter with an Extraterrestrial Other," anthropologist John Traphagan seeks an analogue for our attempts to comprehend extraterrestrial civilizations in Western efforts to understand Japanese culture. As noted earlier, in standard SETI scenarios, contact occurs across vast interstellar distances, on time scales of decades, centuries, or millennia. Contrary to the stereotype of anthropologists encountering members of other cultures face-to-face, learning their language in the process, the American anthropologist Ruth Benedict, a key interpreter of Japanese culture to the West, relied largely on data gathered by others for the research she was commissioned to do by the U.S. government during World War II. Unable to observe and interact with her subjects as anthropologists traditionally do, Benedict instead analyzed the transcripts of interviews with Japanese Americans in internment camps in the American Southwest. Despite these limitations, Benedict's book

The Chrysanthemum and the Sword provided keen insights into the Japanese mind, though much of the theoretical framework for her interpretations was drawn from her earlier book, *Patterns of Culture*.[5]

Information about an extraterrestrial civilization would be far more restricted, Traphagan argues, and our desire to rapidly assess the nature of our interstellar interlocutors will be strong. In spite of limited data we may have about an extraterrestrial civilization immediately after detecting a radio signal from another world, we can expect the news of the contact to be widely and rapidly disseminated. While anthropologists and other scholars attempt to make plausible inferences about the nature of this alien intelligence, public impressions—based more on humans than on the extraterrestrials themselves—will quickly form. When this phenomenon is compounded with "image management" on the part of the extraterrestrials, we will have to be even more cautious about assuming that our initial evaluations of extraterrestrials accurately reflect their true nature.[6]

If we make contact with an extraterrestrial civilization, anthropologist Douglas Raybeck argues that we have much to gain by studying the varied ways that diverse terrestrial cultures have responded to contact with more technologically advanced societies right here on Earth. In his "Contact Considerations: A Cross-Cultural Perspective," Raybeck considers a variety of stances we might take upon making contact with an extraterrestrial civilization, drawing lessons from Western colonial relationships with the Japanese, Iroquois, Chinese, Aztec, and Māori cultures. An indigenous society's willingness to absorb elements of another civilization can be either adaptive or insufficient to survive culturally intact, Raybeck argues. The Japanese, being both experienced and adept at incorporating new cultural practices even when doing so entailed significant social change, provide an especially good example of the flexibility needed when encountering an extraterrestrial civilization. Nevertheless, openness to other cultures does not guarantee a successful engagement; the Iroquois were also flexible and resourceful in dealing with other cultures but were ultimately defeated by a numerically and technologically superior adversary.

---

5. See Ruth Benedict, *The Chrysanthemum and the Sword: Patterns of Japanese Culture* (Boston: Houghton Mifflin, 1946); and Ruth Benedict, *Patterns of Culture* (Boston: Houghton Mifflin, 1934).

6. The messages we have sent into space thus far focus on humans' achievements and portray our species in a positive light. For an argument that we should transmit messages describing aspects of humankind which we often avoid, see Douglas Vakoch, "Honest Exchanges with ET," *New Scientist* 202, no. 2705 (22 April 2009): 22–23.

An isolationist stance can also fail, Raybeck argues, as it did when China's unwillingness to treat Western countries as equals resulted in a serious underestimation of their capabilities. Yet another danger arises when the invader can exploit existing divisions within an indigenous civilization, as was manifest in the case of the Aztecs.

Perhaps the best model for encountering extraterrestrials, Raybeck suggests, comes from the Māori, whose resistance to British incursions gained them the respect of their enemies while helping them to retain their pride after succumbing to more sophisticated organization and weaponry. The implications of Raybeck's analysis are considerable: although each terrestrial culture may have a natural approach to encountering aliens, some responses may be more effective than others. Given the probable technological superiority of any extraterrestrial civilizations we are likely to contact, we would be wise to consider all of our options.

In parallel with the diverse manifestations of culture we see on Earth, Traphagan argues in his second chapter, "Culture and Communication with Extraterrestrial Intelligence," that we should also anticipate multiple extraterrestrial cultures on many other civilization-bearing worlds. He views cultures—whether on Earth or beyond—as continually changing.[7] As a result, they allow for highly individualistic experiences of the world.[8] Consequently, Traphagan casts doubt on the common but often implicit assumption that

---

7. To reflect the transient nature of terrestrial cultures, we may need to abandon the sometimes-implicit goal of designing interstellar messages that express universal truths. For a proposal to send interstellar messages modeled after news stories, see Morris Jones, "A Journalistic Perspective on SETI-Related Message Composition," in *Civilizations Beyond Earth: Extraterrestrial Life and Society*, ed. Douglas A. Vakoch and Albert A. Harrison (New York: Berghahn Books, 2011), pp. 226–235. For an epistolary model of interstellar message construction, in which a series of messages is transmitted over an extended period of time, akin to a series of letters, see Douglas A. Vakoch, "Metalaw as a Foundation for Active SETI," *Proceedings of the Colloquium on the Law of Outer Space* 49 (2007): 537–541.

8. As Traphagan defines it, *culture* is a highly individualized process. To the extent that we wish to communicate this view of culture to extraterrestrials, we must shift our attention from efforts to explain cultural universals and instead focus on individual perspectives. Such an approach is consistent with viewing interstellar messages as works of art, in which the individual artist's vision is valued and seen as valid, even though it may not be shared by others—and in some cases precisely *because* it is not shared by others. For a discussion of related issues, see Douglas A. Vakoch, "The Art and Science of Interstellar Message Composition: A Report on International Workshops to Encourage Multidisciplinary Discussion," *Acta Astronautica* 68, nos. 3–4 (2011): 451–458.

technologically advanced civilizations will each progress toward a unitary culture, unlike the varied cultures we see among contemporary humans. Even on worlds with monolithic, global cultures, he expects room for disagreement between individuals. As a result, he argues that if an extraterrestrial civilization receives a message from Earth, there may be no consensus on whether to respond.

Consistent with arguments made in several of the earlier chapters, Traphagan anticipates significant challenges in understanding the intended meaning of any message from extraterrestrial intelligence; but he contends that this should not be our only goal. Instead, he recommends looking at the messages' implicit meanings, even if we cannot interpret their substantive content. What does their form suggest about how extraterrestrials communicate? And what do the forms of human messages say about us? Might extraterrestrials read the surplus radiation leaking into space from radio and TV transmitters on Earth as an indication that visual and auditory signals figure prominently in human communication? Such a recognition could help message recipients to prepare more intelligible replies, even lacking a comprehension of the specific content of the messages per se. Similarly, the intentional signals already sent from Earth to other civilizations as streams of ones and zeros may highlight the human capacity to think in terms of dualisms. Given that these implicit messages may be more informative than the explicit content, Traphagan encourages additional research on how we might better communicate such tacit meanings to another intelligence.

The closing chapter of this section—"Speaking for Earth: Transmitting Cultural Values Across Deep Space and Time" by psychologist Albert Harrison—argues the benefits of crafting messages to extraterrestrials even if the intended recipients never get them. In contrast to the dominant strategy within the international SETI community of listening for signals from extraterrestrials at radio or optical frequencies, proponents of an approach known as "Active SETI" advocate transmitting intentional signals to other worlds.[9] While terrestrial radio and television signals are being accidentally broadcast into space, as telecommunications grow more reliant on fiber optics and narrowly focused Earth-satellite transmission, these incidental transmissions are expected to become weaker and increasingly rare. Thus, if we wish to make ourselves known to other civilizations, there will be an ever greater need to send intentional signals in the future.

---

9. For an overview of key arguments in the debate about Active SETI, see Kathryn Denning, "Unpacking the Great Transmission Debate," in *Communication with Extraterrestrial Intelligence (CETI)*, ed. Douglas A. Vakoch (Albany: State University of New York Press, 2011), pp. 237–252.

Harrison reviews past attempts to signal our existence to extraterrestrials, ranging from messages borne on several of NASA's Pioneer and Voyager spacecraft in the 1970s to powerful radio transmissions sent from the Arecibo Observatory in Puerto Rico and the Evpatoria Planetary Radar in Ukraine. Indeed, such radio transmission efforts, though intermittent, have proliferated in the past few years—despite heated debates about whether humankind should reveal its existence to potentially hostile aliens.

Harrison also notes parallels between interstellar communication and projects to communicate with our human successors, such as marking nuclear waste sites to be identifiable by our descendants 10,000 years hence, establishing archives on the Moon that could withstand the vicissitudes of terrestrial conflict over the millennia, and launching a satellite designed to return to Earth in 50,000 years. (The latter project, named "KEO" after three phonemes said to be found in all terrestrial languages, was disbanded after the death of its founder, French artist Jean-Marc Philippe.) Whether we are attempting to communicate with distant extraterrestrial civilizations or with the progeny of our progeny, Harrison contends, we can learn much about human interests and values by examining what we hope to convey across the depths of time and space.

The Evolution and Embodiment of Extraterrestrials

In "The Evolution of Extraterrestrials: The Evolutionary Synthesis and Estimates of the Prevalence of Intelligence Beyond Earth," I argue that many astronomers have seen the development of intelligent life as an inevitable occurrence given proper environmental conditions on a planet; and even though such beings would not be identical to humans, we should expect to find significant parallels. A striking contrast to this position is seen in the writings of scientists from other disciplines, who hold widely differing views.

One clue to understanding the differences between the anthropologists, paleontologists, and biologists who speculate on extraterrestrials is suggested by a historical analysis, noting who wrote on the subject. Given the relatively small number of commentators on the topic, it seems more than coincidental that this group includes four of the major contributors to the evolutionary synthesis in the 1930s and 1940s. As I show, the exobiological arguments of Theodosius Dobzhansky and George Gaylord Simpson and, less directly, of H. J. Muller and Ernst Mayr are all related to their earlier work on formulating synthetic evolution. A survey of the views held by later anthropologists, paleontologists, and biologists reveals significant disagreements among them about evolution, disputes that persisted into the 1960s. By the close of the next decade, many but by no means all believed that "higher" life, particularly intelligent life, probably occurs quite infrequently in the universe. This shift in opinion can be attributed to a growing acceptance of the evolutionary synthesis.

In "Biocultural Prerequisites for the Development of Interstellar Communication," anthropologist Garry Chick analyzes the Drake Equation, a heuristic used to estimate the number of civilizations in our galaxy that are capable of interstellar communication. What are the relevant factors, Chick asks, that determine whether an intelligence sophisticated enough to create the technology required to contact other civilizations will evolve on another world? In the process, he demonstrates the importance of being clear about what we mean by *intelligence, culture,* and *technology.*

Rather than focusing on a unitary measure of intelligence, such as a standardized intelligence quotient (IQ), Chick emphasizes that different species may have different forms of intelligence. Dolphins, for example, may have a refined "auditory-musical" intelligence. One is reminded here of the anthropologist and physician team of Doris Jonas and David Jonas, who suggest in *Other Senses, Other Worlds* that alien intelligence dependent on sensory modalities unlike those of humans may have radically different ways of experiencing and conceptualizing their worlds.[10] Similar ideas have been a staple of science fiction as well. Naomi Mitchison's *Memoirs of a Spacewoman,* for example, suggests that radially symmetrical intelligence—in this case brainy starfish—might possess a multimodal logic to match their morphologies, while bilaterally symmetrical species, such as humans, are more prone to view the world in terms of simple dichotomies.[11]

Although mindful of the need to keep a sufficiently broad definition of *intelligence* and *culture* to be open to extraterrestrials with significantly different ways of encountering the world than humans, Chick maintains that the sort of intelligence that leads to advanced technology is rare on Earth and may be just as rare elsewhere in the universe. And no matter how we define *culture,* it is difficult to pinpoint the moment when one culture ends and another begins. To compound this difficulty, the Drake Equation poses an additional challenge: how can we use these data to estimate the lifetimes of independently evolved extraterrestrial civilization?

Chick offers various approaches to determining such quantitative estimates of factors in the Drake Equation—for example, by analyzing historical civilizations or applying datasets such as the Standard Cross-Cultural Sample

---

10. Doris Jonas and David Jonas, *Other Senses, Other Worlds* (New York: Stein and Day, 1976).

11. Naomi Mitchison, *Memoirs of a Spacewoman* (1962; rpt. Glasgow: Kennedy and Boyd, 2011).

to see how often advanced technologies develop.[12] At the same time, Chick cautions that estimates of this sort, however useful they may be in giving some empirical basis to the terms of the Drake Equation, are fraught with difficulties, such as finding societies sufficiently isolated from one another to guarantee truly independent technological development.

Ethologist Dominique Lestel suggests that we can profitably combine two approaches in order to better understand the challenges of interstellar communication. In his chapter, "Ethology, Ethnology, and Communication with Extraterrestrial Intelligence," Lestel recognizes the difficulties of making contact with biologically different organisms and proposes learning from the experiences of researchers who study the communication of chimpanzees, dolphins, and other animals even more distantly related to humans. Despite the divergences between the varied life-forms on Earth, Lestel notes, even species with radically different morphologies can have a significant amount of shared genetic material—something that will not be true of humans and extraterrestrials.

Lestel recommends blending this ethological perspective with an ethnological approach that draws upon the lessons learned by anthropologists who make contact with people from alien cultures. He cautions, however, that an ethnological approach cannot be applied directly. For example, typically (but not always, as we see in Traphagan's chapter on SETI and the production of knowledge) ethnologies are based on face-to-face contact, a situation unlikely to occur with civilizations separated by vast interstellar distances.

Should humans ever receive a message from an extraterrestrial civilization, Lestel predicts that the challenges faced in interpreting those messages could provoke in humans an existential crisis. If the challenges of understanding another civilization turn out to be as great as he expects, Lestel suggests that recognition of this fact in a post-contact world would sharpen our awareness of human understanding's inherent limits—forcing us to reexamine our fundamental presuppositions about epistemology.

Cognitive scientist William Edmondson argues that symbolic communication—in which the connection between sign and signified is arbitrary—is intrinsically limited for communicating with extraterrestrials. In "Constraints on Message Construction for Communication with Extraterrestrial Intelligence,"

---

12. The Standard Cross-Cultural Sample (SCCS) assigns coded variables to elements of 186 representative and relatively independent cultures. The SCCS was developed by anthropologists George P. Murdock and Douglas R. White and first described in their essay "Comparative Ethnographic Data, coded for the Standard Cross-Cultural Sample," *Ethnology* 8 (1969): 329–369. An updated version of Murdock and White's essay is available online at *http://escholarship.org/uc/item/62c5c02n*.

he points out the difficulty of interpreting symbolic artifacts created by other humans, such as the Neolithic and Early Bronze Age rock art of Northumberland or the Voynich manuscript, a late-15th- or 16th-century manuscript that appears to be linguistic in form but remains indecipherable to scholars.

After speculating on the physical environments in which extraterrestrial intelligence might evolve, Edmondson concludes that the factors affecting the propagation of sounds could vary so much from planet to planet as to make audition an unlikely universal. Instead, he argues for messages based on vision, a position that has long been advocated within the SETI community, albeit not without opposition.[13] As one example of a visual message, Edmondson suggests sending a "Postcard Earth," a grid-like collage of color snapshots showing multiple scenes of our world and its inhabitants. Interestingly, several individuals have independently submitted this same type of message to the SETI Institute's online project *Earth Speaks*, in which people from around the world are invited to propose their own messages for first contact with an extraterrestrial civilization. One pictorial message, sent from a participant in Les Ulis, France, shows buildings by a lake in that city, with inset views showing the location of Les Ulis on a map of Earth and then Earth's location in a broader galactic context (see Figure Introduction.1). This proposal from *Earth Speaks* is reminiscent of Edmondson's idea that a technologically advanced civilization may be able

Figure Introduction.1. This *Earth Speaks* message puts the sender's location—the town of Les Ulis, France—in broader geographical and astronomical contexts. *(SETI Institute)*

---

13. For an early argument promoting the use of pictorial messages in interstellar communication, see Bernard M. Oliver, "Interstellar Communication," in *Interstellar Communication: A Collection of Reprints and Original Contributions*, ed. A. G. W. Cameron (New York: Benjamin, 1963), pp. 294–305. For a more recent argument in favor of visual communication with extraterrestrials, see Kathryn Coe, Craig T. Palmer, and Christina Pomianek, "ET Phone Darwin: What Can an Evolutionary Understanding of Animal Communication and Art Contribute to Our Understanding of Methods for Interstellar Communication?," in Vakoch and Harrison, eds., *Civilizations Beyond Earth*, pp. 214–225, esp. p. 219. For a critique of the ease of interpreting pictorial messages, see Douglas A. Vakoch, "The Conventionality of Pictorial Representation in Interstellar Messages," *Acta Astronautica* 46, nos. 10–12 (2000): 733–736.

to recognize images of Earth through direct imaging techniques and thus to connect our messages with its own independent observations of our planet.

The chapters in this volume, then, combine incisive critique with hope that there is a response to the skepticism behind these critiques. Addressing a field that has been dominated by astronomers, physicists, engineers, and computer scientists, the contributors to this collection raise questions that may have been overlooked by physical scientists about the ease of establishing meaningful communication with an extraterrestrial intelligence. These scholars are grappling with some of the enormous challenges that will face humanity if an information-rich signal emanating from another world is detected. By drawing on issues at the core of contemporary archaeology and anthropology, we can be much better prepared for contact with an extraterrestrial civilization, should that day ever come.

CHAPTER ONE

SETI: The NASA Years

John Billingham

Introduction

To this volume dealing with the interplay of archaeology, anthropology, and interstellar communication, I have been asked to contribute a chapter on the story of SETI at NASA.[1] Since I was involved in it from the very beginning to the very end, 1969 to 1994, I can relate here only the highlights of that story. What follows is therefore something of a personal history of SETI in NASA, told in sequential form and omitting names, events, and numerous details due to lack of space.

To anyone who wishes to read a more comprehensive version of the story, I recommend the beautifully written article by Steven J. Dick in *Space Science Reviews*.[2] For even more detail, turn to the references at the end of Dick's

---

1. This chapter was initially prepared in 2000 for the celebration of Frank Drake's 70th birthday; it was recently published in *Searching for Extraterrestrial Intelligence: SETI Past, Present, and Future*, ed. H. Paul Shuch (Berlin, Heidelberg, New York: Springer, 2011), pp. 65–85. All the material in these pages remains as valid today as it was when first written. I am also delighted that Frank, whose name appears more than any other in this chapter, continues to be active at the SETI Institute in Mountain View, California. Frank provided some of the original stimulus for SETI at NASA. At every stage throughout the next quarter-century he participated in making the idea a reality. As the "Father of SETI," he played an active role—especially in the scientific community—in bringing the NASA project to fruition. In the beginning, Ozma was a bold and imaginative new venture in the exploration of the cosmos but was considered by many to be on the fringes of the scientific norm. By 1984, however, SETI was accepted by the scientific community as an exciting intellectual and technical challenge, and Frank was firmly established as the Chair of the SETI Institute's Board of Directors.

2. Steven J. Dick, "The Search for Extraterrestrial Intelligence and the NASA High-Resolution Microwave Survey (HRMS): Historical Perspectives," *Space Science Reviews* 64 (1993): 93–139. Dick is the former Charles A. Lindbergh Chair in Aerospace History at the National Air and Space Museum (2011–2012), Chief Historian at NASA (2003–2009), and Historian of Space Science at the U.S. Naval Observatory (1979–2003). On 1 November 2013, he began a one-year appointment as the Baruch S. Blumberg NASA/Library of Congress Chair in Astrobiology at the Library of Congress's John W. Kluge Center.

article. The events of the final year, 1993–1994, when NASA's SETI program was canceled by Congress, are well chronicled by Stephen J. Garber elsewhere in this book.[3]

1959–1969: Ten Years of Prologue

Giuseppe Cocconi and Philip Morrison published their seminal paper "Searching for Interstellar Communications" in 1959, establishing the radio region of the electromagnetic spectrum as a logical place to search for signals from extraterrestrials.[4] In the very next year, Frank Drake independently conducted Project Ozma, the first search for such signals, at the National Radio Astronomy Observatory in Green Bank, West Virginia.[5] In 1961 the National Academy of Sciences Space Science Board sponsored a small meeting at Green Bank with four objectives: "to examine the prospects for the existence of other societies in the Galaxy with whom communications might be possible; to attempt an estimate of their number; to consider some of the technical problems involved in the establishment of communication; and to examine ways in which our understanding of the problem might be improved."[6] The meeting was notable for many things but especially the genesis of the Drake Equation, the participation of Bernard (Barney) Oliver, and the conclusion that the estimated number of civilizations in the Milky Way capable of communicating with us may be smaller than a thousand or as great as one billion.

In 1963, Nikolai Kardashev conducted the Soviet Union's first search for signals from extraterrestrials.[7] The following year saw the conference on extraterrestrial civilizations at Byurakan in Armenia, organized by Viktor

---

3. See Stephen J. Garber, "A Political History of NASA's SETI Program," chapter 2 in this volume.

4. Giuseppe Cocconi and Philip Morrison, "Searching for Interstellar Communications," *Nature* 184 (19 September 1959): 844–846.

5. Frank Drake, "How Can We Detect Radio Transmission?" *Sky and Telescope* 19 (1960): 26–28, 87–89, 140–143.

6. J. P. T. Pearman, "Extraterrestrial Intelligent Life and Interstellar Communication: An Informal Discussion," in *Interstellar Communication: A Collection of Reprints and Original Contributions*, ed. A. G. W. Cameron (New York: W. A. Benjamin Inc., 1963), pp. 287–293.

7. N. S. Kardashev, "Transmission of Information by Extraterrestrial Civilizations," *Aston. Zhurnal* 41, no. 2 (March–April 1964): 282–287, trans. *Soviet Astronomy–AJ* 8, no. 2 (1964): 217–221, reprinted in *The Quest for Extraterrestrial Life: A Book of Readings*, ed. Donald Goldsmith (1980), pp. 39–47.

Ambartsumian and Kardashev and attended entirely by radio astronomers.[8] May of 1965 saw the first use of the term *CETI*—an acronym for Communication with Extraterrestrial Intelligence—by Rudolph Pesek of the Czech Academy of Sciences in his proposal to the Board of Trustees of the International Academy of Astronautics (IAA) to establish an international symposium on the subject. In 1966, Carl Sagan collaborated with Iosif Shklovskii on an English-language version of Shklovskii's 1962 book *Вселенная, жизнь, разум.* The translation was titled *Intelligent Life in the Universe.*[9] At this time I was Chief of the Biotechnology Division at NASA's Ames Research Center in the San Francisco Bay Area and was becoming aware of scientists in a sister division at Ames called Exobiology, which had been formed a few years earlier by Harold (Chuck) Klein and Richard (Dick) Young. These researchers introduced me to the Shklovskii-Sagan book late in 1968, and it changed my whole life.

1969: The Embryogenesis of SETI at NASA

Through 1969, mulling over *Intelligent Life in the Universe*, I began to realize that NASA Ames might be an ideal home for a program to actively pursue interstellar communication, as it was then known, by designing and using a large-scale radio telescope system to search for signals of extraterrestrial intelligent origin. In the Space Act of 1958, NASA had been specifically charged with the responsibility for conducting the exploration of space. The Exobiology Program had been established at Ames under Chuck Klein and Dick Young. Project Viking was being defined and was to include biology experiments designed to search for evidence of microbial life on Mars. Klein was Project Scientist for these undertakings. Ames already had a strong program in space science. I began to wonder whether it might be possible to build SETI telescopes in space or on the Moon. NASA had the capabilities to carry out all the necessary large-scale science and engineering, and one of Ames's roles was to be at the cutting edge of space exploration. Not least, I thought,

---

8. G. M. Tovmasyan, ed., *Vnzemnye tsivilizatsii: Trudy Soveshchaniia, Biurakan, 20–23 Maia 1964* (Erevan, Armenia, 1965), translated into English as *Extraterrestrial Civilizations: Proceedings of the First All-Union Conference on Extraterrestrial Civilizations and Interstellar Communication, Byurakan, 20–23 May 1964*, trans. Z. Lerman (Jerusalem: Israel Program for Scientific Translation, 1967).

9. Iosif S. Shklovskii and Carl Sagan, *Intelligent Life in the Universe* (San Francisco: Holden-Day, 1966).

NASA and Ames would have the vision and courage to explore the opportunities and perhaps to turn them into an active new venture. I was right.

In September, Hans Mark became director of the Ames Research Center. Mark believed strongly in personal contact, so he visited people in their offices and labs and engineering shops. When he came to find out about my division, I put to him the notion of beginning a study effort on interstellar communication. He thought it was a good idea but advised proceeding slowly and judiciously, since it would be such a new topic at NASA. With the agreement of Chuck Klein, then director of the Life Sciences Division at Ames, we carried out a small initial in-house feasibility study in the summer of 1970 and concluded that there were no impediments. Concurrently, we ran a large summer lecture series at Ames on interstellar communication, with Drake, Sagan, Oliver, A. G. W. Cameron, Ronald N. Bracewell, and others as speakers.[10] In the autumn, I met again with Hans Mark, and we decided to carry out a larger-scale conceptual study in the summer of 1971 under the aegis of the Summer Faculty Fellowship Program in Engineering Systems Design, run jointly every year by Ames and Stanford University and funded by NASA through the American Society of Engineering Education. I was co-director of these programs, together with Jim Adams, professor of mechanical engineering at Stanford. Neither of us had the right technical background for the topic, so we decided to co-opt a third person who knew radio science and engineering. The two principal candidates were Barney Oliver and Frank Drake. Barney, who was then vice president of research and development (R&D) at Hewlett-Packard, won out because of his vast knowledge of radio engineering. I approached him in October and asked if he would take the job. He agreed, with enthusiasm.

1971: Project Cyclops

For 10 weeks during the summer of 1971, 20 physical scientists and engineers (all professors in various related disciplines at colleges and universities around the country) gathered at Ames to conduct "A Design Study of a System for Detecting Extraterrestrial Intelligent Life." Under the inspiring leadership of Barney Oliver, and with advice from visiting experts in radio science and engineering (including Philip Morrison), the team put together a landmark report, which Barney dubbed "Project Cyclops." The report contained 15

---

10. C. Ponnnamperuma and A. G. W. Cameron, eds., *Interstellar Communication: Scientific Perspectives* (Boston: Houghton-Mifflin, 1974).

conclusions, 4 of which are especially relevant here: signaling was vastly more efficient than interstellar travel (the ratio is actually tens of orders of magnitude); the microwave region of the spectrum was the best place to detect incoming signals; the quiet region between the spectral lines of hydrogen and the hydroxyl radical—i.e., between 1420 and 1665 megahertz—was a natural "water hole" for communication between species; and construction of a ground-based phased array for interstellar communication over galactic distances was technologically feasible.

The conceptual design for Cyclops comprised an expandable phased array of 100-meter, fully steerable radio telescopes and a signal processing system that used an optical spectral analyzer to examine the 200-megahertz region of the water hole with a resolution not exceeding 1 hertz. Should it be necessary to build a complete system to achieve the sensitivity required to detect faint narrowband signals from star systems within a radius of 1,000 light-years, namely 1,000 of the 100-meter antennas, then the cost would be between $6 billion and $10 billion, spread over 10 to 15 years. The team also recommended that NASA initiate further scientific and engineering studies, which would lead to a more detailed engineering systems design over a three-to-five-year period.

Interestingly enough, the U.S. National Academy of Sciences and the Academy of Sciences of the USSR sponsored a joint conference on CETI in Byurakan, Armenia, that same September. Some of the key U.S. delegates were Drake, Sagan, and Oliver.[11]

Oliver worked for more than a year to edit and refine the Cyclops report before it was published in 1973.[12] Ten thousand copies were printed, and over the succeeding years it has come to be recognized as a visionary and technological tour de force. (It was later reprinted by the SETI League and the SETI Institute.) At my instigation, the report included an artist's rendering of the 1,000-antenna phased array, designed to occupy a circle 16 kilometers in diameter. This remarkable depiction led to a misunderstanding, which evolved into a myth, that the full array was necessary to detect extraterrestrial intelligence. Many people looked at the picture, looked at the price tag for the full array, and, without reading the fine print, jumped to the conclusion that $6 billion to $10 billion would be needed to detect an extraterrestrial civilization. They were wrong on two counts. First, the array was to be built

11. Carl Sagan, ed., *Communication with Extraterrestrial Intelligence (CETI)* (Cambridge: The MIT Press, 1973).
12. Bernard M. Oliver and John Billingham, *A Design Study of a System for Detecting Extraterrestrial Intelligent Life* (Washington, DC: NASA CR-114445, 1973).

in stages, with searches performed after each stage was completed. So it was possible that a signal would be found with only one dish, at a cost of a few million dollars instead of several billion. Second, even the full-up array might not have detected a signal. In any case, the myth persists even today. But I believe it is on the wane, as Cyclops has now been gradually superseded by the SETI Institute's Allen Telescope Array and by the proposed international Square Kilometer Array.

1972–1974: Early Steps at Ames

Next, I had to find out if NASA would support further studies. With the blessing of Mark and Klein, I put together a Committee on Interstellar Communication at Ames. We were nine, drawn from different divisions and branches. Dave Black was our expert on planetary systems. My deputy was John Wolfe, a space physicist of note. On accepting my invitation to serve, he told me that he had read the Cyclops report from cover to cover in a single night, having been unable to put it down. At this stage we received a boost. The National Research Council (NRC) published its decennial report on astronomy and astrophysics for the 1970s.[13] Prepared under Chairman Jesse L. Greenstein, it included for the first time encouraging words on the future significance of interstellar communication and on studies that might be undertaken in this area. Frank Drake played a major role in preparing this section of the NRC report. By 1974, the Ames committee had produced and sent to NASA Headquarters a comprehensive "Proposal for an Interstellar Communication Feasibility Study." We briefed John Naugle, the NASA Chief Scientist, and his advisors from the scientific community. Barney and I also briefed the NASA Administrator, James Fletcher, and the Associate Administrator for Space Science, Homer Newell. In August of 1974, we received our first funding, in the amount of $140,000, from the NASA Office of Aeronautics and Space Technology.

At this stage it was clear to us that interstellar communication was still generally considered a novelty, a pursuit outside the respectable norms adhered to by most of the scientific community. We therefore decided to conduct a series of science workshops through 1975 and 1976 specifically to outline in greater detail all aspects of a program to detect extraterrestrial intelligence.

---

13. Astronomy Survey Committee, *Astronomy and Astrophysics for the 1970's. Volume 1: Report of the Astronomy Survey Committee* and *Volume 2: Reports of the Panels* (Washington, DC: National Academy of Sciences, 1972–1973).

1975 and 1976: The Science Workshops on SETI

In 1974, after nine years of directing aviation and space biomedical and bio-engineering research, I decided to take a year off in order to devote my time to the nascent SETI program at Ames. Chuck Klein approved and authorized me to hire a secretary. Vera Buescher came on board as the planet's first full-time interstellar secretary. (She remained at SETI until her retirement, as the glue that held us all together.) She and I planned the meetings of the Science Workshops, Philip Morrison agreed to act as chair, and together he and I worked out our goals and objectives and decided whom to invite onto the team. The final membership roster included Ronald Bracewell, Harrison Brown, A. G. W. Cameron, Frank Drake, Jesse Greenstein, Fred Haddock, George Herbig, Arthur Kantrowitz, Kenneth Kellermann, Joshua Lederberg, John Lewis, Bruce Murray, Barney Oliver, Carl Sagan, and Charles Townes. I was executive secretary. Bruce was not on the original list but called from the California Institute of Technology to offer his services, which we were glad to accept. It turned out he had heard a lecture that Barney gave at Caltech on interstellar communication and was very intrigued by it. It also turned out that he was soon to become the director of the Jet Propulsion Laboratory (JPL) in Pasadena.

During 1975 and 1976, we had six 3-day meetings and accomplished much. It became apparent that there was enough interest to fill two additional splinter workshops on extrasolar planetary detection, a neglected field at that time. Jesse Greenstein was named chair and David Black served as the workshops' executive secretary. We also had one splinter workshop at Stanford titled The Evolution of Intelligent Species and Technological Civilizations, an emergent topic in the new domain of exobiology. It was chaired by Joshua Lederberg.

At the fourth SETI science workshop, held in early December of 1975 in Puerto Rico, we discussed names for the new endeavor and accepted John Wolfe's proposal to use "Search for Extraterrestrial Intelligence" instead of "Communication with Extraterrestrial Intelligence." Communication often connotes a two-way or many-way exchange, which was not our immediate goal. Our priority was the search. The acronym SETI stuck and is now in common parlance the world over.

The report of the SETI Science Workshops confirmed the microwave window as a promising place to begin the search and noted that progress in large-scale integrated circuit technology had been so rapid that million-channel, fast-Fourier-transform spectrum analyzers could be used instead of the optical signal processing used in Project Cyclops.[14] Several other conclusions emerged:

1. It is both timely and feasible to begin a serious Search for Extraterrestrial Intelligence.
2. A significant SETI program with substantial potential secondary benefits can be undertaken with only modest resources.
3. Large systems of great capability can be built if needed.
4. SETI is intrinsically an international endeavor in which the United States can take a lead.

Workshop members made the point that the search fell under NASA's mandate. Philip Morrison wrote a stimulating section on "The Impact of SETI" and concluded his preface with the words, "We recommend the initiation of a SETI program now."

In the middle of the workshops, Chuck Klein asked me if I would accept the recently vacated position of Chief of the Exobiology Division at Ames. I was delighted and changed careers forthwith.[15] With the encouraging words of the Morrison report in hand, I established in the division a formally constituted SETI Program Office, with John Wolfe; astronomers Mark Stull and Charles Seeger; sociologist Mary Connors, who was to study the societal aspects of SETI; and Vera Buescher. Barney Oliver and Frank Drake had been participating all along, and Hans Mark continued his support from on high, as did Chuck Klein. Without them there might have been no SETI at NASA.

1977: JPL Joins In

Early in the SETI Science Workshops, everyone assumed that the search method would involve focusing the radio telescope beam continuously for several minutes on selected target stars, thus achieving high sensitivity, as in Project Cyclops. Murray argued forcefully, however, for an additional approach—namely, to sweep the beam across the sky so that total coverage could be realized (at the cost, though, of a reduction in sensitivity of about one thousand-fold). At the fifth meeting in 1976, Oliver gave in—"All right, Bruce, have it your own way"—and the stage was set for the bimodal search strategy, which dominated

---

14. Philip Morrison, John Billingham, and John Wolfe, *The Search for Extraterrestrial Intelligence*, NASA SP-419 (Washington, DC: NASA, 1977).

15. Dick Young, Chief of Exobiology at NASA Headquarters, privately protested that I was "only an M.D." But I think Klein saw a potential expansion of Exobiology to incorporate SETI. In any case, Dick and I had been, and remained, close friends.

SETI at NASA from then on. Murray was by this time director of JPL and suggested that the laboratory join with Ames to conduct SETI.

Discussions between the two Centers began in 1976. Bob Edelson took charge of the JPL program and worked with me for several years. It became apparent that Ames had a strong preference for targeted searches and JPL for sky surveys. Since the approaches were complementary, it made sense to divide responsibility between the Centers. Over the next two-to-three years, the outline of the signal-detection system, based on a multichannel signal analyzer (MCSA), was developed by the engineers who were beginning to come on board. The original plan was to use the same detection system for both searches, though this later proved too difficult and each Center developed its own. For antennas, JPL would use the telescopes at its Deep Space Network at Goldstone in the Mojave Desert, while Ames would use existing large telescopes around the world.

Edelson and I were constantly traveling to NASA Headquarters for all the programmatic and funding discussions. By 1978, the Agency's Office of Space Science had taken over the funding of SETI. At Ames, astronomer Jill Tarter came from Berkeley on a one-year National Academy of Sciences postdoctoral fellowship and then stayed for 15 more. (She currently holds the Bernard M. Oliver Chair for SETI at the Institute.) During her time at Ames, she gradually took over the science of SETI. At JPL, the same function was in the expert hands of Sam Gulkis, a distinguished radio astronomer. In 1979, I organized a two-day conference at Ames devoted to the topic "Life in the Universe," which attracted an overflow crowd.[16] At this meeting Ames and JPL were now able to present a joint paper titled "SETI: Plans and Rationale."[17] The proposed NASA search system would achieve a 10-million-fold increase in capabilities over the sum of all previous searches. The MCSA and its algorithms, at the heart of the system, would now allow a reasonable search of Jill Tarter's "cosmic haystack" for its "needle"—a signal of indisputably extraterrestrial intelligent origin.

1980–1981: The SETI Science Working Group

Ames, JPL, and NASA Headquarters decided that the emerging SETI Program should be carried out with continuing input at a working level from leading

16. John Billingham, ed., *Life in the Universe* (Cambridge: The MIT Press, 1981).

17. John Wolfe et al., "SETI: Plans and Rationale," in *Life in the Universe*, ed. John Billingham, pp. 391–417.

radio scientists and engineers in the academic community. Accordingly, we formed the SETI Science Working Group (SSWG) under the chairmanship of John Wolfe and Sam Gulkis. It met on six separate occasions and in 1984 produced a report containing 17 "Conclusions and Recommendations."[18] This report confirmed the microwave region as preferable; endorsed the bimodal strategy; and envisaged a five-year R&D effort to design, develop, and test prototype instrumentation. Its first conclusion was: "The discovery of other civilizations would be among the most important achievements of humanity." Its last was: "It is recommended that the search for extraterrestrial intelligence be supported and continued at a modest level as a long-term NASA research program." The members of the SSWG were Peter Boyce, Bernie Burke, Eric Chaisson, Thomas Clark, Michael Davis, Frank Drake, Kenneth Kellermann, Woody Sullivan, George Swenson, Jack Welch, and Ben Zuckerman. Significant contributions came also from Michael Klein, who took over from Edelson as manager of the JPL SETI Program in 1981; Kent Cullers, leader of the Ames MCSA signal-detection/algorithm development team; Paul Horowitz from Harvard (who had spent a year on sabbatical at Ames and developed "Suitcase SETI"); Allen Peterson from Electrical Engineering at Stanford; George Morris and Ed Olsen from JPL; two other postdocs who had spent a year at Ames, Ivan Linscott and Peter Backus (both of whom were to join the Ames team); and of course Barney Oliver and Jill Tarter.

Dissidents Emerge

By now SETI was becoming better known and more respected in the scientific community. There were still skeptics, however, and Frank Tipler argued on a number of grounds that the number of coexisting civilizations in the galaxy was vanishingly small.[19] In 1978 the program received a "Golden Fleece" award from Senator William Proxmire (D-WI), and our funding suffered accordingly. Our position was always that we do not know the number of other civilizations and that the only way to answer the question is to carry out a search. Drake and Oliver argued that interstellar travel and colonization were too expensive and that radio communications were vastly more

---

18. Frank Drake, John H. Wolfe, and Charles L. Seeger, eds., *SETI Science Working Group Report,* NASA-TP-2244 (Washington, DC: NASA, 1984), p. xiii.

19. See, e.g., M. H. Hart and Ben Zuckerman, eds., *Extraterrestrials—Where Are They?* (New York: Pergamon Press, 1982); and Frank J. Tipler, "Extraterrestrial Intelligent Beings Do Not Exist," *Quarterly Journal of the Royal Astronomical Society* 21 (1980): 267–281.

efficient over interstellar distances.[20] Morrison spoke out for the empiricism of Western science: "It is fine to argue about N [in the Drake Equation]. After the argument, though, I think there remains one rock hard truth: whatever the theories, there is no easy substitute for a real search out there, among the ray directions and the wavebands, down into the noise. We owe the issue more than mere theorizing."[21]

Nevertheless, in the fall of 1981, Proxmire introduced an amendment to the NASA budget that eliminated all 1982 funding for SETI. At this stage, I had to prepare a termination plan, which was somewhat disheartening. But Hans Mark, then Deputy Administrator of NASA, called a key meeting in Washington with all the senior people from the Agency and leaders from the scientific community, who made the decision to put SETI back into NASA's 1983 budget request to Congress. So I prepared a reinstatement plan. As the budgetary process continued through 1982, Carl Sagan and others were able to convince Proxmire of the validity of the endeavor, so he did not oppose it again.

SETI was and still remains an easy target at which to snipe. While scientists can argue persuasively that life is widespread throughout the galaxy, we cannot quantify the probability of SETI's success. There is, however, no question that an unequivocal discovery of extraterrestrial intelligence would be of the most profound significance for humankind. In spite of this, we have continued over the years to face opposition from a few skeptics in Congress. Much of the resistance we encountered was of a political nature and happened because SETI was such a small element of the NASA budget—ultimately 0.1 percent—that it lacked the broad-based political support of larger NASA projects.[22] SETI also was of such intense interest to the general public that it often figured prominently in the media, which sometimes ridiculed our search for mythical "Little Green Men." What we have actually been searching for, of course, is unassailable evidence of the existence of an extraterrestrial technological civilization, born of cognitive intelligence. The anatomical and physiological structure of the extraterrestrials is a topic of major theoretical interest, but what matters most for our search is that these beings will have figured out, almost certainly a long time ago, how to build powerful radio transmitters.

---

20. See Frank D. Drake, "N Is Neither Very Small nor Very Large," in *Strategies for the Search for Life in the Universe*, Astrophysics and Space Science Library, vol. 83, ed. M. D. Papagiannis (Dordrecht, Netherlands: D. Reidel, 1980), pp. 27–34; and Bernard M. Oliver, "Galactic Colonization and Other Flights of Fancy," *IEEE Potentials* 13, no. 3 (1994): 51–54.

21. Steven J. Dick and James E. Strick, *The Living Universe: NASA and the Development of Astrobiology* (New Brunswick, NJ: Rutgers University Press, 2004), p. 144.

22. See Stephen J. Garber, "A Political History of NASA's SETI Program," chapter 2 in this volume.

1982–1983: Good News

In 1982, Carl Sagan published in *Science* magazine a petition signed by 70 scientists, including seven Nobel Prize winners, from around the world calling for international cooperation in and support of a systematic SETI program. They said: "No a priori arguments on this subject can be compelling or should be used as a substitute for an observational program. We urge the organization of a coordinated, worldwide, and systematic search for extraterrestrial intelligence."[23]

In 1982 the decennial report of the Astronomy Survey Committee (also known as the Field Report) strongly supported SETI as one of seven "Moderate New Programs" for the 1980s.[24] Their specific recommendation was for "an astronomical Search for Extraterrestrial Intelligence (SETI), supported at a modest level, undertaken as a long-term effort rather than a short-term project, and open to the participation of the general scientific community." The Committee had a special Subcommittee on SETI, which interacted at some length with our academic leadership, Drake, Oliver, Tarter, and many others. At this time the new director of Life Sciences in the Office of Space Science and Applications at NASA Headquarters was Jerry Soffen, who had been the Project Scientist for the Viking mission to Mars. Encouraged by the growing support from the scientific community, he accepted our proposal for the first of the five years of R&D funding that had been recommended by the SETI Science Working Group; so our budget for 1983 came in at $1.65 million. Don DeVincenzi, a key figure in exobiology science management at Ames, went to join Soffen in the Life Sciences Division at NASA Headquarters and became Chief of Exobiology there and a most capable SETI Program Manager. Also at this time, and in spite of some competition between the Centers, Ames and JPL and Headquarters got together and agreed that Ames would be the lead Center for SETI in NASA; and so it was until the program was canceled in 1993.

Two other major events occurred in 1983. Barney Oliver retired from Hewlett-Packard and accepted my invitation to join Ames as Deputy Chief of the SETI Program Office. I found a special civil-service position that fitted him perfectly—it was called "expert." I was delighted with his decision,

---

23. Carl Sagan, "Extraterrestrial Intelligence: An International Petition," *Science* 218, no. 4571 (1982): 426.

24. *Astronomy and Astrophysics for the 1980's. Volume 1: Report of the Astronomy Survey Committee* and *Volume 2: Reports of the Panels* (Washington, DC: National Academy Press, 1982–1983), p. 150.

especially since he had no great love for the federal bureaucracy. He used to say that he was not really suited for the job because he was "neither civil nor servile." He had always been close to us, as our principal technical colleague. Now it became a formal arrangement, and everyone benefited. He was the only person in NASA to hold memberships in the National Academies of Sciences and Engineering. Our standing rose in the world. Barney wanted to be a volunteer, but the rules would not allow that; so he was forced to accept a salary!

The second event was the formation of the SETI Institute. This was a brainchild of Tom Pierson, then the director of research administration at San Francisco State University. He consulted with Barney, Jill Tarter, and me and went ahead to establish the Institute as a California research and education nonprofit corporation. Tom next wanted the best person to serve as president and chairman of the board. The best person turned out to be Frank Drake. After serving for many years as director of the Arecibo Observatory, followed by many more years as professor of astronomy at Cornell, Frank was now the dean of science and professor of astronomy at UC Santa Cruz. Frank accepted the position, part time of course, and everyone was delighted. Jack Welch, professor of astronomy at UC Berkeley and director of the Radio Astronomy Laboratory there, became deputy chair of the Institute. Tom Pierson became executive director and ran the Institute with his astonishing flair for leadership. Jill Tarter joined the Institute to spearhead the science, and Vera Buescher followed to become the research assistant to the Institute management.

1983–1987: Five Years of R&D

Unhappily for us, Chuck Klein retired from NASA Ames in 1984. By then he was widely recognized as "the father of exobiology." With funding of about $1.5 million a year, Ames and JPL embarked on an intensive program to define all aspects of SETI in NASA. It was now formally titled the Microwave Observing Project (MOP). I worked with Mike Klein on the programmatic aspects, Barney oversaw the technology, and Jill Tarter and Sam Gulkis were the chief scientists. Elyse Murray joined the Ames team in 1983, and it wasn't long before we realized she was a super secretary.

New spectrometers with resolutions of millions of channels were needed. Some of the original thinking about ways of solving this difficult problem came from Bob Machol, professor of systems at Northwestern University, who had joined us over the years on a series of sabbaticals. He talked with Alan Despain of UC Berkeley. Then Despain and Allen Peterson and Ivan

Linscott at Stanford developed the digital technology for the first Ames MCSA. At Ames, Kent Cullers led the signal-detection team in the design of very sophisticated algorithms to search for both continuous wave and pulsed signals and to reject radio frequency interference, one of SETI's major and continuing problems.[25] The prototype narrowband (1-hertz) signal-detection system had 74,000 channels and was tested on a 26-meter telescope at Goldstone from 1985 to 1987. It succeeded in detecting the 1-watt transmitter on the Pioneer 10 spacecraft at a distance of 4.5 billion miles. At JPL, Mike Klein, ably assisted by engineer Bruce Crow, supervised the corresponding development of their wide-band spectrum analyzer, which was tailored to the needs of the sky survey. From 1985 onward, Klein succeeded in obtaining support from the NASA Office of Telecommunications and Data Acquisition to use part of the Deep Space Network and for some of their engineering development work. This support was to continue for the remainder of the program.

During this period there was a reorganization at Ames, and I became head of an expanded Life Sciences Division, which now included exobiology and SETI; ecosystem science and technology; and space biology, physiology, and medicine. In SETI, Ames and JPL wrote a formal Program Plan, approved by Barney Oliver for Ames and Mike Klein for JPL, which we submitted to Headquarters and which was adopted in March 1987. Jill Tarter played a key role in putting it together, and it was a major milestone. The plan proposed a 10-year, $73.5-million search for narrowband signals. The search was to be composed of two complementary components: a targeted search, carried out by Ames; and a sky survey, carried out by JPL. In addition to the technical, managerial, and administrative details, we made sure that the plan included sections on the following additional material: the intimate link between SETI and exobiology; evaluations from the scientific community; use of the sophisticated instrumentation for radio astronomy and other possible areas; a summary of the manifestations of interest by the public and the media and of the incorporation of SETI into college courses around the country; and an annotated bibliography by Charles Seeger, which included references to the extensive bibliography on SETI that had been published in the *Journal of the British Interplanetary Society* and then continued to appear there for

---

25. Kent Cullers, "Three Pulse/Multiple Stage Continuous Wave Detection Algorithms," in *Bioastronomy—The Next Steps*, ed. George Marx (Dordrecht, Netherlands: Springer, 1988), pp. 371–376.

several more years.[26] I insisted that we include in our NASA budget a Program Plan line item for R&D of future SETI telescopes, searches, and systems at one-tenth of the budget. Although approved at the time, this line item was unfortunately to disappear later in a funding crunch.

SETI at Large

I shall now depart from the chronological history of SETI at NASA to discuss general issues that emerged over the years. Although the NASA program was by far the largest, SETI had gradually appeared in many other places. Drake had carried out his own searches and had sponsored others at Arecibo. Begun in 1973, the observational project at the Ohio State radio telescope, under the direction of John Kraus and Robert Dixon, had become by 1995 the longest-running full-scale SETI project in the United States. In the early 1990s, Dixon had started the imaginative Project Argus, a wide-sky, broad-frequency, low-sensitivity search with small telescopes. Paul Horowitz developed extremely narrow-channel (.05 hertz) instruments for the Harvard radio telescope, beginning with Project Sentinel in 1983, then progressing to META—the Megachannel Extraterrestrial Assay—and finally to the current BETA, with a billion channels. Stuart Bowyer and Dan Werthimer at UC Berkeley have been running Project SERENDIP as a piggyback operation on radio-astronomy projects at Arecibo since 1980.

Outside the United States, SETI projects were carried out in France, Argentina, Italy, Germany, and Japan. These programs and others came to a total of 61 searches worldwide.[27] It should be noted that collectively all of these searches had examined only a minute fraction of astronomical multi-dimensional time search space. In 1991, SETI was still in its infancy. On the

---

26. See E. F. Mallove, R. L. Forward, Z. Paprotny, and J. Lehmann, "Interstellar Travel and Communication – A Bibliography," *Journal of the British Interplanetary Society* 33 (1980): 201–248; Z. Paprotny and J. Lehmann, "Interstellar Travel and Communication Bibliography: 1982 Update," *Journal of the British Interplanetary Society* 36 (1983): 311–329; Z. Paprotny, J. Lehmann, and J. Prytz: "Interstellar Travel and Communication Bibliography: 1984 Update," *Journal of the British Interplanetary Society* 37 (1984): 502–512, 1984; and Z. Paprotny, J. Lehmann, and J. Prytz: "Interstellar Travel and Communication Bibliography: 1985 Update," *Journal of the British Interplanetary Society* 39 (1986): 127–136.

27. Jill Tarter and Michael J. Klein, "SETI: On the Telescope and on the Drawing Board," in *Bioastronomy: The Search for Extraterrestrial Life—The Exploration Broadens*, ed. Jean Heidmann and Michael J. Klein (New York: Springer, 1991), pp. 229–235.

other hand, a real signal might have been detected at any time by any SETI observing project anywhere on Earth.

It had always been our policy to provide, where we could, some level of financial support for these other SETI activities, and we did just that over the years. Another policy was to aim for the highest professional standards in the science and engineering of SETI. To this end, we always engaged with the scientific and engineering communities and made sure that we had a continuing presence at national and international professional conferences, delivering papers and then submitting them to appropriate peer-reviewed journals. Review sessions on SETI have been held at the annual International Astronautical Congress (IAC) since 1972. I was Chairman of the IAA SETI Committee from 1977 to 1994. Every four or five years, we would collect the best papers read at the congresses, have them peer reviewed, and publish them as a special issue of *Acta Astronautica*.[28] The International Astronomical Union (IAU) established a new commission (designated Commission 51) on bioastronomy in 1984, which since then has held scientific meetings trienni-ally. Both Frank Drake and Jill Tarter served as presidents of this commission in the late 1980s.

It had always been apparent to us that the unequivocal discovery of a signal of extraterrestrial intelligent origin would have profound consequences for humankind. Since this was obviously a transnational issue, we brought it up periodically in the IAA SETI Committee and also with colleagues in the International Institute of Space Law. We devised a Declaration of Principles Concerning Activities Following the Detection of Extraterrestrial Intelligence and called it, somewhat loosely, the "SETI Post-Detection Protocols."[29] This list of nine recommendations to SETI investigators, adopted by the IAA in 1989, was endorsed by six major international space societies and, later, by nearly all SETI investigators around the world. In the following years, the Committee worked on a second protocol, which examined questions dealing with the transmission of messages from Earth to extraterrestrial civilizations and recommended that these questions be forwarded to the United Nations' Committee on the Peaceful Uses of Outer Space (COPUOS) for consideration. The basic issues were whether to transmit, either *de novo* or after the detection of

---

28. The SETI special issues of *Acta Astronautica* include vol. 6, nos. 1–2 (1979); vol. 13, no. 1 (1986); vol. 19, no. 11 (1989); vol. 21, no. 2 (1990); vol. 26, nos. 3–4 (1992); and vol. 42, nos. 10–12 (1998).

29. The full text of this declaration is available on the International Academy of Astronautics' SETI Permanent Committee Web site at *http://www.setileague.org/iaaseti/protdet.htm* (accessed 25 June 2013). See also Jill Tarter and Michael A. Michaud, eds., "SETI Post-Detection Protocol," *Acta Astronautica* 21, no. 2 (1990): 69–154.

a signal; what the content of a message might be if transmissions were sent; and how these decisions were to be made. Our document, titled Draft Declaration of Principles Concerning Sending Communications with Extraterrestrial Intelligence and submitted to the IAA in 1995, became a formal Position Paper of the Academy and was endorsed by the International Institute of Space Law.[30] It has now been formally received by COPUOS.

In 1987 at the International Astronautical Federation's 38th Congress, held in Brighton, England, Dr. James Fletcher, then Administrator of NASA, presented a paper on what he imagined his successor might say about space achievements 30 years into the future. In it, he pronounced that the discovery of extraterrestrial intelligence would eclipse all other discoveries in history.

It had been obvious to us since Project Ozma that many questions related to the societal implications of SETI had not yet been addressed. So I asked the distinguished social psychologist Roger Heyns, then director of the Hewlett Foundation and former chancellor of UC Berkeley, to co-chair with me a series of Workshops on the Cultural Aspects of SETI (CASETI). We gathered together a team of specialists in history; theology; anthropology; psychology; sociology; international law, relations, and policy; political science; the media; and education. We met three times in 1991 and 1992 and generated a report titled *Social Implications of the Detection of an Extraterrestrial Civilization*.[31] The report concluded that the issues were important and merited extensive further studies.

1988: The Buildup Begins

In 1988 we saw the signing of the Project Initiation Agreement by NASA, another major step in the bureaucratic approval process. Lynn Griffiths had replaced Don DeVincenzi as Program Manager at NASA Headquarters, and John Rummel became the Headquarters Project Scientist. Funding was now

---

30. The full texts of both the draft and the revision of this position paper are accessible in the "Protocols" section of the International Academy of Astronautics' SETI Permanent Committee Web site: *http://www.setileague.org/iaaseti/protocol.htm* (accessed 25 June 2013). It is also available on the SETI Institute Web site at *http://www.seti.org*.

31. John Billingham et al., eds., *Social Implications of the Detection of an Extraterrestrial Civilization: A Report of the Workshops on the Cultural Aspects of SETI Held in October 1991, May 1992, and September 1992 at Santa Cruz, California* (Mountain View, CA: SETI Press, 1990). The Executive Summary, Principal Findings, and Recommendations can be found at *http://www.seti.org/seti-institute/project/details/cultural-aspects-seti* (accessed 25 June 2013).

running at just under $3 million a year. At Ames, there was another reorganization, and in 1989 I became the full-time chief of the SETI Office, with Barney Oliver at my side as deputy. My first action was to appoint Jill Tarter as our Project Scientist. The SETI Institute, under Drake and Pierson, was playing an increasingly important role.[32] We were completing the R&D phase. Program reviews intensified at the Centers and in Washington. In 1990, SETI took on the status of an approved NASA project, and we began the Final Development and Operations phase. The budget for 1990 was $6 million. The final Project Plan outlined a 10-year search at a total cost of $108 million. We had 140 people working on SETI at Ames and JPL. The search was scheduled to begin on 12 October 1992, the 500th anniversary of Columbus's arrival in America. And so it did.[33]

Speaking of Columbus reminds me that attempts of one sort or another were always being made to reduce our budget. We had constantly to be on guard. We continued to see sniping from individual members of Congress, though also much support. Some in the astronomical community saw SETI as a potential competitor for funding. A frequent question was "Why don't you delay this project until the cost of digital signal processing has come down to a fraction of what it is today?"—to which Oliver replied, "Columbus didn't wait for jets." We actually had another strong argument for not delaying and were able to use it effectively. If we did not get on the air soon, the difficulty of detecting faint signals from other civilizations would increase because of the growing saturation of the radio-frequency spectrum with interference, which in turn would cost progressively more millions of dollars to overcome.

In 1991 the National Research Council published its Astronomy Survey Committee Report for the 1990s and again recommended SETI. In that same year we began building and testing the actual search systems. Tarter and Gulkis finalized the observational plans, advised by an Investigators Working Group of scientists. The 1991 budget rose to $16.8 million. The targeted search was to be conducted at the Arecibo Observatory in Puerto Rico (the plans having been approved by a National Science Foundation peer-review process), and the sky survey would be performed using one of the Deep Space

32. Thomas Pierson, "SETI Institute: Summary of Projects in Support of SETI Research," in *Progress in the Search for Extraterrestrial Life*, ASP Conference Series, vol. 74, ed. G. Seth Shostak (San Francisco: Astronomical Society of the Pacific, 1995), pp. 433–444.

33. For a detailed description of SETI at this time, including science rationale, observational plans, and signal-detection system designs, see John Billingham and Jill Tarter, "Fundamentals of Space Biology and Medicine," in *SETI: The Search for Extraterrestrial Intelligence* (Washington, DC: AIAA; Moscow: Nauka Press, 1993).

Network telescopes at Goldstone in the Mojave desert. I tried at this time to have Michel Klein formally named as Deputy of the NASA SETI Program, but Headquarters said it could not be done. We needed a full-time overall project manager and brought on David Brocker from the Space Science Division at Ames. Reporting to him were Larry Webster, Targeted Search Manager at Ames, and Mike Klein, Sky Survey Manager at JPL. The able Gary Coulter had by this time become Program Manager at NASA Headquarters, replacing the able Lynn Griffiths.

In 1992 the name Microwave Observing Project was changed to High-Resolution Microwave Survey (HRMS) by order of the U.S. Congress. The project was moved from the NASA Headquarters Life Sciences Division to the Solar System Exploration Division, along with Coulter and Rummel. The 1992 budget rose again, to $17.5 million. The signal-detection systems were shipped to the telescopes for final testing. The Ames system was built into a Mobile Research Facility—a trailer—that was trucked to Travis Air Force Base, loaded onto a C-141 transport, flown to Puerto Rico, trucked again to the Arecibo Observatory, and hooked up to the telescope. The basic idea behind the Mobile Research Facility was to be able to take the targeted search to any large telescope anywhere in the world. At the same time, scientists and engineers at JPL assembled and tested their sky-survey instrumentation at Goldstone. Preparations were made for the inauguration of the search. A series of talks were to be given by distinguished people. Invitations went out to them and to the media, and the activity level rose to a crescendo. The brunt of the organization fell on Vera Buescher, who did a wonderful job. We were very busy.

1992: NASA SETI Comes of Age

It was noon on Columbus Day, 1992, at the Arecibo Observatory in Puerto Rico. After a morning of inauguration speeches, including a rousing one from Frank Drake, David Brocker formally initiated the NASA High-Resolution Microwave Survey and pulled the switch to turn on the targeted search system. In a two-way hook-up with the JPL team at Goldstone, where a corresponding inauguration ceremony was underway, Mike Klein did the same for the sky survey. As I said in my briefing to the audience, these new systems were so powerful that they would eclipse the sum of all previous searches within the first few minutes of operation. And so it was.

Both teams spent the next year exploring the sky for signals of extraterrestrial intelligent origin and learning how to deal with the vast flows of data that were analyzed in near real-time. Procedures were worked out for dealing with the chronic radio-frequency interference. Teams of observers and engineers rotated back and forth between the NASA Centers and the observatories. The targeted search completed 200 hours of observations of selected nearby F, G, and K stars. The sky survey conducted observations at X-band and completed a sequence of maps of the galactic plane, primarily at L-band. In August 1993, Jill Tarter and Mike Klein presented a summary of their results at a Bioastronomy Symposium in Santa Cruz, California. They said:

> At both sites the equipment has functioned well, with minor, mostly low-tech glitches. These initial observations have verified the transport logistics for the Targeted Search and provided the first platform for remote observations to the Sky Survey. As a result of the data that have been collected, modifications have been made or planned to the hardware, software, and observing protocols. Both observing programs have encountered signals that required additional observations because they initially conformed to the detection pattern expected for an extraterrestrial signal, but no signals persist as potential candidates at this time. This paper will discuss the lessons we have learned, the changes we are making, and our schedule for continued observation.[34]

Alas, there was to be no continued observation.

The Dissolution of SETI at NASA

Shortly after the Santa Cruz meeting, Senator Richard Bryan (D-NV) introduced an amendment to the 1993 NASA budget eliminating the HRMS program. His argument was based on deficit reduction, and he explained that 150 new houses could be built in Nevada for the same cost. In spite of a vigorous defense of HRMS by Senator Barbara Mikulski (D-MD) and others, the motion was carried. The political complexities of all the issues are covered in detail in the next chapter of this book, "A Political History of NASA's SETI Program."

I now had the unhappy task, for the second time, of putting together a termination plan. Slowly and surely, all the grants and contracts had to be wound down and our team dissolved. It took six months. The total budget

---

34. Jill Tarter and Michael J. Klein, "HRMS: Where We've Been, and Where We're Going," in Shostak, ed., *Progress in the Search for Extraterrestrial Life*, pp. 457–469, esp. p. 457.

for SETI, over all the years, was just under $78 million. In March of 1994 the doors were closed on SETI at NASA.

Epilogue

We had successfully executed Earth's first comprehensive Search for Extraterrestrial Intelligence. We suspect there have been, still are, and will be searches by other intelligent species in the universe. Perhaps some of these searches have been successful, and perhaps communication now exists between these extraterrestrial societies. One day we may join that conversation.

The targeted search was taken over by the SETI Institute in 1994 and continued with funding from private sources. The following year Project Argus, a new all-sky survey (also privately funded), was initiated by the non-profit SETI League, on whose advisory board Frank Drake serves. So Frank Drake, who began it all, continues to hold the torch in his hands. In the year 2014, he still does.

A Political History of NASA's SETI Program[1]

Stephen J. Garber

Humans have always had a curiosity about whether we are unique or whether other intelligent life-forms exist elsewhere in the universe. In 1959 a group of astrophysicists formulated a new approach to answering this question which involved using radio astronomy to "listen" for signs of extraterrestrial intelligent life. Sixteen years later, in 1975, NASA began to fund definition studies for the Search for Extraterrestrial Intelligence (SETI) program. After progressing at a low level of funding for more than a decade, the program was renamed the High-Resolution Microwave Survey (HRMS) and, on Columbus Day, 1992, launched what was intended to be a 10-year, $100-million formal SETI effort. Within a year, Congress abruptly canceled the HRMS program, though aspects of it were continued with private funding.

Why did the NASA SETI/HRMS program—hereafter referred to simply as the SETI program—fail? While debate over the likelihood of finding intelligent extraterrestrial life goes on, most scientists agree that the SETI program constituted worthwhile, valid scientific research. A number of political factors, however, combined to kill the program. Anxiety over the federal budget deficit, lack of support from some segments of the scientific and aerospace communities, and unfounded but persistent claims that linked SETI with nonscientific elements all made the program an easy target in the autumn of 1993.

---

1. First, thank you to Doug Vakoch for suggesting the revision and updating of my prior article on this subject. Thanks also go to the editorial staff of the *Journal of the British Interplanetary Society*, both for publishing an earlier version of this research under the title "Searching for Good Science: The Cancellation of NASA's SETI Program" (*JBIS* 52, no. 1 [1999]: 3–12) and for allowing me to revise that text for this collection.

Searching for Signs of Extraterrestrial Intelligence—
A Brief History

Long before the space age, scientists and engineers pondered ways to answer the question "Are we alone?" In the early 20th century, radio pioneers such as Heinrich Hertz, Nikola Tesla, and Guglielmo Marconi foresaw the possibility of using radio waves for "interplanetary communication," as it was called at the time. In 1919, after observing some unusual radio signals, Marconi tried to determine whether they came from Mars, causing a considerable public stir. Elmer Sperry, head of the Sperry Gyroscope Company, proposed using a massive array of searchlights to send a beacon to Mars, and even Albert Einstein suggested that light rays might be an easily controllable method for extraterrestrial communication.[2]

The age-old question of whether intelligent life exists beyond Earth reached a turning point in 1959. That year, Giuseppe Cocconi and Philip Morrison published a seminal paper in which they suggested that the micro-wave portion of the electromagnetic spectrum would be ideal for communicating signals across tremendous distances in our galaxy.[3] A narrowband frequency could, they theorized, be beamed long distances with relatively minimal power and signal interference. Radio waves travel at the speed of light and are not absorbed by cosmic dust or clouds. Thus, if scientists tuned radio telescopes to the right portion of the spectrum, they might be able to detect a pattern of radio waves that indicated extraterrestrial intelligence. Our own radio and television broadcasts had been drifting into space for a number of years already. While we might pick up such unintentional extraterrestrial signals, Cocconi and Morrison primarily hoped to receive a message deliberately sent by other intelligent beings.

Independently of Cocconi and Morrison, a young astronomer named Frank Drake had also been contemplating radio astronomy as a means of searching for extraterrestrial signals. He decided to test this approach in 1960 by setting up a rudimentary experiment, which he called Project Ozma, at the Green Bank Observatory in West Virginia. While listening over a two-month period to emissions from two nearby stars, Drake was startled to discover a nonrandom signal pattern that potentially indicated ETI. After checking his results, however, he realized that the pattern was a terrestrial one, generated

---

2. Steven J. Dick, "Back to the Future: SETI Before the Space Age," *The Planetary Report* 15, no. 1 (1995): 4–7.

3. Giuseppe Cocconi and Philip Morrison, "Searching for Interstellar Communications," *Nature* 184, no. 4690 (1959): 844–846.

by a secret military radar. Undeterred, Drake persevered with Project Ozma and went on to become one of the leading figures in the SETI field.

The microwave portion of the spectrum seemed to be the logical place to look for extraterrestrial signals, but this still left a broad range of other frequencies. Drake, as well as Cocconi and Morrison, speculated that the optimum wave frequency would be near the spectral emission frequency of hydrogen, the most common element in our galaxy. Soon afterward, scientists adopted a strategy of looking in the "water hole" portion of the spectrum between the emission lines of hydrogen and hydroxyl, the chemical components of water, since water is assumed to be essential for life.[4]

In 1961, Drake gathered a small group of astronomers and other scientists at Green Bank for the first scientific SETI conference. These ten attendees later called themselves members of the "Order of the Dolphin," alluding to a discussion they had had about the dolphin's intellectual capabilities and the evolutionary likelihood of intelligent life. In trying to come up with an agenda for this meeting, Drake produced what became known as the Drake Equation, a formula that estimates the number of potential intelligent civilizations in our galaxy. The equation reads

$$N = R^* \cdot f_p \cdot n_e \cdot f_l \cdot f_i \cdot f_c \cdot L,$$

where N is the number of detectable civilizations in space and the seven other symbols represent various factors multiplied by each other.[5]

Drake himself calculated N to be approximately 10,000. This figure takes into account just the Milky Way galaxy, one of "billions and billions" of galaxies in the universe.[6] As later critics pointed out, scientists have hard data on only one of these variables; the rest continue to be just rough estimates.

---

4. See, for example, Seth Shostak, "Listening for Life," *Astronomy* 20, no. 10 (1992): 26–33, esp. p. 30; and Frank Drake and Dava Sobel, *Is Anyone Out There? The Scientific Search for Extraterrestrial Intelligence* (New York: Delacorte Press, 1992), pp. 42–43.

5. Drake and Sobel, *Is Anyone Out There?*, p. 52. For a discussion of how the Drake Equation has changed slightly over the years, see Steven J. Dick, *The Biological Universe: The Twentieth-Century Extraterrestrial Life Debate and the Limits of Science* (Cambridge: Cambridge University Press, 1996), pp. 428 and 441–442. Linda Billings contends that this formula would be better termed the "Drake Heuristic" because it is a way to think about how many intelligent civilizations may exist, rather than a mathematical calculation per se; see *http://lindabillings. org/gadfly_blog/LindaBillings.org/Capital_Gadfly/Entries/2009/12/10_The_Drake_Heuristic__ Its_Not_Math.html* (accessed 26 April 2013).

6. Drake and Sobel, *Is Anyone Out There?*, p. xv.

Nevertheless, Drake devised the equation simply as a starting point for how to think about searching for extraterrestrial signals.

In the late 1960s, John Billingham, who worked at NASA's Ames Research Center (ARC), began a campaign to get NASA involved in SETI. Billingham had been trained as a medical doctor and had previously done biomedical and life sciences work for NASA, such as designing the liquid-cooled inner garment for the Apollo spacesuits. In 1971, Billingham and Bernard (Barney) Oliver, a former vice president of research at Hewlett-Packard Corporation with a long-standing interest in SETI, authored a detailed NASA study proposing an array of one thousand 100-meter telescope dishes that could pick up radio signals from neighboring stars.[7] Project Cyclops, as it was called, was never adopted, in large measure because of its tremendous $10-billion price tag. An especially unfortunate result of the study was the creation of a widespread misperception that the Cyclops Project required an "all-or-nothing" approach, and thus SETI got nothing for several years.[8]

Four years after this setback, NASA managers judged that the relevant science and technology had matured enough to merit additional investigation. Thus, in 1975, NASA began to fund design studies under the leadership of MIT's Philip Morrison, who had coauthored the seminal *Nature* paper in 1959. The next year, managers at NASA's Ames Research Center established a SETI branch, and scientists and engineers at the Jet Propulsion Laboratory (JPL) also started SETI work. Ames had experience in biomedical research, while JPL had experience tracking deep space missions and easy access to the Deep Space Network antenna for radio astronomy at Goldstone.

The program's troubles in Congress trace back to 1978. That year, while SETI at NASA was still receiving a relatively low level of federal funding,[9] Senator William Proxmire bestowed one of his infamous "Golden Fleece" awards on the program, deriding it as a waste of taxpayer money. In 1981, viewing the SETI program as a foolish enterprise that was unlikely to yield results, Proxmire sponsored an amendment that killed its funding for the next year.

At this point, Proxmire was approached by the famous astronomer Carl Sagan, who had previously dealt with him on "nuclear winter" issues.

---

7. Bernard M. Oliver and John Billingham, *Project Cyclops: A Design Study of a System for Detecting Extraterrestrial Intelligent Life* (Washington, DC: NASA CR-114445, 1971).

8. Drake and Sobel, *Is Anyone Out There?*, p. 139.

9. For an overview of SETI's funding history, see the appendix to this chapter on p. 48. This budget data was supplied by Mr. Jens Feeley, Policy Analyst, NASA Office of Space Science, NASA Headquarters, Washington, DC.

Sagan was able to convince him of the program's scientific merits. Proxmire agreed not to oppose SETI, and Congress reinstated funding for fiscal year 1983 (FY83).

While NASA's SETI program was developing during the 1980s, several privately funded SETI projects were also under way. The Planetary Society, which Sagan had helped to found, provided support for two JPL researchers to conduct SETI observations at a NASA tracking station in Australia. The society also partially funded Paul Horowitz, a Harvard University astronomer who used surplus antennae and computers to build a portable system called "Suitcase SETI," which he later transformed into Project Sentinel and then into the Megachannel Extraterrestrial Assay. Various other projects included the Search for Extraterrestrial Radio Emissions from Nearby Developed Intelligent Populations (SERENDIP), conducted at the University of California at Berkeley, and Ohio State University's "Big Ear" program, which ran from 1973 to 1995. In 1984, the nonprofit SETI Institute was founded in California.

Scientists outside the United States, particularly those in the Soviet Union, were also interested in searching for ETI signals. International conferences were held in 1971 and 1981 in Armenia and Estonia, due in part to the interest of two leading Russian astrophysicists, Iosif Shklovskii and Nikolai Kardashev. In 1965, Soviet astronomers had detected a signal with the apparent hallmarks of ETI, but American scientists determined that it was the result of a naturally occurring phenomenon called quasars. If they had not before, SETI researchers worldwide quickly realized the importance of double-checking their results with colleagues before making any grand pronouncements.[10]

In 1988, NASA Headquarters formally endorsed the SETI program, and technicians at Ames and JPL began to build the necessary hardware. Simultaneously, the Solar System Exploration Division at NASA Headquarters established a working group to form a strategy for finding other planetary systems. This led to the Towards Other Planetary Systems (TOPS) workshops in 1990 and 1992.

By this time, SETI scientists were anxious to begin their search, not only because the preliminary studies had taken many years but also because of a purely technical reason: an increasingly crowded radio spectrum. New commercial communications satellites threatened to create a significant noise problem in the same part of the spectrum where SETI scientists concurred that chances were best to detect extraterrestrial signals. This cluttering was

---

10. For more information on Soviet SETI efforts, see, for example, Drake and Sobel, *Is Anyone Out There?*, pp. 95–115 and 155–156.

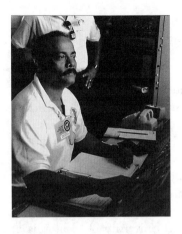

Figure 2.1. High-Resolution Microwave Survey observations begin on 12 October 1992. *(Photo: Seth Shostak)*

likely to worsen, so there was an impetus to start full-fledged "listening" quickly.

While the SETI program had always suffered from a "giggle factor" that derived from its association in the popular press with searches for "little green men" and unidentified flying objects (UFOs), the congressional pressures intensified in 1990. The George H. W. Bush administration requested $12 million for the program in FY91, up from $4.2 million in FY90, to start a full-fledged Microwave Observing Project (MOP). Congressman Ronald Machtley (R-RI) declared, "'We cannot spend money on curiosity today when we have a deficit.'"[11] Silvio Conte (R-MA) stated that he didn't want to spend millions of dollars to find evidence of ETI when one could spend "75 cents to buy a tabloid [with reports of aliens] at the local supermarket."[12] Perhaps the program was lucky to end up with $11.5 million for FY91.

In response to continued political pressure, NASA slightly restructured the program and prepared to start its next SETI effort precisely 500 years after Columbus had "discovered" North America (see Figures 2.1, 2.2, and 2.3). In addition to changing the name from Microwave Observing Project to High-Resolution Microwave Survey, NASA moved HRMS from the Life Sciences Division to its Solar System Exploration Division and made it part of the TOPS program. The House and Senate science committees, as well as the House Appropriations Committee, tried to cancel the program, but it was saved by the Senate Appropriations Subcommittee, in part due to the efforts of Senator Jake Garn (R-UT), who had flown on the Space Shuttle in 1985 and waxed eloquent about his religious convictions in relation to ETI.[13]

---

11. For these and other program budget figures, see the appendix on p. 48. Congressman Machtley is here quoted from Louis D. Friedman, "World Watch," *The Planetary Report* 10, no. 3 (1990): 24–25, esp. p. 24.

12. Friedman, "World Watch," p. 24.

13. Richard A. Kerr, "SETI Faces Uncertainty on Earth and in the Stars," *Science* 258, no. 5079 (1992): 27; Kevin Kelly, telephone conversation with author, 2 July 1997; and William Triplett, "SETI Takes the Hill," *Air & Space* (October/November 1992): 80–86, esp. p. 83.

Figure 2.2. The Arecibo radio telescope, 12 October 1992. *(Photo: Seth Shostak)*

Despite this shaky footing, HRMS was allocated $12 million for FY93 as part of a 10-year, $100-million program that included two main components: a targeted search and an all-sky survey. NASA Ames managed the targeted search component, which was conducted with the radio telescope in Arecibo, Puerto Rico, and was meant to focus on emissions from those nearby stars that scientists viewed as most promising for ETI signals. JPL scientists managed the all-sky survey, which used the Deep Space Network dish at Goldstone to scan the entire Milky Way.

After almost a year of HRMS operations, the program hit a political wall when a prominent opponent sensed an opportune time to strike. On 22 September 1993, Senator Richard Bryan (D-NV), a noted SETI critic, offered a last-minute amendment to kill the program, and the full Senate concurred. A House-Senate conference committee approved the Senate plan, which included $1 million for program termination costs. Bryan issued a press release saying, "This hopefully will be the end of Martian-hunting season at the taxpayer's expense."[14] Seemingly out of nowhere, NASA's SETI efforts were dead.

---

14. See, for example, Debra Polsky, "Team Scrambles To Find New Funds for HRMS," *Space News* (18–24 October 1993): 27; and Steven J. Dick, *The Biological Universe*, p. 469.

Figure 2.3. Bernard Oliver speaks at ceremonies marking the start of the HRMS program in Arecibo, Puerto Rico, on 12 October 1992, with (left to right) John Billingham, an unidentified Puerto Rican official, Oliver, and John Rummel. *(Photo: Seth Shostak)*

While greatly disappointed, program personnel moved quickly and with resolve to continue SETI with private funding. Barney Oliver led a successful campaign to raise money from several wealthy Californians in Silicon Valley, whom he knew from his days at Hewlett-Packard. A number of scientists involved with the project moved over to the nonprofit SETI Institute, which had acted as a NASA contractor. The SETI Institute raised $7.5 million to cover costs of operating a targeted search through June 1995 and began the appropriately titled Project Phoenix, which lasted through 2004.[15] The all-sky survey was discontinued, as was the 10-year HRMS plan, and was replaced by the less-comprehensive observations that the SETI Institute could make contingent upon the vagaries of continued private fund-raising. The cancellation of NASA's SETI program did not end all research in this area (see the "Postscript" section below), but it significantly limited what researchers could accomplish.

---

15. Tom Pierson, e-mail to the author, 13 June 1997.

The Science of SETI

How did other scientists view SETI? A 1991 National Academy of Sciences (NAS) working paper by the Radio Astronomy Panel concluded that even though SETI was not exclusively a radio astronomy program, it contained exciting, valid science. The panel therefore recommended establishing a complementary university-based research program to help NASA develop search algorithms and signal processors.[16] A previous NAS study in 1982 had likewise concluded that SETI was a worthwhile scientific program.[17] In 1982, the journal *Science* published a petition put together by Sagan and signed by 70 eminent scientists, including biologists and biochemists such as Stephen Jay Gould, David Baltimore, and Linus Pauling.[18]

When the discussion stayed on a scientific level, the SETI program was viewed favorably in large measure because those scientists who thought about such matters had reached a strong consensus years earlier about how, where, and when to search for signals. Furthermore, their reasoning was relatively transparent both to scientists from other disciplines and to the general public. Sagan even explained the SETI game plan in an article that made the cover of *Parade* magazine.[19] SETI scientists agreed that a narrowband signal in the radio portion of the microwave spectrum provided the greatest return on investment in terms of traveling farthest with a minimum of power. Narrowing searches down to the water-hole region also made common sense. While other search methods might eventually be developed, in the late 1980s and early 1990s, SETI scientists were eager to start searching in earnest because the formerly quiet microwave spectrum was quickly becoming jammed with the noise of new commercial communications satellites. In short, no major scientific organization seriously disputed SETI's scientific approach.

Still, scientific skeptics tried to exploit the lack of any solid quantitative calculations about the probable existence of an intelligent civilization elsewhere in the cosmos. Even if intelligent life existed, what was the likelihood

---

16. Astronomy and Astrophysics Survey Committee, *Working Papers: Astronomy and Astrophysics Panel Reports* (Washington, DC: National Academy Press, 1991), pp. 1–13.

17. Astronomy Survey Committee, *Astronomy and Astrophysics for the 1980's. Volume 1: Report of the Astronomy Survey Committee* (Washington, DC: National Academy Press, 1982).

18. Carl Sagan, "Extraterrestrial Intelligence: An International Petition," *Science* 218, no. 4571 (1982): 426. See also Drake and Sobel, *Is Anyone Out There?*, Appendix C, pp. 259–265.

19. Carl Sagan, "Scanning the Sky for Alien Civilizations: The Search for Signals from Space," *Parade* (19 September 1993): 1, 4–6. Ironically, this article was published just a few days before Congress passed Senator Bryan's amendment canceling SETI funding.

that these beings could beam a message to us that we could not only receive but understand? If we on Earth were just guessing at these probabilities, or the probabilities were infinitesimal, why bother looking at all?

Ernst Mayr, an eminent biologist who believed that the evolution of intelligent life on Earth was the result of incredibly long odds, cast aspersions on the idea of searching for ETI signals. Mayr went through the Drake Equation and assigned probabilities to the seven conditions expressed by the individual variables. He believed that only two such conditions were at all likely to obtain: that extraterrestrial life is able to originate repeatedly and that habitable exoplanets similar to Earth exist. All the other conditions he rated as improbable, with the exception of extraterrestrial life adapting toward higher intelligence, which he rated as highly improbable. A staunch supporter of Darwinian evolution, Mayr noted that life on Earth originated 3.8 billion years ago, while intelligent life on Earth developed only about half a million years ago. If the "evolutionary soup" had been a few degrees hotter or colder at any one point, we would not be here at all, according to Mayr. Even if ETI did develop, Mayr argued, then a particular intelligent civilization probably would not have the ability to communicate through space. He reasoned that there have been dozens of distinct civilizations on Earth (Greek, Maya, etc.) over the past 10,000 years, yet just one has achieved this technological capability.[20]

Put another way, Mayr argued that since life first appeared on Earth, approximately 50 billion species have evolved, but only one has developed technology: "If intelligence has such high survival value," he asked, then "why don't we see more species develop it?"[21] Back in 1961, however, the members of the Order of the Dolphin had concluded that intelligence did indeed have a high survival value, as shown by the behavior of species such as dolphins.[22] While dolphins presumably are not interested in astronomy, there is another variable, f_c, in the Drake Equation to calculate the fraction of intelligent species who develop the technological means for interstellar communication. Mayr overlooked this variable and attacked SETI, calling it "hopeless" and "a waste of time," and saying, "We have to deal with realities—not pipe dreams."[23]

20. Ernst Mayr and Carl Sagan, "The Search for Extraterrestrial Intelligence: Scientific Quest or Hopeful Folly?," *The Planetary Report* 16, no. 4 (1996): 4–13.

21. Erik Skindrud, "The Big Question: Giant Ears Await Alien Broadcasts," *Science News* 150, no. 107 (September 1996): 152–155, esp. p. 153.

22. Drake and Sobel, *Is Anyone Out There?*, p. 59.

23. Mayr, quoted in Skindrud, "The Big Question," p. 152.

Sagan responded to these comments by allowing that the probability of ETI may be low, but he quoted his 1982 *Science* petition: "No *a priori* arguments on this subject can be compelling or should be used as a substitute for an observational program."[24] Sagan also rebuked Mayr for suggesting that "biologists know better," noting that because "the relevant technologies involve the physical sciences, it is reasonable that astronomers, physicists and engineers play a leading role in SETI."[25] Actually, as this article points out, Sagan had advanced training in biology, having served as a research assistant in the laboratory of the Nobel Prize–winning geneticist Hermann J. Muller.[26]

Mayr turned this argument around by claiming that even though the existence of ETI cannot be established by *a priori* arguments, "this does not justify SETI projects, since it can be shown that the success of an observational program is so totally improbable that it can, for all practical purposes, be considered zero."[27] Similarly, in the fall of 1993, congressional critics such as Senator Bryan noted that, despite almost one full year of HRMS operation and almost two decades of NASA support, SETI had failed to find any "little green men." While the HRMS operation had found no ETI signals after scanning only a small fraction of the sky, this program had been planned as a 10-year effort, and even a decade might not be long enough to find a signal. Sagan argued that Mayr's, and hence Bryan's, line of thinking was the closed-minded equivalent of believing that Earth is at the center of the universe. Ultimately, however, Sagan noted that arguments over the relative probability of receiving an ETI signal are specious, since we can't know whether there are any signals unless we seriously look for them.[28]

Another line of reasoning suggests that instead of looking for ETI signals, we may as well sit back and wait for a more advanced extraterrestrial civilization to visit us. After the Manhattan Project scientists developed the atomic bomb, Enrico Fermi is reported to have asked, "Where are they?" By this, Fermi meant that surely we weren't the only ones to have developed nuclear technology, so why hadn't other extraterrestrial civilizations left traces of their existence? Because our Sun is a medium-age star, SETI researchers believe that if another ETI civilization exists, it stands a good chance of having been

---

24. Mayr and Sagan, "The Search for Extraterrestrial Intelligence," p. 10.

25. Mayr and Sagan, "The Search for Extraterrestrial Intelligence," p. 10.

26. Mayr and Sagan, "The Search for Extraterrestrial Intelligence," p. 5; the byline for Sagan notes that "He is one of the few astronomers with a background in biology" and mentions his working for Muller.

27. Mayr and Sagan, "The Search for Extraterrestrial Intelligence," p. 11.

28. Mayr and Sagan, "The Search for Extraterrestrial Intelligence," p. 13.

around far longer than we have and thus of being more advanced technologically. The Fermi paradox is premised in part on the notion that such advanced ETI civilizations would naturally expand into and colonize space.[29]

Yet perhaps other civilizations would colonize only planets near their own but still very far from us. Barney Oliver, among others, refuted Fermi's paradox, arguing that even for a highly advanced civilization, interstellar travel would be quite difficult because of its immense power requirements.[30] Perhaps they would not colonize at all for a variety of reasons, including the relatively young state of their technology—just as we have not yet colonized space. John Ball, an astronomer at MIT, suggests another possibility, which he dubbed the "zoo hypothesis": that alien civilizations are simply content to watch us from afar.[31]

Whether or not distant civilizations could somehow travel to Earth, the efficiency of radio signals makes that form of indirect communication much more likely. Beyond listening for intended signals, SETI scientists could conceivably find extraterrestrial transmissions that weren't meant for us, comparable to the radio and television signals that have been drifting into space from Earth this past century. As Fermi himself realized, the Fermi paradox may be interesting to contemplate, but it really offers no evidence one way or the other about the existence of ETI.[32]

Skeptics James Trefil and Robert Rood, who try to calculate how long colonization of the galaxy would take, take another cut at the problem. Trefil, a physics professor at George Mason University, and Rood, an astronomy professor at the University of Virginia, used the Drake Equation to calculate the chances of other sentient life-forms in the galaxy at 3 percent. Trefil and Rood believe that if we are now almost capable of building space colonies, an extraterrestrial civilization would probably have done so long ago, due to diminishing resources and crowding on their home planet. They theorize that such colonization further and further into space would continue exponentially through the generations. Thus, in 30 million years, the entire galaxy would be colonized. Assuming the universe is billions of years old, this

---

29. For more on the Fermi paradox, see, for example, Drake and Sobel, *Is Anyone Out There?*, pp. 130–131 and 203.

30. Bernard Oliver, "SETI: Galactic Colonization and Other Flights of Fancy," *IEEE Potentials* 13, no. 3 (1994): 51–54. Drake makes similar calculations in Drake and Sobel, *Is Anyone Out There?*, pp. 61, 119–131.

31. John A. Ball, "The Zoo Hypothesis," *Icarus* 19, no. 3 (1973): 347–349. See also Skindrud, "The Big Question," p. 153.

32. Drake and Sobel, *Is Anyone Out There?*, p. 203.

would be a mere blip on the cosmic timeline.[33] So, again, where are they? For the record, Sagan calculated the length of time it would take a civilization to colonize the galaxy as 5 billion years.[34]

Yet even cynics such as Trefil and Rood see value in ETI searches. Trefil believes in the value of technological spin-offs, while Rood heralds SETI as "a great intellectual adventure into our own origins."[35] Former Senate staffer Kevin Kelly, a less-than-enthusiastic SETI program supporter, felt strongly that the educational component alone, which could get children and their parents excited about science, justified NASA's SETI program.[36] In terms of spin-offs, the Federal Aviation Administration showed interest in adapting SETI frequency-analyzer technologies for air traffic control, while the National Security Agency was curious to learn about new techniques for eavesdropping and code-breaking.[37]

While not vocal supporters of the SETI program, many other scientists felt that a $10 million annual investment was probably worthwhile. For example, Zen Faulks, a University of Victoria biologist, observed that

> the incredible improbability of alien intelligence should be taken into account when deciding how much of our effort SETI should occupy, but I would be disheartened to see the search stopped.... The fallout for all the sciences, especially the biological sciences, would be so gargantuan if we did contact an alien intelligence... that it seems foolish to abandon the entire affair.[38]

At bottom, it could be argued that some of what scientists investigate is based on fundamental beliefs, hunches, or faith that the world works in some logical way. Deciding what is logical when we have little information may be a leap of faith. Thus, Rood has made the interesting argument that most of

---

33. Triplett, "SETI Takes the Hill," p. 84.
34. Lee Dye, "NASA Holds Its Breath and Listens for Other Worlds," *Los Angeles Times/Washington Edition* (7 October 1992), available online at *http://articles.latimes.com/1992-10-07/news/ mn-425_1_radio-astronomy*. This article also notes that Tulane University mathematician Frank Tipler agrees with Trefil and Rood's figure of 30 million years.
35. Triplett, "SETI Takes the Hill," p. 84.
36. Triplett, "SETI Takes the Hill," p. 85.
37. Triplett, "SETI Takes the Hill," p. 85.
38. Zen Faulks, "Getting Smart About Getting Smarts," *Skeptical Inquirer* 15, no. 3 (1991): 263–268; quoted in Donald E. Tarter, "Treading on the Edge: Practicing Safe Science with SETI," *Skeptical Inquirer* 17, no. 3 (1993): 288–296, esp. pp. 289–290.

those who believe in extraterrestrial life may do so because of a psychological need to believe in it.[39] Even if true, this proposition should in no way taint the search for ETI; and no responsible scientist has yet claimed to have found any, just that it is worth looking. Interestingly, Rood has gone on to conduct SETI research himself in the belief that, while a discovery is unlikely, it is still worth searching, since theorizing can't prove or disprove its existence.[40]

Moreover, SETI researchers fully comprehend and appreciate the need to double- and triple-check any potential signals from ETI in case a simpler phenomenon, whether terrestrial or nonterrestrial, could explain them. In addition to this application of the standard scientific principle of "Occam's Razor" to examine the simplest or most likely explanation first, an internationally adopted "contact" protocol calls for data about a potential ETI signal to be widely publicized and distributed so that other scientists may scrutinize and validate it.[41]

Even though SETI scientists are wary of publicizing a strange signal too soon for fear of "crying wolf," the scientific logic is simple: phenomena that cannot be attributed to conventional terrestrial or cosmic sources merit further investigation. As longtime SETI scientist Jill Tarter has said, "It's not a matter of being able to define what identifies intelligence. What constitutes 'credible evidence' is being unable to explain a signal—which you also can't make go away—by any known astrophysics or technology."[42] Again, SETI researchers have long been aware of the perils of debating their program at the "little green men" level and have adhered closely to traditional scientific methods of inquiry.

In addition, many SETI researchers caution that they may not discover an ETI signal anytime soon. Although those such as Drake continue to be very optimistic, simultaneously most researchers know that, by its very nature, the length of a comprehensive search is very hard to predict. Signal processing and other computer technology has continued to change rapidly, NASA's SETI program was a classic example of basic science generating observations and results that would eventually pay off, but when and how was anyone's guess. Program scientists also noted that if a definitive search produced no signs of ETI, this negative result would in itself be very important. Although HRMS certainly was not a definitive search, it was tens of thousands of times

39. Drake and Sobel, *Is Anyone Out There?*, p. 208.

40. Drake and Sobel, *Is Anyone Out There?*, p. 208.

41. Tarter, "Treading on the Edge," pp. 293–295.

42. Jonathan Eberhart, "Listening for ET: What if the Message Comes?," *Science News* 135, no. 19 (1989): 296–298, esp. p. 297.

more comprehensive than any previous efforts. Yet, as Jill Tarter has noted, the program was in the unenviable position of having to petition Congress for more funding on the basis of previous "failures."[43]

Unfortunately for SETI, even John Gibbons, President Clinton's science advisor, demonstrated a surprising misunderstanding of the nature of SETI. In February 1994 he opined: "We've done a lot of observing and listening [for alien signals] already, and if there were anything obviously out there, I think we would have gotten some signal [by now]."[44] Gibbons made these comments after Congress had already canceled funding for SETI, so it is possible he was posturing after the fact. Nevertheless, either nobody properly briefed Gibbons, or he was never interested enough to learn anything about SETI.

It is also well known that few scientists or engineers serve in Congress. One analysis of the membership of the 103rd Congress (1993–1995) by a SETI scientist showed that it contained more former undertakers (four) than former scientists (one) or engineers (three).[45] The only former scientist, Congressman, George Brown, Jr. (D-CA), viewed SETI as "valid science."[46]

The Political Story Behind the Congressional Cancellation

The SETI program represents a unique case study. By all accounts, it was properly managed, scientifically valuable, and had a relatively small budget. By contrast, the Superconducting Super Collider, which Congress also canceled at about the same time, was a multibillion-dollar program that was controversial among physicists and suffered from significant mismanagement. Agencies such as NASA or the National Science Foundation do not always renew investigators' grants, but why would Congress choose to dismantle a low-cost research program that was already staffed and operational?

Ironically, the first factor was SETI's size. At the height of the program, it received $12.25 million annually, which at the time worked out to less than 0.1 percent of NASA's total budget—a drop in the bucket compared to the billions spent on other types of space science or defense research and

---

43. Jill Tarter, e-mail message to author, 16 July 1997.

44. Keay Davidson, "Scientists Gather in S.F., This Time on a Note of Hope," *San Francisco Examiner* (17 February 1994), p. A4.

45. Jill Tarter, e-mail message to author, 16 July 1997.

46. Leonard David, "The Search Begins," *Final Frontier* (February 1993): 25–27 and 53–54, esp. p. 54.

development programs.[47] SETI's small budget meant that few contractors were involved. Since the SETI program people prided themselves on being self-reliant and developing much of their own hardware and software,[48] there were no major engineering support contracts or big aerospace firms to lobby Congress on the program's behalf. Although the program might have been "lean and mean," it provided little political "pork" in the form of jobs in congressional districts around the country.

The SETI program was also a casualty of intensified congressional and public anxiety over the ballooning federal budget deficit. In 1993 the new Clinton administration and Congress were taking a hard look at overall federal spending. Congress was searching for programs that would be easy to cut. While $12 million in one year obviously would hardly erase the deficit, the program's $100 million price tag over 10 years sounded more like "real money" and wasteful to boot if one characterized it as searching for "little green men."

The latter half of 1993 was also a particularly trying time for NASA politically. During that summer and autumn, NASA had barely won two bruising battles over continuation of the multibillion-dollar Space Station program and the Advanced Solid Rocket Motor program. The Hubble Space Telescope was still suffering from its spherical aberration problem.[49] In short, after waging these larger battles, NASA had little political ammunition left to defend a small program such as SETI. While top NASA officials such as Daniel Goldin, who had been the Administrator since May 1992, and Wesley Huntress, a planetary scientist who had been the Associate Administrator for Space Science for the previous six months, publicly supported SETI, it was more a question of how hard they could afford to push. Linda Billings, a former support contractor for the program at NASA Headquarters, believes that the SETI program administrators didn't fully appreciate that the fate of

---

47. Historical budget data for NASA as a whole are available in Appendices D1–D3 of the annual *Aeronautics and Space Report of the President*; see, for example, the FY07 edition of this report, available online at *http://history.nasa.gov/presrep.htm*.

48. Gary Coulter, telephone conversation with author, 17 July 1997.

49. See, for example, Robert W. Stewart, "House OKs Space Station by 1 Vote," *Los Angeles Times*, 24 June 1993, available at *http://articles.latimes.com/1993-06-24/news/mn-6643_1_space-station* (accessed 26 April 2013); and U.S. General Accounting Office, *Shuttle Rocket Motor Program: NASA Should Delay Awarding Some Construction Contracts*, Rep. GAO/NSIAD-92-201, ed. Mark E. Gebicke (April 1992), available online at *http://archive.gao.gov/d32t10/146526.pdf* (accessed 26 April 2013). The first Hubble servicing mission took place in December 1993.

this project was just one of many issues for congressional staffers and that they therefore didn't see the need to engage proactively with their perceived and actual allies on Capitol Hill.[50]

The program was also contending with the "giggle factor." Despite the program's well-attested scientific validity, it was easy for opponents to make jokes at its expense. SETI program researchers hated this, of course, but once the dialogue descended to this level, it became harder and harder for the program to be taken seriously. In addition, the nature of the search program meant that no immediate or definitive results were likely; still, this was another source of criticism.

While the cancellation of congressional funding in 1993 might have seemed abrupt, SETI had in fact suffered political difficulties for a number of years. Senator Bryan was not the first member of Congress to ridicule or try to cancel the program: Proxmire and Conte were just a few of the others. One key Hill staffer heavily criticized the program after the fact, calling it a very narrowly focused rifle-shot program that was supported only by those elitist people who worked on it.[51]

Perhaps even more problematic were adversaries such as Senator Bryan, who did not want to debate the program's merits in earnest. Bryan apparently felt that he had all the information he needed to make a decision. SETI program administrators knew that Bryan was opposed to the project and tried repeatedly to talk with him or his staff. A decade earlier, Sagan had been able to win over Proxmire, but this time Bryan simply refused to meet with anyone associated with SETI. According to Jill Tarter, she and other program researchers had been working with NASA's legislative affairs office for over a year to arrange such a meeting with Bryan and Huntress, only to

---

50. Linda Billings, telephone conversation with author, 10 July 1997; and Linda Billings, e-mail messages to author, 21 July 1997 and 9 June 2011. Billings also wrote a chapter entitled "From the Observatory to Capitol Hill," covering the political history of SETI to 1990, in *First Contact: The Search for Extraterrestrial Intelligence*, ed. Ben Bova and Byron Preiss (New York: Plume Penguin Books, 1990).

51. Kevin Kelly, conversation with author, 2 July 1997. During this conversation, Kelly dismissed the claim by SETI supporters that "if this doesn't get funded by Congress, it won't get done" as being false, since the SETI Institute was able to continue Project Phoenix with private funds. Project Phoenix, however, continued only the targeted search portion of NASA's SETI program; the all-sky survey had to be dropped due to lack of funding. Kelly also asserted that doing ground-based astronomy is not part of NASA's primary mission, but even most casual observers would probably concede that looking for ETI aligns with NASA's overall mission more closely than with that of any other agency.

be caught off guard when Bryan's office finally called at the last minute and nobody from NASA was available.[52] As program manager Gary Coulter put it, he never knew of anyone initially opposed to SETI who, after listening to the proponent's side of things, did not at least move to a neutral position. In other words, he felt that Bryan was not "fighting fairly."[53]

In 1993, SETI also had a problem beyond the halls of Congress: it was an unconventional program that did not fit neatly into any specific scientific discipline whose members could support it when times got tough. SETI had begun under the aegis of NASA's Life Sciences Division, in part because of John Billingham's interest. Once it was restarted as HRMS in 1992, it was moved to the Solar System Exploration Division, but some planetary scientists did not receive it warmly because they felt that it did not "come with its own money" in a time of tight budgets.[54] That is to say, some TOPS program scientists did not want to be "tainted" by SETI's problems.[55]

Because SETI was an astrobiology program that used the tools and techniques of radio astronomy, neither the biology nor the astronomy communities fully embraced it.[56] According to one observer, the average radio astronomer saw SETI as a distraction.[57] A 1991 decade-long survey of astronomy projects by the National Academy of Sciences called the search for ETI very exciting but cautioned that the "speculative nature of the subject" demanded especially innovative technology development and careful peer review.[58] While some critics singled out such language as a

---

52. Jill Tarter, e-mail message to author, 23 July 1997.

53. Coulter, personal communication, 17 July 1997.

54. Jill Tarter, e-mail message to author, 23 July 1997.

55. Steven Dick, e-mail message to author, 17 July 1997.

56. For an excellent discussion of the distinctions among astrobiology, SETI, exobiology, and so forth, see Linda Billings, "Are We All There Is? Astrobiology in Culture," paper presented at the American Association for the Advancement of Science Annual Meeting in San Diego, CA, 20 February 2010. A copy of this paper has been deposited in the NASA Historical Reference Collection at the NASA History Program Office, NASA Headquarters, Washington, DC. Billings believes that more clarity about these differences will lead to better public understanding and appreciation of this scientific research. As she concludes, "astrobiologists will do well to be mindful of public interest in their research; consider why people are interested; and tend to the task of communicating clearly, and meaningfully, about their work" (p. 10).

57. David H. Smith, telephone conversation with author, 7 July 1997. Smith has been a staff officer of the Space Studies Board at the National Academy of Sciences since 1991.

58. Astronomy and Astrophysics Survey Committee, *The Decade of Discovery in Astronomy and Astrophysics* (Washington, DC: National Academy Press, 1991), p. 62; also available online

less-than-resounding endorsement, this was largely because SETI didn't fall naturally into the domain of the commission members, who were mostly conventional nighttime astronomers, with the notable exception of Frank Drake.[59] Unfortunately, few people or groups exist who are both willing and able to stand up in support of basic scientific research. Despite former program official John Rummel's conviction that there were a few such people, he also believes that they were surprised by the political tactics of Senator Bryan.[60] Whether the SETI program was managed by NASA life scientists or astronomers was less significant than the fact that neither discipline supported it wholeheartedly at this formative stage. With all these factors entering into the political equation, it is hardly surprising that Congress canceled funding for the SETI program in 1993.

Postscript

"Although HRMS was a very small project by NASA standards, it dwarfed all other SETI efforts combined."[61] Compared to the $100 million or more that it typically cost to build and launch a spacecraft, $12 million was indeed a very modest annual budget. NASA funding for SETI had hovered in the $1 million to $2 million range for about a decade before it jumped to $4.42 million in FY90, $11.5 million in FY91, $12.25 million in FY92, and $12 million in FY93 (see appendix). Up until the congressional cancellation, NASA was the main government sponsor of SETI research, and private funding had not been very significant.

After Congress eliminated federal support for the SETI program, the SETI Institute was able to take over the targeted search portion of HRMS in 1994, aptly renaming the revived effort as Project Phoenix. High-profile private donors from the computer industry, such as Paul Allen, William Hewlett,

---

at *http://www.nap.edu/openbook.php?record_id=1634&page=62* (accessed 26 April 2013). This report is often informally referred to as the "Bahcall Report," after the committee's chairman, John Bahcall.

59. Kevin Kelly, conversation with author, 2 July 1997; and David H. Smith, conversation with author, 7 July 1997.

60. John Rummel, letter to author, 21 July 1997. Rummel was the SETI Program Scientist at NASA Headquarters from 1987–1993.

61. The quotation comes from an unattributed article titled "The Search for Extraterrestrial Intelligence: A Short History," published online by the Planetary Society; a hard copy of this article will be processed in the NASA Historical Reference Collection.

Gordon Moore, Barney Oliver, and David Packard, as well as many other individuals contributed funds, and NASA loaned equipment to the SETI Institute to make Phoenix possible.[62]

Project Phoenix scientists began their observations in February 1995, using the Parkes radio telescope in Australia. Two Northern Hemisphere campaigns followed, using the National Radio Astronomy Observatory and the Arecibo facility in Puerto Rico. Phoenix scientists targeted nearby Sun-like stars and observed approximately 800 stars, as well as specific exoplanets discovered after Project Phoenix began. For each star, almost two billion channels were analyzed. Phoenix scientists developed the cutting-edge technique of "real-time interference monitoring," using a second radio telescope to confirm any promising signals. Project Phoenix concluded its three observing campaigns in March 2004.[63]

In 2001, Paul Allen, a cofounder of the Microsoft Corporation, provided $25 million as seed funding for what became known as the Allen Telescope Array (ATA), a planned set of 350 radio astronomy dishes for SETI research. The SETI Institute then raised another $25 million to build the first 42 dishes, which began operating in 2007. The ATA may eventually be able to search nearby stars approximately 100 times faster than Project Phoenix and

---

62. Jill Tarter, "The Search for Extraterrestrial Intelligence," *Annual Review of Astronomy and Astrophysics* 39 (2001): 511–548, esp. pp. 536–537; David Whitehouse, "Radio search for ET draws a blank," 25 March 2004, available at *http://news.bbc.co.uk/2/hi/science/ nature/3567729.stm* (accessed 26 April 2013); and *http://www.seti.org/node/662, http:// www.seti.org/seti-institute/project/details/project-phoenix, http://www.seti.org/seti-institute/ project/details/project-phoenix-frequently-asked-question*, and *http://www.seti.org/seti- institute/project/details/seti-history* (accessed 18 October 2013).

63. For more on Project Phoenix, see the following pages on the SETI Institute Web site: *http:// www.seti.org/seti-institute/project/details/arecibo-puerto-rico-1998-2004, http://www.seti. org/seti-institute/project/details/green-bank-west-virginia-1996-1998, http://www.seti.org/ seti-institute/project/details/parkes-australia-1996*, and *http://www.seti.org/seti-institute/ project/details/project-phoenix-frequently-asked-question* (accessed 18 October 2013); hard copies of these online sources will be processed in the NASA Historical Reference Collection. See also "The Search for Extraterrestrial Intelligence: A Short History"; and Whitehouse, "Radio search for ET draws a blank." The first exoplanet, 51 Pegasi, was discovered in 1995. See, for example, "Exoplanet History – From Intuition to Discovery," NASA Jet Propulsion Laboratory, *http://planetquest.jpl.nasa.gov/page/history* (accessed 18 October 2013); a hard copy of this article will be processed in the NASA Historical Reference Collection.

could expand Project Phoenix's search net to 100,000 and perhaps to as many as 1,000,000 nearby stars.[64]

Another setback for SETI scientists occurred in spring 2011, when budget cuts by the National Science Foundation (NSF) and the State of California forced them to mothball the ATA equipment. The approximate annual cost of ATA's daily operations was $1.5 million in addition to $1 million allotted annually for scientific analysis and research. The NSF cut its support by 90 percent and the State of California also cut funding for Berkeley's Radio Astronomy Laboratory, which partnered with the SETI Institute in the planning and operation of the ATA from 2004 to April 2011.[65]

This crisis was followed by another SETI comeback in December 2011, when the ATA was brought out of hibernation. Through a *SETIStars.org* fund-raising campaign that yielded $200,000 and a separate collaboration with the Air Force, the SETI Institute was able to bring the ATA back online. Scientists can now use the ATA's unique capabilities to analyze the tens of millions of wavelengths emitted from the more than 1,200 exoplanets recently identified by the Kepler spacecraft, dozens of which could potentially support life.[66]

Not all of the consequences of the NASA SETI program's cancellation proved to be negative. Among the positive outcomes were increased funding from the Planetary Society for all-sky searches, such as Paul Horowitz's Project

---

64. See *http://www.seti.org/ata* (accessed 26 April 2013); Seth Shostak, "Searching for Science: SETI Today," *International Journal of Astrobiology* 2, no. 2 (2003): 113; and Lisa M. Krieger, "SETI Institute to Shut Down Alien-Seeking Radio Dishes," *The San Jose Mercury News*, 26 April 2011, available at *http://www.mercurynews.com/ci_17926565* (accessed 18 October 2013). See also *http://www.seti.org/seti-institute/project/details/general-overview* and *http://www.seti.org/seti-institute/project/details/fact-sheet* (accessed 18 October 2013).

65. Krieger, "SETI Institute to Shut Down Alien-Seeking Radio Dishes"; and Tom Pierson, e-mail message to SETI Institute supporters, 22 April 2011, posted at *http://archive.seti.org/pdfs/ATA-hibernation.pdf* (accessed 26 April 2013).

66. See "SETI Search Resumes at Allen Telescope Array, Targeting New Planets," *http://www.seti.org/node/905* (accessed 26 April 2013); Jenny Chynoweth, "Thank you, SETIStars!," 5 October 2011 SETIStars blog post, *http://info.setistars.org/2011/10/gearing-up-for-the-ata-re-launch* (accessed 26 April 2013); Dennis Overbye, "Search Resumes for Evidence of Life Out There," *New York Times*, 5 December 2011; "AFSPC Explores Allen Telescope Array for Space Surveillance," *http://www.seti.org/node/905* (accessed 3 July 2013) and *http://www.afspc.af.mil/news/story.asp?storyID=123150121* (accessed 3 July 2013). The last Web site is an Air Force news release showing that even in 2009, the Air Force was considering using the ATA for "space situational awareness."

BETA (Billion-channel Extraterrestrial Assay) at the Harvard-Smithsonian Center for Astrophysics; the formation in 1994 of the nonprofit SETI League, which just a year later initiated Project Argus, another new, privately funded all-sky survey; and continued expansion of the Search for Extraterrestrial Radio Emissions from Nearby Developed Intelligent Populations (SERENDIP), begun in 1979 at UC Berkeley.

Concurrent with the growth of computing power, SERENDIP projects have increased the bandwidth and number of channels they search, effectively broadening the search net.[67] In 1999, researchers at the University of California initiated the SETI@home project, utilizing the power of distributed computing to process SETI observational data.[68] Using the project's screensaver software on their personal computers, members of the public can process discrete batches of data. This crowdsourcing approach was obviously designed to build a broad public constituency for SETI research.

As befits such international scientific efforts, scientists and volunteers from countries around the globe have also been involved in SETI. Australia brought SERENDIP equipment to the Parkes radio telescope, and for a time scientists there were involved in the SERENDIP project. Nations such as France, Argentina, and Italy are sponsoring more modest SETI efforts. In years past, the Soviet Union sponsored a significant amount of SETI research; more recently, however, Russian support has dwindled to a trickle.[69]

---

67. For a good recent summary of optical SETI efforts, see Curtis Mead and Paul Horowitz, "Harvard's Advanced All-sky Optical SETI," in *Communication with Extraterrestrial Intelligence*, ed. Douglas A. Vakoch (Albany: State University of New York Press, 2011), p. 125. See also David Koerner and Simon LeVay, *Here Be Dragons: The Scientific Quest for Extraterrestrial Life* (New York: Oxford University Press, 2000), p. 165. Bruce Murray, a former director of the Jet Propulsion Laboratory, was one of the founders, along with Carl Sagan and Louis Friedman, of the Planetary Society in 1980. See *http://www.planetary.org/about* (accessed 26 April 2013) and "The Search for Extraterrestrial Intelligence: A Short History." Murray's reasoning is that we should not assume too much about extraterrestrial intelligence by focusing searches on nearby stars with Earth-like exoplanets. For more information on the SETI League, see "What is *The SETI League, Inc.*?" at *http://www.setileague.org/general/whatis.htm* (accessed 26 April 2013); "What is *Project Argus*?" at *http://www.setileague.org/argus/whargus.htm* (accessed 26 April 2013); and *http://www.setileague.org* (accessed 26 April 2013). For more information on SERENDIP, see *http://seti.berkeley.edu/SERENDIP* and "SERENDIP V.v Installation Report," at *http://seti.berkeley.edu/serendip-vv-installation-report* (both accessed 26 April 2013).

68. See, for example, *http://seti.berkeley.edu/setiathome/aboutseti* (accessed 26 April 2013).

69. Koerner and LeVay, *Here Be Dragons*, pp. 172–173; and "History of SETI," *http://www.seti.org/seti-institute/about-seti/press-materials/backgrounders/history-of-seti*.

Since the congressional cancellation, the general public's and the scientific community's interest in and appreciation for astrobiology has significantly increased.[70] A notable episode from 1996 was that of the "Mars rock," a meteorite discovered in Antarctica which scientists at that time believed might contain Martian microfossils (a possibility that remains unproved), and a subsequent meeting chaired by then–Vice President Gore with national experts on the scientific and societal implications of potential extraterrestrial life.[71] Over the past 15 years the number of known exoplanets has risen dramatically from a small handful to more than 800 confirmed, with more than 1,200 potential exoplanets identified by the Kepler spacecraft scientific team as of July 2013.[72]

NASA's Origins program, consisting of several large space telescopes, began gearing up in the late 1990s.[73] NASA Administrator Dan Goldin believed that in some ways, biology was the future of space, and he encouraged employees to study biology since few had any biological training in the mid-1990s.[74] In 1996, NASA began a formal Astrobiology Program,

---

70. The 1997 film *Contact*, directed by Robert Zemeckis, can be seen as cultural evidence of this trend. Based on Carl Sagan's novel of the same name, *Contact* features a leading character modeled on SETI scientist Jill Tarter. The film grossed over $170 million; see *http://www.imdb.com/title/tt0118884* (accessed 26 April 2013).

71. See Kathy Sawyer, *The Rock from Mars: A True Detective Story on Two Planets* (New York: Random House, 2006); "Statement of Vice President's Space Science Symposium, December 12, 1996," copy in file 9009, NASA Historical Reference Collection, NASA Headquarters, Washington, DC; and Steven J. Dick and James E. Strick, "The Mars Rock," chapter 8 in *The Living Universe: NASA and the Development of Astrobiology* (New Brunswick, NJ: Rutgers University Press, 2004), pp. 179–201.

72. See *http://exoplanet.eu/catalog.php* (accessed 26 April 2013) and *http://kepler.nasa.gov/news/keplerinthenews/index.cfm?FuseAction=ShowNews&NewsID=102* (accessed 26 April 2013).

73. See, for example, the 1997 fact sheet at *http://www.jpl.nasa.gov/news/fact_sheets/origins.pdf* (accessed 26 April 2013).

74. Goldin kicked off a three-part biology colloquium at NASA Headquarters in 1998 by noting that a "biological revolution" will take place in the 21st century, analogous in scale to the changes brought about by physics and engineering in the 20th century. The colloquium featured such notables as Bruce Alberts, head of the National Academy of Sciences from 1993 to 2005. See "Talking Points of Mr. Goldin for the Biology Colloquium," file 32164, NASA Historical Reference Collection, NASA Headquarters, Washington, DC. See also the 12 January 1998 edition of the *NASA HQ Bulletin*, also available in the NASA Historical Reference Collection.

building on exobiology and more than 35 years of research by NASA scientists.[75] Then in 1998, Goldin established the virtual NASA Astrobiology Institute (NAI), which is centered at Ames Research Center and currently consists of more than 700 scientists and faculty at 15 different sites.[76] In addition to the NAI, NASA's Astrobiology Program now includes three other research elements: Exobiology and Evolutionary Biology, Astrobiology Science and Technology for Exploring Planets, and Astrobiology Science and Technology for Instrument Development.[77] One of the goals enunciated in the Astrobiology Program's 2008 road map calls for scientists to "determine how to recognize signatures of life on other worlds."[78] In pursuit of this objective, NASA has awarded a few small grants to SETI Institute scientists for non-SETI astrobiological research.[79]

In the mid-1990s the SETI Institute split its work into two main divisions: the Center for SETI Research and what later became known as the Carl Sagan Center. Barney Oliver had died in 1995 and bequeathed a significant sum of money to the SETI Institute, which helped to establish the astrobiology program.[80] It is also possible that after the congressional debacle of 1993, the SETI Institute chose to separate these two areas of research so that its astrobiology work and its very organization could better survive politically.

---

75. See *http://astrobiology.nasa.gov/about-astrobiology/* (accessed 26 April 2013).

76. See, for example, *http://astrobiology.nasa.gov/nai/about/* (accessed 26 April 2013); and Dick and Strick, *The Living Universe*, pp. 19–20.

77. See *http://astrobiology.nasa.gov/about-astrobiology/* (accessed 26 April 2013). Thanks also to Linda Billings for pointing out the relationship between NASA's Astrobiology Program and the NAI.

78. The road map is available at *http://astrobiology.nasa.gov/roadmap/* (accessed 26 April 2013). This site links to a version of David J. Des Marais, Joseph A. Nuth III, et al., "Focus Paper: The NASA Astrobiology Roadmap," *Astrobiology* 8, no. 4 (2008): 715–730. Goal 7 (detailed on pp. 729–730) is to "identify biosignatures of distant technologies."

79. Marc Kaufman writes, in *First Contact: Scientific Breakthroughs in the Hunt for Life Beyond Earth* (New York: Simon and Schuster, 2011), that "NASA and the National Science Foundation have reopened their grant competition to SETI projects" (p. 13) without providing a source for this information. NASA Astrobiology Institute Director Carl Pilcher clarified the probable meaning of this in an e-mail dated 27 May 2011. According to Tom Pierson, Jill Tarter did receive a principal investigator–level grant through NASA's Science Mission Directorate's peer-review process for developing some specific SETI technology, and there may have been a couple of other similar grants (telephone conversation with author, 3 June 2011).

80. See *http://www.seti.org/page.aspx?pid=235* and *http://www.seti.org/page.aspx?pid=237* (accessed 26 April 2013); Tom Pierson, telephone conversation with author, 3 June 2011.

Overall, astrobiology has clearly come into its own as an accepted scientific field of study supported by the government, while SETI research has had to "fly under the radar" by making do with a patchwork of private support. The government has awarded grants for principal investigator–level SETI proposals, yet no significant efforts to resurrect NASA funding for a dedicated SETI project have occurred since 1993.[81] Somehow, it seems that SETI remains tainted by the congressional politics of the early 1990s, while astrobiology has enjoyed a much higher public profile.

Overall, since 1993, scientists have managed to perform some smaller-scale SETI research. Simultaneously, astrobiology has experienced tremendous growth and acceptance as a scientific discipline. Public funding was again withdrawn from SETI research in 2011, this time in the case of the Allen Telescope Array. Yet within a year, private fund-raising and a collaboration with the Air Force combined to revive that particular SETI project.

What can we learn about the intersection of politics and science from this SETI case study? One obvious lesson is that good science does not always triumph on its own merits. Communicating one's case effectively on Capitol Hill is always important, and nobody should be surprised to learn that politics often trumps policy, in science as in other fields. Advocates of SETI research certainly hope that future congressional and public debate over basic science programs will be conducted in a more open, better-informed manner.

---

81. Douglas Vakoch, e-mail message to author, 13 May 2011; and Tom Pierson, telephone conversation with author, 3 June 2011.

CHAPTER TWO, APPENDIX

Funding History for the NASA SETI Program

SETI Area Funding ($K)	FY75	FY76	FY77	FY78	FY79	FY80	FY81	FY82	FY83	FY84
SETI Microwave Observing Project	140	310	400	130	300	500	1895	0	1800	1500
Definition/R&D	140	310	400	130	300	500	1895	0	1800	1500
Program/ Project C/D	0	0	0	0	0	0	0	0	0	0

SETI Area Funding ($K)	FY85	FY86	FY87	FY88	FY89	FY90	FY91	FY92	FY93	TOTAL
SETI Microwave Observing Project	1505	1574	2175	2403	2260	4233	11500	12250	12000	56875
Definition/R&D	1505	1574	2175	2403	0	0	0	0	0	14632
Program/ Project C/D	0	0	0	0	2260	4233	11500	12250	12000	42243

Note: FY92 and FY93 figures are for the High Resolution Microwave Survey (HRMS). In October 1993, Congress directed NASA to discontinue the HRMS program. *(Credit: Jens Feeley, NASA Headquarters Office of Space Science, June 1997.)*

CHAPTER THREE
_____

The Role of Anthropology in SETI
A Historical View[1]

Steven J. Dick

Three events mark the beginning of the modern era of the Search for Extraterrestrial Intelligence (SETI): 1) the publication of the landmark paper by Giuseppe Cocconi and Philip Morrison, "Searching for Interstellar Communications," in *Nature* in 1959, suggesting that a search be carried out at the 21-cm radio wavelength; 2) Frank Drake's Project Ozma in 1960, which conducted the first such search at Green Bank, West Virginia; and 3) a small but now legendary conference at Green Bank in 1961, where the feasibility of a search was discussed and the Drake Equation was first proposed as a method for estimating the number of communicative civilizations in our Milky Way galaxy. Modern SETI was born during those three years, 1959–1961, setting the agenda for the field over much of the next 50 years.[2]

By the 1960s, when modern SETI began, anthropology as a discipline was almost a century old. The word *anthropology* derives from the Greek *anthropos*, meaning "man" or "mankind," which indicates that the discipline is meant to encompass the study of humans. One might well ask, then, why it should apply to the extraterrestrial life debate, which obviously deals with nonhumans. The answer is that in its broadest sense anthropology has developed a set of approaches to and methods for analyzing cultures and cultural evolution. Any intelligent species that may exist beyond Earth is likely to have developed culture. If, as many SETI proponents expect, that culture turns out to be millions of years old, cultural evolution will have taken place, with all that implies for development, communication, cultural diffusion, and so on. All of these phenomena are areas of study that anthropologists, along

_____

1. This chapter is adapted from Steven J. Dick "Anthropology and the Search for Extraterrestrial Intelligence: An Historical View," *Anthropology Today* 22, no. 2 (2006): 3–7.

2. Steven J. Dick, *The Biological Universe: The Twentieth-Century Extraterrestrial Life Debate and the Limits of Science* (Cambridge: Cambridge University Press, 1996), pp. 414–431.

with their colleagues in the social and behavioral sciences, have refined over the past century for terrestrial cultures.[3]

In this paper, I examine the role that anthropology has historically played in SETI, and how the two intellectual cultures of natural scientists and social scientists made contact. I argue that these historical interactions bode well for beneficial mutual interactions between anthropology and SETI in the future. What has been lacking is a *systematic* approach applying anthropology to the Search for Extraterrestrial Intelligence. There is considerable evidence that such a study will benefit both disciplines.

Beginnings

It would seem *self evident* that the social sciences, and anthropology in particular, have the potential to illuminate a subject so centrally concerned with societies and cultural evolution, even if the setting happens to be extraterrestrial. Yet, the historical record shows that the social sciences played no important role in SETI's first decade. This circumstance undoubtedly reflects a variety of factors, including C. P. Snow's "two cultures" phenomenon, increasing specialization already in full swing in the early 1960s, and plenty of problems on Earth for social scientists to tackle. Thus, while the Green Bank conference included astronomers, physicists, a biochemist, an engineer, and even a specialist on dolphin communication (John Lilly), no one represented the social sciences or humanities. This is hardly surprising when one considers that the conference organizer was the National Academy of Sciences, an organization devoted largely to physical science and mathematics.

What is interesting, however, is that the social sciences, stimulated by these early activities and discussions, did play a peripheral role in SETI almost from its modern beginnings. It is no accident that the first article of anthropological interest to SETI was published in *Nature* in 1962 and cited the Cocconi and Morrison article. It was entitled "Interstellar Communication and Human Evolution" and authored by Robert Ascher and Marcia Ascher, respectively an anthropologist and a mathematician at Cornell, the home institution of Cocconi and Morrison. Significantly, this article was included in the first essay collection on the topic of SETI, a volume edited by the astrophysicist A. G. W. Cameron, published in 1963, and entitled *Interstellar Communication*. The article's inclusion was a *de facto* recognition by at least one natural scientist that

---

3. On the development of anthropology in the context of the social sciences, see Roger Smith, *The Norton History of the Human Sciences* (New York: W. W. Norton, 1997).

the social sciences might have something to add to the embryonic SETI debate. The article argues that models founded on our knowledge of human evolution might contribute to SETI endeavors. In particular, the authors suggest an "analogy between prehistoric contact and exchange, and hypothesized extraterrestrial contact and exchange."[4] In early prehistory, when biologically distinct hominid populations existed, they point out, contact "occurred between technologically similar but biologically diverse populations. In later prehistory contact was usually initiated by those populations with advanced techniques and equal exchange was rare." This history, they suggest, might shed light on the nature of contact with extraterrestrial civilizations. Such comparisons bring with them all the problems of analogy, but the Aschers' article pioneered the idea that anthropology might aid SETI through a study of human evolution.

Meanwhile a NASA-commissioned study, published in 1961, had broached another possible role for the social sciences in SETI—assessing the impact of the discovery of extraterrestrial intelligence. Written as part of a mandate in the National Aeronautics and Space Act to examine the effects of the space program on American society, a brief section discussed the implications of discovering life beyond Earth. The social science authors viewed the recently completed Project Ozma (which had no connection to NASA) as having popularized and legitimized speculation about the impact of such a discovery on human values. The Brookings report authors emphasized that reactions by both individuals and governments to radio contact with an alien intelligence would likely depend on religious, cultural, and social backgrounds, as well as on the content of the message received. In a statement often cited since, the authors warned that substantial contact could trigger a foreboding effect: "Anthropological files contain many examples of societies, sure of their place in the universe, which have disintegrated when they had to associate with previously unfamiliar societies espousing different ideas and different life ways; others that survived such an experience usually did so by paying the price of changes in values and attitudes and behavior."[5]

---

4. Robert Ascher and Marcia Ascher, "Interstellar Communication and Human Evolution," *Nature* 193, no. 4819 (1962): 940–941, reprinted in *Interstellar Communication*, ed. A. G. W. Cameron (New York: W. A. Benjamin, 1963), pp. 306–308, esp. p. 307.

5. *Proposed Studies on the Implications of Peaceful Space Activities for Human Affairs, Prepared for the National Aeronautics and Space Administration by the Brookings Institution*, Report of the Committee on Science and Astronautics, U.S. House of Representatives, 87th Congress, 1st session, 24 March 1961 (Washington, DC: GPO, 1961), pp. 215–216. The report was prepared under the direction of Donald N. Michael, a social psychologist "primarily responsible for the interpretations, conclusions, and recommendations in, and the final drafting of this report" (p. viii).

This statement begs for elaboration and documentation. Over the past four decades, anthropology has certainly tackled the problem of cultural contact among terrestrial societies. But it has not systematically studied the possible effects of extraterrestrial contact.

Already by the early 1960s, then, two roles had been identified for anthropology in the context of SETI: the study of human evolutionary models as analogies for extraterrestrial contact and the study of its potential repercussions. Both roles embedded the problems and the promise of analogical thinking but, cautiously undertaken, held potential for further research.[6]

Early SETI Overtures to Social Science

These ideas lay mostly fallow during the tumultuous decade of the 1960s, when only two SETI searches were carried out, one in the United States and one in the Soviet Union. The realization gradually dawned on SETI proponents that the social sciences might be useful, even essential, to their discussions. Nowhere was this more true than in the case of the cultural components of the Drake Equation, which embodies all facets of cosmic evolution, including astronomical, biological, *and* cultural. In particular its last two components—the probability of the evolution of technologically sophisticated civilizations and the lifespans of such civilizations—were clearly in the realm of the social sciences. This realization was in evidence at an international meeting on CETI (Communication with Extraterrestrial Intelligence) held in the Soviet Union in 1971 and organized by Carl Sagan, Phil Morrison, Frank Drake, and their Soviet colleagues. It was sponsored jointly by the National Academies of Sciences of the United States and the USSR at a time when the Cold War was still very hot. Among those at the meeting were such luminaries as Francis Crick, Tommy Gold, Freeman Dyson, Gunther Stent, and Marvin Minsky. But also included in that landmark meeting were two anthropologists, Kent Flannery of the University of Michigan and Richard B. Lee of the University of Toronto, as well as historian William H. McNeill

---

6. On the use of analogy in astrobiology, see articles and references in Douglas A. Vakoch, ed., *Astrobiology, History and Society: Life Beyond Earth and the Impact of Discovery* (Heidelberg: Springer, 2013). For a contemporary view of these problems in connection with the space program, see Bruce Mazlish, ed., *The Railroad and the Space Program: An Exploration in Historical Analogy* (Cambridge, MA: The MIT Press, 1965), passim. For the general use of analogy in thinking see Douglas Hofstadter and Emmanuel Sander, *Surfaces and Tensions: Analogy as the Fuel and Fire of Thinking* (New York: Basic Books, 2013).

of the University of Chicago. There they debated the natural scientists about the evolution of technical civilizations. No conclusions were reached, but the natural scientists were clearly interested in what the social scientists had to say.[7]

At least token representation of the social sciences became quite common at gatherings where extraterrestrial intelligence was discussed. When NASA sponsored a 1972 symposium at Boston University titled "Life Beyond Earth and the Mind of Man," anthropologist Ashley Montagu was among the speakers His topic was the prospective reaction of humans to the discovery of extraterrestrial intelligence. Montagu concluded that "it is the communication we make at our initial encounter that is crucial." He recommended that no government official be allowed to participate in any way in responding to a signal but rather that "independent bodies be set up outside governmental auspices, outside the United Nations, operating possibly within or in association with a university, whose object shall be to design possible means of establishing frank and friendly communicative relations with beyond-Earthers." (The SETI Institute was founded 12 years later with message construction eventually becoming one of its activities.) Furthermore, Montagu counseled,

> I do not think we should wait until the encounter occurs; we should do all in our power to prepare ourselves for it. The manner in which we first meet may determine the character of all our subsequent relations. Let us never forget the fatal impact we have had upon innumerable peoples on this Earth—peoples of our own species who trusted us, befriended us, and whom we destroyed by our thoughtlessness and insensitivity to their needs and vulnerabilities.[8]

Montagu's point was again a plea for the study of culture contacts.

In the mid-1970s the scientific community and NASA in particular were taking a more serious interest in SETI.[9] The guiding light of SETI at NASA was John Billingham at NASA's Ames Research Center in Moffett Field,

---

7. See Carl Sagan, ed., *Communication with Extraterrestrial Intelligence (CETI)* (Cambridge, MA: The MIT Press, 1973), passim, esp. pp. 85–111.

8. Ashley Montagu, "Comments," in *Life Beyond Earth and the Mind of Man: A Symposium*, ed. Richard Berendzen (Washington, DC: NASA SP-328, 1973), pp. 24, 25.

9. Steven J. Dick and James E. Strick, *The Living Universe: NASA and the Development of Astrobiology* (New Brunswick, NJ: Rutgers University Press, 2004), pp. 131–154; and Steven J. Dick, "The Search for Extraterrestrial Intelligence and the NASA High Resolution Microwave Survey (HRMS): Historical Perspectives," *Space Science Reviews* 64, nos. 1–2 (1993): 93–139.

California. It was he who organized a series of workshops, chaired by Philip Morrison, with the goal of getting a NASA SETI program off the ground, complete with NASA funding. Part of that effort was a workshop on cultural evolution, which was chaired by Nobel laureate Joshua Lederberg and included anthropologist Bernard Campbell. The workshop focused on the evolution of intelligence and technology. The summary of the workshop, published in the landmark NASA volume *The Search for Extraterrestrial Intelligence*, edited by Philip Morrison, John Billingham, and John Wolfe, asserted that "our new knowledge has changed the attitude of many specialists about the generality of cultural evolution from one of skepticism to a belief that it is a natural consequence of evolution under many environmental circumstances, given enough time."[10] The cultural evolution panel discussed what evolutionary factors were responsible for hominid intelligence: warfare, communication and language, the predatory nature of life on the savannah. Arguing that evolutionist George Gaylord Simpson had been too pessimistic, they even quantified the probability that both intelligence and technology would evolve, assuming life had originated on any given planet. That probability, they said, was 1 in 100. Campbell contended that planets capable of producing intelligent civilizations "must have heterogeneous and time-variable environments," since on Earth evolution does not occur when environments are stable and homogeneous.

Three years later Campbell participated in yet another landmark NASA meeting on "Life in the Universe," also organized by John Billingham and held at NASA Ames. Here he discussed the evolution of technological species on Earth in an attempt to gain insight into the question of extraterrestrial technological species. He described four stages of early technology development, ranging from prototechnology (tool use and modification) and technology itself (tool manufacture) to pyrotechnology (fire control and metal industries) and energy control. He argued that in an extraterrestrial context, prototechnology would likely be common wherever animals have evolved, but more advanced technology would probably occur only among strongly social species. Technology, he concluded, "is adaptive, cumulative and generally progressive. At its simplest it is older than reason. At its most advanced, it is the product of cooperative undertakings by large numbers of highly intelligent organisms."[11]

---

10. Philip Morrison, John Billingham, and John Wolfe, eds., *The Search for Extraterrestrial Intelligence (SETI)* (Washington, DC: NASA-SP-419, 1977), pp. 49–52; for the agenda and a list of participants in the Workshop on Evolution of Intelligent Species and Technological Civilizations, see pp. 275–276.

11. Bernard Campbell, "Evolution of Technological Species," in *Life in the Universe*, ed. John Billingham (Cambridge, MA: The MIT Press, 1981), pp. 277–285, esp. p. 285.

Early Social Science Overtures to SETI

Sporadic though they were, these early efforts through the 1970s demonstrated the relevance of anthropology to SETI and constitute recognition of that fact by the scientific community that sponsored them. However, they hardly tapped the richness that anthropology holds for SETI. Were there proactive efforts on the part of social scientists to tackle the subject, rather than waiting to be invited to a SETI meeting? The first substantial evidence of such interest appears in the proceedings of a symposium at the 1974 American Anthropological Association (AAA), published in 1975 as a popular trade book titled *Cultures Beyond the Earth*. The book's subtitle, *The Role of Anthropology in Outer Space*, is somewhat misleading for several reasons: only two of its eight authors were card-carrying anthropologists, it is a mixed volume including fictional stories as well as factual analysis, and it is not in any sense systematic. But it does include a stimulating foreword by futurist Alvin Toffler and an afterword by anthropologist Sol Tax; it was sponsored by the AAA as part of a "Cultural Futuristics" symposium; and, most important of all, it contains ideas that were at the time new and sophisticated. In his foreword, for example, Toffler pointed out that "what we think, imagine or dream about cultures beyond the earth not only reflects our own hidden fears and wishes, but alters them." He saw the book as important because "it forces us to disinter deeply buried premises about ourselves."[12] This is a straightforward but important point, one that we do not explicitly address often enough. Contemplating extraterrestrial cultures forces us to do that, raising, as Toffler said, "the critique of our cultural assumptions to a 'meta-level.'" Moreover, he argued, the cultures that anthropology traditionally studies are all human and less technologically advanced; analyses of such cultures leave vast areas of life unilluminated by contrast or comparison. Toffler went even further, asserting that extraterrestrial anthropology

> calls into question the very idea of cultures based on a single epistemology, of single time tracks or merely human sensory modalities. It forces questions about intelligence and consciousness. It makes one wonder whether our assumptions about probability apply universally. In the course of all this, it also begins to give intellectual shape to the whole question of space exploration and its relationship to our world.[13]

---

12. Alvin Toffler, foreword to *Cultures Beyond the Earth: The Role of Anthropology in Outer Space*, ed. Magoroh Maruyama and Arthur Harkins (New York: Vintage Books, 1975), pp. vii–xi, esp. p. vii.
13. Toffler, foreword in Maruyama and Harkins, eds., *Cultures Beyond the Earth*, p. ix.

This profound statement gives some indication of anthropology's unrealized potential in relation to SETI.

It is one thing for a futurist to say such things. But in his afterword, Sol Tax, professor of anthropology at the University of Chicago, endorsed and elaborated these ideas. Extraterrestrial anthropology, he said,

> removes itself from our planet to view "human nature" as a whole. It envisions the opportunity to study the human behavior and the change or development of human cultures under extra-terrestrial conditions; to test the applicability of anthropological knowledge to the design of extraterrestrial human communities; and to develop anthropological models for quite different species of sentient and intelligent beings by using, on a higher level, the comparative methods by which we have come to understand each earthly culture in contrast to others.

Moreover, Tax noted, "Only when we have comparisons with species that are cultural in nonhuman ways—some of them maybe far more advanced than we—will we approach full understanding of the possibilities and limitations of human cultures." Nor was this a fruitless undertaking, because "even if we have no contact with nonhuman cultures in the immediate future, the models that we meanwhile make require that we sharpen the questions that we ask about human beings."[14] Studies of culture among animals are of course also relevant here, especially in the evolution of culture, but they inevitably fall in the more primitive direction. Contemplation of extraterrestrial cultures allows us to approach the problem from the direction of more advanced cultures, emphasizing that humans may not be on the upper end of a cultural spectrum that includes species from other planets.

Between Toffler and Tax in this volume were two anthropologists, Roger W. Wescott and Philip Singer. Wescott pointed out that anthropology brings both strengths and weaknesses to the ETI problem. Among the strengths is the range of its inventory of cultures, primitive and literate, extant and extinct. Among the weaknesses is the fact that in his view anthropology tends to study the primitive and prehistoric more than the modern cultures. SETI and space programs are the purview of modern industrialized countries, and anthropologists are less accustomed to operating within this context, much less with advanced extraterrestrial civilizations. In a broader sense, however, the tools of anthropology are

---

14. Sol Tax, afterword in Maruyama and Harkins, eds., *Cultures Beyond the Earth*, pp. 200–203, esp. pp. 202–203.

applicable. Wescott broached another problem with anthropology's entry into the SETI realm, one that concerned the natural scientists also in their time: "Just as exo-biologists now run the risk of being called ex-biologists," he wrote, "so may anthropologists with extraterrestrial interests find themselves regarded with suspicion by the more conservative members of their own profession."[15] Wescott also called attention to the anthropological relevance of studying cultures and subcultures in Earth orbit, in lunar orbit, and on the lunar surface. It is this aspect of extraterrestrial communities that Philip Singer addresses in the same volume.[16] This view particularly resonates now, almost 40 years later, in light of NASA's current interest in sending humans to Mars.

More substantial and influential than the 1974 AAA meeting on cultures beyond the Earth was the response to a crisis for SETI after the mid-1970s. The crisis was the so-called Fermi paradox, which asserts that if the galaxy is full of intelligent life, given the billions-of-years timescales involved, then at least some intelligence should have colonized the galaxy and should have arrived on Earth by now. Yet we do not see them, so "where are they?" Many scientists concluded in the 1970s and 1980s that this argument provided strong empirical evidence that extraterrestrials do not exist—"empirical" because we do not observe them on Earth (unless one accepts the evidence for UFOs, which SETI enthusiasts studiously avoid).[17] The discussion of interstellar colonization was joined by physical scientists, who calculated colonization rates and other relevant factors. But the "diffusion" of cultures was primarily a problem for social scientists and a problem familiar to cultural anthropologists.

One anthropologist in particular took up the challenge. Ben Finney, professor of anthropology at the University of Hawai'i and later chair of that department, was well known for his work on Polynesian migrations.

---

15. Roger W. Wescott, "Toward an Extraterrestrial Anthropology," in Maruyama and Harkins, eds., *Cultures Beyond the Earth*, pp. 12–26, esp. pp. 13–14.

16. Philip Singer and Carl R. Vann, "Extraterrestrial Communities—Cultural, Legal, Political and Ethical Considerations," in Maruyama and Harkins, eds., *Cultures Beyond the Earth*, pp. 83–101.

17. For the Fermi paradox crisis in SETI, see Dick, *The Biological Universe*, pp. 443–454. The original articles in the mid-1970s stating the paradox are Michael H. Hart, "An Explanation for the Absence of Extraterrestrials on Earth," *Quarterly Journal of the Royal Astronomical Society* 16 (1975): 128–135; and David Viewing, "Directly Interacting Extra-Terrestrial Technological Communities," *Journal of the British Interplanetary Society* 28 (1975): 735–744. A collection of articles on the subject is found in Michael H. Hart and Ben Zuckerman, *Extraterrestrials: Where are They?* (New York: Pergamon Press, 1982), 2nd ed. (Cambridge: Cambridge University Press, 1995). For a thorough discussion of possible answers to the Fermi paradox, see Stephen Webb, *Where is Everybody? Fifty Solutions to the Fermi Paradox and the Problem of Extraterrestrial Life* (New York: Copernicus Books, 2002).

He began his path-breaking work with the NASA SETI community in the mid-1980s, commencing perhaps the most sustained connection of a single anthropologist with SETI. Under a National Research Council program to bring university scientists into government labs, Finney applied anthropological methods to SETI's assumptions. He challenged some of its assumptions on the basis of terrestrial experience with deciphering ancient Egyptian and Mayan inscriptions.[18]

Most important was the book *Interstellar Migration and the Human Experience*, edited by Finney and Eric Jones. The result of a conference on interstellar migration held in 1983 at Los Alamos National Laboratory (LANL), where Jones worked as an astrophysicist, this collection of essays concentrated on yet another aspect of SETI, the possibility of interstellar colonization. Finney and Jones invited anthropologists, demographers, historians, paleontologists, and philosophers as well as astronomers, physicists, and machine intelligence specialists to discuss the subject of interstellar migration. Among the anthropologists were Joseph Birdsell, Nancy Tanner, and Finney himself. On the basis of humanity's evolutionary and historical past, and its characteristic expansionary, technologically innovative, and inquisitive nature, Finney and Jones made this prediction in the volume's epilogue: "Mankind is headed for the stars. That is our credo. Our descendants will one day live throughout the Solar System and eventually seek to colonize other star systems and possibly interstellar space itself. Immense problems—technical, economic, political, and social—will have to be solved for human life to spread through space." They recognized the dangers of hubris and of repeating discredited expansionary and imperialistic themes of history. Yet they concluded that "although we obviously cannot predict that human descendants will colonize the entire Galaxy, we are betting that they will try."[19] This dispersion of humanity among the stars would bring not only cultural diversity but also new species descended from humans, as well as new cultures. They did not resolve the Fermi paradox. But whether life on other planets turns out to be alien or descended from humans, anthropologists and social scientists in general will surely be anxious to study cultures beyond Earth.

---

18. Ben Finney and Jerry Bentley, "A Tale of Two Analogues: Learning at a Distance from the Ancient Greeks and Maya and the Problem of Deciphering Extraterrestrial Radio Transmissions," *Acta Astronautica* 42, nos. 10–12 (1998): 691–696, reprinted in expanded form as chapter 4 of this volume.

19. Ben R. Finney and Eric M. Jones, eds., *Interstellar Migration and the Human Experience* (Berkeley: University of California Press, 1985), pp. 333–339, esp. pp. 338–339.

The Past 25 Years: Mutual Benefits?

Over the past quarter century the interaction of SETI and the social sciences can only be described as sporadic. At professional meetings of the International Astronautical Federation (IAF) and the International Astronomical Union (IAU) and at international bioastronomy meetings with a variety of sponsors, social science has been only an occasional companion to the natural sciences. The proceedings of the IAF SETI Committee sessions, published as special issues of *Acta Astronautica,* sometimes represented anthropological or societal interests, especially in the 1980s and 1990s. Finney, for example, continued to examine the probable effects of contact from an anthropological point of view.[20] A series of triennial international bioastronomy meetings inaugurated in 1984, with the IAU as an occasional sponsor, began to show an interest in social science aspects of SETI with its 1993 meeting, again focusing on consequences of the discovery of ETI but also touching on other aspects.[21] And, more generally, University of Hawai'i sociologist David Swift undertook a series of revealing interviews with SETI pioneers that remains a rich resource for future work.[22]

In the early 1990s, on the eve of the inauguration of the NASA SETI program in October 1992, John Billingham led a series of workshops on "Cultural Aspects of SETI," known as the CASETI Workshops. For the first time social scientists were fully integrated into the discussion of the implications of contact with extraterrestrials. Four focus groups were formed to address history, human behavior, policy, and education, each with a mix of

---

20. Ben Finney, "The Impact of Contact," in *SETI Post-Detection Protocol,* ed. Jill Tarter and Michael Michaud, *Acta Astronautica* 21, no. 2 (1990): 117–121. This volume represents papers from 1986–1987 presented at the IAF SETI meetings.

21. For example, a section titled "SETI: Societal Aspects" at the 1993 meeting included papers by Ivan Almar, "The Consequences of Discovery: Different Scenarios," and Steven J. Dick, "Consequences of Success in SETI: Lessons from the History of Science," both of which were later published in *Progress in the Search for Extraterrestrial Life,* ed. G. Seth Shostak, ASP Conference Series, vol. 74 (San Francisco: Astronomical Society of the Pacific, 1995), pp. 499–506 and 521–532. Among other social science papers, the 1999 meeting included a paper by Douglas A. Vakoch, "Three-Dimensional Messages for Interstellar Communication," which was published in *Bioastronomy '99: A New Era in Bioastronomy,* ed. G. A. Lemarchand and Karen Meech, ASP Conference Series, vol. 213 (San Francisco: Astronomical Society of the Pacific, 2000), pp. 623–628.

22. David W. Swift, *SETI Pioneers: Scientists Talk About Their Search for Extraterrestrial Intelligence* (Tucson: University of Arizona Press, 1990).

natural and social scientists. The three recommendations produced by the history group (which included historians John Heilbron, Steven Dick, Karl Guthke, Jill Conway, and Ken Kenniston; anthropologist Ben Finney; and SETI scientist Kent Cullers) are relevant here:

1. It is important that NASA study appropriate analogies drawn from earlier human experience, while emphasizing that they are rough guides for thinking about SETI and not precise predictors of the future.

2. Study should be concentrated on analogies based on the transmission of ideas within and between cultures in preference to analogies based on physical encounters.

3. NASA's educational programs should place SETI within the historical context of humankind's effort to comprehend its place in the universe and to understand the nature and possibility of other intelligent life.[23]

The second recommendation, in particular, posed a challenge to the conventional thinking that radio contact with ETI would be analogous to physical culture contacts on Earth, an idea elaborated at a bioastronomy conference in 1993, the year following the conference.[24] A few individuals have tackled SETI from the social science perspective. In *After Contact: The Human Response to Extraterrestrial Life*, psychologist Albert Harrison led the way, showing how fields such as psychology, sociology, and anthropology can be used as an aid to thinking about implications of contact, an approach that may be generalized to astrobiology. In particular he advocates an approach called Living Systems Theory, in which what we know about organisms, societies, and supranational systems on Earth can be used to discuss the outer-space analogues of aliens, alien civilizations, and the galactic club. While he does not himself tackle the anthropological aspects, Harrison recognizes their potential role.[25] Canadian futurist Allen Tough has undertaken research on the impact of "high-information" contact with extraterrestrials and has encouraged such

23. John Billingham et al., eds., *Social Implications of the Detection of an Extraterrestrial Civilization:, A Report of the Workshops on the Cultural Aspects of SETI held in October 1991, May 1992, and September 1992 at Santa Cruz, California* (Mountain View, CA: SETI Press, 1999).

24. For more on this issue, see Dick, "Consequences of Success in SETI: Lessons from the History of Science," in Shostak, ed., *Progress in the Search for Extraterrestrial Life*, pp. 521–532.

25. Albert A. Harrison, *After Contact: The Human Response to Extraterrestrial Life* (New York and London: Plenum, 1997), pp. 5–8 and 151.

research through specialized conferences on the subject.[26] More recently, the Canadian anthropologist and archaeologist Kathryn Denning has not only provided a variety of keen anthropological insights into SETI but has also become a respected member of the SETI community.[27]

The work of Douglas Vakoch on interstellar message construction, with its emphasis on the relation between language and culture, has much in common with linguistic anthropology.[28] Vakoch has also been instrumental in rallying the anthropology community to the study of SETI. The session titled "Anthropology, Archaeology and Interstellar Communication" at the 2004 annual meeting of the American Anthropological Association—30 years after the previous AAA meeting on the subject—demonstrates the possibility of a larger role for anthropologists in SETI. That role ranges from the scholarly to the popular; among the best-known anthropological contributions to SETI are the science-fiction novels of anthropologist Mary Doria Russell.[29]

In the most general sense it is cultural evolution that drives the relationship between SETI and anthropology. If, as most SETI proponents believe, non-human intelligence in the universe is millions or billions of years old, we know only one thing for certain: cultural evolution will have occurred. One can speculate on exactly what the result might have been. The universe may, for example, be postbiological, full of artificial intelligence, precisely because one must take cultural evolution into account.[30] But, given intelligence beyond the Earth, the fact of the occurrence of extraterrestrial cultural evolution is

---

26. Allen Tough, ed., *When SETI Succeeds: The Impact of High-Information Contact* (Bellevue, WA: Foundation For the Future, 2000).

27. For a recent example of her work, with numerous references, see Kathryn Denning, "Social Evolution," in *Cosmos and Culture: Cultural Evolution in a Cosmic Context*, ed. Steven J. Dick and Mark Lupisella (Washington, DC: NASA SP-2009-4802), pp. 63–124.

28. Douglas A. Vakoch, "Constructing Messages to Extraterrestrials: An Exosemiotic Perspective," *Acta Astronautica* 42, nos. 10–12 (1998): 697–704; Vakoch, "The View from a Distant Star: Challenges of Interstellar Message Making," *Mercury* 28, no. 2 (1999): 26–32; Vakoch, "The Dialogic Model: Representing Human Diversity in Messages to Extraterrestrials," *Acta Astronautica* 42, nos. 10–12 (1998): 705–710; Vakoch, "The Conventionality of Pictorial Representation in Interstellar Messages," *Acta Astronautica* 46, nos. 10–12 (2000): 733–736. These are only a sampling of Vakoch's many articles over the past 15 years.

29. See Mary Doria Russell, *The Sparrow* (New York: Villard Books, 1996), and *Children of God: A Novel* (New York: Villard Books, 1998).

30. For a more detailed discussion of this idea, see Steven J. Dick, "Cultural Evolution, the Postbiological Universe, and SETI," *International Journal of Astrobiology* 2, no. 1 (2003): 65–74.

not open to doubt and is fundamentally a problem of anthropology. SETI is at the center of the question of cultural evolution in a cosmic context, and the study of culture in relation to cosmos may in time illuminate both terrestrial and extraterrestrial cultures.[31]

Summary

Historically anthropology has made sporadic contributions to SETI in the following areas, each of which should be systematically elaborated:

1. *Evolution of Technological Civilizations.* Using empirical data from terrestrial cultures, anthropologists can shed light on the likelihood of the evolution of technological civilizations, their natures, and their lifespans. This is a problem of physical anthropology, and the potential of this approach has been realized since the early 1960s.

2. *Cultural Contact.* Using analogical studies of cultural contacts on Earth, anthropologists may illuminate contact scenarios with ETI, extending cultural anthropology to the extraterrestrial realm. However, because SETI envisions remote radio contact with ETI, rather than physical contact, the transmission of ideas may provide a better model for SETI. Should physical contact be made in the distant future with cultures beyond Earth, cultural anthropology and even archaeology will become more directly relevant.

3. *Interstellar Message Decipherment and Construction.* Philip Morrison has argued that deciphering an interstellar message may be a long-term project, requiring the efforts of many scholarly disciplines to complete. Linguistic anthropology has a role to play both in deciphering and constructing interstellar messages.

4. *Cultural Diffusion.* Analogical studies of human migration on Earth may illuminate the Fermi paradox of extraterrestrial civilizations. Beyond SETI, migration studies will also be applicable to extraterrestrial human cultures wherever they may be established. A start on these topics has been made with the volume *Interstellar Migration and the Human Experience.*

All of these approaches belong under the rubric of cultural evolution and relate directly to the study of SETI as the third component of the Drake Equation. Whether applying the data and lessons of terrestrial cultural

---

31. Steven J. Dick and Mark Lupisella, eds., *Cosmos and Culture: Cultural Evolution in a Cosmic Context* (Washington, DC: NASA SP-2009-4802).

evolution to extraterrestrial cultures, tackling the implications of extraterrestrial cultural contact and communication, or studying human migration in a biological or a postbiological universe, anthropology has much to offer both in terms of data and approach. Other branches of the social sciences may prove useful in the long-term future. For example, should physical contact be made with extinct extraterrestrial civilizations, the methods of archaeology will become relevant. Soviet SETI scientists have especially emphasized this in the context of extraterrestrial artifacts that might be discovered in the exploration of the solar system. In any case, anthropologists are uniquely qualified by knowledge and training to contribute to SETI. In turn, the extraterrestrial perspective that many of us in the SETI field have found so invigorating also has much to offer the discipline of anthropology, both in expanding its boundaries, its insights, and its tools and in reassessing cultures on Earth and seeing them anew.

Finally, the participation of anthropologists in SETI fits into the larger project of bringing the social sciences and humanities into SETI.[32] This endeavor could advance E. O. Wilson's idea of "consilience," the unity of knowledge. Ben Finney has made this point, arguing that SETI "has the potential for playing a major role in transcending intellectual boundaries."[33] In my 40 years' experience working in this field, I have found nothing that has greater potential to unify knowledge than the idea of extraterrestrial intelligence. Moreover, the appeal of the idea to students makes SETI an ideal tool for implementing a unified knowledge curriculum in schools, work already being done at the SETI Institute and elsewhere.

---

32. Albert Harrison et al., "The Role of the Social Sciences in SETI," in Tough, ed., *When SETI Succeeds*, pp. 71–85.

33. Edward O. Wilson, *Consilience: The Unity of Knowledge* (New York: Alfred A. Knopf, 1998); Ben Finney, "SETI, Consilience and the Unity of Knowledge," in Lemarchand and Meech, eds., *Bioastronomy '99*, pp. 641–647; reprinted in Tough, ed., *When SETI Succeeds*, pp. 139–144.

CHAPTER FOUR

A Tale of Two Analogues
Learning at a Distance from the Ancient Greeks and Maya and the Problem of Deciphering Extraterrestrial Radio Transmissions[1]

Ben Finney and Jerry Bentley

Preface

During the mid-1980s I spent a little over a year working in a trailer parked near the huge wind tunnels at NASA's Ames Research Center on the shores of San Francisco Bay. A sign written in large bold letters and displayed in one of the trailer's windows—"ET, Phone Home"—hinted that something out of the ordinary might be going on inside. In fact, the trailer served as an overflow office for NASA's fledgling SETI program, which was then developing the means to detect radio signals hypothesized to have been sent by extraterrestrial civilizations. I was there to work alongside SETI researchers, using my anthropological background and knowledge to assess their rationale and procedures for trying to establish contact with extraterrestrials, as well as to consider the possible impacts on humanity if the enterprise succeeded. At that time I had already conducted a number of unusual research projects, most recently reconstructing a Polynesian voyaging canoe and sailing it over legendary migration routes to resolve issues about Polynesian migrations. Yet working at Ames alongside SETI astronomers, physicists, computer specialists, and

---

1. A version of this chapter was published earlier in a special issue of *Acta Astronautica*; see Ben Finney and Jerry Bentley, "A Tale of Two Analogues: Learning at a Distance from the Ancient Greeks and Maya and the Problem of Deciphering Extraterrestrial Radio Transmissions," *Acta Astronautica* 42, nos. 10–12 (1998): 691–696. The opening section here ("Preface") is a new addition, written by Ben Finney specifically for this collection.

others in their daring quest to contact the ultimate "others" proved to be an even more exotic and thought-provoking experience.

The epiphany that had steered me indirectly toward SETI came in 1978 when I was writing up an experimental canoe voyage from Hawai'i across the equator to Tahiti, navigated without instruments or charts. By then linguists, archaeologists, and others had made good progress in tracing the migration of ancestral Polynesians from Southeast Asia into the open Pacific, and our voyaging research was beginning to provide data and insights supporting the hypothesis that Polynesians had intentionally explored and settled the Pacific—as opposed to the then-popular null hypothesis that their canoes and navigation methods were so crude that they could only have been castaways driven eastward by wind and current. Nonetheless, I realized that for want of precise information on what the ancient voyagers actually thought, said, and did, we would never know exactly why and how they pushed the human frontier so far into the ocean. That's when it hit me that if I was truly interested in human migration into new habitats, and not just the Polynesian experience, then I had an opportunity to study firsthand the beginnings of a much more portentous migration that might eventually take humanity beyond Earth and into the cosmos.

But I could hardly write a grant proposal to study "space migration" and expect to get it funded by the National Science Foundation or any other agency that supports anthropological research. Instead, I started reading the literature on human spaceflight and attending space conferences. At the 1980 congress of the International Astronautical Federation (IAF) held in Rome, I wandered into a fascinating symposium on SETI, a topic I had only vaguely heard about. Papers by John Billingham, Jill Tarter, and others immediately intrigued me because they offered the prospect of humans expanding into space intellectually rather than attempting the daunting (and, according to Barney Oliver, energetically impossible) task of physically migrating to other star systems. Afterward I corresponded with Billingham, the head of SETI at Ames, about how I might participate in the NASA effort, and he recommended that I apply for a grant from a program of the National Research Council designed to allow university scientists to spend a year in government laboratories. But just after I submitted my proposal, Wisconsin Senator William Proxmire struck. He awarded SETI a "Golden Fleece" as a foolish waste of government funds and contributed to the demise of NASA's program. When funding was restored two years later, I was offered a fellowship and went to work in the SETI trailer.

As a resident anthropologist, I wanted to learn about SETI, much as I would about any other culture I had chosen to study. In addition to studying the science and technology involved in sending and receiving messages, above all I sought to understand the ideas and logic behind searching for extraterrestrial messages, deciphering any messages detected, and deriving useful information from these. This meant reading the scholarly literature on SETI, which at that time was sparse; attending SETI conferences; interviewing SETI scientists and technicians; listening to them discuss issues among themselves; and presenting papers at SETI symposia about my research. However, I did not take the antagonistic approach of so-called science studies as then practiced by a group of sociologists bent upon exposing what they considered to be the epistemological naïveté and dangerous hubris of scientists. If anything, I was biased in favor of SETI and those who were involved in what I regarded as a noble quest. Nonetheless, I did find some of the SETI scientists' thinking questionable—especially when they employed analogies based primarily on Western experience to speculate about the nature of ET civilizations and behavior.

For example, according to SETI advocates, many of the civilizations that might be contacted will be so many light-years away that the prospect of any meaningful conversations with distant ET interlocutors would be very dim. For the foreseeable future, we will therefore just listen. Furthermore, because of NASA's vulnerability to public criticism, in the mid-1980s SETI researchers at Ames studiously avoided even talking about sending messages into the cosmos. They feared that any such transmissions would be perceived by the public as exposing Earth to potentially hostile aliens, and that citizens' anxieties could, when expressed in letters to their representatives, bring the wrath of Congress down on NASA. (Of course, as Frank Drake pointed out, we were already giving our position away through powerful radar and television transmissions.) Accordingly, these scientists went out of their way to emphasize that they would attempt only to receive messages and not to transmit them. For those who asked how it would be possible to learn anything from listening to messages sent tens, hundreds, or thousands of years ago, they had an ingenious answer: "But we have already had the experience of learning from the ancient Greeks through one-way messages from the distant past." They were referring to the transmission of classical Greek science and learning to Western Europe in late medieval and Renaissance times through the intermediary of Arab scholars and others who had studied and translated ancient Greek texts.

As much as I was intrigued by this analogy, I could not help but think that the challenge faced by medieval Western Europeans learning at a distance from ancient Greeks was trivial compared to the task of deciphering and understanding interstellar messages. I thought that a more useful terrestrial analogy might be derived from the efforts to decipher ancient scripts of cultures far removed from the classical world I had a case in mind: the long struggle to translate the hieroglyphs carved on ancient Maya temples and vividly painted on pottery and pages of the few codices that survived Spanish colonization. While working toward my doctorate in the early 1960s, I had studied ancient Maya culture and the attempts to decipher the hieroglyphs. By then scholars had cracked the Maya's numbering system and their elaborate calendrical cycles based on the apparent movements of the Sun, Venus, and other heavenly bodies. Particularly because some scholars were then speculating that Maya writing might turn out to be primarily mathematical, calendrical, and astronomical-astrological in nature, the Maya case seemed like a much closer parallel to SETI issues than protracted ancient-to-medieval European knowledge transfers.

However, I didn't get around to investigating the Maya case until long after I had left the SETI trailer and returned to my university duties in Hawai'i. In 1994 John Billingham asked me to present a paper at a SETI session to be held later that year at the International Astronautical Federation congress in Jerusalem. He suggested that I might address the analogy between SETI and the delayed transfer of knowledge from ancient Greece to medieval Europe. "Well," I replied, "I could, but I would rather focus on the Maya case," and explained why. John agreed, so off I went to the library to catch up on the latest advances in Mayan decipherment studies.

Indeed, I did find the Maya case relevant to SETI thinking but not at all in the way I had previously imagined. The expectations that Maya writing would turn out to be primarily mathematical, calendrical, and astronomical in content did not pan out. Instead it proved to be largely focused on the histories of kings, ruling dynasties, and their wars. Furthermore, it became apparent that a fundamental fallacy had delayed the translation of Maya hieroglyphs, the same one that had for so long kept scholars from reading Egyptian hieroglyphic writing. This was the assumption that the glyphs represented ideas as a whole independent of spoken language. In both cases, it was not until scholars approached the glyphs as symbols for the phonemes and morphemes of speech, studied the modern languages descended from ancient Egyptian and Mayan, and discovered translation keys (such as Egypt's famous Rosetta Stone) that they were able to decipher the hieroglyphic texts. I therefore wrote my paper as a cautionary tale for SETI scientists who believed that extraterrestrial radio messages would be readily decipherable because they would mainly be mathematical and scientific in content and form.

Never have any of my conference papers caused such uproar. During the question-and-answer period, I was lectured on prime numbers and physical constants and told I ought to know that science and mathematics are universal languages that must be shared by any truly intelligent life-form. Jean Heidmann, the ebullient astronomer who was chairing the session, interjected that civilizations anxious to share their experience and knowledge didn't need to send mathematical and scientific primers. All they had to do was transmit their encyclopedia, which other truly intelligent beings should be able to understand with the aid of powerful computer algorithms. Only at the end of the discussion did someone come to my defense, a semiotician and computer specialist. "Of course," he calmly observed, "you need a key to decipher a totally alien message." Nonetheless, Heidmann and the rapporteurs of the session recommended that my paper be submitted for publication in *Acta Astronautica*. The reviewers recommended publication, although one suggested that in focusing so much on the Maya case I had not really explained the delayed transmission of knowledge from ancient Greece to Western Europe. Accordingly, I recruited Jerry Bentley, the founding editor of the *Journal of International History* and a historian who takes a global view of human events, to analyze more fully the knowledge transfer from ancient Greece to medieval Western Europe. Our joint paper, reprinted here with minor revisions, was subsequently published in *Acta Astronautica*.

Introduction

Can encounters between terrestrial civilizations help us think about making radio contact with extraterrestrial civilizations? The commonly suggested examples of the brutal impact of technologically powerful invading peoples on indigenous populations do not directly apply since radio contact would be intellectual only. There is, however, a type of encounter between terrestrial civilizations that occurs without any physical contact and involves the passive transmission of knowledge from one civilization to another without any possibility of an actual conversation. Here on Earth such encounters have occurred whenever scholars have been able to decipher ancient texts—be they written in books, engraved on stone or clay, or painted on pottery—and learn from the extinct civilizations that had produced them. One such encounter occurred during medieval times when Western European scholars began to learn about ancient Greek philosophy and science from translated texts. Since the knowledge gained from these texts is said to have stimulated Western learning and the development of modern science, SETI theorists have proposed this case as an analogue for how we might intellectually benefit from deciphering and studying radio transmissions from an advanced extraterrestrial civilization without (or before) attempting two-way communication.[2]

---

2. J. L. Heilbron, J. Conway, K. Cullers, B. Finney, and S. Dick, "History and SETI," in *Social Implications of the Detection of an Extraterrestrial Civilization: A Report of the Workshops on the Cultural Aspects of SETI Held in October 1991, May 1992, and September 1992 at Santa Cruz, California*, ed. J. Billingham et al. (Mountain View, CA: SETI Institute, 1990), pp. 1–26.

From Ancient Greece to Medieval Western Europe

During classical times, Greek learning spread throughout the Mediterranean basin. After the collapse of the Roman Empire in the 5th century AD, the study of Greek philosophy and science largely disappeared in Western Europe, along with an understanding of the Greek language itself. Knowledge of classical Greek philosophy and science was fully maintained, however, in the Byzantine and Arab worlds. Greek scholars of the Byzantine Empire continued to study classical texts, and until the fall of the empire in AD 1453, they maintained a lively tradition of commenting on classical authorities and adapting them to contemporary needs. Meanwhile, beginning in the 7th century AD, Arab peoples encountered classical Greek thought—along with classical Persian and Indian learning—as they expanded to the north, east, and west under the banner of Islam. Muslim scholars translated the works of Aristotle, Plato, and other classical Greek scholars into Arabic, and during the next half millennium sought to reconcile Islamic values with the secular traditions of Greek philosophy and science, as well as with Indian medicine and mathematics.

During the medieval period, Western European scholars were therefore able to turn to the Byzantine Empire and centers of Islamic scholarship in Sicily and Spain to recover knowledge of classical Greek learning.[3] For example, Islamic scholarship played a major role in bringing Aristotle to the attention of Roman Catholic philosophers and theologians. Although the Neoplatonic thoughts of Ibn Sina, or Avicenna (AD 980–1037), commanded the most respect in the Arab world, the works of those Islamic philosophers who looked to Aristotle for inspiration suggested the possibility of a powerful synthesis between analytical thought and religious faith. The most influential was Ibn Rushd (AD 1126–1198), also known as Averroes, who produced voluminous commentaries on Aristotle. Ibn Rushd spent most of his career in Cordoba, Seville, and Marrakesh, where Jewish scholars became familiar with his work. They discussed it widely among themselves and helped make it known among Christian scholars, some of whom undertook their own translations of the texts from Arabic to Castilian. Having thus become aware of the explanatory power of Aristotle's thought, Christian philosophers and

---

3. R. R. Bolgar, *The Classical Heritage and Its Beneficiaries* (Cambridge: Cambridge University Press, 1954); J. M. Hussey, *Church and Learning in the Byzantine Empire* (New York: Russell and Russell, 1963), pp. 867–1185; F. E. Peters, *Aristotle and the Arabs* (New York: New York University Press, 1968); J. R. Hayes, *The Genius of Arab Civilization: Source of Renaissance*, 3rd ed. (New York: New York University Press, 1992).

theologians embarked on the remarkable venture of scholasticism—the effort to synthesize Aristotle and Christianity.

Direct knowledge of Aristotle in Western Europe came as much from Greek as from Islamic sources. The Latin translations of Aristotle from Islamic Sicily and Spain, made mostly by Jewish scholars, were less than satisfactory since they passed Aristotle's original Greek through both Arabic and Latin filters. Thus, whenever possible, Roman Catholic theologians sought to obtain translations of Aristotle made directly from Greek texts; St. Thomas Aquinas (AD 1225–1274), for example, commissioned many such works. Many of these translations came from the Byzantine Empire, while others came from Greek texts preserved in the libraries of Islamic Sicily and Spain. Nevertheless, translations from Arabic remained in circulation until Renaissance humanists prepared fresh versions from Greek texts during the 15th, 16th, and 17th centuries.

Islamic scholarship also stimulated Western European interest in classical Greek science. In Sicily, Spain, and the Middle East, Western Europeans learned about Islamic science and medicine, which drew on both Greek and Indian traditions. They called for translations of Ptolemy, Galen, Hippocrates, and other classical scientists. Again, polyglot Jewish scholars and translators from various schools prepared many of these translations, working from original Greek texts when available and otherwise from Arabic translations of the Greek originals. The understanding of classical Greek science that resulted from these efforts profoundly influenced Western Europe from the 12th century through the 16th century, by which time, however, Copernicus and Vesalius were on the verge of launching Western European science and medicine on altogether new trajectories that were to surpass scholastic studies based on classical Greek texts.

Does the role played by this roundabout transmission of classical Greek learning to medieval Western Europe in stimulating the development of learning and science there provide a useful analogue for thinking about the possible impact of texts transmitted by advanced extraterrestrials on modern science and learning? At best the answer would seem to be a highly qualified maybe. To state the obvious, the ancient Greek philosophers and scientists; their Arab, Byzantine, and Jewish successors and translators; and the Western European scholars who received this learning were close cultural cousins of the same biological species, who could readily learn each other's languages and decipher each other's writing systems. By contrast, the gulf that would separate us—barring some extraordinary convergence—from any extraterrestrials whose radio transmissions might be received would surely be immense. This suggests that if we are to employ terrestrial analogues for learning from extraterrestrial civilizations, we should examine cases around the globe in which the cultural/linguistic gap between long-dead scholars and later ones who attempt to decipher and learn from old texts is significantly greater than that between ancient Greek writers and medieval Western European readers.

Breaking the Maya Code

The saga of attempts by European and American scholars to decipher the inscriptions left by the ancient Maya and then enter into their intellectual world provides just such a case to consider, for the cultural gulf between 19th- and 20th-century students of the ancient Maya and the ancient Maya themselves is about as great as can be found on this globe between civilizations past and present. The Maya are thought to be descendants of northern Asian peoples whose colonization of the Americas started some 20,000 or more years ago. Well after these emigrants had spread from Alaska to Tierra del Fuego, high cultures based on intensive agriculture arose in the Andes, along the west coast of South America, and in the Mesoamerican region of Mexico and Central America. Although some have posited Chinese or Southeast Asian influence on New World high cultures, most scholars hold that they developed independently from those of the Old World.

Archaeologists call the civilization from which come the bulk of the known Mayan inscriptions "Classic Maya." It flourished in the lowlands of southern Mexico, Guatemala, Belize, and western Honduras from about AD 250 to around AD 900. Scattered throughout this region are the architectural remains—consisting of temples, pyramids, stelae, and other structures—of numerous administrative and ceremonial centers. The societies that built and occupied these centers are generally described as primitive kingdoms or incipient city-states, ruled over by divine kings and often at war with one another. The autochthonous development of Classic Maya civilization came to an end by the 9th century. By that time one after another of the Maya kingdoms had collapsed, and their central places were abandoned to the tropical forest. Exhaustion of tropical soils by the burgeoning populations of these kingdoms, climate shift, peasant revolt, and invasion from highland Mexico have all been proposed, singly or in combination, to account for this collapse. During the "post-classic" period, Maya peoples continued living throughout the region but without the great centers and high culture of the classic era, except in the north of the Yucatan Peninsula, where Mexican-influenced civilization briefly flourished until the time of the Spanish conquest.

Despite the Spanish takeover and the subsequent impact of imported diseases, direct colonization, and cultural suppression, some three million Maya now live in Mexico and Central America. Most of them still speak Mayan languages and retain, if on an attenuated level, many of the belief structures, though not the scripts, of their ancestors.[4] In the 1820s, 1830s, and 1840s explorers from Europe and the United States began to "discover," with the help of Maya guides, long-abandoned ceremonial centers of the classic era, which by then had been covered by the tropical forests for centuries. Carved in relief on the tall stelae and on the walls and lintels of some buildings, the explorers found what appeared to be elaborate inscriptions composed of a long series of hieroglyphs. These inscriptions, plus similar symbols painted on plaster-covered bark pages of the few codices that escaped destruction by the ravages of time and of zealous Spanish priests, and those painted on excavated pottery urns, constitute the entire corpus of textual materials over which scholars have been laboring for a century and a half.

Only recently, however, have these researchers succeeded in cracking the Maya code. Why has it taken so long? According to Mayanist Michael Coe, scholars were misled by their belief that the hieroglyphs (often referred to simply as "glyphs") with which the Maya wrote were "ideographic" in the sense that each conveyed an *idea* directly to the mind without regard to speech.[5] This same "ideographic myth" also held up the decipherment of Egyptian hieroglyphic writing. In the 3rd century AD the Neoplatonist philosopher Plotinus marveled at how the ancient Egyptians could express their thoughts directly in their seemingly pictographic hieroglyphs without the intervention of "letters, words, and sentences." "Each separate sign," he proclaimed, "is in itself a piece of knowledge, a piece of wisdom, a piece of reality, immediately present."[6] These words, republished in Florence the year Columbus reached the New World, inflamed the Renaissance imagination about the wisdom of ancient Egypt, where people could express their thoughts in pictorial form without the intervention of writing. Athanasius Kircher, a German Jesuit who taught mathematics and Hebrew in Renaissance Rome, made widely admired "translations" of Egyptian hieroglyphs, which, as the Egyptologist Sir Alan Gardiner put it, "exceed all bounds in their imaginative folly." Without a true key to the hieroglyphs, Kircher could arbitrarily assign any meaning to them he wished.[7]

Not until the 1820s did the brilliant linguist Jean-François Champollion finally show the way toward translating the Egyptian hieroglyphs. Using the

---

4. M. D. Coe, *The Maya*, 5th ed. (London: Thames and Hudson, 1993).

5. M. D. Coe, *Breaking the Maya Code* (London: Thames and Hudson, 1992).

6. Quoted here from M. Pope, *The Story of Decipherment* (London: Thames and Hudson, 1975), p. 21.

7. Pope, *The Story of Decipherment*, pp. 28–33; A. Gardiner, *Egyptian Grammar*, 3rd ed. (Oxford: Griffith Institute, 1957), pp. 11–12.

newly discovered Rosetta Stone—on which in 196 BC the same message had been inscribed in Hieroglyphic Egyptian, Demotic Egyptian, and Greek—and his considerable linguistic skills, he was able to read the hieroglyphs as a phonetically written form of a once-spoken language, not as a collection of ideographs divorced from speech.[8] Hence, in a classic work on the newly discovered Maya ruins, John Lloyd Stephens wrote of the great classic Maya center of Copan: "One thing I believe, that its history is graven on its monuments. No Champollion has yet brought to them the energies of his inquiring mind. Who shall read them?"[9]

The Abbé Brasseur de Bourbourg made one of the first attempts. He had discovered a manuscript written in the 16th century by Diego de Landa, the bishop of Yucatan, just after its conquest by Spain. In its pages Brasseur thought he had found a key for deciphering Maya writing. De Landa had redrawn the glyphs and transliterated into Spanish the names of the days in the Maya 260-day calendar and the names of the months of their 360-day solar year. In addition, he recorded, or thought he did, the Maya symbols for each letter of the Spanish alphabet. However, whereas Brasseur was on the right track in his calendrical translations, he was more wrong than right when he interpreted the noncalendrical glyphs as phonetic letters of a Mayan alphabet instead of what they apparently were: attempts by de Landa's Maya informants to find a Maya symbol that, when spoken, more or less matched the Spanish pronunciation of each letter in the Spanish alphabet.[10]

Whereas Champollion had been an expert linguist and knew Coptic, the modern Egyptian language descended from ancient Egyptian, neither Brasseur nor any of the other would-be epigraphers who followed him had the requisite linguistic skills and knowledge of Mayan languages to be the New World Champollion. Many of them even denied that it was necessary to know linguistics or any Mayan language because they believed that the glyphs were not symbolic of speech but were pure ideographs, as had previously been claimed for Egyptian hieroglyphs. As late as 1950, Sir Eric Thompson maintained that the non-numerical/calendrical Maya glyphs did not express anything as mundane as language but instead symbolized mystical-mythological

---

8. J.-F. Champollion, *Précis du Système Hiéroglyphique des Anciens Égyptiens* (Paris: Imprimerie Impériale, 1824).

9. John Lloyd Stephens, *Incidents of Travel in Central America, Chiapas, and Yucatan*, 2 vols. (London: John Murray, 1841), vol. 1, p. 159.

10. C. É. Brasseur de Bourbourg, *Relation des Choses de Yucatán* (Paris: Durand, 1864); C. É. Brasseur de Bourbourg, *Manuscrit Troana: Étude sur le Système Graphique et la Langue des Mayas* (Paris: Imprimerie Impériale, 1869–1870); Coe, *Breaking the Maya Code*, pp. 101–106.

concepts.[11] His revival of such Neoplatonist nonsense might seem laughable except for the fact that his power and influence among Mayanists of his day enabled him to single-handedly block for several decades all attempts to read the Mayan script as a written form of once-spoken languages.[12]

Two years after Thompson's pronouncement, however, Yuri Knorozov, a brilliant Russian epigrapher outside the circle of Western European and American Mayanists, published a stunning paper that pointed the way toward using linguistic analysis and knowledge of Mayan languages to decipher the inscriptions.[13] He found that the principles of Mayan writing were similar to those operating in other hieroglyphic systems. However pictographic they might seem (and probably were in origin), the glyphs had come to stand for either phonetic-syllabic signs or morphemes (the smallest meaningful units of speech) and could be read with the help of knowledge gained from the study of surviving Mayan languages. Since then a new generation of Mayanist scholars—linguists, art historians, archaeologists, and ethnographers, as well as specialized epigraphers—have followed Knorozov's lead and have begun to read the inscriptions with some facility and to learn about Mayan politics, wars, religious practices, and other facets of this fascinating culture.

Michael Coe, whose analysis I have followed here, emphasizes how critical the linguistic approach has been to this decipherment, as it has been to every other deciphered ancient script. He even goes so far as to state categorically that "no script has ever been broken, that is, actually translated, unless the language itself is known and understood."[14] Coe offers as a case in point the inscriptions of the Etruscan inhabitants of central Italy before the rise of the Roman state. There are over 10,000 funerary inscriptions in Etruscan written in a script similar to that of the early Greeks and, like Greek, ultimately derived from Phoenician writing. But no one has discovered a "Rosetta Stone" with parallel texts in Etruscan and Latin or any other known language.[15] Apparently, the Romans never bothered to describe and analyze the language of their Etruscan subjects. As a result, declares Coe, "Etruscan can be read, but it has never been translated."[16] Those who might object that Chinese writing, with its

11. J. E. Thompson, *Maya Hieroglyphic Writing: An Introduction* (Washington, DC: Carnegie Institute of Washington, 1950), p. 295.

12. Coe, *Breaking the Maya Code*, pp. 124–144.

13. Y. V. Knorozov, "Drevnyaya pis'mennost' Tsentral'noy Ameriki [Ancient Writings of Central America]," *Sovetskaya Etnografiya* 3, no. 2 (1952): 100–118.

14. Coe, *Breaking the Maya Code*, p. 44.

15. C. Holden, "Etruscan Tablet Interpreted," *Science* 269, no. 5226 (1995): 925.

16. Coe, *Breaking the Maya Code*, p. 44.

tens of thousands of characters, must surely be ideographic should read John DeFrancis's *The Chinese Language*, in which DeFrancis demystifies Chinese characters by demonstrating that these figures—despite their pictographic beginnings—have evolved to be primarily phonetic-semantic symbols.[17]

Discussion

The Maya case appears to undermine SETI scientists' hopes of actually translating the messages they are working to detect. If we have been unable to translate ancient human scripts without some knowledge of the spoken language they represent, what prospects have we of being able to comprehend radio transmissions emanating from other worlds for which we have neither "Rosetta Stones" nor any knowledge of the languages they encode?

One way out of this dilemma of deciphering absolutely alien languages that is commonly suggested in the SETI literature revolves around two assumptions: first, that advanced intelligent beings capable of communicating by radio must share with us the same basic logical processes and employ numbers and understand physics at least as well as we do; and, second, that those extraterrestrials anxious to establish interstellar radio contact would deliberately avoid natural languages and develop artificial ones based on presumably shared reasoning processes and scientific knowledge. In 1960 Hans Freudenthal composed a *Lingua Cosmica* (*Lincos*) that was, he said, based solely on pure logic and was therefore decipherable by other intelligent beings.[18] Mathematician C. L. DeVito and linguist R. T. Oehrle subsequently proposed that beings from different star systems who have developed radio telescopes, and who therefore must share a basic understanding of mathematics and science, could begin to communicate in an artificial language built on such fundamental scientific facts as the nature of chemical elements, the melting and boiling points of pure substances, and the properties of gases. They asserted that these putative interstellar interlocutors could then progress to such basic physical units as grams, calories, kelvins, and so on, after which, as DeVito and Oehrle put it, "more interesting information can be exchanged."[19]

---

17. J. DeFrancis, *The Chinese Language: Fact and Fantasy* (Honolulu: University of Hawai'i Press, 1984).

18. H. Freudenthal, *Lincos: Design of a Language for Cosmic Intercourse: Part 1* (Amsterdam: North-Holland Publishing, 1960).

19. C. L. DeVito and R. T. Oehrle, "A Language Based on the Fundamental Facts of Science," *Journal of the British Interplanetary Society* 43, no. 12 (1990): 561–568.

The necessary assumption behind such an argument is that of the psychic unity of all intelligent species, or at least of all those who have entered a radio-communicative stage. Rather than directly challenging this crucial assumption, as have some commentators on the SETI enterprise,[20] let us assume enough convergent scientific intelligence that beings from disparate star systems could begin to recognize transmitted symbols for numbers, physical and chemical constants, and the like. Would this shared knowledge necessarily lead to "more interesting information"? Would it be possible to progress from mathematical and physical verities to discussions of biologies, cultures, and histories? Might it even be possible, as many SETI advocates hope, for such young civilizations as ours to learn from older and presumably wiser civilizations how to survive technological adolescence?

A closer examination of the Maya case may again yield an illuminating parallel. Brasseur de Bourbourg's early success in understanding the rudiments of Maya numerical notation and calendrical reckoning eventually led to a comprehension of Maya mathematics, which are based on vigesimal numeration symbolized by dots indicating one and bars indicating five and a zero marker, as well as recognition of their facility for plotting calendrical cycles of the Sun, Moon, and Venus.[21] But this breakthrough did not lead to the translation of the bulk of the Maya texts. On the contrary, it seems to have impeded the full translation of Maya because it reinforced the idiographic fallacy that all the glyphs represented ideas without any relationship to language. This fallacy led to some interesting ideas, such as the notion that an elaborately carved and inscribed "altar" from the ceremonial center of Copan portrayed the proceedings of an astronomy congress devoted to correlating solar and lunar cycles. Linguistically oriented scholars have since discovered, however, that the carvings on this artifact actually represent the 16 dynastic rulers of Copan and their reigns.

We have presented this terrestrial tale not to suggest the impossibility of deciphering messages from extraterrestrials. Rather, we offer it as a warning against a facile acceptance of the analogy between SETI and the delayed

---

20. See, for example, W. H. McNeill, "Remarks," in *Communication with Extraterrestrial Intelligence: CETI*, ed. Carl Sagan (Cambridge, MA: The MIT Press, 1973), pp. 342–346; J. C. Baird, *The Inner Limits of Outer Space* (Hanover, NH: University Press of New England, 1987), p. 133; and A. Westin, "Radioastronomy as Epistemology: Some Philosophical Reflections on the Contemporary Search for Extraterrestrial Intelligence," *The Monist* 70, no. 1 (1988): 88–100.

21. F. G. Lounsbury, "Maya Numeration, Computation, and Calendrical Astronomy," in *Dictionary of Scientific Biography*, ed. C. C. Gillespie, 15 vols. (New York: Charles Scribner, 1980), vol. 15, pp. 759–818.

transmission of classical Greek learning to Western Europe. We must think about the formidable prerequisites of deciphering extraterrestrial messages and consider the possibility that whole domains of knowledge may remain opaque to us, despite our best efforts, for a very long time. If terrestrial analogues are to be employed in relation to SETI, then we should explore the wide range of human experience around the globe and not focus solely on familiar cases that appear to reinforce our most earnest hopes.

CHAPTER FIVE

Beyond Linear B
The Metasemiotic Challenge of Communication with Extraterrestrial Intelligence

Richard Saint-Gelais

A Semiotic Outlook on SETI

Communication, as we all know, is a touchy business between human beings. So there is reason to doubt that it would be an easy thing across the universe. In this essay I will try to describe a set of theoretical problems that might affect communication with extraterrestrial intelligences. I will also attempt to map the chief difficulties that arise when we look at the phenomenon (or more exactly the hypothesis) of communication between what will be, in all likelihood, profoundly different species. These difficulties are often expressed in terms of epistemic and sensorial incompatibility between interstellar interlocutors who will belong to species and cultures so different that the common ground necessary to communication could be very small indeed. We do not know whether extraterrestrial beings will perceive and conceptualize their reality in ways similar to ours, using the same cognitive categories, or even whether they will communicate through visual and acoustic channels.

I should state at the outset that my position is similar to the epistemic skepticism just mentioned. But my perspective will be slightly different from, though not incompatible with, the epistemic perspective. I will apply the theories and methods of semiotic analysis to the problem of interstellar communication, focusing on signs, language, meaning, and interpretation. A simple—but simplistic—conception of communication defines it as a production phase followed by a reception phase, an encoding and then a decoding of a given meaning through a message that is seen as a vehicle for this content. But understanding a message is not extracting something physically present in the signs. It entails, rather, the integration of these signs into an interpretive frame that enables the recipient to give them meanings—meanings that the recipient has to elaborate, not extract. Take, for instance, a very simple and frequently encountered sign that consists of two equilateral triangles placed base to base and pointing in opposite directions, one left, the other right; these two triangles are sometimes separated by a vertical line. As repeated experiences with undergraduate students have shown me, a reproduction of this sign on the blackboard meets only with perplexity until I offer them the clue "Suppose this is something you see in an elevator," providing an interpretive context that allows them to recognize the triangles as the conventional symbol for opening doors.

An important part of the interpretive context is knowledge of the language to which the signs belong. Semioticians have insisted that meaning depends on the code or system used to interpret the sign. For instance, a vertical stroke may mean, among other things, the number one (when interpreted as part of the arithmetical notation system), the first-person pronoun (when taken as an English word), the torso of a man or woman (when viewed as part of a matchstick figure), or the idea of verticality. In a "bottom-up" model of interpretation, this processing of individual signs is a first step, followed by more complex operations requiring a syntactic competence, i.e., a practical knowledge of the rules governing the combinations of signs.[1] As any student of a foreign language notices, though, understanding a sentence is not simply a matter of adding up the dictionary definitions of individual words in that sentence. It calls for a grasp of the interrelationships among these words and of the function each plays in the structure of the sentence. What makes this operation rather complex is that it is not as linear as the bottom-up model suggests: interpreters do not process isolated meanings *before* asking how to coordinate them into a global signification; a tacit hypothesis about the global syntactic pattern already guides the identification of the meaning and function of words. So there is a constant oscillation between bottom-up and top-down operations, in which inferences about a global and abstract pattern (within a sentence, text, or narrative) guide the expectation and recognition of the successive elements that make up this structure. For instance, the French word *loupe* may be either a noun (meaning "magnifying glass") or a form of the colloquial verb *louper* (meaning "to miss"). But the reader of a sentence in which the word *loupe* appears rarely wonders which of these meanings is

---

1. Bottom-up (or "data-driven") models of cognition assume that the processing of information starts with fundamental units, from which higher-order structures are inferred. The opposite strategy is the top-down (or "theory-driven") processing model, where a hypothesis about the global structure (a sentence pattern, for instance) guides the treatment of lower-level units. On both strategies, see Jerry Fodor, *The Modularity of Mind* (Cambridge: The MIT Press, 1983).

being invoked: the syntactic context, and what he infers from it, leads him to recognize the correct meaning instantly. *Sherlock Holmes examina le sol avec une loupe*: "Sherlock Holmes examined the ground with a magnifying glass"; *Il loupe tous ses examens*: "he flunks all of his exams."

The consequences these considerations have for interstellar communication are quite obvious. Such communication, if it is to be successful, must overcome the difficulties inherent in an exchange where sender and recipient do not share a common language; the latter cannot rely on an already established language competence with which to work out the meaning of the message but must instead start with the message itself and try to infer from it, conjecturally, the lexical and syntactic rules that endow it with meaning.[2] From the sender's point of view, the challenge is to conceive a message that will include, somehow, the interpretive context necessary for it to make sense. In other words, the sender must, apparently, produce this semiotic paradox: a self-interpreting message.

The difficulty is greater still because, even before the recipients tackle the intricacies of interpretation, they must identify the message as a semiotic (rather than natural) phenomenon. Normally, in a shared cultural context, this identification does not require conscious thought. For instance, each language selects an array of phonetic or graphemic patterns that count as signs so that users of this language know not only where to look for but how to easily recognize articulated signs when they see (or hear) them. For instance, the Turkish alphabet distinguishes between dotted and dotless *I*, treating each of these characters as a significant linguistic unit. In English, where no such distinction holds, a dotless *I* would seem to be merely the result of carelessness on the part of the writer. So a sign must not only be correctly interpreted but must also be recognized as a sign in the first place. When sender and recipient share an interpretive context (modes of perception, type and structure of language, cultural assumptions, and so on), this context functions as an implicit cue, as a kind of meta-sign signifying *this is a sign*. It is precisely this semiotic confidence that becomes problematic with interstellar communication, in which sender and recipient are compelled to question the invisible assumptions that underlie the production and reception

---

2. So this would seem a radical case of bottom-up treatment of information, but we must not forget that eventual recipients would have their own abstract cognitive frames, which they would tentatively (or unconsciously) mobilize, in a top-down fashion, when processing our messages. This would also apply to our own attempts at deciphering interstellar messages, as Stanislaw Lem brilliantly shows in his science-fiction novel *His Master's Voice*, trans. Michael Kandel (San Francisco: Harcourt Brace Jovanovich, 1983).

of signs. More precisely, it confronts the sender with the challenge of devising messages that include what is normally *outside* messages: a sign that acts as an index (*this is a sign*) and, to some extent, as code (*it must be interpreted that way*) to the whole message. Creating such a message is no small task. It implies the conception of messages that incorporate self-interpreting devices, signs that do not require an external interpretive system in order to be correctly identified and interpreted. We may therefore say that communication with extraterrestrial intelligences entails, per se, a form of altruism, an altruism that is not necessarily expressed on the level of *content*[3] but is embodied in the sender's endeavor to facilitate the recipient's task by trying both to see the message from the perspective of a hypothetical other and to imagine the obstacles that such a recipient may face. This is a discreet, albeit strong, form of collaboration, one that goes beyond the expression of altruistic values or the sharing of information, because it is the message's configuration rather than its content that anticipates potential difficulties at the recipient's end and tries to attenuate them.

Deciphering Ancient Scripts

The question, of course, is: to what extent is this possible? A comparison with the opposite, noncooperative situation—the deciphering of coded messages or inscriptions written in extinct languages—may provide a fresh look at the problems involved.[4]

---

3. For a detailed proposal along this line, see Douglas A. Vakoch and Michael Mantessa, "An Algorithmic Approach to Communicating Reciprocal Altruism in Interstellar Messages: Drawing Analogies Between Social and Astrophysical Phenomena," *Acta Astronautica* 68, nos. 3–4 (2011): 459–475.

4. Kathryn Denning makes a similar point: "If we can effectively isolate what makes a message decipherable, then we can compose messages with those anticryptographic properties in mind"; see her "Learning To Read: Interstellar Message Decipherment from Archaeological and Anthropological Perspectives," chapter 6 in this volume. On the decipherment of ancient languages, see Johannes Friedrich, *Extinct Languages*, trans. Frank Gaynor (New York: Philosophical Library, 1957); John Chadwick, *The Decipherment of Linear B* (1958; rpt. Cambridge: Cambridge University Press, 1990); and Andrew Robinson, *Lost Languages. The Enigma of the World's Undeciphered Scripts* (2002; rpt. New York: Thames & Hudson, 2009). For an account of a famous case of decipherment, see F. H. Hinsley and Alan Stripp, eds., *Code Breakers: The Inside Story of Bletchley Park* (Oxford: Oxford University Press, 1993).

At first glance, the difficulties involved in the decipherment of coded messages or ancient scripts suggest a rather pessimistic view of the interstellar communication challenge, for if it took specialists many years to solve the enigma of writing systems devised by human beings (without, in the latter case, any intent to conceal the meaning of the utterances), it seems unrealistic to imagine that our messages could be easily understood by beings whose culture, history, and even biology will differ vastly from ours. How can we be sure that some well-meaning interpreter will not misread our intended message?[5]

On a semiotic level, the similarity between the three kinds of situations is readily apparent. Deciphering inscriptions in unknown languages or messages in secret codes implies coping with strings of signs without having any prior knowledge of the encoding rules, so recognizing these rules become one of the ends (instead of the means, as is usually the case) of the interpretive process. The decipherer of unknown languages tries to establish the phonetic and/or semantic value of symbols. The decipherer of secret messages seeks to identify the principle governing the replacement and/or permutation of letters. So both activities can be compared to the reception of an interstellar message and the task of interpreting it without having a prior idea of the encoding rules, if any, governing the production of the signals.

I use the word *signal* instead of *sign* because at the early stage of interpretation, decipherers must still identify the relevant semiotic units. They are confronted with signals—i.e., material manifestations of some kind (strokes on clay tablets, microwaves of a certain frequency)—that *may* be signs.[6] A sign is more abstract in nature: it is a semiotic configuration that is relatively independent of the concrete signals that embody it because it is defined by a limited number of relevant features, whereas the signal that manifests it exhibits supplementary—and, from the point of view of the code, unnecessary—features. The word *please* may be shouted or whispered; it may be pronounced with an Oxford or a French accent; it is always the same word, the same linguistic sign. For someone who does not know the code, however, nothing in the utterance indicates whether the relevant feature here is not

5. Chadwick's account of the decipherment of Linear B (*The Decipherment of Linear B*, pp. 26–32) is particularly useful in that it relates not only the successive breakthroughs that finally led to the solution but the sad story of failed attempts, some by distinguished scholars who were so convinced of the validity of their initial hypothesis that they forced it on the material to be deciphered.

6. "In information theory, the term *signal* corresponds to the *sign vehicle* of semiotics.... This signal or information vehicle…is opposed to the sign since it is only its physical embodiment" (Winfred Nöth, *Handbook of Semiotics* [Bloomington: Indiana University Press, 1995], p. 80).

instead the whispering. To recognize a given sign from its signal is one of the feats that are accomplished automatically and unconsciously by those mastering the code but which become uncertain and difficult for those who do not. This is precisely the case when the first steps are taken toward understanding an unknown script, as John Chadwick shows in this passage from *The Decipherment of Linear B*:

> [E. L. Bennett's] outstanding contribution [to the decipherment of Linear B] is the establishment of the signary; the recognition of variant forms and the distinction of separate signs. How difficult the task is only those who have tried can tell. It is easy enough for us to recognize the same letter in our alphabet as written by half a dozen different people, despite the use of variant forms. But if you do not know what is the possible range of letters, nor the sound of the words they spell, it is impossible to be sure if some of the rare ones are separate letters or mere variants.[7]

At first glance, the remarkable achievements of Champollion, Georg Friedrich Grotefend, and others seem to contradict the thesis that the understanding of signs depends on prior familiarity with a language's underlying code. Were these men not able to decipher the hitherto unreadable hieroglyphs and cuneiform? Without underestimating their exploits, we should note that they *did*, in fact, start with some knowledge and (eventually valid) assumptions. First and foremost, they knew that they were dealing with human artifacts, signs made by human beings who shared with them a wide range of anthropological and cultural notions and categories. Some of these shared characteristics may remain entirely unnoticed as long as we are steeped in a given culture or semiotic context. Let us take, for instance, the kinds of writing systems human cultures have developed. It is possible to determine, just from the *number* of different characters a language possesses, the type of writing system that underlies it. If there are between 20 and 40 characters, it is an alphabetical system; if there are approximately 100 characters, we have a syllabic system in which each symbol transcribes a syllable (e.g., *ta, te, ti, to*). Ideographic systems require many more than 100 characters: Mandarin, for instance, has at least 60,000. So it is possible, provided enough inscriptions have been found, to identify the *type* of writing system even before it is deciphered. This is a nice example of what Charles Sanders Peirce called an abduction, a piece of reasoning that takes a startling fact and extrapolates

---

7. Chadwick, *The Decipherment of Linear B*, p. 39.

a more or less bold guess from it.[8] But this guess is undeniably informed by the fact that we humans have used these three kinds of writing systems. We cannot expect all writing systems in the universe to follow these lines, if only because the phonological apparatus of extraterrestrial beings may be quite different from ours; their languages may have more or fewer phonetic units than ours or may rest on a physiological basis unrelated to articulated sound. It is not at all certain that extraterrestrial civilizations use alphabetical systems of notation; nor can we assume, even supposing they do use alphabets, that their signaries include a similar number of units to ours.

Another crucial help for the decipherers of extinct human languages comes from the foothold that the decipherer can obtain from bilingual documents (e.g., the Rosetta Stone) and/or from identifiable proper names (of kings and countries, for instance). Since we cannot use the bilingual method (we would have to know an extraterrestrial language already) and proper names would be unrecognizable, the comparison remains an imperfect one. But we may draw more encouragement from cases in which the decipherment was successful even though no bilingual inscriptions could be found and in which both the language and the characters were unknown. The most famous of these is the case of Linear B, a writing system found on clay tablets on the island of Crete, deciphered by Michael Ventris in the 1950s on the basis of important groundwork laid by Alice Kober.

As Kober had done before him, Ventris used a purely formal method, grouping together words with the same beginning and then deducing—or rather abducting—which grammatical variations the different endings corresponded to (e.g., gender, number, etc.). Eventually he produced a grid on which the phonetic value of each sign was recorded. This grid led to Ventris's unexpected discovery that Linear B symbols transcribed a very ancient form of Greek.[9]

This conclusion to the story undermines an initially promising comparison between ancient scripts and extraterrestrial communication. Ventris did not know in advance what the language "behind" Linear B was, but of course he could recognize it, however different it was from Classical Greek, when he "saw" it—i.e., when enough evidence was accumulated to reveal the relationship. We cannot, of course, expect such recognition across interstellar distances.

---

8. "Abduction is the process of forming an explanatory hypothesis.... Deduction proves that something *must* be; Induction shows that something *actually is* operative; Abduction merely suggests that something *may be*" (Charles Sanders Peirce, *Collected Papers*, 8 vols. [Cambridge: Cambridge University Press, 1965], vol. 5, p. 106).

9. See Chadwick, *The Decipherment of Linear B*, pp. 40–66.

Peirce's Three Categories of Signs

My discussion of unknown languages has so far touched upon only one category of signs, namely, conventional signs. So it seems appropriate to look at a more comprehensive view, such as the one proposed at the end of the 19th century by Charles Sanders Peirce, who is now considered, along with the Swiss linguist Ferdinand de Saussure, as one of the two "founding fathers" of semiotics. Peirce's model encompasses a larger array of signs than does Saussure's, which is essentially preoccupied with verbal signs and so cannot account for images, traces, and so on. The generality of Peirce's classification is thus more suited to situations in which we may presume neither what kind of signs our "extraterrestrial correspondents" will send or expect to receive nor what kind of conception they may entertain regarding meaningful communication.

Peirce distinguishes among three types of signs: *index*, *icon*, and *symbol*. An index is a sign that has a causal link, or at least a "contact," with its object. For instance, a footprint in the snow is an index of the foot that made it and, by extension, of the presence of someone walking in a certain direction. (An experienced interpreter of footprints—a hunter or a detective, for instance—may determine more characteristics, such as the approximate weight of the animal or person responsible for a given trace.) An example of the weaker relation, contact, would be an arrow in a road sign: the direction of the arrow is an index of the portion of space at which it points.

The second category of signs is that of icon. It is variously defined as a sign having a relationship of similarity with the object it depicts or sharing some (but not all) of the object's properties. The "sharing of properties" definition of icons suggests that a recipient could, by observing an iconic sign, arrive at some conclusions concerning the features of the object depicted. By contrast, the "similarity" definition leads to a less optimistic outlook: similarity rests on a form of convention,[10] and we cannot know whether the recipients share any of our pictorial habits and principles. Our images could very well seem transparent to us while appearing opaque to others—including, as we know, human beings from other cultures and time periods.

We come finally to the third Peircean category, symbol. Symbols are signs that refer to their object only by means of a convention (or, as Peirce puts it, a Law). These are often called "arbitrary signs," such as those of language (the word *dog* has no causal link to the animal thus named, nor does it resemble a dog). It is essential to note that it is the code, the arbitrary system of Law,

---

10. See Douglas A. Vakoch, "The Conventionality of Pictorial Representation in Interstellar Messages," *Acta Astronautica* 46, nos. 10–12 (2000): 733–736.

that gives symbols their status and significance. Let us return for a moment to the two *I*s of the Turkish alphabet. On encountering his or her first dotless *I*, a tourist in Turkey might mistake it for a printing error or, in handwritten cases, attribute it to haste on the writer's part. The tourist's ignorance of this feature of the writing system would make the absence of the dot seem to be an accident, not an integral part of a writing system. But if the same tourist stumbles again and again on occurrences of this curious letter, he will eventually cease to regard it as a mistake; the very regularity of this form would then mark it not only as intentional but as a likely element of a writing system.

While only sentient beings can create symbols, they do not express themselves exclusively through them (blushing, for instance, is an index). Besides, a sign acting as a symbol can simultaneously function as another type of sign. We have just seen that pictorial representation is in part contingent on conventions, so images that human beings draw, paint, etc., are both icons and symbols. Here is another example. If I write *Je serai là à 5 heures* on a piece of paper and leave the paper on a table, it means, even for someone who does not understand French, that a human being has been in that room. The piece of paper and its written marks thus act also as an index. Another example would be hieroglyphs: the sign for *to cut* resembles a blade, so it is an icon; but the link between this image *of an object* and the *action* of cutting involves a convention, so it is also a symbol.

Now, only icons and symbols seem to be of real importance to us here, for the meanings we would like to communicate (such things as the position of Earth in the galaxy or mathematical formulae) would require either icons or symbols or, more likely, both. We should not count out indices too soon, however, since the first task is to devise signals that will stand an optimal chance of being perceived as intentional messages. So the aim is to ensure that our signals are taken as indices not of a natural phenomenon but rather of a will to communicate. An artifact such as the Voyager spacecraft cannot be mistaken for a natural phenomenon, but in the case of electromagnetic radiation such a mistake cannot be ruled out; so the sender of the latter must ensure that the configuration of the message reduces the risk of such a basic misunderstanding. I do not think a purely negative approach could work here: we may avoid any configuration that could be confused with interstellar "noise," but doing so cannot guarantee that the remaining configurations would not resemble electromagnetic phenomena unknown to us. There must therefore be some kind of metasemiotic cue, some "mark" that clearly "says" *This is a message.* The difficulty lies in encoding this metasemiotic marker in a way that ensures its recognition and correct decoding. It is clear that this metasemiotic cue cannot consist of symbols (in the Peircean sense of the word): being conventional and thus interpretable only by those familiar with the adequate set of rules, symbols would require on the part of the recipients a knowledge that we cannot presuppose.

Showing and Telling

At this point, a comparison with cryptology may yet become useful. At first glance this situation looks quite different since the sender—a spy, say—must send a message that his intended recipient will be able to decipher but which, to other recipients, will remain unintelligible (e.g., a text made of a jumble of letters) or will seem to convey an innocuous meaning or will not even look like a message.[11] But this obvious difference covers a less obvious similarity. Of course, our spy cannot mask the semiotic status of his message by simply adding a header that says, *This is not a message* or *This is just an ordinary letter that I am writing to a friend of mine*, just as the sender of an interstellar message, conversely, cannot simply declare that what follows is a meaningful message. Both kinds of messages must *convey* these metasemiotic assertions but cannot in any way *state* them. This requirement may be linked to an old distinction in literary studies, that between "showing" and "telling": a good writer devises ways to show things, for instance the feelings of his characters, whereas the debutant or clumsy writer will plainly tell them.[12] To give a simple example: the blunt novelist will affirm that a character lacks empathy, instead of putting him, as a more skillful writer would likely do, in fictional situations where the character might show empathy but does not do so. We can see the link between Percy Lubbock's showing and Peirce's notion of index: the "showing" mode of narration consists in giving indices, instead of direct statements, about what the writer wants to convey.

---

11. "I think with special pleasure of his [Arthur Conan Doyle's] sending one of his books to prisoners of war in Germany with an accompanying letter explaining that the first couple of chapters might be slow but the story would improve about Chapter 3. The intelligent prisoners were shrewd enough to divine that this meant something. Beginning with Chapter 3 they held the pages to the light and saw that Doyle had laboriously pricked out certain letters with a needle. Reading these in succession they spelled out messages of what was happening at home" (Christopher Morley, *The Standard Doyle Company* [New York: Fordham University Press, 1990], p. 112).

12. "The art of fiction does not begin until the novelist thinks of the story as a matter to be *shown*, to be so exhibited that it tells itself" (Percy Lubbock, *The Craft of Fiction* [1921; New York: Viking, 1957], p. 62).

What in literature is only a matter of taste (and literary reputation) becomes, in the world of spies and that of interstellar communication, quite crucial. We cannot *say* to extraterrestrials that our signals are not interstellar noise; we must find ways to *show* it. In other words, the configuration of the message needs to lead its recipients to the conclusion that the message was sent deliberately. We cannot *tell* them how to interpret the signals correctly but must *show* them how, in some way or another. This cannot be done by an external meta-message, a "how-to" framing device, but must be done *by the primary message itself*. In other words, the message needs to *embody* its metasemiotic frame.

Let's turn again to the spy's problem. His secret messages, to be efficient, must be difficult to decipher; this could be ensured by the use of an alphabetic substitution and/or permutation system resulting in a meaningless sequence of letters. In some situations, as we have seen, they must even dissimulate the fact that they are dissimulating something. A string of letters, "PSTVO CABDF," say, could achieve the first goal but not the second. It is interesting here to note that, when the Second World War broke out, the United States put a ban on all postal chess games and crossword puzzles for the obvious reason that ciphered messages could easily have appeared to be innocent exchanges in such a context.[13] But it should be stressed that, had the censorship bureau's employees been familiar with the rules of chess, they would immediately have spotted the bogus sequence of movements that a coded message would inevitably have entailed. (I remember a spy novel from my teenage years, *Langelot et l'avion détourné*, that relied on this discrepancy.)

Interpretants and Meaning

All this goes to show that the conspicuousness of a sign is largely contextual, which is bad news for the interstellar communication challenge because the reception context is a parameter the sender cannot control and about which he has virtually no clue. From there, two courses of action present themselves: devise a context-free sign, or devise signs that compensate for the ignorance of context. The first path points toward the search for universals, that is, signs that do not depend on a specific context—or at least not too specific a context—in order to be recognized as signs and to stand a chance of being correctly interpreted; hence the preference expressed by many experts for mathematics as a basis for communication. Whether they are right is an

---

13. See Frank Higenbottam, *Codes and Ciphers* (London: English Universities Press, 1973), p. 17.

anthropological question rather than a semiotic one, so I will leave it out of this discussion.

The second way is to think up self-contextualizing messages—or, in other words, self-interpreting signs. A self-interpreting sign is easier conceptualized than created. Let's consider, for instance, the pictograms imagined by H. W. Nieman and C. Wells Nieman, which would be sent as sequences of pulses that correspond to the dots into which an image has been decomposed.[14] In order to reconstruct the correct image, the recipients would need first to convert the linear signal into a bi-dimensional structure and then to interpret that structure to determine what it might signify or represent. I will not dwell here on the much-discussed problems pertaining to the recognition of visual signs. I would just like to address the prior (and allegedly simpler) problem of recognizing a two-dimensional structure embedded within a one-dimensional signal. Frank Drake imagined an easy and ingenious way to point to this, by making the total number of dots equal the product of two prime numbers, say 17 and 23, so that the transmitted message can be construed only as a 17-by-23-cell grid. Such a signal is as close as we may come to a message embodying an interpretive instruction. It assumes only a basic knowledge of prime numbers, which is not asking too much.

So this instruction looks promising, but only insofar as the recipient deduces that the signal corresponds to a *rectangular* grid. Why not a triangular or hexagonal grid? Our convention of drawing and painting on rectangles may not be as universal as we think.[15] Whatever the probability of extraterrestrial artists using three- or six-sided frames, this analysis shows that any configuration (here, the product of prime numbers) acts as a sign only by virtue of some assumption; we may invent astute ways to reduce the number of assumptions, but we must give up the idea of devising an assumption-free message. A perfectly self-interpreting sign is an impossibility: whatever "help" a signal may offer on its correct handling and interpretation, there will always have to be, on the part of the recipient, an interpretive jump—one that we can hope for but cannot count on unless we devise signs that do the (metasemiotic) job; but these in turn would have to be themselves correctly interpreted, and so on. The recursive dimension of communication cannot be bypassed, except precisely by the kind of interpretive bets that Peirce calls abductions and that are the work of the interpreter, not of the sign alone.

---

14. For a presentation and discussion of this scheme, see Douglas A. Vakoch, "The View from a Distant Star: Challenges of Interstellar Message-Making," *Mercury* 28, no. 2 (1999): 26–32.

15. This reflection has been suggested to me by René Audet.

This conclusion should come as no surprise to a Peircean semiotician, because for Peirce a sign does have a reference (and a meaning) only by virtue of its being interpreted. I recall his oft-quoted definition:

> A sign, or *representamen*, is something that stands to somebody for something in some respect or capacity. It addresses somebody, that is, it creates in the mind of that person an equivalent sign, or perhaps a more developed sign. That sign which it creates I call the *interpretant* of the first sign. The sign stands for something, its *object*.[16]

A sign refers to its object through the interpretant. The interpretant is not the person interpreting the sign, but rather the new sign through which the interpreter makes sense of the sign. Let me illustrate this with a simple example, that of smoke and fire. Smoke is obviously a sign (an index, more precisely), and fire the object to which it refers. It would seem that smoke refers by itself to the fire. But smoke only *results*, by a physical relation, from fire. In order for smoke to have a *semiotic* relation to fire, it is necessary for an interpreter to produce an interpretant linking both, for example, the phrase: "Oh, there is fire here!" From our perspective, Peirce's theory has the sobering implication that a sign does not *include* its meaning: it has one only insofar as it is *attributed* a meaning through the elaboration of an (appropriate) interpretant by its recipient. Providing such an interpretant to our interstellar message would not suffice for this further sign—and its status as the message's interpretant—would require its own interpretant, and so on.

Here the distinctions between symbols, icons, and indices again become useful. In the case of symbols, the gap from sign to meaning is maximal since nothing in the sign's appearance or physical nature gives any clue as to its object, which is linked to the sign by virtue of an arbitrary correlation. Without knowledge of the adequate code, a symbol (for instance, the word *Himmelblau* for someone who does not know German) remains opaque. The recipient of such a sign cannot arrive at its correct interpretant unless he or she is provided one, by, for instance, consulting a dictionary. The interpretation of indices requires a grasp not of a culturally determined code but of an empirical knowledge that may be shared across cultures and even, in certain cases, across species: the animals that flee when they smell smoke clearly understand the significance of this index as we do. The leap from icons to their interpretations is probably somewhere in between, not

---

16. Peirce, *Collected Papers*, vol. 2, p. 135.

as important as in the case of symbols but less automatically performed than in the case of indices.

Icons stand relatively close to their objects, for some of their observable characteristics correspond to features of what they depict. For instance, the images of the human body proposed by Douglas Vakoch resemble a human figure in that they show a head (represented by two superposed squares at the top), two arms (each represented by three diagonally disposed squares), and so on.[17] Still, we can expect no direct reconstitution of the object by an extraterrestrial recipient but at best a series of correct conjectures: that this is an image; that what it depicts is one figure (the one that appears in black in Vakoch's illustrations) and not the five shapes left in white (which, to us, are an indifferent background of the intended image); that this is a schematic image of the body of the sender of the message; that the two sets of diagonally disposed squares are part of this body (and not, say, objects or other beings clinging to the central figure); and so on. But the recipient, however intelligent and cooperative, may fail to make what we consider the correct assumptions—thus arriving at what to us would seem "wrong" interpretants—or, in the worst case scenario, may fail to make any assumption at all—in which case the sign would not even be recognized as such.

This discussion about symbols, icons, and indices does not inevitably lead to the conclusion that interstellar messages should include only the easier-to-interpret kinds of signs. We must remember that a message is composed not of one isolated sign but of (sometimes complex) combinations of signs, which may contribute to their mutual elucidation. This is precisely the idea behind Vakoch's proposal of a sequence of frames, each of which would contain six distinct areas: one for the picture; four for different parts of speech (nouns, verbs, adjectives, and adverbs); and one for the interrelationship between two successive frames (a meta-sign, then). Here we have a combination of icons (the shape of a human body, or of parts of it) and symbols: nouns for what is shown in the picture, adjectives for properties of that object (e.g., *high*, *low*, etc.), verbs for actions performed by the character between two successive frames, and adverbs for characteristics of that action (*fast*, *slow*). At first it may seem dubious that a recipient could establish a correlation between a given symbol and

---

17. See Douglas A. Vakoch, "Possible Pictorial Messages for Communication with Extraterrestrial Intelligences," *Journal of the Minnesota Academy of Science* 44 (1978): 23–25. More recently, Vakoch has commented on the narrative dimension of his proposal in "A Narratological Approach to Interpreting and Designing Interstellar Messages," *Acta Astronautica* 68, nos. 3–4 (2011): 520–534.

what it is intended to designate, or even that this recipient could identify it as a symbol and not as part of the picture. What may decisively help this eventual recipient is the mutual interpretation that parts of the message provide for one another (but an interpretation that must still be understood, i.e., interpreted, as such) and the systematic interplay of repetition and variation between frames, which will give recipients the opportunity to make conjectures—abductions—that the subsequent frames may either confirm or inform, in the latter case pressing the recipients to revise their previous hypotheses. Whereas Vakoch stresses the narratological structure of the sequence (the very simple story of an anthropomorphic character raising and lowering an arm, closing and opening an eye), I would stress its interactive aspect—the fact that it not only solicits (as any message does) interpretations but also offers a trial-and-error game in which conjectures, perplexities, and even mistakes may contribute to a gradual and tentative understanding.

Once a message like Vakoch's is devised, it should be submitted to several human interpreters who are unaware of its meaning. This test would give the designers an idea, however approximate, of the "decipherability" of their message, but it would also (and more crucially, I think) give them an inkling of the various and unexpected paths interpreters may explore when trying to make sense of it.

Unintended Clues

The admission that part of the process has to be entrusted to the recipient and the devising of messages that take the interactive nature of interpretation into account are, in my view, the keys to solving the difficulties outlined in this article. We cannot dictate, control, or even imagine the conditions, presuppositions, and results of the interpretation of our messages to extraterrestrials. But we can offer recipients the opportunity to try various strategies, even if this implies a risk that the paths they will follow are not the ones we would have expected or chosen for them. What we know of interpretation shows that this inability to control reception is always the case anyway, and that it is not necessarily a bad thing. A widespread conception of communication rests on the premise that successful reception of a message is one that recovers the meaning its sender meant to convey through it. But the history of the decipherment of unknown languages shows that things are never so simple, and that oblique ways of reading sometimes lead to unexpected breakthroughs. In his book on extinct languages, Johannes Friedrich points out that the direction in which a script should be read can sometimes be deduced from the empty space at the end of an inscription's last line.[18] Here we have an index, a sign caused by its object: the direction of writing is concretely responsible for which side of the last line is left blank. But this is not so conspicuous a sign that it does not require a piece of abductive reasoning.

Strange as it may seem, I see in this small example some grounds for hope regarding interstellar communication. We tend to conceptualize communication with extraterrestrial intelligences in terms of the successful transmission of *intended* meanings. But the production and reception of signs cannot be restricted to an intentional plane. An important feature of most indices is their unintentional nature. This applies not only to natural signs, such as smoke, but also to consciously produced signs, which always include an indexical aspect besides what the sender meant to say. The tourist confronted with a dotless *I* may, as we have seen, conclude erroneously that it is a mistake; but this hypothesis becomes less and less plausible as he or she encounters more dotless *I*'s, repetition of which becomes an index of the regular nature of this sign, even if this indication never crossed the mind of the texts' authors.

This example shows once again the centrality of interpretation. Peirce's insistence on the role of the interpretant implies that a sign, as soon as it is recognized as such (which is already the result of an interpretation), is subject to an endless and often unexpected interpretive process. This will certainly be so if, by chance, our signals are received by intelligent beings, whatever their physiology or culture. We can rely, up to a certain point, on the ingenuity of recipients. While they may not understand particular things we want to communicate, they may instead recognize and interpret, maybe even fruitfully, some clues we have left quite unintentionally. The Sumerian scribe who left a portion of the line empty could not possibly imagine that he was leaving a sign that would be read and utilized many centuries later by an archaeologist. SETI's situation is not really much different. From the experience of decipherers of extinct languages, it seems that sending as many and as various messages as possible is the best strategy, the one that offers the greatest chance at the recipient's end. The content of our messages may be far less important than the number and the variety of messages we send, if only because they will give the recipients more opportunities to compare and test their abductions about past messages against new examples. In the absence of feedback, this may be the best course of action when devising our interstellar "messages in a bottle."

18. Johannes Friedrich, *Extinct Languages* (New York: Philosophical Library, 1957), p. 91.

CHAPTER SIX

Learning To Read
Interstellar Message Decipherment from Archaeological and Anthropological Perspectives

Kathryn E. Denning

Introduction

Human musings about Others in faraway lands, from distant times, and on other worlds predate academic disciplines by thousands of years. The locations may be different, but the questions at the heart of the matter—*What do Others know of their worlds? What do They do there? How can We learn about Them?*—are the same. It is not surprising, therefore, that anthropology, archaeology, and SETI share certain core issues. It is also not surprising that anthropologists/archaeologists and SETI scientists understand and address these core issues differently, given their divergent disciplinary orientations.

These convergences and divergences provide a space for some very interesting interdisciplinary discussions.[1] My primary focus in this paper is on just one of many intersections of anthropology, archaeology, and SETI: interstellar messages.[2] I aim to highlight some assumptions about message decipherability and decipherment that appear in the SETI literature and that tend

---

1. I discuss some of these intersections at length in Kathryn Denning, "Social Evolution: State of the Field," in *Cosmos and Culture: Cultural Evolution in a Cosmic Context*, ed. Steven J. Dick and Mark Lupisella (Washington, DC: NASA, 2010), pp. 63–124; Kathryn Denning, "Unpacking the Great Transmission Debate," in *Communication with Extraterrestrial Intelligence*, ed. Douglas A. Vakoch (New York: SUNY Press, 2011); Kathryn Denning, "Being Technological," *Acta Astronautica* 68, nos. 3–4 (2010): 372–380; Kathryn Denning, "Ten Thousand Revolutions: Conjectures about Civilizations," *Acta Astronautica* 68, nos. 3–4 (2011): 381–388; and Kathryn Denning, "L on Earth" in *Civilizations Beyond Earth: Extraterrestrial Life and Society*, ed. Douglas A. Vakoch and Albert A. Harrison (New York: Berghahn Books, 2011), pp. 74–83.

2. Although I have elsewhere discussed in detail some of the other intersections among these three fields of research, the present chapter was written in 2004–2006 and has been only minimally updated.

to be contradicted by anthropology and archaeology. These contradictions stem from differences in the use of Earth analogues, in frameworks regarding linguistic meaning, and in epistemological orientations. I argue that by drawing from different disciplinary traditions, we can strengthen the conceptual groundwork for interstellar message decipherment.

Anthropology, Archaeology, and SETI

At the time of writing, there have been no confirmed signals of intelligent extraterrestrial origin, but then again, scientific SETI is a recent endeavor.[3] Over the past several decades, an impressive body of scientific work on astrobiology and on SETI has emerged; a growing community of scientists has been rationally and meticulously working through the possibilities, creating and testing hypotheses.[4] Many scientists are actively engaged in searches, and powerful new equipment is being developed. And as one SETI researcher has put it, "as the power of [SETI] searches continues to increase, so does

---

3. Two events marked the start of modern SETI: first the publication of Giuseppe Cocconi and Philip Morrison's article "Searching for Interstellar Communications," *Nature* 184, no. 4690 (1959): 844–846; and, second, Frank Drake's Project Ozma, a radio telescope search begun in 1960 at the National Radio Astronomy Observatory in Green Bank, West Virginia. But, as Peter Chapman-Rietschi notes, there were earlier suggestions in the scientific searches made by Ernest W. Barnes in 1931 and by Fred Hoyle in 1950, and in another 1959 article by S. S. Huang published in *American Scientist*; see P. Chapman-Rietschi, "The Beginnings of SETI," *Astronomy & Geophysics* 44, no. 1 (2003): 1–7. For a description of the prescient deliberations of Konstantin Tsiolkovsky in 1933, which were apparently suppressed by the Soviet regime, see B. Finney, V. Lytkin, and L. Finney, "Tsiolkovsky and Extraterrestrial Intelligence," *Acta Astronautica* 46, nos. 10–12 (2000): 745–749. For concise descriptions of the earlier history of SETI ideas, see Steven J. Dick, "Extraterrestrial Life and our World View at the Turn of the Millennium," Dibner Library Lecture, Smithsonian Institution Libraries (2000), available at *http://www.sil.si.edu/silpublications/dibner-library-lectures/extraterrestrial-life/etcopy-kr.htm*. See also David Grinspoon, *Lonely Planets: The Natural Philosophy of Alien Life* (New York: HarperCollins, 2004). For more details, see Steven J. Dick, *The Biological Universe: The Twentieth-Century Extraterrestrial Life Debate and the Limits of Science* (Cambridge: Cambridge University Press, 1996).

4. In 2004, the NASA Astrophysics Data System listed more than 600 SETI-related articles in refereed journals (Mark Moldwin, "Why SETI Is Science and UFOlogy Is Not: A Space Science Perspective on Boundaries," *Skeptical Inquirer* 28, no. 6 [2004]: 40–42). In summer 2011, that total exceeded 1,000; see *http://adsabs.harvard.edu/abstract_service.html*.

the probability of discovering an extraterrestrial civilization."[5] Another SETI scientist has recently reckoned that, because of very rapidly improving search technology, astronomers will detect signals within a single generation, if ever. That is to say, if there's anyone "out there" for us to find, we will likely know before 2030.[6] And whether we find neighbors or not, either way, the result will be significant.

Those directly involved in the search are busy developing and implementing new technologies for scanning the skies and analyzing data. Their overall task seems clear: search as much territory as thoroughly and efficiently as possible. But is there anything that other researchers can usefully do while Earth waits for a signal that may or may not come? In particular, what might anthropologists and archaeologists contribute?

While scarce in comparison with those from the physical and biological sciences,[7] contributions to SETI from the social sciences have been steady. Social scientists and SETI scientists have addressed a multitude of SETI-related social topics, including the social effects of the search, psychological correlates to beliefs about ETI, the social impact of a detection event, the uses of SETI in education, characterization of long-lived societies, what people would want to learn from ETI, global political decisions about whether to reply to a message, and the formulation of post-detection protocols.[8]

---

5. J. Billingham, "Cultural Aspects of the Search for Extraterrestrial Intelligence," *Acta Astronautica* 42, nos. 10–12) (1998): 711–719, esp. p. 711.

6. Seth Shostak, "When Will We Detect the Extraterrestrials?," *Acta Astronautica* 55, nos. 3–9 (2004): 753–758.

7. Billingham, "Cultural Aspects of the Search for Extraterrestrial Intelligence," 711.

8. For a particularly wide-ranging review, see Albert Harrison, *After Contact: The Human Response to Extraterrestrial Life* (New York: Plenum, 1997). An excellent overview of cultural aspects of SETI is provided by a SETI scientist in Billingham, "Cultural Aspects of the Search for Extraterrestrial Intelligence," pp. 711–719. Of particular note here is Billingham's comment that "the time is ripe to begin a thorough examination of 'SETI and Society'...[since] the number of authors who have published on these issues can be counted on the fingers of a few terrestrial hands" (p. 713). For the social effects of the search, see A. Tough, "Positive Consequences of SETI Before Detection," *Acta Astronautica* 42, nos. 10–12 (1998): 745–748. For the psychological correlates to beliefs about ETI, see Douglas A. Vakoch and Y.-S. Lee, "Reactions to Receipt of a Message from Extraterrestrial Intelligence: A Cross-Cultural Empirical Study," *Acta Astronautica* 46, nos. 10–12 (2000): 737–744. For the social impact of a detection event, see John Billingham et al., eds., *Social Implications of the Detection of Extraterrestrial Civilization: A Report of the Workshops on the Cultural Aspects of SETI* (Mountain View, CA: SETI Press, 1999); G. Seth Shostak, "Media Reaction to a SETI Success," *Acta Astronautica* 41, nos. 4–10 (1997): 623–627. On the uses of SETI in education, see Edna

Similarly, anthropologists and archaeologists have also been involved in the discussion ever since the emergence of modern scientific SETI efforts. The Drake Equation, often referred to as the cornerstone of modern SETI, is formulated in such a way that the estimated average lifespan of advanced civilizations strongly affects the estimated number of civilizations that might be sending interstellar communications. And indeed, it was on the issue of civilizations' life-spans that anthropologists and archaeologists contributed to formal SETI debates as early as 1971.[9] Recently, anthropologists and archaeologists have worked on SETI-related topics through assessment of the possible evolutionary paths to intelligence; review of historical precedents for contact between civilizations; simulations of contact; and, in this volume, consideration of the challenges of interstellar message decipherment and composition.[10]

DeVore et al., "Educating the Next Generation of SETI Scientists: Voyages through Time," *Acta Astronautica* 53, nos. 4–10 (2003): 841–846. On characterizing long-lived societies, see Albert Harrison, "The Relative Stability of Belligerent and Peaceful Societies: Implications for SETI," *Acta Astronautica* 46, nos. 10–12 (2000): 707–712. See also A. Tough, "What People Hope to Learn from Other Civilizations," *Acta Astronautica* 46, nos. 10–12 (2000): 729–731.

9. Kent Flannery and Richard Lee participated in an early CETI symposium: see Carl Sagan, ed., *Communication with Extraterrestrial Intelligence (CETI)* (Cambridge: The MIT Press, 1973). Other anthropological contributions to the discussion from the 1970s are outlined in Charles F. Urbanowicz, "Evolution of Technological Civilizations: What is Evolution, Technology, and Civilization?," paper presented at a 1977 symposium titled "The Search for Extraterrestrial Intelligence (SETI)," held at Ames Research Center, Moffett Field, California; the full text of this paper is available at *http://www.csuchico.edu/~curban/Unpub_Papers/1977SETIPaper. html.* Discussions of human evolution that derive from work in physical anthropology appear frequently in SETI literature.

10. On evolutionary paths to intelligence, see, for example, Garry Chick, "Biocultural Prerequisites for the Development of Interstellar Communication," chapter 13 in this volume; Lori Marino et al., "Intelligence in Astrobiology," *http://intelligence.seti.org*; Kathryn Denning and Lori Marino, "Getting Smarter about Intelligence," *Astrobiology* 8, no. 2 (2008): 389–391; and Douglas Raybeck, "Predator-Prey Models and the Development of Intelligence," paper presented at the SETI Institute, Mountain View, California, on 20 November 2004.

For three recent studies of historical precedents for cross-cultural contact, see Douglas Raybeck, "Contact Considerations: A Cross-Cultural Perspective," chapter 9 in this volume; Kathryn Denning, "The History of Contact on Earth: Analogies, Myths, Misconceptions," paper presented at the 61st International Astronautical Congress of the International Astronautical Federation 2010 (paper no. IAC-10-A4.2.2); and Kathryn Denning, "Is Life What We Make of It?" in *The Detection of Extra-terrestrial Life and the Consequences for Science and Society,*

But there is more to be done, as Ben Finney contends in his argument for further consilience between SETI scientists and social scientists.[11] All of the work done thus far in social scientific areas will prove to be crucial preparation if a detection event ever *does* occur, when a cascade of challenges would rapidly follow and multidisciplinary expertise would be needed. But even if a SETI detection event *never* occurs, this research still benefits us by enhancing our understanding of how we represent ourselves and how we measure the limits of our self-knowledge. This is, arguably, the ultimate project in abstracting principles about language, symbolization, cognition, and interpretability; about civilizations and what makes them develop the way they do; and about the evolution of technology.

There is another reason for anthropologists and archaeologists to add their voices to SETI discussions, and that is simply that their subjects are often invoked as examples of potential SETI outcomes. SETI discussions rely heavily on Earth analogues for predictions of the effects of contact and the challenges of understanding radically different kinds of communication. Specialists in Earth cultures, past and present, can contribute meaningfully to these discussions by unpacking those analogies and considering how best to use them.[12]

Using Earth Analogues Effectively

SETI researchers must speculate extensively. After all, there is as yet no accepted evidence of extraterrestrial intelligence. Therefore, it is not surprising that—as with many fascinating topics for which data are presently insufficient and implications are far-reaching—there is diverse and sometimes vehemently polarized thinking among scientists on many SETI issues, including

---

ed. Martin Dominik and John C. Zarnecki, *Philosophical Transactions of the Royal Society A* 369, no. 1936 (2011): 669–678, available at *http://rsta.royalsocietypublishing.org/ content/369/1936/669.full.*

On simulations of contact, see, for example, the long-running annual conference described at *http://www.contact-conference.com.*

11. Ben Finney, "SETI, Consilience and the Unity of Knowledge," in *Bioastronomy '99: A New Era in the Search for Life*, ASP Conference Series, vol. 213, ed. G. Lemarchand and K. Meech (San Francisco: Astronomical Society of the Pacific, 2000).

12. For one example of such an analysis, see John W. Traphagan, "Anthropology at a Distance: SETI and the Production of Knowledge in the Encounter with an Extraterrestrial Other," chapter 8 in this volume.

the probability of being contacted by other intelligences, what extraterrestrials could be like, and the wisdom of sending interstellar messages.[13]

This range of arguments and assertions is of considerable interest because it is not a consequence of data or their interpretation. Rather, much of the diversity in scientific SETI discourse stems, I believe, from alternative forms of reasoning, and also from the different Earth-based analogues (human and otherwise) that SETI researchers use in building their conceptual models of ETI. These influential analogues and varied reasoning processes comprise a fascinating and important substrate to SETI.[14]

The problem with analogies is that they are highly persuasive, inherently limited, and easily overextended. They therefore constitute a significant source of error in cultural understanding. For example, people often assume that Others are very much like themselves. This attitude can be called ethnocentrism, or it can be construed as an analogy—to oneself and one's own culture—which has been taken too far. A related problem is the single exotic example, generalized so that all Others are understood to be essentially the same. Anthropology offers theory, methods, and a wealth of cross-cultural data that can help us to avoid these errors. It emphasizes the diversity of human culture and experience while also seeking to make it comprehensible. Accordingly, in relation to SETI, Earth analogues are best used in sets, as illustrations of the diversity of behavior among intelligent beings. Single analogies are rhetorically useful in illustrating a point, for example, that contact could have unintended and potentially disastrous consequences, as it did when Columbus arrived in the Americas—but sets of analogies have the power to tell us something that we don't already know or suspect—for example, patterns distilled from the full range of contact phenomena that have been observed in human history. Using sets gives us the option of finding common

13. Some background on SETI scientists may be found in David Swift, *SETI Pioneers: Scientists Talk About Their Search for Extraterrestrial Intelligence* (Tucson: University of Arizona Press, 1990). For an interesting assessment of the reasoning involved in SETI, see André Kukla, "SETI: On the Prospects and Pursuitworthiness of the Search for Extraterrestrial Intelligence," *Studies in History and Philosophy of Science, Part A* 32, no. 1 (2001): 31–67. David Koerner and Simon LeVay also vividly describe some differences of opinion in *Here Be Dragons: The Scientific Quest for Extraterrestrial Life* (New York: Oxford University Press, 2000).

14. This subject is covered at length in Denning, "Social Evolution: State of the Field," in Dick and Lupisella, eds., *Cosmos and Culture* (see n. 1 above for full citation).

principles in cross-cultural comparisons, via deduction, rather than assuming all cultures to be essentially similar, based on induction from single cases.[15]

My comments below are generated partly by this distinction between induction up from single cases and deduction down from multiple cases, and partly by the anthropological principle that culture is endlessly variable and that we make assumptions about the cognitive worlds of others at our own risk.

The Decipherability of Interstellar Messages

What if SETI telescopes actually pick up a signal from a distant star system? Could we understand it? Should we respond to it? If so, what should we say, and how? Should we just go ahead and call them without waiting for them to call first?

For many years, SETI's emphasis has been on listening, known as "Passive SETI," rather than on transmitting, known as "Active SETI," although some messages have already been sent into space. The subject of whether further communications should be sent at all has been much discussed in recent years within the SETI community, but broadcasting has continued, and approaches to the problem of message content and encoding—that is, what to say and how to say it—have evolved considerably. Discussions about the form and content of interstellar messages, both outgoing and incoming, have a long history, dating back to at least the early 1800s.[16] These dialogues are ongoing, with some very interesting interdisciplinary work on the challenges of creating messages that ETI might find intelligible.[17]

Many have argued that we need not worry too much about optimally encoding our messages to ETI or about decoding their hypothetical messages

---

15. For one such exploration, see Raybeck, "Contact Considerations: A Cross-Cultural Perspective," chapter 9 in this volume.

16. For a concise review of ideas about message construction from 1826 onward, see Douglas A. Vakoch, "Constructing Messages to Extraterrestrials: An Exosemiotic Perspective," *Acta Astronautica* 42, nos. 10–12 (1998): 697–704. Another overview can be found in Brian McConnell, *Beyond Contact: A Guide to SETI and Communicating with Alien Civilizations* (Cambridge: O'Reilly UK, 2001).

17. See, for example, Douglas A. Vakoch, "The Art and Science of Interstellar Message Composition," *Leonardo* 37, no. 1 (2004): 33–34; and other papers in the same issue. See also abstracts here: "Encoding Altruism: The Art and Science of Interstellar Message Composition," *http://publish.seti.org/art_science/2003/*.

to us. If, as is commonly assumed in SETI circles, extraterrestrial civilizations turn out to be vastly older and more advanced than we are, then perhaps they will be kind enough to construct their messages in such a way that we can comprehend them (as in Carl Sagan's book *Contact*), and perhaps they will have no difficulty comprehending whatever we say, however we say it. For example, Brian McConnell surmises: "Since it's a reasonable assumption that a civilization capable of receiving an interstellar message is probably pretty smart, it's also reasonable to assume that, given enough time to understand the [alphanumeric] documents, they will be able to learn the meaning of many of the words in our vocabulary."[18] Seth Shostak has similarly argued that we needn't focus on short, simple messages, as "any decent extraterrestrial engineer would be able to decode our television signals, and would probably find them more informative than simple pictograms."[19] Certainly these assertions *could* be true, but the anthropological perspective suggests that they are not *necessarily* true, or even *likely* to be true, given the cultural embeddedness of language and images. For example, the word *dog* has no necessary connection to a dog, and not everyone interprets a picture in the same way.

Thus, it is also possible that outgoing and incoming signals could be utterly incomprehensible to their respective recipients. But it seems illogical to concede this without making an effort; that would be equivalent to shrugging and not answering the cosmic telephone, saying that it is enough to have simply heard it ring. Unquestionably, in the context of SETI, there would be value in recognizing an artificial signal and seeing patterns in it even without understanding the content.[20] There is a similar truth in archaeology, as Paul Wason has pointed out, for there is much that we can learn from symbolic behavior without necessarily being able to decipher its specific meaning.[21] However, that is something of a consolation prize.

I therefore take the position that the intertwined tasks of composing intelligible interstellar messages and deciphering such messages are neither

---

18. McConnell, *Beyond Contact*, p. 369.

19. G. Seth Shostak, "SETI at Wider Bandwidths?" in *Progress in the Search for Extraterrestrial Life*, ed. G. Seth Shostak, ASP Conference Series, vol. 74 (San Francisco: Astronomical Society of the Pacific, 1995), pp. 447–454.

20. Cipher A. Deavours, "Extraterrestrial Communication," in *Extraterrestrials: Science and Alien Intelligence*, ed. E. Regis (Cambridge: Cambridge University Press, 1987), pp. 201–214. See also John Elliott, "Detecting the Signature of Intelligent Life," *Acta Astronautica* 67, nos. 11–12 (2010): 1419–1426.

21. See Paul K. Wason, "Inferring Intelligence: Prehistoric and Extraterrestrial," chapter 7 in this volume.

trivial nor impossible—in other words, I consider these challenges worthy of attention. I regard the challenge of decipherment as primary, for if we can effectively isolate what makes a message decipherable, then we can compose messages with those anticryptographic properties in mind. In defining what makes a message decipherable, we have recourse to multiple fields of study, including cryptology and archaeology.

In cryptology, generally speaking, original text is called *plaintext*, which is then encrypted via a *keytext* to create a *cryptotext*. Any two out of these three will reveal the third.[22] Given a cryptotext, one would then proceed with standard cryptanalytic methods, which "have their roots in the inherent properties of language." The usual sequence of attack with cryptotexts is "determination of the language employed, the general crypto system, the specific key, and the plaintext."[23] Cryptanalysis is essentially a distillation of classic scientific method,[24] but, like any method, it has limitations. Thus, there are cryptosystems that are perfectly secure, i.e., that result in indecipherable messages. In the realm of cryptanalysis, decipherability requires that the cryptotext provide some information about the plaintext—even just fragments of indirect information—without the keytext.

In archaeology we have a wider range of scenarios, with a tremendous variety of writing systems, languages, symbols, and communication purposes, and so the methodological repertoire is correspondingly wide. Archaeologists do, however, generally agree that to be decipherable, an inscription must include at least one known language or the names of historical figures.[25]

While cryptological and archaeological methodologies would undoubtedly be useful in deciphering an interstellar message, we cannot assume that these tools alone would be sufficient to accomplish the task. Powerful computers would help, but even the artificial intelligence of the future could be challenged by completely unknown languages and symbolic systems, which might not succumb to brute computational and methodological force.

A more comprehensive strategy for deciphering interstellar messages could begin with a compilation of the problem-solving strategies and scenarios we have already encountered on Earth along with a careful consideration of the disciplinary frameworks within which these are situated.

---

22. F. L. Bauer, *Decrypted Secrets: Methods and Maxims of Cryptology*, 3rd ed. (Berlin: Springer, 2002).

23. Bauer, *Decrypted Secrets*, p. 218.

24. As Bauer observes, cryptanalysis is "a prototype for the methods in science" (*Decrypted Secrets*, p. 438).

25. P. T. Daniels and W. Bright, eds., *The World's Writing Systems* (Oxford: Oxford University Press, 1996), pp. 142–143.

Different Disciplinary Perspectives on Redundancy and Revealing Knowledge

Douglas Vakoch has noted a predictable yet fascinating polarization on the subject of interstellar messages: mathematicians and physical scientists are often confident that the problems of decoding and optimal encoding can be solved and propose new ways of doing so, whereas social scientists and humanities scholars tend to critique those approaches and state that the problems are fundamentally insoluble.[26] Philosophically speaking, this is a sure indication of something intriguing and worth exploration. Why such different opinions? An example may help to locate the origins of these divergences and suggest some interesting areas for further exploration.

Jean Heidmann, a prominent SETI thinker and a highly accomplished astronomer at the Paris Observatory until his death in 2000, suggested transmitting the *Encyclopedia Britannica* into space, displaying little concern for decipherability. The *Encyclopedia* pages, Heidmann said, are:

> essentially a linear string of typographic signs (the text) and a set of bidimensional arrays of pixels (the illustrations) whose coding is elementary. The alphabetical coding can be deciphered using just a few pages, as well as the grammatical structures. The illustrations are also obviously decidable by any ETs using bidimensional information from their own environment. The coupling between text and illustrations will easily provide information nearly *ad infinitum.*[27]

Heidmann's optimism is enviable. But his statement is fascinating to me because it seems so clearly and definitely *wrong* from an anthropological perspective, given that reading texts and interpreting images are not even *human* universals.[28] Yet Heidmann was obviously a very sophisticated thinker in his field, and many shared his opinions. His argument has recently been extended by Shostak, who advocates sending the contents of the Google

---

26. Vakoch, "Constructing Messages to Extraterrestrials," pp. 697–704.

27. Jean Heidmann, *Extraterrestrial Intelligence*, ed. Storm Dunlop, 2nd ed. (Cambridge: Cambridge University Press, 1997), pp. 202–203.

28. For constructive skepticism about Heidmann's argument, see Douglas A. Vakoch, "The Dialogic Model: Representing Human Diversity in Messages to Extraterrestrials," *Acta Astronautica* 42, nos. 10–12 (1998): 705–710.

servers into space, since they include enough redundant information to ensure their decipherability.[29]

Vakoch suggests that the optimism of scientists on this matter of decipherability "reflects well the continued accomplishments of science and technology in the contemporary world," although this confidence could do with tempering, since fundamental assumptions do need periodic re-evaluation.[30] But is this view of decipherability simply a result of the optimism of scientists in our era of incredibly rapid scientific progress? Or is it rather a reflection of the tendency among SETI scientists, noted above, to believe that any ETI with whom we exchange signals will be much more technologically advanced than we are? Conversely, does the skepticism of scholars in the humanities and social sciences result from a lack of appreciation for mathematical arguments regarding the likely age of ETI or from an underestimation of recent advances in computing, techniques in cryptography and signal processing, and the might of deductive logic? Perhaps. But I suspect there are additional factors at work here.

The difference of opinion also reflects epistemological diversity—differences in how we believe we can know the world. Where does knowledge lie? How is it obtained? Is it merely uncovered in the world, or is it created in the mind? A reprise of the "Science Wars" and a great deal of Western philosophy might be of use here in outlining disparate views on these questions, but in the interest of brevity, I will simply assert my own view that not all knowledge is the same. Some knowledge is discovered more than it is made; some is made more than it is discovered. We are not dealing with the same kind of knowledge all the time. Not all knowledge can be deduced through sheer logic and computational might. Some knowledge, like the meaning of a picture or the relationship of a word to a thing, is cultural and arbitrary. This variable is crucial when considering what sorts of methods are appropriate to a given situation.

Heidmann's view—and perhaps some others like it—seems at least partly born of confidence that the redundancy inherent in written language and the redundancy of coupling text with images are enough to ensure decipherability. This idea may originate with Claude Shannon's work in information theory, as his research has influenced not only SETI researchers but cryptologists as well.[31]

29. G. Seth Shostak, "What Do You Say to An Extraterrestrial?," Space.com/SETI Institute (2 December 2004), *http://www.space.com/searchforlife/seti_whattosay_041202.html.*

30. Vakoch, "Constructing Messages to Extraterrestrials," pp. 697–704.

31. C. E. Shannon's 1948 classic, "A Mathematical Theory of Communication" (*Bell System Technical Journal* 27, nos. 3–4 [1948]: 379–423 and 623–656) is frequently cited in scientific SETI documents.

But a theory can easily break down when applied in new contexts, and there is indeed a shift in context here. To what, exactly, is this theory about redundancy in language being applied in Heidmann's example above? Not to the discovery of a pattern in an interstellar signal nor to the identification of a pattern as the work of an intelligence—either of which would be an appropriate use of the theory—but to the recovery of *specific information* from an interstellar message. This begs further attention.

It is perfectly true that redundancy aids recognition of a signal as a language or a code, and this recognition is crucial to SETI. However, Shannon's method provides only a quantitative measure of the complexity of a language or signaling system—*not a translation.*[32] And while it is axiomatic in cryptology that redundancy helps in deciphering a text, the task of decipherment/cryptanalysis is to move from an encoded text to the original text—*not from text to meaning.* To get from text to meaning, we need to understand the language. Put another way, redundancy's primary function is to reduce noise or permit correction in the case of imperfect transmission; it improves the signal-to-noise ratio but does not provide for the conversion of signal to information.[33] And, as Richard Saint-Gelais notes, the conversion of signal to information involves semiotic issues that cannot be bypassed via method.[34]

Broadly speaking, this observation suggests that the matter of SETI and signals—either outgoing or incoming—occupies a tricky intersection, where paradigms, methods, and disciplines meet. It may be that concrete examples from Earth can help us to puzzle through the theoretical problems of decipherment.

Analogues from Anthropology and Archaeology: The Rosetta Stone and Mathematics

The archaeological process is itself a useful illustration of the matter of interpretation. In contrast to the classic model of scientific discovery—i.e., "reading the book of Nature," uncovering information that exists independent of the observer—archaeology is now held by many to exemplify a different

---

32. Brenda McCowan, Laurance Doyle, and Sean F. Hanser, "Using Information Theory to Assess the Diversity, Complexity, and Development of Communicative Repertoires," *Journal of Comparative Psychology* 116, no. 2 (2002): 166–172.

33. Thomas Sebeok, *I Think I Am a Verb: More Contributions to the Doctrine of Signs* (New York: Plenum, 1986), p. 170.

34. Richard Saint-Gelais, "Beyond Linear B: The Metasemiotic Challenge of Communication with Extraterrestrial Intelligence," chapter 5 in this volume.

kind of reasoning process. Interpretation begins "at the trowel's edge"; the archaeologist is an integral part of the discovery.[35] The material remnants, the signs, of past lives have no inherent meaning without a living mind acting upon them. The encyclopedia of the ancient world cannot simply be read or translated. It needs modern coauthors.

In a more concrete sense, the archaeological record is useful as a collection of poorly understood signals, where the problem lies in bridging the gap between symbol and meaning. Many have made this connection, noting that archaeology as well as cryptology could provide useful information about how to decipher an incoming message from ETI and how best to encode an outgoing message to ETI. The case of the Rosetta Stone, for example, is frequently invoked in the SETI literature.

Carl Sagan argued that mathematics, physics, and chemistry could constitute a cosmic Rosetta Stone: "We believe there is a common language that all technical civilizations, no matter how different, must have. That common language is science and mathematics. The laws of Nature are the same everywhere."[36] Following Sagan, many SETI researchers have proposed that we should use mathematics or physical constants as a basis for communication with ETI: since we won't have names or historical events in common, a universal principle or property would have to serve as a "virtual bilingual" or a "crib." Discussion of this subject has been lively. As Vakoch observes:

> The dominant position among astronomers and physicists is that conveying information between two civilizations will be relatively straightforward because both species will share basic conceptions of mathematics and science. Scholars in the humanities and social sciences typically contend the opposite: that even mathematics and science as we know them may be specific to humans, and that it may be impossible to develop systems of communication across species.[37]

---

35. Ian Hodder, *The Archaeological Process: An Introduction* (Oxford: Blackwell, 1999).

36. Carl Sagan, *Cosmos* (New York: Random House, 1980), p. 296.

37. Vakoch, "Constructing Messages to Extraterrestrials," p. 697. Early explorations of mathematics as the *lingua franca* were carried out by Drake, Oliver, and Morrison in the early 1960s. Among the first to discuss the idea were Iosif Shklovskii and Carl Sagan in *Intelligent Life in the Universe* (London: Holden-Day, 1966). A particularly useful hierarchy of coding levels, beginning with astrophysical coding and only gradually working up to alphabets, mathematics, and images, can be found in James M. Cordes and Woodruff T. Sullivan, III, "Astrophysical Coding: A New Approach to SETI Signals. I. Signal Design and Wave Propagation," in Shostak,

True to form as a social scientist, albeit a hopeful one, I must note that even if the laws of nature are the same everywhere, as Sagan believes, and even if all technical civilizations understand some of them, these circumstances cannot ensure all the secondary conditions that would be necessary for successful communication. Even if two different intelligences were expressing the same single scientific principle, understood by each of them in exactly the same way—which seems scarcely imaginable—there would be a good deal of luck and inference involved in establishing this beginning point. And, of course, just as language has a cultural context, so does math.[38] Thus, there is a potential incommensurability problem—perhaps the notion of a universal math is, in the words of historian W. H. McNeill, rather chauvinistic.[39]

I do not think, however, that an anthropological perspective requires us to abandon the matter there. On the contrary, anthropology can offer useful Earth analogues, specifically, those of ethnomathematics.[40] Modern astronomy and physics use Western mathematics, but other mathematical systems have existed on Earth, with very different ways of understanding and expressing the world. The fact that none of these systems *did* produce modern technology, such as radio telescopes, does not *necessarily* mean that they *could not have* done so; that failure could be as easily due to historical contingencies and interruptions to their development as to anything inherent in the systems themselves. Until a qualified scholar undertakes the project of considering whether or not, for example, ancient Mayan mathematics might eventually have produced an understanding of electromagnetic radiation or advanced geometry, this point is moot. In the meantime, simply learning about radically different forms of mathematics here on Earth would extend the range of analogies SETI researchers can draw upon, and thus could be of use. It would demonstrate the diverse possibilities for mathematical representation.

But if human math and science do not look like extraterrestrial math and science, then the Rosetta Stone analogy will not hold up. We must

ed., *Progress in the Search for Extraterrestrial Life*, pp. 325–342. McConnell also supposes that "idiot-proofing" messages would involve a multistage process beginning with math and Boolean logic (*Beyond Contact*, pp. 357–358).

38. B. Martin, "Mathematics and Social Interests," in *Ethnomathematics: Challenging Eurocentrism in Mathematics Education*, ed. A. Powell and M. Frankenstein (1988; rpt. Albany: SUNY Press, 1997), pp. 155–172.

39. Vakoch, "Constructing Messages to Extraterrestrials," pp. 697–704.

40. See, for example, M. Ascher, *Mathematics Elsewhere* (Princeton, NJ: Princeton University Press, 2002); and M. Ascher, *Ethnomathematics: A Multicultural View of Mathematical Ideas* (Pacific Grove: Brooks/Cole, 1991).

also remember that the Rosetta Stone was but one of several pieces in the hieroglyphs puzzle, the others being inscriptions from other artifacts, such as the Philae Obelisk, and Champollion's knowledge of ancient Greek and Coptic Egyptian.[41]

Archaeological Decipherments

To observe that the Rosetta Stone is not a straightforward analogy is not to say that we cannot learn anything of use from archaeological decipherments. It is to say, rather, that the general analogy between archaeological decipherments and potential interstellar messages should be explored more fully.

For example, we know that successful decipherment in archaeology has required accurate copies of scripts, a familiar language, proper names of historical figures known from neighboring cultures that left interpretable records, and bilingual or multilingual inscriptions.[42] These features parallel the standard needs of decryption—clean signals without noise, plus keys and cribs—and are thus to be expected. But just as significantly, successful decipherment has also required the shedding of assumptions about how a symbol connects to a language. Any connection between a sign and what it signifies is a matter of convention. Does a sign represent a spoken sound? Does it represent a physical thing that it resembles? Does it represent an idea? Does it sometimes represent one of these and sometimes another? Puzzling through these problems has required scholars to abandon fundamental concepts about alphabets and images.[43]

Several ancient scripts have yet to be deciphered, such as the Indus script, the Rongorongo script, Linear A, Linear Elamite, Jurchen, Khitan, and some Mesoamerican scripts. Sometimes a key piece of information is missing, such as the language being represented. Sometimes there just isn't enough of a

---

41. Richard B. Parkinson, *Cracking Codes: The Rosetta Stone and Decipherment* (London: British Museum Press, 1999).

42. Daniels and Bright, eds., *The World's Writing Systems*, pp. 142–143. For comments on the slightly different Linear B scenario, see also Saint-Gelais, "Beyond Linear B," passim.

43. See, for example, Cyrus H. Gordon, *Forgotten Scripts: How They Were Deciphered and Their Impact on Contemporary Culture* (New York: Basic Books, 1968); Roy Harris, *The Origin of Writing* (London: Duckworth, 1986); Joyce Marcus, *Mesoamerican Writing Systems: Propaganda, Myth, and History in Four Ancient Civilizations* (Princeton, NJ: Princeton University Press, 1992); Parkinson, *Cracking Codes*; and Kurt Ross, *Codex Mendoza: Aztec Manuscript*, with commentary (Barcelona: Miller Graphics, 1978).

script to do much with it. The best methods in the world cannot bridge certain gaps. This situation is humbling but no cause for despair. It simply means that we have more work to do to find information that can bridge those gaps. But sometimes our approach itself may be inadequate; the problem may be an unidentified supposition we have not yet examined. For example, in the case of the Indus script, we have 4,000 texts with plenty of redundancy, but the sheer quantity of information has not enabled linguists or cryptologists to decipher it. Recent analyses suggest that the entire framing of the Indus script has been incorrect, which might explain why none of the many attempts at decipherment (more than 100 published since the 1800s) has met with much acceptance.[44] The problem, as suggested by Steve Farmer and others, could be that the Indus symbols are not a script at all; that is, perhaps there is no direct correlation between the Indus symbols and a language.[45] The symbols were clearly meaningful but not necessarily in the same way as, for example, the hieroglyphic or cuneiform inscriptions that have been deciphered. It *could* be a case of discordance between the signs, their modern-day viewers' assumptions about types of meaning, and modern methods of accessing meaning.

Cases such as the frustrating Indus script are just as instructive as the classic, successful decipherments of hieroglyphs, Linear B, or cuneiform. If we choose only one of these analogies to inform our projections of an interstellar decipherment project, we limit ourselves unduly. In a related discussion, Ben Finney and Jerry Bentley elegantly argue that when considering the potential impact of ET radio transmissions upon human society, we "should explore the wide range of human experience around the globe and not focus solely on familiar cases that appear to reinforce our most earnest hopes."[46] More specifically, they make the case that the modern West's learning from classical

---

44. Steve Farmer, Richard Sproat, and Michael Witzel, "The Collapse of the Indus-Script Thesis: The Myth of a Literate Harappan Civilization," *Electronic Journal of Vedic Studies* 11, no. 2 (2004): 19–57.

45. Farmer, Sproat, and Witzel, "The Collapse of the Indus-Script Thesis," passim. Then again, a brute-force computing approach may be yielding results: see also a contrary view in Rajesh P. N. Rao et al., "Entropic Evidence for Linguistic Structure in the Indus Script," *Science* 324, no. 5931 (2009): 1165, available at *http://www.sciencemag.org/content/324/5931/1165.full*; and Rajesh P. N. Rao, "Probabilistic Analysis of an Ancient Undeciphered Script," *Computer* 43, no. 4 (2010): 76–80, available at *http://homes.cs.washington.edu/~rao/ieeeIndus.pdf*. The debate continues.

46. Ben Finney and Jerry Bentley, "A Tale of Two Analogues: Learning at a Distance from the Ancient Greeks and Maya and the Problem of Deciphering Extraterrestrial Radio Transmissions," chapter 4 in this volume.

Greek sources is probably not a good analogue for ET decipherment and its consequences, and that the case of Mayan hieroglyphs is a better example, given that the decipherment was tremendously difficult and is still underway.

I agree with their intention, which is not to declare interstellar message decipherment impossible but to insist that it may not be simple. And I support their suggestion to look at difficult decipherments. But further, I would suggest that we should focus not just on decipherment successes but also on *failures*. Successes confirm that, given adequate data, established methods work much of the time. Failures indicate a space in which we can learn, information we must acquire, theory we must build, and assumptions we must identify and discard.

SETI Begins at Home

It has been said that "SETI begins at home," and I concur.[47] In considering interstellar message composition and decipherment, why not make the best possible use of all the Earthly data and methods we have? There are many areas in which anthropology and archaeology can contribute to SETI thinking; we share the fundamental tasks of learning what not to take for granted and developing methods through which we can comprehend very different minds. Earth's cultures, used appropriately, can provide useful analogies for expanding our thinking about ETI. And perhaps considering our local unsolved puzzles will help us to build the strongest possible strategies for reading interstellar mail.

---

47. Lori Marino, "SETI Begins at Home: Searching for Terrestrial Intelligence," in Shostak, ed., *Progress in the Search for Extraterrestrial Life*, pp. 73–81.

CHAPTER SEVEN

Inferring Intelligence
Prehistoric and Extraterrestrial

Paul K. Wason

Introduction

Different as they may be in other respects—sources of data, research tools, academic training—what the fields of archaeology and the Search for Extraterrestrial Intelligence (SETI) do have in common is at the core of their respective enterprises: the study of intelligent beings without benefit of firsthand observation. Archaeological analysis is conducted without direct contact with living beings, with few if any written communications to aid the study; and it is accomplished by constructing bridging arguments that span great distances of time, space, culture, and, in the case of our hominid ancestors, biology. While we can imagine other kinds of contact with extraterrestrial intelligence, these basic but important features of archaeology likely apply to SETI, too—at least for the time being.

I cannot guess whether any of the insights earned through the development and practice of archaeology may prove useful to scholars seeking evidence of extraterrestrial intelligence. The differences between the two ventures may simply overwhelm what they have in common. But I believe there are at least analogical connections. In particular, to the extent that approaches in archaeology uncover evidence of intelligence as a phenomenon per se, and not of humanness specifically, some insights from this discipline could be transferable to SETI.

Uncovering evidence of human activity in the past is of course the primary goal of archaeology, but doing so often means inferring intelligence or some aspect of it, such as agency, purpose, design, choice, the expression of meaning, or the ability to communicate. Archaeological work can help to reveal one or another of these aspects of intelligence and, perhaps, not just human agency but agency itself. There may thus be some hope of generalizing, and these approaches may provide a basis for the development of analogous approaches in SETI.

In the following sections I offer a series of archaeological vignettes that illustrate some of the more promising avenues to explore and a few of the issues that may be faced. One might think it more helpful if I were to offer instead some kind of identification key to intelligence, perhaps a set of 10 infallible signs of human activity. Whether or not this is even possible, the creation of such a key or set would certainly be more difficult than it seems at first. Archaeologists in fact do not often identify the criteria they use for demonstrating intelligence or for drawing any other conclusion about human activity except in very specific discussions about the materials at hand. When surveying large areas for archaeological sites, our eyes are naturally drawn to circles and straight lines, to regularly shaped formations (or at least those shaped differently from the background terrain). In looking at rocks, bones, or other materials that are potentially artifacts, we seek symmetries, regularity, evidence of the use of tools rather than teeth, and so on. But we cannot use the presence of these features as a generalized key for inferring human activity. One cannot, for example, say something as straightforward as that circular structures must be human-made (or made by an intelligent agent). And even if generalizations of this kind were possible, it is not clear they could be transferred for use in the world of astronomy, where circles, symmetries, and regularities abound.

For this chapter, my examples are at a broader level and more in the manner of "lessons learned" than prescriptive advice. First, I consider briefly an instance in which archaeology may seem to have failed on its own terms. This is not very comforting for those of us who want to use archaeology in the service of SETI. But I also suggest a way out. My second vignette considers the equally troubling issue of ethnographic analogy. Protests to the contrary notwithstanding, I believe archaeology cannot be done at all without drawing analogies to known living human groups. This notion, too, would seem to make the relevance of archaeological approaches to SETI a very great stretch indeed—but, again, I don't think this makes it impossible. The next vignettes, which explore the importance of intellectual and physical contexts, expectations for a solid scientific argument, and the implications of symbolism for understanding communications, will perhaps help to close on a more optimistic note.

When Archaeological Methods Don't Seem to Work—Even When Studying Humans

Archaeology begins with certain advantages over the Search for Extraterrestrial Intelligence. Its practitioners now have a century and a half of experience inferring the past activity, thoughts, and intentions of intelligent agents. Although archaeologists can't observe these intelligent beings "in action," they do have an abundance of material remains and the contexts of their former use. And most obviously, they already know a great deal about these beings quite independently of the archaeological work itself.

Yet even so, archaeology has not always succeeded in its efforts. Worse, it is not always possible to tell whether researchers are even on the right track. Consider the Paleolithic cave art of southern Europe that scholars have been studying for more than a century. Many theories have been offered concerning what these paintings are all about (what they mean, why they were painted, and so on), but there is no agreement at this point—which raises the following question: What hope do we have of communicating with extraterrestrials if we have such a hard time understanding symbolic imagery produced in Europe as recently as 12,000 years ago by members of our own species?

This is a valid question, certainly. But for several reasons the situation is not nearly as bleak as all that. First, though we may not have solved all the riddles, we have made some progress; it has hardly been a century of effort without insight. Admittedly, there are some things we may never learn about Paleolithic cave art. I fully agree with Clifford Geertz, who characterizes art as a "local matter."[1] One need only think of Leonardo da Vinci's *The Last Supper*. As David Lewis-Williams observes, this painting has rather little to do with a group of hungry men, but what chance would someone unfamiliar with Christianity have of knowing what it really is about?[2] While Geertz has an important point, perhaps it does not apply to everything we may wish to know. Why stop at "local," after all? Why not claim, as is sometimes done, also with good reason, that art is "personal" and no one can ever understand someone else's art or someone else's response to art? Why not admit, for that matter, that the artist herself does not really "understand" what she has created, art being a somewhat intuitive affair? Surely there is some truth to each of these perspectives. But while there are some things that I as an individual will never know about a given work of art, this limitation doesn't mean that I cannot know anything about it, or that what I do know about it is somehow less true for being incomplete.

The same can be said for insider cultural knowledge at the local level: there are some things outsiders will never know, but this fact does not mean one can never learn anything about another culture. Admittedly, the all-or-nothing

---

1. Clifford Geertz, "Art as a Cultural System," *Modern Language Notes* 91, no. 6 (1976): 1473–1499, esp. p. 1475; Paul K. Wason, "Art, Origins of," in *Encyclopedia of Science and Religion*, vol. 1, ed. J. Wentzel Vrede van Huyssteen (New York: Macmillan Reference USA, 2003), p. 31.

2. David Lewis-Williams, *Discovering South African Rock Art* (Cape Town: David Philip Publishers, 1990).

way I phrased the *Last Supper* example is a bit misleading. A viewer will, yes, miss much if he or she knows nothing about Christian theology, but one doesn't need that "local" knowledge to realize there is a lot more going on in this painted scene than the satisfaction of hunger.

So my second and perhaps more important reason for optimism about humans' ability to understand cosmic cross-cultural communications is that our frustrations with Paleolithic art have mostly had to do with the difficulty of understanding the message's content, what is being communicated. No one denies that these paintings are the work of human agents, produced through purposeful activity and carrying meaning. We can infer the existence of intelligences, and we can learn much about them simply from looking at these works of art, even without knowing what the images "mean" in the sense of what their creators were trying to express in them, or understanding the cosmology behind this sophisticated symbolic activity—the latter perhaps being truly "local knowledge."

Ethnographic Analogy: Knowledge of the Ways of Intelligent Creatures

Ethnographic analogy is using what we already know about human material culture to interpret what we discover in archaeological contexts. Most valuable for prehistorians have been analogies with the ways of traditional peoples around the world known to us through the field of ethnography (hence the name), but of course archaeologists apply analogies to what they themselves think and do at least as much, even if they aren't always aware of doing so. Ethnographic analogy was actually a key to the beginnings of the field in the first place, and to the recognition of human antiquity by Europeans. For hundreds of years Europeans appear to have been oblivious to the existence of stone tools. Presumably many people saw them. At least it is hard for me to believe that no stone axes, spear points, or arrowheads turned up in plowed fields, dried streambeds, or eroded hillsides. But, as William Stiebing observes, there is no mention of them prior to the 16th century. People apparently "did not notice them. To them such things were just so many more rocks."[3] Writings from the 16th century indicate that people were noticing anomalies, for example, that rocks which we would now recognize as stone tools, differed substantially from others in the land-

---

3. William H. Stiebing, Jr., *Uncovering the Past: A History of Archaeology* (Buffalo, NY: Prometheus Books, 1993), p. 29.

scape. These objects were widely referred to as *fairy arrows* or *elf-shot* or, by those less given to specifying a cause in terms of personal agency, *thunderbolts*. In his classic book *The Idea of Prehistory*, Glyn Daniel quotes an explanation offered by Ulisse Aldrovandi in the mid-16th century. Aldrovandi described objects we would now label stone tools as "due to an admixture of a certain exhalation of thunder and lightning with metallic matter, chiefly in dark clouds, which is coagulated by the circumfused moisture and conglutinated into a mass (like flour with water) and subsequently indurated by heat, like a brick."[4] And "these rather surprising words," as Daniel puts it, "were written by a man who has been described as the greatest zoologist of the Renaissance period."[5] I cannot resist quoting one more example in which the use of jargon also seems inversely proportioned to useful information conveyed; a man named Tollius from about the same time period "claimed chopped flints to be 'generated in the sky by a fulgurous exhalation conglobed in a cloud by the circumposed humour.'"[6]

Even while such things were being pondered, other scholars were proposing that these objects were ancient tools. The reasoning these proto-archaeologists offered in support of such a view turns out to be very important—an analogy with similar tools used by the Native Americans. Once the connection was made, it is no surprise that this view rapidly became the standard one. Ethnographic analogy saved the day in this case, as it often does, and in the process represented a major step toward what would become the academic field of prehistory.

In one sense this is not good news for SETI—that it could require analogies with known activities of specific cultures to correctly interpret these rocks as products of intelligent human activity. But I suggest this is only half the story. If we dig a little deeper, we see that even those who did not recognize them as tools did understand that something about the rocks needed to be explained. In retrospect, the superstitious common people who dubbed them *elf-shot* or *fairy arrows* were, in an odd sort of way, more perceptive and closer to the core truth than those who concocted naturalistic or mechanistic explanations. For they recognized the most important point, namely, that these items are indeed the products of intentional beings, purposeful agents.

How do people recognize intentionality and purposeful agency? As noted earlier, the archaeological literature seems to have largely neglected

---

4. Ulisse Aldrovandi, quoted here from Glyn Daniel, *The Idea of Prehistory* (Cleveland, OH: The World Publishing Company, 1962), p. 47

5. Aldrovandi, *The Idea of Prehistory*, p. 47.

6. Aldrovandi, *The Idea of Prehistory*, p. 47.

this question. In part this neglect may be due to the fact that archaeology has often tried to follow the social science model of research, which seeks overarching trends and external causation. Until recent years archaeology seriously undervalued agency, giving more attention to broad cultural and ecological forces than to individual initiative. Another reason archaeologists can work so hard, often successfully, to recognize intelligent agency and purposive behavior yet give so little attention to "how" we actually make inferences concerning intelligent agents, may be that it is actually quite difficult. At heart, it is not really an archaeological problem but an issue of cognition. In the final section, I offer a few thoughts in this direction as well as suggestions for future research, based on recent cognitive science. But it seems clear, both from those who spoke of elf-shot and from contemporary archaeology, that we are often quite capable of recognizing the products of intelligence even when we cannot clearly articulate what we are using as evidence.

As for the skeptics, they were on the wrong track altogether, though their motivation was reasonable enough, in that it was the fairies of which they were skeptical. Even so, their response is useful. Those who tried to explain stone tools as things formed in clouds by various processes with intimidating names clearly understood there was something special about them in need of explanation. They simply did not allow themselves to attribute it to intelligence. Had I lived at that time, I may well have been in this group—but only because the problem was framed in such a way as to limit the options to lifeless mechanical action or fairies.

It is not easy to see what you are not looking for, or to know what it is you do not know, and both the strengths and weaknesses of ethnographic analogy grow from this conundrum. Ethnography expands our vision of what is humanly possible—or at least what has been tried by other humans—but cannot expand our vision much further than that. It is likely enough that even in the Paleolithic there were social forms not represented among ethnographically known peoples, so what of a distant planet? As has often been said, if we depend too heavily on ethnographic analogy, we lessen our chances of discovering the true range of forms human society has taken.

Intellectual Context

Like most aspects of culture, our *intellectual culture*—the intellectual context in which our view of the world is formed—frees us to explore new ideas in disciplined and creative ways. At the same time, it constrains our search by restricting what we are predisposed to believe is possible. One example of how intellectual context can affect our approach to and success with archaeological interpretation is found in the next episode of this brief history of the understanding of stone tools. While the idea that they were tools—by analogy with those of Native Americans—became accepted, scholars at first did not appreciate their great age. Their true nature, so to speak, could not be recognized, as the existence of a Paleolithic origin simply did not fit with what everyone "knew" to be true.

How might this point be relevant for SETI? First, and rather generically, intellectual context has the same relevance for SETI as for any other science: it can be liberating or limiting, but major breakthroughs in difficult problems often come about when that context is transcended, when someone thinks the previously unthinkable. This link recognizes Thomas Kuhn's much-repeated principle that the data supporting scientific theories are "theory-laden," described and interpreted in the light of theoretical expectations.[7] Even our choice of what counts as data—indeed, even what we are able to "see" out of the myriad bits of information that come our way in any experiment—is interpreted according to our assumptions about what we expect to see. But this inescapable bias does not warrant the discouraging view that even scientific findings are just relative, as Imre Lakatos asserted.[8] We are not trapped hopelessly in our web of assumptions, and the way out is to be pushed by unexplainable data to rethink the theoretical assumptions. Such "thinking the unthinkable" is undoubtedly difficult, but it is possible.

Second, and rather more specifically, the importance of intellectual context to our ability to see what we are not looking for does suggest a possible solution to the Fermi Paradox. Perhaps like those fine scholars of the 18th century who had myriad evidence for prehistoric human activity but could not imagine it, we, too, have evidence of extraterrestrial intelligence but somehow cannot recognize it. Now, I realize these are dangerous words. "Doesn't this guy know that *Men in Black* is fiction?" you may ask, or "Does he want us to take stories of abductions and ancient astronauts seriously?" All claims I am aware of concerning evidence for "aliens" – including the kinds of things people like to talk about once they learn I am an archaeologist—make the rather different assertion that the aliens are among us, or have been in the past. They are not proposing untapped sources of information. And they seem to me to be perfect examples of being caught in a current intellectual

---

7. Thomas Kuhn, *The Structure of Scientific Revolutions*, 2nd ed. (Chicago: University of Chicago Press, 1970).

8. See Nancey Murphy, *Theology in an Age of Scientific Reasoning* (Ithaca: Cornell University Press, 1990); Nancey Murphy and George F. R. Ellis, *On the Moral Nature of the Universe: Theology, Cosmology and Ethics* (Minneapolis: Fortress Press, 1996), pp. 10–13.

context, a current context of some kind anyway. Attributing the Nazca Lines in Peru to aliens has as much to do with cultural prejudice as attributing ancient artifacts to elves or fairies because doing so was somehow easier than imagining prehistoric humans living here before us.

But what might we discover if we could break out of our intellectual context? This is a question that SETI researchers must ask constantly—wondering, for example, whether even something as simple as tuning to a different radio frequency could be the key to discovering data about ETIs that have surrounded us all along. Perhaps it is not technology that sets all our limits.

Physical Context

What turned the tide in European scholarly appreciation of prehistoric humanity was the physical context: specifically, tools found in undisturbed sediments and in clear association with the remains of extinct mammals. This discovery, along with a growing appreciation for Earth's age, yielded a broadening and shifting of the intellectual context—perhaps even something of a revolution in the intellectual context of Europe. Pierre Teilhard de Chardin, one of the excavators of Peking Man, expressed beautifully the ability to conceive of the antiquity of humanity as "a surprisingly recent conquest of the modern mind":

> Today we smile as we think of the thrills and triumphs experienced by our great predecessors when in 1864 they first observed, on a fragment of mammoth tusk, the carved outline of the mammoth itself—definite testimony, over man's own signature, that man...had known and hunted the fabulous and (to the scientist of the period) fabulously ancient animal.[9]

Physical context remains central in all archaeological research at several levels. Any day-to-day work also depends on the context created by existing knowledge. Contexts in this sense flood our meager data with all manner of associations and additional conclusions that flesh them out into a picture of human activity. Archaeologists do not read "raw" data—almost anything we might wish to say about a find is an interpretive conclusion. When I come across another broken stone in my garden in Pennsylvania

---

9. Pierre Teilhard de Chardin, "The Idea of Fossil Man" in *Anthropology Today: An Encyclopedic Inventory*, ed. A. L. Kroeber (Chicago: University of Chicago Press, 1953), p. 93.

and determine it to be a projectile point, I receive a message from the past that is rich and deep and easy to read. My mind is filled with images of woodland longhouses, villages with smoke curling lazily into the blue sky as small clusters of people work on various tasks, a group of men returning with two deer from a hunt, children and dogs playing all around. The tool does not tell me all this by itself but because it is in a context. Had I found a tool, perhaps vaguely similar in appearance, in a garden in India, the context of associations would be rather different. Similarly, in the study of human evolution, a great deal can be said about a primate and its lifestyle from something as small as a tooth, for the "parts" of an organism are even more tightly knit than the "parts" of a culture.

To take just one more example, what we accept as conclusions can depend on the broader context of what is already known. Debates continue about the anthropogenic nature of finds. For example, the Calico Hills site in California is said by Ruth Simpson to be some 250,000 or more years old. This estimate is way out of line with anything else we know about the peopling of North or South America. No firm dating to earlier than 12,000 years ago had been accepted until 2000, when Thomas Dillehay conclusively demonstrated that the Monte Verde site in southern Chile is at least 15,000 years old (and possibly a good deal older).[10] This date, too, may well change—after all, an archaeologist can almost never say, "This is the oldest," but only "This is the oldest evidence yet discovered." It is, however, very unlikely (for a host of reasons unrelated to the Calico Hills site in itself) that humans lived in the New World a quarter of a million years ago.

A similar line of reasoning holds for the Meadowcroft Rockshelter in southwestern Pennsylvania. Some of the radiocarbon dates came back at about 19,000 years. This dating is also out of line with previous estimates but not as dramatically so, especially now that the long-standing 12,000-year barrier has fallen. In the case of Calico Hills, Simpson's dating is solid, but it may not be a site at all, for only stone tools have been found there, and it is not entirely clear that they are tools. More likely they are "geofacts," naturally broken rocks that mimic the appearance of artifacts. As for Meadowcroft, this is a complex Paleoindian archaeological site, but it is still hard to accept a date of 18,000 years ago. At the moment, the most likely explanation is that the carbon sample was contaminated natural coal, giving the materials an appearance of much greater age. Because stratigraphically the layer with

---

10. For an excellent presentation by the excavator of the Monte Verde site, with references to the strangely difficult-to-find technical literature, see Thomas D. Dillehay, *The Settlement of the Americas: A New Prehistory* (New York: Basic Books, 2000).

the older date does not otherwise seem to be so much older than the other layers, this theory is quite plausible. On the other hand, the excavation was done with exceptional care by an archaeologist (James Adovasio) who well understood what was at stake. To put it another way, this site may be every bit as old as it seems, and the problem lies instead with our intellectual context.[11]

SETI is also conducted within a web of interrelated empirical knowledge and under a set of intellectual expectations, a context that renders some ideas more or less plausible. Obvious as this circumstance may seem when stated in this way, it has a significant effect on research. We have seen this phenomenon in exobiology, a line of study that has been rendered more interesting by the recent discoveries of extremophiles on Earth. I would suggest then that, contrary to the view held by many who regard SETI with interest from the outside, the "success" of the SETI enterprise is not really an "all-or-nothing" matter. Firm evidence of even simple life beyond Earth will render the existence of intelligent life somewhat more plausible, in much the way existing knowledge of the peopling of the New World renders certain proposed site dates more or less plausible.

Acceptable Approaches to Scientific Argument

Alison Wylie, perhaps the foremost philosopher of archaeology, has analyzed archaeologists' reasoning process.[12] Some arguments are like chains—they follow link by link by logical link. But if one link fails, whether through faulty logic or lack of evidence, the whole argument falls apart. Science is portrayed in this metaphor as a formal, sequential testing of hypotheses. Such a process does not work well in the practice of archaeology, which, as Lewis-Williams notes, "is, almost by definition, the quintessential science of exiguous evidence."[13]

In practice, Wylie points out, archaeologists use an approach to reasoning that more closely resembles the weaving of strands to form a cable. No individual strand *does* stretch, and no individual strand of reasoning *needs* to stretch, from raw data to firm conclusion. Rather, the whole cable, if well

---

11. J. M. Adovasio and Jake Page, *The First Americans: In Pursuit of Archaeology's Greatest Mystery*, (New York: Random House, 2002). For an excellent overview of issues concerning the first human colonization of North and South America, see David J. Melzer, *First Peoples in a New World: Colonizing Ice Age America* (Berkeley: University of California Press, 2010).

12. Alison Wylie, "Archaeological Cables and Tacking: The Implications of Practice for Bernstein's 'Options Beyond Objectivism and Relativism,'" *Philosophy of Science* 19, no. 1 (1989): 1–18.

13. David Lewis-Williams, *The Mind in the Cave: Consciousness and The Origins of Art* (London: Thames and Hudson, 2002), p. 102.

constructed, bridges larger gaps than the individual strands ever could. The separate arguments also help to confirm or challenge one another. As well as enabling or sustaining, this method is also constraining (in a useful way) in that the pieces really do have to fit together. Some speculation that may seem plausible given one type of evidence just will not work as the whole package fits together. To take one telling example, archaeologists often rely very heavily on studies of ceramics. Marion H. (Harry) Tschopik traced the continuity of Andean Aymara ceramics of the Puno region over five centuries, and what he discovered was quite surprising:

> If the data furnished by the Aymara ceramic tradition *taken alone and by itself* were our only evidence of change (which of course is not the case), the Inca era in the Puno region would have passed virtually unrecorded, and Spanish contact would have appeared to have been slight or fleeting. By and large, Aymara ceramics have been modified to a far less extent than other, and more basic aspects of Aymara culture.[14]

This understanding of the reasoning process is in some respects valuable for any field of study with large gaps in its data, and it is thus highly relevant to any future SETI signal detection. To forestall hopeless confusion should we receive a message from beyond Earth—indeed, even to help us have hope of recognizing a communication when we see one—we need to consult every strand of evidence and use every type of reasoning available to understand it. This, I trust, is obvious enough, but I mention it because in some fields the "context" in terms of expectations about how good science is done can work against weaving various clues together from diverse sources, often with the dismissive claim that since none of the clues really makes the case on its own, the case has not been made.

The Importance of Symbolism

Although I have, without apparent hesitation, just made page-length forays into intellectual history and the philosophy of science, two areas outside my expertise, I must preface this section by saying that the study of symbolic representation, the cognitive skills involved, and the approaches to

---

14. Marion H. Tschopik, "An Andean Ceramic Tradition in Historical Perspective" (1950), quoted here from Paul K. Wason, *The Archaeology of Rank* (Cambridge: Cambridge University Press, 1994), p. 34.

understanding are areas whose potential contribution to the inference of intelligence is matched only by the immensity and complexity of the literature on these subjects. Still, they cannot be avoided when considering this topic.

The study of symboling is important to the archaeological inference of intelligence—if only for the obvious reason that producing symbols requires intelligence. One problem—and this is perhaps at the root of worries about understanding any communication—is that symbols can, and often do, have an arbitrary (or at least a conventional rather than conceptual) relationship to the things they symbolize. While this relationship is arbitrary, it is not necessarily random. Indeed, when it comes in the form of language, symboling is extraordinarily systematic. So the arbitrariness or conventional nature of the connection does not mean we can never figure out what is being said through symbols. As suggested concerning the study of cave art, if we can recognize something as the product of symbolic behavior, we have learned a great deal already without having the slightest idea what the symbols mean: we know that there is an individual capable of high-level intelligent activity, that this individual was trying to communicate, and that this individual is therefore a social being.

Consider the decipherment of ancient languages written in scripts like Egyptian (or, more recently, Mayan) hieroglyphics. It might seem that symbolism and communication of ideas routinely expressed in complex symbolism would be the worst possible way to go about constructing messages for non–Earth-based intelligences. But this pitfall is not easily avoided. We may send messages expressing pure mathematics, or perhaps scientific knowledge, but these concepts must be communicated in a medium that will, of necessity, be symbolic. (Sending pictures is another way to go, although it does assume certain sensory commonalities.) But it might make a difference whether or not the symbols are in systematic form (like a language), for otherwise the problems resulting from their arbitrary relation to their referents will be multiplied. While mathematics does not include a grammar as such, surely the concepts and their symbolic representations are systematically related, even if not in the same way as "natural" languages.

On the other hand, it is unlikely to be easy in any case. Writing, for example, has the advantage of representing a very systematic set of symbols. Yet, it is in effect a symbol system representing another symbol system (the language itself) representing the ideas. Kathryn Denning points out elsewhere in this book that no ancient form of writing has ever been deciphered without some knowledge of the language in which it was written.[15] This fact is impor-

---

15. Kathryn E. Denning, "Learning to Read: Interstellar Message Decipherment from Archaeological and Anthropological Perspectives," chapter 6 in this volume.

tant, and somewhat discouraging, in light of the probability that interstellar messages will also engage at least two layers of symboling.

Again, to recognize something as a symbolic communication, we do not need to actually understand the content, and thus may not need to get through these two layers. But from the perspective of those constructing the messages, this issue may be more important, assuming that we want to be understood if at all possible and not merely recognized as intelligent. Given this difficulty inherent in messages communicated via writing or other symbol systems, it may be that messages with only one layer of symbolism could be easier to understand.

Humans do often use symbols to express ideas that cannot be articulated verbally or mathematically. In archaeology, evidence of symbolic activity—artworks especially, which are usually related to religious or spiritual issues—typically tells us most about past thought and intelligences. We can learn a great deal from the fact of the symboling behavior, as noted already, and also from its nature and characteristics, even without being able to decipher what is being expressed. And while ideas concerning matters aesthetic, moral, religious, and poetic seem to be the ones in which human cultures vary most, in fact there is often substantial commonality. I realize this seems counterintuitive to most of us, especially to people like me, who can never seem to get the point of poetry, or to people who think of religion in terms of squabbles over doctrines rather than in terms of its connection to the human spiritual sense. But the point is easily illustrated: we may not know what the artists of Lascaux or Altamira were saying specifically, but when we see their work, we "feel" something, often described as the universal human spirit shared across the millennia. But it is just as conceivable that it is the spirit of intelligent, purposive beings, a spirit, perhaps, shareable over even greater spans of time and space.

I hasten to add that I am not confusing feeling with knowing, as is so common in popular discourse. I am suggesting something more like the following: creating messages such that ETIs could recognize our use of symbols and thus our intelligence, should be possible. Transmission of specified, objective knowledge through written language is certainly worth trying, but if our experience in deciphering ancient scripts is any indication, it will not be easy for an intelligent being out there to get through the two layers of symbolism to the content of the message. Communicating as the artists (symbolists) of Lascaux did, with but one layer of symbols, won't get across a concrete, specified body of data either, but it could convey useful insight about us, perhaps more than a rich, language-based message that can't be read. Anthropologists and archaeologists are largely agreed that religion is a human universal. Thus, there is an argument to be made for designating religion as a topic for interstellar communication. On portions of the planet where exponents of contemporary academia live, religion is regarded as a rare aberration, or perhaps as an early evolutionary stage. But on Earth as a whole this is not true; indeed it would be an error of great proportions to think so. Religious people are not uncommon even among the sophisticated ranks of scientists. Like every other aspect of culture, religion comes in many flavors; but this variety does not mean there is no common basis for religion or that it has no referent outside the human subjective self. Such conclusions follow no more logically than they do when the same idea is applied to some other area of human culture, such as food. The fact that humans often eat radically different things does not contradict the fact that eating is a universal, much less the existence of nutritional sources outside of our bodies.

In his entertaining introduction to astrobiology, *Sharing the Universe: Perspectives on Extraterrestrial Life*, Seth Shostak raises the question of "ET's religion."[16] He makes the important point that whether or not ET has religion depends on what religion is: if it is a useful survival tool, it will likely evolve on other worlds; but if, like music, it is mainly a contingent by-product of other evolved capabilities, it may be unique to humans and not a universal feature of intelligent life. Shostak then adds, "Of course, if they do, there's little chance that the specifics of ET's faith will mimic our own, any more than his appearance will resemble ours."[17]

I am inclined to think otherwise (including about music). If religion is essentially a survival mechanism for humans, it would be a highly contingent feature of human psychology, and thus its evolution elsewhere would seem implausible. Religion is likely to be widespread throughout the universe only if it refers to some reality beyond the peculiarities of the *Homo sapiens* brain. And if it does, then it may well have features in common wherever found.

If religion and spirituality really refer to something outside of our brains—a creator God, for example—then it could well be the case that an ETI would have a sort of spirituality or religion and that it might even be recognizable as such. I have elsewhere defined religion as the human cultural response to the real or perceived supernatural.[18] Mine is only one of hundreds of definitions offered, but it is useful to remember that religion really is a human phenomenon—a feature of human cultures—and it varies as much as our

---

16. G. Seth Shostak, *Sharing the Universe: Perspectives on Extraterrestrial Life* (Berkeley: Berkeley Hills Books, 1998), pp. 99–100.

17. Shostak, *Sharing the Universe*, p. 100.

18. Paul K. Wason, "Naturalism vs. Science in the Anthropological Study of Religion," *Omega: Indian Journal of Science and Religion* 3, no. 1 (2004): 27–58.

cultures do. But my definition does not reduce religion to nothing but culture right from the start; it leaves open the possibility that religion refers to important facets of reality that are not as easily recognized via other cultural forms of knowing.

Perhaps what we should be looking for is any place where human nature intersects with a deeper reality (and so would not represent human nature alone). If there is a creator God, then this Being might constitute a connection between us and ETIs, via our respective religions, despite the likelihood of extensive differences between us in other respects. Similarly, if there are real meanings and purposes in the universe—love, quest, purpose, or whatever—these, too, are potential connections. As with religion, all the examples I can think of are disputed. I believe music or mathematics could work if there is a fundamental reality to, for example, harmony, as could mathematics if, as George Ellis and some other scholars suggest, math exists objectively, not just in the human brain, and so is discovered rather than invented.[19] The nature of these features of reality is as disputed a point as the existence of God, it seems; and if it happens that music or mathematics is an arbitrary invention of the human mind, then neither may serve as a connection with extraterrestrial beings.

Conclusions and Next Steps

To return to a crucial question, how, specifically, do we recognize intelligent agency and purpose? Recall that archaeologists regularly find items of unknown function, yet these researchers have no problem agreeing that the items are the product of human activity. In this instance the inference is clearly not from known function to demonstration of human agency. Often enough, we argue endlessly about an object's functions, never questioning its having been the product of human activity. There must be some other feature of these tools, that tells us this piece of stone is a naturally fractured rock and that one is a tool. Do we need ethnographic analogy to make this determination? Is our conclusion based on what we know about humans—including implicit insight gained from the researcher actually being one of these creatures—or is it based on a deeper recognition of intelligence or purpose or agency? As with the matter of elf-shot, I think it is often the latter.

---

19. George F. R. Ellis, "True Complexity and Its Associated Ontology," in *Science and Ultimate Reality: Quantum Theory, Cosmology, and Complexity*, ed. John D. Barrow, Paul C. W. Davies, and Charles L. Harper, Jr. (Cambridge: Cambridge University Press, 2004), pp. 607–636.

In his fascinating book titled *Why Would Anyone Believe in God?*, Justin Barrett reviews the literature on what cognitive psychologists like to call the *human agency detection device*.[20] Students of cognition give us reason to believe humans are attuned to things that have a personal source. Being on the lookout for agency, so to speak, is often a subconscious process, which may account for our difficulty in clarifying exactly *why* we think something is an agent. During my archaeological training, I was often told, in effect, "just work with the materials and eventually you will see it." And though I would have preferred a straightforward identification key, this turned out to be good advice.

It is entirely reasonable—from the point of view of both natural selection and common sense—that our minds would work this way. In his book *Faces in the Clouds*, Stewart Guthrie asserts that religion is essentially anthropomorphism.[21] I find many of his observations concerning our intellectual predispositions both interesting and helpful. I particularly like an example which runs something like this: If you see an object ahead on the trail and think it is a bear but it turns out to be a rock, you have not lost much. But if you think it is a rock and it is really a bear, that is a different matter. In such a world as ours, where we cannot always identify bears and rocks with certainty, it is reasonable to assume natural selection will favor the one who is predisposed to recognize living, purposive agents.

There are good selectionist reasons for being able to detect agency and personality whenever they are seen. But we cannot have perfect knowledge. Ideally, it would be a rock, and the person walking along would know it is a rock at first sight; but ours is an uncertain world, and we inevitably err a portion of the time. All else being equal (visual acuity, level of intelligence, reaction time, and running speed, for example), natural selection could well favor those who err on the side of overestimating agency and purpose in the world around us.

Following the lead of cognitive scientists, including those associated with the promising field of evolutionary psychology and the new cognitive science of religion (of which Barrett is one of the founders), I suggest that what the archaeologist is "seeing" when identifying one lump of rock as a tool and another as a naturally occurring stone is evidence not just of humanity in the concrete (and, for our purposes, narrow) sense but of intention, purpose, the work of an agent with a plan. We see, for example, repeated regular blows

---

20. Justin L. Barrett, *Why Would Anyone Believe in God?* (Lanham, MD: AltaMira Press, 2004).
21. Stewart Guthrie, *Faces in the Clouds: A New Theory of Religion* (Oxford: Oxford University Press, 1993).

and chips, something that would result from an intelligent being *trying to do something*, not from a rock tumbling down a hillside due to frost erosion and the work of gravity.

To the extent that this is true, it is very encouraging, for it suggests that part of being an intelligent, purposive agent is a deeply evolved ability to recognize the work of other intelligent, purposive agents, even, perhaps, if they are not *Homo sapiens* from planet Earth. It would work equally well the other way around, for any intelligent being will be a purposive agent and will therefore have evolved under conditions favoring the ability to recognize other agents and distinguish their work from other forms of causation.

CHAPTER EIGHT

Anthropology at a Distance
SETI and the Production of Knowledge in the Encounter with an Extraterrestrial Other

John W. Traphagan

Throughout much of its history, anthropology has explicitly focused its intellectual gaze upon the understanding of seemingly "alien" others whose languages, beliefs, patterns of living, and social structures have been viewed as remote from the societies of the industrial West—England, France, Germany, and the United States—in which the discipline developed. In the formative years of anthropology, ethnographers did not normally have the capacity to be in direct contact with the others who were the object of their studies. Indeed, early "armchair" anthropologists of the 19th century, such as James Frazer, E. B. Tylor, and Lewis Henry Morgan (although Morgan did also conduct some direct data collection among the Iroquois in addition to the armchair variety of research), worked under conditions not entirely unlike those of SETI researchers today; limitations in technology (specifically transportation and communications technologies) dramatically restricted the types of interaction accessible to social scientists interested in contacting and understanding a distant other. Communication was slow, requiring weeks or months for anthropologists in the United States or Britain to request and then receive information from individuals (often missionaries) living in distant places. When data were eventually received, such as the kinship data collected by Morgan in the mid-19th century from numerous parts of the world, interpretation was based largely upon theoretical frameworks and assumptions that had a decidedly Western tinge—specifically, social Darwinism and cultural evolution of a Spencerian variety, with their overtly teleological underpinnings associated with progress. These frameworks and assumptions were difficult to test using the methods of direct contact and participant observation that would later become the foundation of ethnographic research.[1]

---

1. Thomas R. Trautmann, *Lewis Henry Morgan and the Invention of Kinship* (Berkeley: University of California Press, 1988); Herbert Spencer, *Social Statics: The Conditions Essential to Human Happiness Specified, and the First of Them Developed* (1954; rpt. New York: A. M. Kelly, 1969), p. 1851.

Although the 19th-century style of armchair anthropology was replaced by ethnographic fieldwork in the early 20th century, instances of anthropology at a distance continued to occur, the most notable being Ruth Benedict's attempt to develop an understanding of the seemingly—to American eyes—intensely alien Japanese during World War II, conducted under the auspices of the U.S. government and published in 1946 as *The Chrysanthemum and the Sword*.[2]

In this chapter I explore one avenue through which anthropology and, more specifically, the subdiscipline of cultural or social anthropology can contribute to SETI research. Michael A. G. Michaud has noted that the social sciences are an area of intellectual inquiry that has not been sufficiently tapped in reference to SETI.[3] Here, I want to suggest that one of the most potent ways the social sciences in general and anthropology in particular can contribute to SETI is through analogy, using an analysis of anthropology's own history of contact as a framework for thinking about potential contact with an extraterrestrial civilization. While it is extremely important to contemplate the content and type of interstellar message we might construct, it is equally important to consider the context of interpretation in which such a message will be conveyed and interpreted, as well as how any response might be interpreted by scientists and others on planet Earth. Rather than simply an act of discovery, initial contact with any extraterrestrial intelligence will also create a new context in which knowledge is generated and understood. The context of initial contact will be formed on the basis of very limited data and, inevitably, interpreted through the lenses of our own cultures and the theoretical frameworks that are in vogue among intellectuals and others at the time contact occurs.

In order to explicate this point, I will consider the type of "anthropology at a distance" evident in the early and, to a lesser extent, middle years of the discipline, focusing on the work of Ruth Benedict during World War II as an example of how the complex interplay between assumptions, data, and misinterpretations can become established as authoritative knowledge about and understanding of an alien civilization. The central point of this chapter is that Japan, as a culture and a civilization, was not simply revealed by Benedict;

---

2. See Ruth Benedict, *The Chrysanthemum and the Sword: Patterns of Japanese Culture* (Boston: Houghton Mifflin, 1946). It is important to recognize that Benedict herself was not trying to represent the Japanese as incomprehensibly alien. Rather, her primary aim was to show that if we understood the cultural logic at the foundation of Japanese society, we could understand the behaviors and their motivations that seemed so alien to Americans during the war.

3. Michael A. G. Michaud, *Contact with Alien Civilizations* (New York: Copernicus Books, 2007), p. 327.

it was in many respects created out of this interplay, at least as far as the American perspective is concerned (and, although not specifically relevant to this paper, to some extent the Japanese perspective as well).[4] I will argue that the initial contact and subsequent interaction between extraterrestrials and humans (including SETI researchers, politicians, scholars outside of SETI, and the general public) will involve a similar production of knowledge about the alien other. Awareness of this hazard and the ability to reflexively think about our own role in constructing an alien culture, particularly where great distances and time delays are insurmountable with current technology, are of fundamental importance in reducing the risk of misunderstanding and misinterpretation.

Ruth Benedict and the Invention of Japanese Culture

Anthropologist Marvin Harris has noted that the beginnings of anthropology are to be found in the inspiration of the natural sciences and the scientific method. At the foundation of anthropology is an assumption that sociocultural processes are governed by "lawful principles" that can be understood in terms of causality and that are discoverable by an objective observer.[5] Early formulations of culture grew out of the research of scholars who saw distinct cultures as relatively bounded entities, and they posited culture as largely deterministic, fundamentally shaping the behaviors and thought patterns of the people inhabiting a particular context. Much recent work tends to see culture as fluid and having very permeable boundaries (if we can really think in terms of boundaries at all), conceptualizing it as a process of invention in which particular "cultures" arise out of an intersubjective dialectic between the individual and his or her social environment.[6] The anthropologist is not remote from this process but, instead, can become actively involved in the invention of a particular culture—understood as an analytical category as well as a popular framing of a particular social group—through translating, interpreting, and writing about what he or she observes, as well as through the daily interaction associated with the activity of fieldwork.

---

4. To some extent, even the perspective of postwar Japanese citizens on their national culture has been influenced by Benedict's assessment; see Sonia Ryang, *Japan and National Anthropology: A Critique* (London: RoutledgeCurzon, 2004), p. 29.

5. Marvin Harris, *The Rise of Anthropological Theory* (New York: Harper and Row, 1968), p. 1.

6. Roy Wagner's *The Invention of Culture*, rev. ed. (Chicago: University of Chicago Press, 1981) is one study among many that have addressed this issue over roughly the past 30 years.

Nowhere, perhaps, is the issue of the anthropologist herself as research instrument more evident than in the studies Ruth Benedict conducted during World War II on Japanese culture. To begin, Benedict's work is, if not exactly armchair anthropology, a latter-day expression of "anthropology at a distance." As most anthropologists and other scholars who work on Japan know, Benedict was commissioned in the early 1940s by the U.S. government to provide a report that would explain Japanese behavior and could thus be used to predict enemy responses during what was, by 1944, the anticipated invasion of Japan. In other words, her work was to be an explanatory guide in the project of social engineering that would become the Occupation of Japan.

Considerably less well known among the general public, and even among some scholars with interests in Japanese culture, is how Benedict's research was done. First, Benedict did not conduct a study of Japanese culture or society through traditional ethnographic methods of participant observation; instead, due to the war, she was forced to turn to what appeared to be the next best thing—Americans of Japanese descent who were confined to internment camps in the desert Southwest. Obviously, in retrospect, this should raise red flags about Benedict's study. As Eiko Ikegami recently pointed out, Benedict's research subjects, when faced with an authority figure representing the same government that had removed them from their homes and imprisoned them in the camps, were "passive and cautious in their replies to her questions."[7] Interestingly, this issue was not addressed by most scholars who reviewed Benedict's book; a few noted the problem, but in general it was overlooked or ignored. It is only recently that open discussion has ensued about how Benedict's research contains flawed conclusions in part because the conditions of her data collection were limited by her inability to make direct contact with individuals within the Japanese cultural context.

For my purposes here, it is not important to go into details about the empirical and interpretive errors that exist in *The Chrysanthemum and the Sword*. Ryang notes many of the problems and demonstrates that Benedict's development of linguistic data from Japanese is not supported by either sociological or historical data. She tends to select words from her informants and from literature without contextualizing the terms or understanding how they are conceptually used by Japanese, but in her work these terms tend to become keywords for representing and understanding Japanese culture and behavior.[8] More important than the specific errors in Benedict's research is

---

7. Eiko Ikegami, "Shame and the Samurai: Institutions, Trustworthiness, and Autonomy in the Elite Honor Culture," *Social Research* 70, no. 4 (2003): 1351–1378, esp. p. 1370.

8. Ryang, *Japan and National Anthropology*, p. 33.

the fact that she takes a totalizing approach to representing Japan: specific words, ideas, or concepts evident in sources such as Japanese literature are used to broadly explain, often in a single brushstroke, all or most elements of Japanese behavior. In part this approach is a consequence of the theoretical framework Benedict uses, as well as a general lack of detailed empirical data about Japan upon which to base her conclusions.

While the study's flaws are significant, a more salient point is that *The Chrysanthemum and the Sword* becomes, as Ryang notes, "paradigmatic," playing "a crucial role in the postwar social science discourse on Japan" both among Japanese and non-Japanese scholars.[9] Indeed, so thorough was the assumption that Benedict had accurately presented Japanese culture that it was only rarely noted that her research had not focused on Japanese people. Attitudes toward *The Chrysanthemum and the Sword* at the time of its publication are summed up in a 1947 review written by John Embree, himself a well-known anthropologist of Japan, in which he states: "Dr. Benedict, with the soft words of a fox spirit, leads the reader into the forest of Japan and before he knows it she has him bewitched into believing that he understands and is familiar with every root and branch of Japanese culture."[10]

When I first read this comment, I thought it might be sarcastic, but throughout the review Embree's only real criticism of Benedict's book concerns her failure to recognize that Japan is an old culture while the United States is a new one, itself a rather dubious observation since Japan underwent a radical social transformation in the second half of the 19th century.[11] He goes on to state, "The frontiersman and the nomad are more likely to be individualistic braggarts than is the village bound peasant who must face his same neighbor day after day.... A man of an old peasant culture such as the Japanese is likely to be more meticulous in his etiquette and sense of reciprocal duty."[12] In Embree's view, Benedict allowed us to gain entrance into an almost impenetrable cultural "forest" vastly different from ours because it

---

9. Ryang, *Japan and National Anthropology*, p. 48.

10. John Embree, "Review of *The Chrysanthemum and the Sword*," *Far Eastern Survey* 16, no. 1 (1947): 11.

11. In one sense, Embree is correct that Japan has a much longer history than the United States, but the U.S. Constitution remained in force throughout a period in which Japan experienced two radical social transformations: the Meiji Restoration of 1868 and the industrialization of Japanese society following the U.S. Occupation, with its associated political and social changes. The second of these transformations was happening as Embree was writing, and both raise questions about the meaningfulness of describing Japan as old and the United States as new.

12. Embree, "Review of *The Chrysanthemum and the Sword*," p. 11.

was a "peasant" society based upon village social organization (I'm not quite sure where Tokyo and Osaka fit into that forest) as opposed to urban, individualistic American social organization. And she did this while dealing with the considerable limitations that were inevitable at the time of her research.[13]

Interestingly enough, in another review where he compares Benedict's book to a book by Andrew W. Lind on Japanese communities in Hawaiʻi, Embree takes for granted the idea that Benedict did, in fact, explicate Japanese cultural patterns and behaviors through her research.[14] Indeed, Benedict, although clearly identifying her fieldwork locale, ultimately represents her work as if it were about Japanese rather than Japanese-American people and cultural values, and, as is apparent in Embree's review and those of other scholars at the time, this representation went largely uncontested,[15] although John Morris in his 1947 review points out that "in normal circumstances no one would think of writing a serious book without first spending a considerable time observing at first hand the actual behavior of the people concerned."[16] Morris quickly puts this problem aside and lauds *The Chrysanthemum and the Sword* as "the most important contemporary book yet written on Japan. Here, for the first time, is a serious attempt to explain why the Japanese behave the way they do."[17]

These examples clearly demonstrate that *The Chrysanthemum and the Sword* became, as noted above, the cornerstone of the ethnographic, and nonethnographic, corpus of Western scholarship on Japan, despite its lack of sound empirical data. Benedict's contemporaries largely took her work at face value and accepted as a given the idea that she had produced a study of Japanese culture. The problems inherent in having to do "anthropology at a distance" were overlooked by Benedict's colleagues and by many of those who

---

13. It is worth noting that Embree backed away from his support for Benedict's work a few years later, shortly before his death in the early 1950s. See Ryang, *Japan and National Anthropology*, pp. 35–40.

14. John Embree, "Review of *Hawaii's Japanese* and *The Chrysanthemum and the Sword*," *American Sociological Review* 12, no. 2 (1947): 245–246.

15. Erwin H. Ackerknecht, "Review of *The Chrysanthemum and the Sword*," *The Quarterly Review of Biology* 22, no. 3 (1947): 246; Paul H. Clyde, "Review of *The Chrysanthemum and the Sword*," *The American Political Science Review* 41, no. 3 (1947): 585–586; Embree, "Review of *The Chrysanthemum and the Sword*"; Raglan, "Review of *The Chrysanthemum and the Sword*," *Man* 48 (1948): 35.

16. John Morris, "Review of *The Chrysanthemum and the Sword*," *Pacific Affairs* 20, no. 2 (1947): 208–210, esp. p. 209.

17. Morris, "Review of *The Chrysanthemum and the Sword*," p. 208.

became interested in Japanese culture; instead of being challenged, her book shaped the major questions posed and studies produced by "Japanologists," most notably the focus on the Japanese psyche or personality (self) that dominated research on Japan into the 1990s and continues at present.[18] By the 1980s, anthropologists began moving away from Benedict's construction of Japanese culture, but her work has been cited hundreds of times and continues to be cited, particularly in cross-cultural psychological studies, not as a book about Japanese Americans during World War II but as a book about Japanese people and their culture.[19]

In essence, the publication of *The Chrysanthemum and the Sword* initiated a process by which the Western concept of Japanese culture was invented. Benedict's work identified what would be considered the basic elements and core values associated with Japanese culture and the Japanese psyche for years to come, and a great deal of the scholarship produced during that period supported Benedict's conclusions, either directly or indirectly. As people read and followed her work with further research, analysis, and publication, a sense of Japanese culture and Japanese behavior being accurately and completely represented in the basic ideas put forth by Benedict prevailed in communities of scholars working in areas such as cross-cultural psychology and cross-cultural communication, as well as in the broader community of nonscholars who were simply interested in Japan. In short, Benedict's at-a-distance take on Japan became Japan itself for many, and perhaps the majority, of Americans throughout most of the second half of the 20th century. This influence cannot be overstated: Benedict's work was central to the U.S. government's approach to reorganizing and engineering Japanese society after the war and was widely read by an American public interested in understanding the enemy they had just conquered and whose country they were now occupying.

However, what was being created was not a true understanding of Japan, if such an understanding of any culture is actually possible. Rather, what was created was a notion of Japanese culture that reflected values and psychological orientations—with an emphasis on the concept of shame—that seemed important to Benedict. Indeed, the book is an application of theories she developed in an earlier work, *Patterns of Culture*, in which she used psychological idioms (although not Freudian in nature) as a means of creating

---

18. Ryang, *Japan and National Anthropology*, passim.
19. Perhaps most striking is that when the book is cited today, its conclusions are often presented as constants of Japanese culture, impervious to historical circumstances, such as the influence of American concepts of individualism that became common during and after the Occupation, despite the fact that the book was published more than 60 years ago.

configurations or categories of cultural types that, in turn, were imprinted in the minds of those living in a particular cultural milieu. In other words, Benedict's understanding of how culture works and what culture is should be seen as a direct result of the academic context, with its considerable interest in psychology, in which she was trained at Columbia during the 1920s and which continued to be a significant focus as her career developed.

Consequences of Anthropology at a Distance for SETI

This foray into the history of anthropology has a direct bearing on how we might think about an encounter with an extraterrestrial technological civilization. The wartime conditions under which Benedict conducted her research eliminated the possibility of doing true ethnography in the form of participant observation and long-term fieldwork. Indeed, few of the data she relied on were actually collected by her; instead she borrowed data collected by psychological anthropologist Geoffrey Gorer from interned Japanese Americans in the relocation camps during the war as well as data gathered by another psychological anthropologist, Weston La Barre, although she did collect some interview data of her own.[20]

As noted above, given the lack of empirical data and the limited scholarly resources available on Japanese culture and behavior,[21] as well as her general tendency toward emphasizing (psychologically oriented) theory over data, Benedict essentially took the little she had and worked it into the theoretical framework she had developed in her earlier book, *Patterns of Culture,* which categorized Native American cultures on the basis of personality traits associated with a particular group of people. Benedict's study of Japan, from afar, set in motion a conceptualization of Japan and the Japanese people that has influenced scholarship and policy-making related to that society up to the present day. And a great deal of what she wrote has turned out to be either a very simplistic representation/explanation of Japanese culture or fundamentally inaccurate; yet her work continues to be influential.

If we turn to a bit of speculation about our initial encounter with an extraterrestrial intelligence, it is not difficult to imagine an analogous process

---

20. Ryang, *Japan and National Anthropology,* p. 17; Geoffrey Gorer, "Themes in Japanese Culture," *New York Academy of Sciences,* ser. II, vol. 5 (1943): 106–124; Weston La Barre, "Some Observations on Character Structure in the Orient: The Japanese," *Psychiatry* 8, no. 3 (1945): 319–342. Neither Gorer nor La Barre were trained as Japan scholars.
21. See Ryang, *Japan and National Anthropology,* p. 16.

occurring. The first scientists to encounter a signal from an extraterrestrial intelligence will likely receive a limited amount of data. If we simply capture a signal that is not directly aimed at attracting the attention of an alien civilization (such as our own), then it may be extremely difficult to develop a clear sense of what we are looking at. This is not simply a matter of translation; even if we can infer specific meanings of linguistic constructs that correspond to something in our own language, we will have no cultural framework with which to interpret how those meanings apply to an alien society. Even mathematics, the language of science, is not without its own difficulties in terms of interpretation.[22] In the case of Benedict, who knew she was dealing with another human society that had the same basic structures (albeit different in their manifestations) as American society—systems associated with religion, kinship, government, etc.—a lack of sufficient data and an inherent tendency to fit an alien culture into a framework that made sense to an American mind led to a casting of Japanese culture along particular lines that had many flaws.

The odds are that, without an understanding of an extraterrestrial culture—one derived from hard data rigorously analyzed—we will interpret what we find in terms of values, structures, and patterns of behavior associated with our own culture (itself a problematic idea since there is no single human culture on Earth). In some respects, we have already started this process in our reasonable attempt to think about the nature of ETI—the notion of an asymmetry of age between ETI and ourselves is based on an assumption that the rate of progress on Earth should be fairly standard elsewhere.[23] However, given the differences that exist among human cultures in terms of how we perceive, interpret, and categorize our surroundings, it is reasonable to think that a truly alien society would consist of beings who do these things in ways unlike those of humans.[24] Perhaps these differences, when combined with distinct biology, would lead to rates of development much faster, or much slower, than has been the case on Earth. The capacity to "do" culture in a relatively consistent way among human beings, even with all of the differ-

---

22. See Carl L. DeVito, "On the Universality of Human Mathematics," in *Communication with Extraterrestrial Intelligence*, ed. Douglas A. Vakoch (Albany: State University of New York Press, 2011), pp. 439–448; and C. L. DeVito and R. T. Oehrle, "A Language Based on the Fundamental Facts of Science," *Journal of the British Interplanetary Society* 43, no. 12 (1990): 561–568.

23. See Douglas A. Vakoch, "Integrating Active and Passive SETI Programs," in Vakoch, ed., *Communication with Extraterrestrial Intelligence*, pp. 253–278.

24. Douglas Vakoch, "Culture in the Cosmos," *Space.com*, 3 May 2007, available at *http://www. space.com/searchforlife/seti_culture_070503.html*.

ences we find in specifically how culture is done, is heavily dependent upon a common set of sense organs. Neurological studies have shown that differential experiences and forms of stimulation during developmental processes shape the connections among neurons and thus influence the construction of the neural networks that are basic to human behavior and thought. What would "culture" look like when applied to a being with different sense organs and possibly a very different natural and social environment from ours?

If the first message we encounter happens to be an intentional attempt on the part of an alien civilization to contact another intelligent species, then it is reasonable to expect that such a message will be limited in content. Douglas Vakoch notes that the few messages humans have already sent into space have been rather limited, and a bit warped, in terms of their representation of our own civilization, showing chiefly the brighter sides of humanity and ignoring social ills such as war and poverty.[25] Even if extraterrestrials try to represent themselves in an objective manner, any intentional message we receive will almost certainly have subjective qualities and represent an alien civilization in a way that will influence how we construct an understanding of their messages and, beyond that, of their civilization.

Regardless of the type of communication received, we humans are most unlikely to receive a message and simply take it at face value without speculating on the nature of those who sent it. Benedict, like armchair anthropologists before her, was a trained interpreter and theorist of culture and behavior, but the conditions of her research on Japan and her lack of understanding of the Japanese language made it difficult for her to gain an accurate picture of the culture and people about which she wrote. Furthermore, her subjective interests in a particular theoretical framework influenced her management of the data she did obtain and led her to organize her understanding of Japan in a way that fitted her assumptions about how cultures work. This is understandable, particularly when one is dealing with limited data. However, this process will not be restricted to a few scholars and policy-makers and gradually released to the public.[26] Instead, as Seth Shostak points out, should contact occur, knowledge of the event will quickly become evident to a wide audience, most likely well before SETI scientists are even certain that the

---

25. Vakoch, "Integrating Active and Passive SETI Programs," pp. 253–278.

26. For an interesting discussion of some policy issues related to SETI, see Mark L. Lupisella, "Pragmatism, Cosmocentrism, and Proportional Consultations for Communication with Extraterrestrial Intelligence," in Vakoch, ed., *Communication with Extraterrestrial Intelligence*, pp. 319–332.

signal has really come from an extraterrestrial intelligence.[27] Contact will become widely known and reflected upon by media pundits long before anthropologists and other scientists whose expertise is the interpretation of different cultures are able to understand and analyze whatever content might exist in a signal. In short, the invention of an alien culture will begin almost the moment that contact is made.

If we ever do receive a message from an extraterrestrial intelligence, we will be faced with the same problem that Benedict and earlier anthropologists working at a distance encountered: limited data. In addition, we will face the problem of a time lag—but not the lag of several months experienced by armchair anthropologists of the 19th century. Instead, we will deal with time lags of years, decades, centuries, or millennia between message and response. If we think about the study of Japan, the course of which was so heavily influenced by the work of Benedict even though access to new data has been readily available over the past 60 years, it is easy to imagine how long stretches with few or no data could lead humans to create an image of an extraterrestrial civilization based largely upon our own theories and expectations about how culture and behavior work. Michaud notes that scientists "should not let belief or preference triumph over evidence," but in the case of extraterrestrials this will be a challenging task.[28] Indeed, the vast majority of what we will "know" about ET, if contact happens, will be our own inventions based upon very limited data and then elaborated over the long waiting periods between contacts.

27. Seth Shostak, "Contact: What Happens if a Signal is Found?," *Space.com*, 17 August 2006, available at *http://www.space.com/searchforlife/seti_whatif_060817.html*.

28. Michael A. G. Michaud, "The Relevance of Human History," in Vakoch, ed., *Communication with Extraterrestrial Intelligence*, p. 315.

CHAPTER NINE

Contact Considerations
A Cross-Cultural Perspective

Douglas Raybeck

Introduction

Within the scientific community as well as in the popular press and among science-fiction writers, the existence of extraterrestrials and the possibility of communicating with them have long been matters of intense interest. This interest has led to such projects as the Search for Extraterrestrial Intelligence (SETI), which continues to be a focus of attention for many scientists despite the challenges of finding sustained funding for this field of research.[1] Practitioners of the physical, social, and behavioral sciences have all theorized and speculated about the nature of extraterrestrial intelligence and the problems involved in inter-sentient communication.[2] The general consensus has been that the universe is very likely to host other intelligent beings, that some of these will be more technologically advanced than humans, and that some are trying even now to locate other intelligences.

In the science-fiction community, images of extraterrestrials have varied in form, intelligence, and intention. They range from the beneficent aliens of Julian May, who wish only to elevate humanity and facilitate our participation

---

1. Ronald D. Ekers et al., eds., *SETI 2020: A Roadmap for the Search for Extraterrestrial Intelligence* (Mountain View, CA: SETI Press, 2002); Philip Morrison, John Billingham, and John Wolfe, eds., *The Search for Extraterrestrial Intelligence: SETI* (Washington, DC: NASA SP-419, 1977); Albert A. Harrison and Alan C. Elms, "Psychology and the Search for Extraterrestrial Intelligence," *Behavioral Science* 35 (1990): 207–218; Douglas Raybeck, "Problems in Extraterrestrial Communication," paper presented at the 9th annual CONTACT conference, held on 5–8 March 1992, in Palo Alto, California.
2. See, for example, Carl Sagan, ed., *Communication with Extraterrestrial Intelligence* (CETI) (Cambridge: The MIT Press, 1973); and for one example of the many discussions of ETI by social and behavioral scientists, see Albert A. Harrison, "Thinking Intelligently About Extraterrestrial Intelligence: An Application of Living Systems Theory," *Behavioral Science* 38, no. 3 (1993): 189–217.

in an intergalactic "milieu," to the malevolent extraterrestrials of Greg Bear, who travel about the universe locating intelligent life-forms and destroying them before they can become future competitors.[3] Generally, however, images of aliens in fiction and within the scientific community are positive. It is widely believed that if a sentient form can achieve the degree of civilization necessary to support interstellar communication, it is unlikely to be characterized by hostile intentions.

In all likelihood, should we have an encounter with an alien intelligence, that experience will be neither physical nor continuous. Rather we are most apt to find either a message or a remote probe.[4] In either event, acknowledging the current strictures of space-time and of Relativity Theory, there will be a significant lag between exchanges of information. Given the improbability of physical contact with aliens, there would seem to be little chance for hostile confrontations, even if intelligent extraterrestrials had untoward motives, as is quite possible.[5]

Instead the pertinent question appears to be how will we respond to the knowledge, and its inherent challenge, that there are other intelligences out there? This paper seeks to explore that issue by utilizing analogies from Western colonial adventures in Asia, the Americas, and New Zealand to construct differing scenarios of contact. Our own sociocultural variability may be as important as the diversity of those who may contact us. As we shall see, some cultures appear better equipped to deal with the profound questions likely to be posed by another intelligent life-form.

The relevance of anthropology to SETI has been well argued by Steven Dick and by John Traphagan in other chapters of this volume. Kathryn Denning has also demonstrated the pertinence of archaeology to several of the issues with which SETI is concerned, and her argument that "SETI begins at home" is clearly one that the present chapter supports.[6]

---

3. Julian May, *The Metaconcert* (New York: Ballantine Books, 1987); Julian May, *The Surveillance* (New York: Ballantine Books, 1987); Greg Bear, *The Forge of God* (New York: TOR, 1987).

4. See, for example, Albert A. Harrison, *After Contact: The Human Response to Extraterrestrial Life* (New York: Plenum, 1997).

5. Douglas Raybeck, "Predator-Prey Models and Contact Considerations," paper presented at the 11th annual Contact conference, held 18–20 March 1994 in Santa Clara, California.

6. Steven J. Dick, "The Role of Anthropology in SETI: A Historical View," chapter 3 in this volume; John W. Traphagan, "Anthropology at a Distance: SETI and the Production of Knowledge in the Encounter with an Extraterrestrial Other," chapter 8 in this volume; Kathryn E. Denning, "Learning to Read: Interstellar Message Decipherment from Archaeological and Anthropological Perspectives," chapter 6 in this volume.

Colonial Cultural Contacts

For many centuries European societies had comparatively few technological advantages over the developed societies of the East. Asian cultures were technologically superior to Western societies in many respects until the early modern period, when Europeans began to excel in shipbuilding, cartography, navigation, and the design and manufacture of artillery. By coupling naval and military superiority with good management, state support, and often ruthless policies, the West was able to impose its will upon other cultures and to extract a great deal of wealth.[7]

I believe physical encounters with extraterrestrials are highly unlikely, but I am concerned with the manner in which we will discern and react to the discovery of a nonhuman intelligence. A brief review of some of the more notorious examples of European and U.S. colonialism may enrich our discussion of the possibilities of first contact with extraterrestrial intelligence. Of particular interest here is how the members of various cultures perceived and responded to outsiders who often possessed technologies that made them seem magical. The examples appear instructive.

Aztec

The cultural contact between the Aztecs and the conquistadors is perhaps the most extreme example on record of misinterpreted intentions. At the time of contact with the Spanish in the 16th century, the Aztecs had created a highly stratified empire with tributary states and a great deal of specialization. They were noted for literacy, a complex calendar, magnificent architectural structures, and other accomplishments.

Aztec mythology included a deity called Quetzalcoatl who, it was believed, would come from the East with pale countenance and strange beasts. When Hernán Cortés arrived in 1519, the Aztec ruler at the time, Montezuma II, and members of the priestly class declared that he was a god and that his companions also were divine.[8] This misperception was encouraged by Cortés, who began to pass himself off as that god. Montezuma identified Cortés as a deity in part because the explorer had landed in Mexico on the calendar day of Quetzalcoatl's birth. This timing was no

---

7. Daniel J. Boorstin, *The Discoverers* (New York: Random House, 1983); Robert Van Niel, *Java Under the Cultivation Systems: Collected Writings* (Leiden: KITLV Press, 1992).

8. George C. Vaillant, *Aztecs of Mexico: Origin, Rise and Fall of the Aztec Nation* (1941; New York: Doubleday, 1944).

accident. Cortés had heard tales of Quetzalcoatl and had gambled on being mistaken for the Aztec god.[9]

Cortés had already made an alliance with a traditional enemy of the Aztecs, the Indians of Tlaxcala. No doubt the Spanish found the Tlaxcalans worthy as allies because they had found them worthy as opponents. When the Tlaxcalans had been wrestling with the question of the possibly divine nature of the Spanish, one of the more experimentally minded war leaders had resolved the issue by holding a Spanish soldier under water until he drowned.[10]

Unlike previous Aztec rulers, who are described as great warriors, Montezuma II was a weak and indecisive man, more interested in sorcery and philosophy than in war. Instead of attacking the Spaniards, he tried to assert power over them by trickery, magic, and gifts; when these means failed, Montezuma allowed Cortés to enter the island capital of Tenochtitlán unchallenged and received him in his court. Montezuma was taken prisoner without resistance, but the brutal conduct of the invaders aroused the anger of the city's inhabitants. The Aztecs managed to drive the foreigners out for a short while, but during the ensuing battle, Montezuma died under mysterious circumstances; he was killed either by the Spaniards or by his own people.[11]

Moral: Try to assess the new guys on the block accurately, and don't give them any opportunity to exploit existing divisions. Indeed, the likelihood that many nations will seek to gain a monopoly on interactions with extraterrestrial intelligence is apt to be one of humanity's greatest problems.

Japanese

Until the middle of the 19th century, Japan was an agrarian, peasant society ruled by warlords (*daimyo*) in the service of an overlord (*shogun*). Daimyo, in turn, were served by the samurai, a traditional warrior class whose name derives from the Japanese word for service. Medieval samurai were generally illiterate rural landowners who farmed between battles. Some developed the necessary skills for bureaucratic service, but most did not. During the shogunate of the Tokugawa family (1600–1868), the samurai as a class were transformed into military bureaucrats and were required to master administrative

---

9. Buddy Levy, *Conquistador: Hernán Cortés, King Montezuma, and the Last Stand of the Aztecs* (New York: Bantam Books, 2008).

10. Eric R. Wolf, *Europe and the People Without History* (Berkeley: University of California Press, 1982).

11. Warwick Bray, "Montezuma II," *Grolier Multimedia Encyclopedia*, Grolier Online at *http://gme.grolier.com/article?assetid=0197695-0* (accessed 28 June 2013).

skills as well as military arts. As hereditary warriors, they were governed by a code of ethics: *bushido*, meaning "the way of the warrior," defined service and conduct appropriate to their status as elite members of Japanese society.[12]

The first European to reach Japan was a Portuguese explorer named Fernão Mendes Pinto, who arrived there in 1543; just two years later the Portuguese established the first trade route between Japan and Europe. Shortly afterward, Jesuit missionaries introduced Roman Catholicism. Christianity conflicted with feudal loyalties, however, and by 1639 had been completely banned.[13] At that point all Europeans except the Dutch were expelled from Japan, and the Dutch traders permitted to remain were interned on an artificial island so that the Japanese might better study their economic practices.[14] The Japanese could accomplish all this largely because they were a centralized polity.

Japan's traditional class structure placed merchants at the bottom of a four-tiered system, where they were carefully controlled by the ruling elite. This privileged class, while dependent upon merchants for trade, feared their economic power.[15] The Japanese class system and other cultural elements had been adapted from Chinese practices. Indeed, for centuries Japan had borrowed significant cultural elements from China, including aspects of Chinese science, philosophy, and literacy.[16]

The social structure was strongly patrilineal, with a rule of primogeniture: the eldest son inherited the family land, and younger sons moved elsewhere to seek employment. Marion Levy has argued that this combination of features made it possible for Japan to modernize rapidly. Not only did Japan have prior experience emulating and adopting the cultural patterns of others, but its social organization created a cadet class of younger brothers ready to be trained for industry, and its merchants were waiting to be freed from the economic and behavioral fetters that bound them.[17]

---

12. William B. Hauser, "Samurai," *Grolier Multimedia Encyclopedia*, Grolier Online at *http://gme. grolier.com/article?assetid=0255830-0* (accessed 28 June 2013).

13. Nam-lin Hur, *Death and Social Order in Tokugawa Japan: Buddhism, Anti-Christianity, and the Danka System* (Cambridge, MA: Harvard University Press, 2008).

14. Harumi Befu, *Japan: An Anthropological Introduction* (San Francisco: Chandler Publishing Company, 1971).

15. Chie Nakane, *Japanese Society* (Berkeley: University of California Press, 1970).

16. Milton W. Meyer, *Japan: A Concise History* (Lanham, MD: Rowman and Littlefield, 1993).

17. Marion J. Levy, "Contrasting Factors in the Modernization of China and Japan," in *Economic Growth: Brazil, India, Japan*, ed. Simon Kuznets et al. (Durham, NC: Duke University Press, 1955), pp. 496–536.

In 1868, in reaction to U.S. Commodore Matthew Perry's incursions of the mid-1850s and Japan's consequent concessions to the West, Japanese samurai overthrew the Tokugawa shogunate and reestablished the rule of the Meiji emperor. What followed was one of the most dramatic examples of sociocultural change in history. Within two generations, Japan transformed itself from a feudal backwater to a world power by making major changes in its traditional culture and social structure.

Moral: Here the example suggests that prior experience with borrowing cultural elements may promote a flexible response to sociocultural challenges, even when they involve significant adaptation.

Chinese

China is a highly patricentric culture in which descent is patrilineal, power is patripotestal, inheritance follows the male line, major ancestors included in ancestor worship are exclusively male, and Confucianism exalts manliness and masculine virtues.[18] When Europeans were still wearing urine-cured hides and painting their faces blue, China was already a complex, centralized polity.

The name *Middle Kingdom* expressed China's self-image as a nation positioned midway between heaven and hell.[19] Because China dominated the region, it demanded and received preferential treatment from neighbors it viewed as vassal states. Indeed, several states in Southeast Asia paid annual tribute and routinely requested assistance from China to mediate regional disputes.[20]

When Western influence first appeared in the shape of travelers such as Marco Polo, it was seen by the Chinese as a harmless novelty. As Western governments became aware of the vast resources China possessed, they pressed its rulers to open up the country to trade; but the Chinese continued to believe that all outsiders were barbarians compared to residents of the Middle Kingdom. As late as 1793, China's Qianlong emperor rejected the idea of trade with Europe on the grounds that the West had nothing

---

18. Arthur Cotterell and David Morgan, *China's Civilization: A Survey of Its History, Arts, and Technology* (New York: Praeger Publishers, 1975); Joel Coye, Jon Livingston, and Jean Highland, eds., *China Yesterday and Today* (New York: Bantam Books, 1984).

19. David Bonavia, *The Chinese* (New York: Penguin Books, 1980); Robert Hunt, ed., *Personalities and Cultures: Readings in Psychological Anthropology* (Garden City, NY: The Natural History Press, 1967); William H. McNeill and Jean W. Sedlar, eds., *Classical China* (New York: Oxford University Press, 1970).

20. Donald K. Swearer, *Southeast Asia* (Guilford, CT: Dushkin Publishing Group, 1984).

his country needed.[21] This attitude could not long be maintained, however, and by the early 20th century, European hegemony in Asia was well established.[22]

The Qing emperors had attempted to conduct diplomatic and commercial relations with the European powers within the traditional framework of the tribute system and had sought to confine foreign trade to the single port of Canton in the south. The British, the most active European traders, were also among the most active smugglers of opium into China. The seizure and destruction by Chinese authorities of all foreign opium at Canton precipitated the First Opium War of 1839–1842. At its conclusion, the emperor was forced by the Treaty of Nanjing to capitulate to a British naval force, cede Hong Kong to Britain, open several ports to unrestricted trade, and promise to conduct all future foreign relations on the basis of equality. China was also compelled to recognize the principle of extraterritoriality, by which Westerners in China were subject only to the jurisdiction of their own country's consular court.[23] As a result of these events, China was treated by Westerners as politically and economically inferior until the mid-20th century.

Moral: China's unwillingness to deal with European powers as equals and its inability to perceive the threat implicit in Western technology had serious repercussions, some of which still influence contemporary Chinese attitudes toward trade and outsiders.[24]

Iroquois

The matrilineal Iroquois nations were among the most politically complex cultures in North America. When Europeans first encountered them in the early 17th century, the Iroquois were composed of five separate nations: the Cayuga, Oneida, Onondaga, Seneca, and Mohawk; somewhat later the Tuscarora also came to be considered as part of the Iroquois Confederacy.

---

21. Joel Coye, Jon Livingston, and Jean Highland, eds., *China Yesterday and Today* (New York: Bantam Books, 1984); Walter A. Fairservis, Jr., *The Origins of Oriental Civilization* (New York: Mentor Books, 1959).

22. Michel Oksenberg, "The Issue of Sovereignty in the Asian Historical Context," in *Problematic Sovereignty: Contested Rules and Political Possibilities*, ed. Stephen D. Krasner (New York: Columbia University Press, 2001), pp. 83–103, esp. p. 89.

23. Howard J. Wechsler, "China, History of," *Grolier Multimedia Encyclopedia*, Grolier Online at *http://gme.grolier.com/article?assetid=0061010-0* (accessed 29 June 2013).

24. Sumie Okazaki, E. J. R. David, and Nancy Abelmann, "Colonialism and Psychology of Culture," *Social and Personality Psychology Compass* 2, no. 1 (2008): 90–106.

Living in fortified villages, they raised corn, hunted game, and controlled a territory ranging from the Atlantic Coast to the Mississippi Valley, as far north as the St. Lawrence Valley.[25]

Traditionally, Iroquois women were the principal participants in agriculture and were also active in some aspects of governance. Iroquois men traveled frequently, sometimes for war parties but more often to engage in diplomacy. The Iroquois Confederacy was governed by 50 sachems. The ruling council did not interfere with individual tribes, which were overseen by sachem representatives, but it did make policy for the Confederacy. Council decisions were unanimous and required consensus. Not surprisingly, oratory was valued and the Iroquois were widely regarded as skilled public speakers.[26]

In the 17th century the Iroquois rejected the European missionaries who had hoped to convert them to Christianity. After access to firearms was made possible by divisions between the European powers, the Iroquois, whose military tactics were often superior, battled European soldiers to a stalemate. Both the French and English regarded the Iroquois as the most diplomatically astute and militarily dangerous of all the northeastern groups with which they came into contact.[27] Further, the Iroquois, while eager to possess European technology, were selective in their approach to cultural borrowing. They took those elements they wanted, such as firearms, tools, and tribute; but, unlike many other Native American tribes, they refused to emulate European culture until long after the original contact period.

The Iroquois tended to support the English against the French, but increasingly they found advantage in playing one foreign power off against the other. This strategy foundered during the Revolutionary War, when the Americans, incensed by Iroquois support for England, attacked Iroquois villages using tactics similar to those employed by Native Americans, and with a degree of viciousness that has seldom been equaled.[28]

Moral: The Iroquois initially responded to European incursions as well as any of the cultures I have discussed thus far. Their contact with and openness to other cultures, their flexibility, and their resourcefulness initially stood them in good stead. Ultimately, however, the Iroquois were simply overpowered by a force that was numerically and technologically superior.

---

25. James W. Bradley, *Evolution of the Onondaga Iroquois: Accommodating Change, 1500–1655* (Lincoln: University of Nebraska Press, 2005).

26. Anthony F. C. Wallace, *The Death and Rebirth of the Seneca* (New York: Vintage Books, 1972).

27. Wallace, *The Death and Rebirth of the Seneca.*

28. Wallace, *The Death and Rebirth of the Seneca.*

Māori

The Māori of New Zealand speak a language related to both Tahitian and Hawaiʻian. They are probably descended from travelers who left Hawaiʻi and who eventually reached the islands they called Aotearoa sometime around AD 900.[29] At the time of Captain James Cook's visit in 1769, the Māori population was an estimated 100,000 to 250,000, divided into about 50 tribes, each occupying separate territories. The Māori were village-dwelling gardeners who stored sweet-potato crops. Three social classes existed: aristocrats, commoners, and slaves captured in war. Differences in rank were associated with supernatural power, or *mana*. Religious knowledge and activities were also graded, with priests (*tohunga*) functioning as key figures. Traditional art forms included decorative wood carving—such as those seen on Māori longhouses and great canoes—poetry and storytelling, chanting, dancing, and singing.

By the end of the 18th century, European seal and whale hunters were establishing shore bases on both islands. Soon after came traders in search of timber and flax. Inevitably, perhaps, a series of clashes followed in which the Māori were very badly treated: reports of atrocities committed by sailors and adventurers became so alarming to the Anglican Church that it established a mission and then petitioned the British government to appoint a resident administrator of the islands in 1833.

By then, however, the Māori had already come to regard Westerners as dangerous and untrustworthy. One of the first commodities they traded for in quantity was weaponry, and in 1825 they managed to rebuff the first serious British attempt at colonization. Māori were accustomed to organized conflict, and many of their villages were located on hilltops, palisaded and surrounded with fighting trenches.[30] When the British regiments attacked, they were met by accurate gunfire from both trenches and palisade. The Māori took great pride in their ability to repel British troops, and on one notorious occasion they sent down gunpowder and musket balls to a company of British soldiers that, having run out of ammunition, was about to break off hostilities.[31]

The process of colonization led, especially on the North Island, to clashes with those Māori, who, with good cause, disputed the alleged purchase of land by the New Zealand Company. Sporadic warfare broke out, and disorder and uncertainty prevailed for some 12 years. But in time, British troops quelled

---

29. Robert C. Suggs, *The Island Civilizations of Polynesia* (New York: New American Library, 1960).

30. Caroline Phillips, *Waihou Journeys: The Archaeology of 400 Years of Maori Settlement* (Auckland: Auckland University Press, 2000).

31. Suggs, *The Island Civilizations of Polynesia*.

the "fire in the fern," as these Māori Wars were called, and Māori resistance to British authority ceased. The Treaty of Waitangi, which was signed on 6 February 1840 by some but not all of the Māori chiefs, gave the Māori a disadvantageous position.

After the signing of the treaty came a long period of protest and gradual adjustment. Māori morale was buoyed in part because there had been no formal surrender but rather a negotiated accession. The Māori now number about 565,000 (2006 Census) and represent more than 14 percent of New Zealand's population. Recently, the New Zealand government made a settlement with the Maori that addressed the inequities of the 1840 treaty and provided compensation in the form of large land tracts and cash.[32] Generally, New Zealanders of European descent have supported attempts to improve the economic situation of the Māori people.

Moral: The Māori resisted British incursions in a fashion that not only earned the respect of their adversaries but also allowed them a pride that sustained them when they were finally overwhelmed by disease, superior technology, and organization.[33] Reacting forcefully to clear injustice and violations of reciprocity can eventually benefit a disadvantaged group.

Back to the Future

When I, and many others, began to express a professional interest in the possibility of extraterrestrial intelligence, we were often met by indulgent smiles. As Douglas Vakoch does a fine job of demonstrating in chapter 12 of this collection, our interest is neither new nor unwarranted; at the same time, as Albert Harrison shows in chapter 11, this interest is not without a range of accompanying concerns.[34]

Most serious astronomers and cosmologists are convinced that we are unlikely to be the only intelligent life in the universe. NASA's Kepler mission

---

32. Yvonne Tahana, "Iwi 'Walks Path' to Biggest Ever Treaty Settlement," *The New Zealand Herald*, 25 June 2008.

33. James H. Liu et al., "Social Identity and the Perception of History: Cultural Representations of Aotearoa/New Zealand," *European Journal of Social Psychology* 29, no. 8 (1999): 1021–1047.

34. See Douglas A. Vakoch, "The Evolution of Extraterrestrials: The Evolutionary Synthesis and Estimates of the Prevalence of Intelligence Beyond Earth," chapter 12 in this volume. On the concerns that the topic of ETI raises, see Albert A. Harrison, "Speaking for Earth: Projecting Cultural Values Across Deep Space and Time," chapter 11 in this volume.

to identify Earth-like planets has already met with some significant success.[35] However, it is a *big* universe and scientists are split about the probability of an actual encounter with an alien intelligence.[36] Nonetheless, all are generally agreed that such an encounter would have enormous consequences for humanity, and most such scenarios are positive. It is this consensus that fuels the SETI project. Once sponsored by the federal government, SETI now operates with private funding.

SETI researchers are currently enlisting the assistance of interested computer owners around the world. It is possible to download a program called SETI@home, which in turn can download chunks of data from radio observatories and then analyze that data for a meaningful pattern that could suggest intelligence.[37] The results of the analysis are then returned by the computer owner to the SETI scientists, providing them with a free and powerful means to expand their information-processing base.

Probes and Possibilities

Given the strictures on space travel imposed by problems arising when one approaches a percentage of the speed of light, our first encounter with extraterrestrials will almost certainly be via a messaging system of some sort. I believe the biggest obstacle to current searches involves the limitations of our technology. It may not be possible to recognize that a message is being sent since there are a variety of media that could be employed, and aliens may well employ a medium that we have yet to recognize. How would we have responded a century ago to radio transmissions, a half-century ago to microwaves, a quarter-century ago to binary laser pulses? The obvious answer is we wouldn't have been aware that there was anything to which to respond. We cannot recognize and deal with messages conveyed through a medium that we have yet to discover. Unfortunately, a technologically advanced civilization

---

35. William J. Borucki et al., "Characteristics of Planetary Candidates Observed by *Kepler*, II: Analysis of the First Four Months of Data," *The Astrophysical Journal* 736, no. 1 (2011): 1–111, available at *http://arxiv.org/abs/1102.0541v2*.

36. Harrison, *After Contact*; Sagan, ed., *Communication with Extraterrestrial Intelligence*; Seth Shostak, "Are We Alone?: Estimating the Prevalence of Extraterrestrial Intelligence," in *Civilizations Beyond Earth: Extraterrestrial Life and Society*, ed. Douglas A. Vakoch and Albert A. Harrison (New York: Berghahn Books, 2011), pp. 31–42.

37. The SETI@home program can be found at *http://setiathome.ssl.berkeley.edu*.

may employ a very advanced medium, as a means of identifying species and civilizations with which more promising exchanges might take place.

In addition to the purely technological problems with recognizing messages, there is the difficulty of decoding them. Since alien intelligences have necessarily developed in an alien environment, we can expect them and their mental processes to be markedly different from our own, probably so different as to impede communication.[38] Fortunately, while there is not space to discuss the details here, there are means by which we may be able to overcome communications problems, positing only that an alien intelligence can recognize binary distinctions, a fundamental aspect of information processing.[39]

Assuming that we recognize signals emanating from an intelligent extraterrestrial source, our next difficulty will involve the enormous time lags in sending and receiving messages. According to our present understanding, no message can exceed the speed of light, and while that speed is nothing to be challenged by a tortoise, the lag will necessarily be measured in years, possibly decades. The strategic problems such a lag imposes are considerable and have serious consequences for productive communications and for exchange.

Let me indulge in a final terrestrial parallel from the history of British colonialism. A promising young administrator of the British East India Company (BEIC), Stamford Raffles, was due to return to England, having served his tour in Batavia in Indonesia.[40] He stopped at a fishing village on an island in the Strait of Malacca and noted a large natural harbor in a location that ensured access to both the East and the West and that could affect, if not control, much of the shipping between the two. He immediately dispatched a letter to the BEIC and Foreign Office requesting permission to establish a port, and since it would be several months before he could receive a response, he set about developing the port and area trade. In the mid-19th century, Britain was heavily involved with the enormous Indian subcontinent and had no desire to establish outposts in Southeast Asia. Further, Britain had no wish to offend or risk alienating its Dutch allies, who already had a strong presence on the Malay Peninsula. The answer returned to Raffles was "no." However, by this point the port was already making a significant profit and challenging Malacca for primacy.

---

38. Douglas Raybeck, "A Possible Solution to Communication Problems: Part 2," *SETIQuest* 2, no. 3 (1996): 9–11, esp. p. 10.

39. Douglas Raybeck, "Problems in Extraterrestrial Communication," *SETIQuest* 2, no. 2 (1996): 19–21.

40. Emily Hahn, *Raffles of Singapore* (Garden City, NY: Doubleday, 1946).

Raffles believed the new circumstances of this emergent economic power might sway the bureaucrats at BEIC, and he wrote them back, citing the growth in population and in trade and the favorable location of the site. While the British and Dutch entered into negotiations on this issue, Raffles continued to expand trade. Within a year his profit was over $4,000,000, and his little port had grown to 10,000 inhabitants. Within five years, while Dutch-controlled Malacca made $2,500,000, the island port generated revenue of $22,185,000. Even the British bureaucracy proved capable of recognizing a windfall when one fell on them, and they gave Raffles permission to continue with the establishment of Singapore.[41]

This kind of scenario strongly suggests that our most meaningful interaction with extraterrestrial intelligence will be through a perspicacious robot probe equipped to seek out other intelligence and to conduct trade where possible. The existence of such an instrument would certainly imply a civilization technologically in advance of ours. However, while such a civilization could be greatly advanced compared to us, this is not a necessary postulation. Several authorities believe that, within the next 75 years, we will possess the capability to send such probes ourselves.[42]

We need not make the Aztec error and presume that extraterrestrials who contact us possess godlike powers or even represent an enlightened civilization.[43] They may come from a civilization as politically, culturally, and ethnically divided as our own. However, for purposes of initial interaction, this diversity may not be salient, as we are liable to be contacted by a single sociocultural entity.

Trade and Tremors

The one precious commodity that has no mass yet can be traded between all sentients is information. This is why we can anticipate the arrival, at some point, of an intelligent probe, designed to collect information for later

41. N. J. Ryan, *The Making of Modern Malaya: A History From Earliest Times to Independence* (Kuala Lumpur: Oxford University Press, 1965).

42. K. Eric Drexler, *Engines Of Creation* (Garden City, NY: Anchor Press/Doubleday, 1986); B. Haisch, A. Rueda, and H. E. Puthoff, "Inertia as a Zero-Point Field Lorentz Force," *Physical Review A* 49 (1994): 678–694; Oliver W. Markely and Walter R. McCuan, eds., *21st Century Earth: Opposing Viewpoints* (San Diego: Greenhaven Press, 1996).

43. Douglas Raybeck, "Predator-Prey Models and Contact Considerations," paper presented at the 11th annual Contact conference, held 18–20 March 1994 in Santa Clara, California.

transmission back to its point of origin. No doubt the probe will also be equipped to evaluate the circumstances it confronts and to assess what sorts of information can appropriately—and safely—be exchanged. Exchange, trade, will be the main motivation for contact. Of course, some information can be obtained by observation, without any human agents. However, efficiency in gathering information and the ability to assess its importance and organize it coherently would greatly benefit from our active participation.

Perceptions of the potential represented by such contact can be expected to vary among nations and to raise a series of ethical and international legal issues.[44] Each country will want to profit from exchanges, and a dominant theme, given the sad state of the international scene, may well be weaponry. However, if we can assume a modicum of rational self-interest on the part of an intelligent probe, this is just the sort of information it would be unwilling to release. This leaves a variety of issues ranging from health and longevity to environmental control. Different nations will undoubtedly have varying priorities in this regard. There may even be countries that wish to trade for such esoteric elements as music and philosophy.

The reactions of various nations to the trading possibilities will be critical in shaping the initial interactions with a nonterrestrial sentient. Nations will likely differ in both perspective and manner as they approach the goal of communicating with an extraterrestrial intelligence. All nations will make assessments of the intentions of the probe and will evaluate whether it is apt to be threatening or benign.[45] Fortunately, a promising means of assessing intentions has recently been suggested.[46] Even though the possibility that the sentients responsible for constructing the probe may well be aggressive, the probe itself will probably not pose a threat. As mentioned earlier, Greg Bear has posited malevolent extraterrestrials who send destructive probes about the universe to locate intelligent life-forms and destroy them.[47] Short of this scenario, however, such probes are apt to be complex collectors of information. One of their functions may well be to identify sentients who could pose a future threat to them.

---

44. Douglas A. Vakoch, "Responsibility, Capability, and Active SETI: Policy, Law, Ethics, and Communication with Extraterrestrial Intelligence," *Acta Astronautica* 68, nos. 3–4 (2011): 512–519.

45. Raybeck, "Predator-Prey Models and Contact Considerations."

46. Douglas A. Vakoch and Michael Matessa, "An Algorithmic Approach to Communicating Reciprocal Altruism in Interstellar Messages: Drawing Analogies between Social and Astrophysical Phenomena," *Acta Astronautica* 68, nos. 3–4 (2011): 512–519.

47. Bear, *The Forge of God*.

The responses of most major nations will likely feature a degree of military/political paranoia. Although it seems improbable that the probe would express bellicose intent, or be capable of significant hostile action (remember, we need not anticipate enormously advanced technology to accept the probability of contact), most governments will respond with a conservative posture, fearing at least trickery and at most some form of cataclysm. Given the manner in which our technologically superior nations have treated other members of their own species, there could be grounds for real concern.[48]

It would make sense to nominate the United Nations or some other agency as the spokes-entity for the planet, but the UN has become an unwieldy bureaucracy with both staunch supporters and vociferous opponents, and there exists no other agency acceptable to all powers. That Earth may not speak with one voice could put us in a difficult bargaining position, as countries will probably vie with each other for greater access to the probe's store of information. It is extremely plausible that the probe might be in a better position to influence trade terms than will the various nations of Earth.

Practical Ponderings

While the United States may have a technological advantage in complex communication systems, this advantage may prove insignificant should real possibilities for trade arise. Indeed, given the ubiquity of the Web and the access to information it provides, poor countries can assert their right to trade as easily as rich ones. Probably, those nations who might better succeed in such a trading situation will possess some cultural and social qualities that the United States lacks. Their internal politics may be more consistent and their world view more accepting of differences. Other countries may also lack some of the United States' handicaps. The U.S., along with many other Western nations, tends to make dichotomous judgments that can oversimplify complex situations.

As our brief review of the Iroquois Confederacy and Japan indicated, there is considerable utility in coordinating a unified response to the possibility of trade. A centralized polity can foster such a response, assuming that, like those of Japan and the Iroquois and unlike that of the United States, the governance structure is not overly bureaucratic. Exempting a few idealistic and intellectual oddballs, the principal concern of most people and most nations will be profit.

---

48. Raybeck, "Predator-Prey Models and Contact Considerations."

As it did among the Japanese and the Iroquois, a history of prior cultural borrowing could encourage an open attitude toward trade. Nonetheless, as Japan has abundantly demonstrated, this element does not hinder an ethnocentric world view. What it does do is to make borrowing and adopting new elements a pragmatic issue rather than an ideological one.

A level of balanced heterogeneity is desirable. By that I mean it would be useful if a nation contains peoples of differing ethnicities and languages who are neither particularly advantaged nor disadvantaged within the social structure. Such a situation would probably further a genuine respect for differences, and this could be a useful perspective in dealing with an extraterrestrial intelligence. I would like to report that our planet is replete with examples, but such is not the case. This condition is not only rare; it is probably not fully realized anywhere on Earth, and we have 4,000 cultures.[49]

Finally, the strangest observation of all, in communications with an alien probe, poor nations should enjoy an advantage over rich ones. My reasoning here simply reflects the propensities of those in control to wish to remain so and, if possible, to augment their power.[50] Thus, wealthy nations such as ours will have to contend with a variety of powerful special interests, each trying to gain some advantage in the unfolding scenario and each *desperately worried that new information may undercut its market position*. Who could be more threatened by cheap energy than Standard Oil, Shell, the oil cartels, etc.? Who would be more endangered by inexpensive transport than Detroit and other auto and truck manufacturers? How will drug companies, insurance companies, power suppliers, unions, and others respond to the challenges posed by new information? Should they be unable to benefit directly from the new information, they will endeavor at least to maintain the status quo. Since we possess the best government money can buy, we in particular will find our efforts at trade hindered by the divisive acts of entrenched corporate interests.

One final bit of advice in what is liable to be a future bargaining session: don't forget the lesson taught us by the Māori and by the confident manner with which they greeted British colonizers. Despite probable disparities in

---

49. To some degree this condition was approached in Java a generation ago and among some elements of Pakistani society earlier. For the case of Java, see Benedict R. O'G. Anderson, *Mythology and the Tolerance of the Javanese* (Ithaca, NY: Modern Indonesia Project, Cornell University, 1965). On Pakistan, see Fredrik Barth, *Ethnic Groups and Boundaries* (Boston: Little Brown and Company, 1969).

50. Kevin Avruch et al., "A Generic Theory of Conflict Resolution: A Critique," *Negotiation Journal* 3 (1987): 37–96; Michael Banton, *Political Systems and the Distribution of Power* (New York: Frederick A. Praeger Publishers, 1965).

technology and knowledge between ourselves and the extraterrestrials who send a probe to contact us, we should not view ourselves as helpless pawns. Reciprocity is the most fundamental principle of human interaction.[51] It is therefore one apt to be appreciated by any sentient.[52] If we encounter difficulties in the bargaining process, they will more probably emanate from our own differences and our own politics than from the machinations of an intelligent probe. Of course, if we place ourselves in weak bargaining positions, it seems probable that another would take advantage of that. Wouldn't you?

51. Lawrence Becker, *Reciprocity* (Boston: Routledge and Kegan Paul, 1986); Karl Polanyi, Conrad M. Arensberg, and Harry W. Pearson, eds., *Trade and Market in the Early Empires* (New York: The Free Press, 1957); and W. V. Quine and J. S. Ullian, *The Web of Belief*, 2nd ed. (New York: Random House, 1978).

52. Harrison, "Thinking Intelligently About Extraterrestrial Intelligence" ; Harrison, *After Contact*; Vakoch and Matessa, "An Algorithmic Approach to Communicating Reciprocal Altruism in Interstellar Messages."

CHAPTER TEN

Culture and Communication with Extraterrestrial Intelligence

John W. Traphagan

Recent research focusing on how humans might construct interstellar messages to communicate with an extraterrestrial intelligence has raised interesting opportunities to think about the manner in which contact and culture intersect. Douglas Vakoch, for example, asks the important question of whether music, the seemingly universal "language" shared by humans, could provide a means of communicating or whether it might be incomprehensible to beings with different types of sense organs and who evolved different ways of dealing with the exchange of information through sound.[1] It has also been widely thought that mathematics would provide an excellent means of communication. As Carl DeVito has observed, in order for extraterrestrial intelligent beings to construct the equipment necessary for radio transmissions, it would seem likely that they would need a thorough understanding of mathematics.[2] Other researchers have suggested exploration of potential cognitive universals, such as aesthetics or spiritual ideas as a basis for developing strategies in SETI research.[3] In each case, however, questions remain as to whether the mathematics, aesthetics, or spirituality of an extraterrestrial

---

1. Douglas Vakoch, "Celestial Music?," *Space.com*, 22 December 2000, available at *http:// archive.seti.org/epo/news/features/celestial-music.php* (accessed 12 June 2013); Douglas Vakoch, "Will ET's Math Be the Same as Ours?," *Space.com*, 11 January 2001, available at *http://archive.seti.org/epo/news/features/will-ets-math-be-the-same-as-ours.php* (accessed 12 June 2013). See also Douglas A. Vakoch, "An Iconic Approach to Communicating Musical Concepts in Interstellar Messages," *Acta Astronautica* 67, nos. 11–12 (2010): 1406–1409.

2. Carl L. DeVito, "On the Universality of Human Mathematics," in *Communication with Extraterrestrial Intelligence*, ed. Douglas A. Vakoch (Albany: State University of New York Press, 2011), pp. 439–448, esp. p. 439.

3. Guillermo A. Lemarchand and Jon Lomberg, "Communication Among Interstellar Intelligent Species: A Search for Universal Cognitive Maps," in Vakoch, ed., *Communication with Extraterrestrial Intelligence*, pp. 371–295, esp. p. 371.

being will be mutually intelligible with our own, even if the underlying principles are the same.

Marvin Minsky argues that certain basic capacities and characteristics will be typical of any intelligent being: these include self-awareness; problem-solving capacity; analytical skills; and the abilities to describe the world, explain phenomena, accumulate and exchange information, allocate scarce resources, and plan ahead.[4] While this argument makes a great deal of sense, an important issue is missing that must be considered: all of these capacities involve culture, and culture is highly variable even among humans, who are, from a biological perspective, relatively uniform.

Philosopher Thomas Nagel's discussion of the question "What is it like to be a bat?" is illustrative when considering this issue. Nagel notes that, while consciousness of experience occurs at many levels of animal life, experiencing what it is to *be* another form of animal life is essentially impossible.[5] Bats, of course, are designed to experience the world through echolocation, using sonic feedback from their own screeches to discriminate among objects in the world and thus to construct in their brains some type of model or understanding of their environment. Echolocation mediates the manner by which bats enact the capacities that they have, such as planning ahead to avoid ramming into obstacles or identifying mosquitoes to eat. In other words, *how* they plan and *how* they identify things are based on a model of the environment that is, in turn, based on the interpretation of sonic echoes as the means by which to spatially locate and identify objects (in contrast to humans, who primarily interpret light reflections to accomplish the same goals).

Nagel defines the problem this way: because we lack the capacity to echolocate, we are fundamentally incapable of knowing how bats experience the world we both inhabit. We can *imagine* what it is to be a bat, but we cannot *know* what it is to be a bat or what a bat's experience of the world is really like, because we are incapable of processing and interpreting information in the way that bats do. The same can be said for other animals, such as dogs, that are much closer to humans in terms of their sense organs. Hound dogs have approximately 10 times the number of scent receptors that humans do and have different visual and aural abilities. With these senses, how does a

---

4. Marvin Minsky, "Communication with Alien Intelligence," in *Extraterrestrials: Science and Alien Intelligence*, ed. Edward Regis (New York: Cambridge University Press, 1985). The full text of this article is available at *http://web.media.mit.edu/~minsky/papers/AlienIntelligence.html* (accessed 12 June 2013).

5. Thomas Nagel, "What Is It Like to Be a Bat?," *The Philosophical Review* 83, no. 4 (1974): 435–450.

dog construct the world? Are his "images" or conceptualizations of the world primarily based on interpretation of scent or sound (note the difficulty we have, being largely visual animals, in imagining the world without the notion of an image coming into the picture) as opposed to the interpretation of visual images?

Even among humans who share the same apparatus for sensing the world (keep in mind that people who are blind or deaf, for example, do not share the same apparatus), the things that people choose to focus on when constructing their world can vary considerably from one culture to another. For example, when English speakers count, we focus only on the number of a particular object: one sheet of paper, two sheets of paper, three sheets of paper; one pencil, two pencils, three pencils. We also emphasize the difference between one object and multiple objects. For some reason that is lost to the ages, it matters to English speakers that, when counting things, one addresses only the issue of *how many* and that, when categorizing parts of the world, one differentiates between a single object of a particular kind and many of those objects.

By contrast, Japanese speakers approach counting things in the world quite differently. First, the Japanese language does not need to distinguish between one and more than one object. This is implied by the fact that numbering of things does not involve plurals in most cases. There is one car, two car, three car; or one tree, two tree, three tree; and so on. Second, the issue of *how many* is not distinct from the issue of the structural form that the object one is counting takes in the world. Thus, to count things like sheets of paper or compact discs in Japanese, one counts *ichi-mai, ni-mai, san-mai*, meaning "one thin, flat thing; two thin, flat thing; three thin, flat thing." If one wants to count things like pencils or pipes, one counts *ippon, ni-hon, san-bon*, indicating "one cylindrical thing, two cylindrical thing, three cylindrical thing." There are counters for large machines, small machines, large animals, small animals, and, to the irritation of native English speakers who want to learn Japanese, many different forms found in the world.

The point here is that even among two human languages, the approach to something as simple as counting differs significantly, although by no means beyond the point of mutual comprehension. We can translate counting in Japanese to counting in English by rendering *enpitsu ippon* as "one pencil" and *kuruma ni-dai* as "two cars." While this is a perfectly clear and reasonable translation for these objects and for the quantity of them, something interesting happens in the process—we lose basic interpretive and classificatory information about how Japanese people perceive what is important in counting things. Furthermore, we encounter this difference despite the fact that Japanese and English speakers do all of the things that Minsky identifies as being fundamental to intelligence. How would we translate counting between humans and, say, a race of intelligent beings who process sensory data through echolocation? Would counting—and, more generally, mathematics—necessarily be constructed in the same way humans do this by such beings? Given their manner of processing the world, perhaps they would be quite interested in shape and size or sonic qualities when counting. Would a bat-like intelligent species count "one large sound-absorbent thing, two large sound-absorbent thing," or "one small sound-reflective thing, two small sound-reflective thing"?

While it seems entirely reasonable that the underlying principles of symbolic systems such as mathematics or music would be understood by both humans and an alien intelligence, the way in which a particular being acquires and processes sensory data will influence its construction of any system to describe what is being processed. Furthermore, the elements of the world that are deemed important in a particular culture, which are, in turn, shaped by the sensory organs available to a particular species of beings, will also influence cognition and the manner in which individuals in that society classify and construct their world around elements that matter more or less.[6]

Whether it is counting, music, or mathematics, the question of how to communicate is not simply one of the mediums through which ideas are exchanged or the capacity to carry out certain functions necessary to understanding and manipulating an environment that is consistent in the universe that both beings inhabit. Instead, it is one of recognizing an interpretive context or framework for communication that will work when it is quite possible that the mode of communication and interpretation—of receiving and analyzing information—natural to an extraterrestrial life-form will differ significantly from our own. At the root of this issue is the question of how culture factors into that process of interstellar communication and the construction of interstellar messages.

What is Culture?

The definition of *culture* is usually assumed rather than explicated, not only in the literature dealing with SETI but also in more general scholarly and non-scholarly discussions of intercultural communication among human societies.

---

6. I am at this point ignoring the possibility of an alien intelligence in which individuality is not important or where—along the lines of *Star Trek*'s Borg—the civilization is organized as a collectivity. This issue is best left to another paper.

It is essential, however, that we, as cultural beings, rigorously consider what we mean by *culture* when addressing the issue of how to communicate with an unknown other. The culture concept, as it is used in popular media and many areas of scholarship, is largely used as a homogenizing category that tends toward essentialist representations of both other societies and those of the individuals who are writing.[7]

Anthropologists have long recognized the complexity associated with identifying the characteristics of any particular "culture" and have debated not only the extent to which one can consider culture bounded but also the meaning of *culture* as both an empirical and an analytical category. These debates have often divided anthropologists about how the concept should be used and what it actually represents in terms of human social organization and behavior. As James L. Watson points out, early usage of the term in anthropology centered upon the idea that culture is a shared set of beliefs, customs, and ideas that are learned and that unify people into coherent and identifiable groups.[8] In this sense, then, culture represents a form of collective or social memory that links past, present, and future. This formulation represents culture as fairly deterministic in shaping human behavior within a particular—and bounded—society.

Contemporary anthropologists have created theoretical constructs that posit culture as being much less static than the type of definition given above implies. People are not only unified but may also be divided by their customs and beliefs even when they ostensibly belong to the same culture. Rather than the deterministic "thing" reified in earlier concepts of culture developed by anthropologists and still widely used in other fields of scholarship, culture is better understood as a process by which people continually contest and reinvent the customs, beliefs, and ideas that they use, collectively, individually, and often strategically, to characterize both their own groups and those of others.[9] In short, culture is in a constant state of flux. Furthermore, it involves not only subjective interpretation of events and experiences but also individual agency as people negotiate and manipulate their social environments.

---

7. Essentialism is often defined as the tendency to reduce a group of people to specific characteristics, values, or features that all members of that group are assumed to exhibit.

8. James L. Watson, ed., *Golden Arches East: McDonald's in East Asia* (Stanford, CA: Stanford University Press, 1997).

9. See Sherry Ortner, *Anthropology and Social Theory: Culture, Power, and the Acting Subject* (Durham, NC: Duke University Press, 2006); V. Prashad, "Bruce Lee and the Anti-Imperialism of Kung Fu: A Polycultural Adventure," *Positions* 11, no. 1 (2006): 51–90.

That said, it is important to recognize that culture is the primary lens through which humans acquire sensory data and organize those data into useful patterns and systems. Bruce Wexler, in a recent discussion of sensory deprivation and brain development, notes that the relationship of an individual to his or her environment is so extensive that making a hard and fast distinction between the two is quite problematic.[10] Because humans now inhabit an environment that is more artificial than organic, modern children develop their cognitive abilities in response to stimuli that are predominantly cultural rather than natural Culture does not simply provide a set of ideas, rules, or concepts that shape behavior; it provides an environment of behaviors that people observe and that, in children at least, influences the physiological development of the brain.

The fact that culture is both fluid and highly individualized does not mean that culture is either analytically unapproachable or impossible to understand and characterize. Indeed, culture is so central to how humans and, I would argue, any intelligent being functions that it is essential to attempt a definition, even if only a provisional one.[11] *Culture, from my perspective, is a complex of social and ideational fields of constructs that exist within individual minds, that are negotiated and developed in reaction to personal experience mediated by particular sensory apparatuses, and through which individuals organize and interpret sensory data as symbols and concepts that are, in turn, used for further organization and interpretation.* These fields are interconnected regions of memory that are used to translate concrete experience into domains of abstract and subjective reasoning and feeling. In short, culture involves the individual process of triangulating memory, which is inherently personal and idiosyncratic, with experience, which can be either individuated or collectivized.

For example, when an American sees a baseball game, he is likely to conjure up a variety of images or memories, both personal and shared, which may contribute to the status of baseball within the consciousness of individual Americans as culturally significant. One person might think of civil rights and Jackie Robinson, or the come-from-behind victory of the Red Sox over the

---

10. Bruce E. Wexler, *Brain and Culture: Neurobiology, Ideology, and Social Change* (Cambridge, MA: The MIT Press, 2006), p. 39.

11. Humans are not the only animals on Earth who exhibit culture or cultural variation. Chimpanzees make use of rudimentary tools and in some cases isolated groups use different tools and techniques for activities such as gathering ants. See Wexler, *Brain and Culture*, p. 184; and Beghan J. Morgan and Ekwoge E. Abwe, "Chimpanzees Use Stone Hammers in Cameroon," *Current Biology* 16, no. 16 (2006): R632–R633.

Yankees in the 2004 American League Championship Series. Another might think about pleasant afternoons playing Little League ball, or displeasure with a spouse who spends hours in front of the television watching major league games. The specific memories that one associates with the sport are idiosyncratic; a single woman won't have memories of a husband who spends too much time watching baseball on TV, even if she is well aware that there are husbands whose behavior is interpreted this way. A Red Sox fan may consider the Dodgers/Angels interleague rivalry but could regard it as trivial in comparison with memories of Ted Williams or hatred of the Yankees, which, in turn, are based on remembered experiences of past encounters between Williams and the Yankees. One need not have played or even watched baseball to have memories related to the game and to understand its meanings within American culture, but it is necessary to know baseball as an idea in order to create linkages with other areas of one's life and to derive meaning from those linkages. It is in the subjective and personal interpretation of experience and the generation of personal abstractions or linkages between experience and interpretation that we find culture.

The idea that some memories or ideas are shared, such as a baseball game, is based upon the assumption that most people have had some similar experience associated with the thing in question. But if one considers the example of a sporting event carefully, it becomes clear that each person at the ballpark or arena has a different experience. For example, each seat is oriented at a unique angle to the field, creating distinct visual and aural perspectives on the action; the experience from an outfield bleacher seat and the experience from a box seat directly behind home plate are radically different. Furthermore, a variety of other activities are going on during the game: people are having conversations, passing around a beach ball, taking a nap, getting beer or peanuts, chasing a nearby foul ball, or shouting obscenities at the umpires. To put it briefly, at what appears to be the collective event of a baseball game, no two members of the audience experience the game in precisely the same way. The same can be said for the players, each of whom perceives the game from a different position on the field or from the bullpen or bench.[12]

This example should not be taken as an isolated one—each particular experience is embedded in a vast matrix of constructs that exists within each person's own collection of experiences. The formula $F = ma$ that we learn in high-school physics class is part of the collection of experiences shared by

---

12. For a related discussion of baseball and collectivization, see John W. Traphagan, *Rethinking Autonomy: A Critique of Principlism in Biomedical Ethics* (Albany: State University of New York Press, 2012), p. 16.

most Americans and people in many other societies, although certainly not shared by all humans. Study and learning are direct experiencings of the world and are reflected in this example as the reified abstractions (such as *force*) that have become part of the logic of modern science and specifically physics. As the knowledge of individual experience becomes shared knowledge among certain groups of people, it is organized and constructed (re-collected) within the framework of an assumed, collectivized logic, which in many cases may be accepted as consisting of unequivocal maxims of human experience, or *doxa*, as sociologist Pierre Bourdieu terms the natural and unquestioned in relation to culture, even when that logic is not actually shared among all humans or even by various groups within a particular society.[13]

In short, the experience of the baseball game or the formula $F = ma$, rather than being collective, is collectivized as the participants generate an abstraction (construct) about a shared experience (watching a game, learning a formula, etc.). While the experience that I have with my son sitting next to me at a Red Sox game may be reasonably similar to his, that of the drunken fan two rows behind us may be quite different from ours; however, we may still collectivize the experience as communal because we do share the fact of having attended the game and, if we are both Red Sox fans, of having pulled for our team. We also share some level of common understanding of the game and how it is played; however, my son's knowledge of the game is considerably deeper than mine because he is an accomplished player—he sees many things that I miss because he has a type of experience I lack. And other fans may know little or nothing about the game or be knowledgeable enough to keep score.

The central point here is that culture is contained not in an ephemeral social milieu but in the heads of the people who define their own selves in terms of a particular set of contextually shaped constructs (ideas, memories, and behaviors). As a result, culture is idiosyncratic. There is neither an American culture nor a Japanese culture nor an extraterrestrial culture. Instead, there are multiple and varied constructions and interpretations of the social milieu in which intelligent beings live. Many of these constructions and interpretations are collectivized and are thus viewed as being shared by the members of any arbitrarily defined social group. The fact that these interpretations overlap to some (variable) extent and generate predictable behaviors and selves that are mutually identified and consistent with observable behaviors leads people to

---

13. Pierre Bourdieu, *Outline of a Theory of Practice* (Cambridge: Cambridge University Press, 1997); Henry Margenau, *The Nature of Physical Reality: A Philosophy of Modern Physics* (1950; rpt. Woodbridge, CT: Ox Bow Press, 1977).

think of culture as being "out there"—transcending the individual, existing in its own right, and governed by its own laws.[14]

Implications for SETI Research

There are several themes running through the above discussion that have relevance for SETI and CETI research. First, culture is not distinct from biology—the sensory apparatus that individuals use significantly shapes their experience of the world and the manner in which they experience and construct cultural ideas and patterns of behavior. Second, culture represents a context for linking memory, experience, and predictability (past, present, and future) into an interpretive framework that people use to deal with their surroundings. Third, culture is neither bounded nor constant; instead, it is in a continual state of change or flux. Finally, culture is not consistent; it is an amalgam of individual experiences, interpretations, and memories that are treated as though they are consistent but that actually involve considerable variation at the individual level.

When thinking about potential contact with an extraterrestrial intelligence, one can draw several conclusions from this type of understanding of

---

14. In addition to avoiding assumptions about one's own culture as collective and "out there" in the world, it is important to recognize that the culture concept can at times be used in ways that freeze difference in a manner similar to concepts such as *race* and *ethnicity*. The culture concept, when viewed in terms of collectivity rather than as a process that involves some level of collectivization of ideas and behaviors, can become a way of reifying an "other" that is inherently contrasted to the "self"—whether it is the "self" of the Western anthropologist, of Western society, or of another society—as people attempt to contrast, often strategically, their own world with the worlds and ideas of other societies. Abu-Lughod argues against cultural labels that homogenize the experience of women and, thus, obscure the worlds that women create and within which they interact. This idea can be extended more broadly as a strategy to avoid homogenizing categories, such as "Korean culture" (or American, Japanese, German, etc.), that inherently obscure the variations existing within the heads of individual Koreans and the complexities of their own interpretations of something or somethings—an abstraction— that is/are represented as Korean culture by both Korean and foreign observers of Korean society. In one sense, there is no such thing as "Korean culture"; but there is a sense in which many Korean people, under certain circumstances, *tend* to interpret their surroundings in similar ways and construct their worlds on the basis of assumptions about what is natural and normal behavior. See L. Abu-Lughod, "Writing Against Culture," in *Recapturing Anthropology: Working in the Present*, ed. R. Fox (Santa Fe, NM: School of American Research Press, 1991).

culture. First, when we ask such questions as "Will ET be altruistic?" or "Will ET be bent upon eradicating inferior beings from the galaxy?" we are probably barking up the wrong tree. For example, Frank Drake argues that any highly organized group of people will necessarily require altruism, because the ability to put the needs of the social whole ahead of one's own needs is a prerequisite to creating any organizational structure.[15] There are, of course, some problems with this formulation; the most notable of which is the recognition that group and individual needs are not always necessarily at odds and, thus, that individuals may align themselves with the needs of the group *only* when those needs correspond with their individual interests.[16] I may align my own interests with those of administrators in my university simply because they write my paycheck, not because I necessarily agree in every case with their decisions about university policies and practices. In other words, being "altruistic" may simply be a form of selfish behavior. Drake also makes the important point that the definition of what constitutes altruistic behavior may vary considerably from one society to another. Ethnographic research has shown repeatedly that there is no necessary mapping of one society's conceptualizations of the good or the altruistic onto those of another society, and it is not at all unusual for such concepts to be contradictory even within a particular society.[17]

My aim here is not to enter into a discussion of whether alien societies will be altruistic. Rather, it is to point out that questions and debates about the likely character of an alien civilization assume that aliens will be quite uniform in their attitudes toward their own world and toward the encounter with an intelligent other. Reflection on our own case, and the above discussion of culture and cognition, make it clear that if they are anything like us, this will not necessarily be true. Indeed, much of the literature on contact

---

15. Frank Drake, "Altruism in the Universe?," available at *http://archive.seti.org/seti/projects/imc/encoding/altruism.php* (accessed 12 June 2013).

16. For a fascinating exploration of altruism from both biological and cultural perspectives, see Barbara Oakley et al., eds., *Pathological Altruism* (New York: Oxford University Press, 2011).

17. For excellent examples of this, see Anthony P. Glascock, "When Is Killing Acceptable: The Moral Dilemma Surrounding Assisted Suicide in America and Other Societies," in *The Cultural Context of Aging: Worldwide Perspectives*, 2nd ed., ed. Jay Sokolovsky (New York: Bergin and Garvey, 1997), pp. 56–70; Anthony P. Glascock, "By Any Other Name, It Is Still Killing: A Comparison of the Treatment of the Elderly in America and Other Societies," in *The Cultural Context of Aging: Worldwide Perspectives*, ed. Jay Sokolovsky (New York: Bergin and Garvey, 1990), pp. 43–56; and John W. Traphagan, *Taming Oblivion: Aging Bodies and the Fear of Senility in Japan* (Albany: State University of New York Press, 2000).

with extraterrestrial intelligence tacitly assumes that an alien civilization will be culturally unified, *unlike* our own world. The idea behind this hypothesis seems to be that progress leads to greater levels of unified organizational structure, but this assumption derives from human, and particularly Western, perspectives that reflect a teleological notion of cultural evolution in which there is a universal outcome to processes of cultural change. "Advanced," in this formulation, becomes inexorably associated with "culturally and politically unified."[18]

In essence, this is a very anthropocentric approach that assumes an underlying similarity in all intelligent beings, in the ways in which "culture" is expressed, and in how culture shapes civilizations. However, if we do look at our own world as an analogue of what we might find elsewhere, we must face the fact that we could be dealing with a world fragmented into different cultural frameworks, much as our own is, and consisting of beings who may not respond to contact with us in a uniform way. Technological advancement on Earth has not always been associated with increased political and social integration (think World Wars I and II). Even if the experience of our planet is dissimilar to that of another world, it seems reasonable to think that we will be dealing with beings shaped by common memories (among themselves) and who will share, but who will also debate and contest, ideas developed within the frameworks of those common memories and experiences about what to do with the fact of having contacted humans. This problem is exacerbated when we take into account the strong likelihood that alien beings may have sensory organs that are quite different from our own and, thus, may process experience and translate that experience into cultural frameworks in a way different from our own. And even if such experiences and memories can be seen as "common," they must be understood in the manner identified above as being highly particularistic and based on individual experience, unless, of course, we encounter an alien society in which individual beings are cognitively integrated in some way and, thus, actually do share a single experience of the world. In that situation, the

---

18. One good example of this in the scholarly literature on SETI appears in Steven Dick's interesting article "The Postbiological Universe" (*Acta Astronautica* 62, nos. 8–9 [2008]: 499–504, esp. p. 500), in which he works from the assumption that a "central goal" of cultural evolution is increasing intelligence. The idea that cultures necessarily evolve, rather than change, is based upon Western (cultural) notions about the nature of human social organization in which certain social structures are more advanced than others and there is a directionality that implies improvement to the flow of cultural change.

meaning of *culture* for such a being becomes extremely difficult for humans to understand or even imagine.[19]

One proposed solution to this problem depends on members of both societies sharing the capacity for symbolic interaction. In order for the transfer of information to occur, intelligent beings need to be able to make one thing stand for another thing. If humans were incapable of making the color red stand for the command to stop, we would have a very difficult time transferring the information needed to make driving reasonably safe most of the time. In this example, as in much of the symbolic activity of humans, the linkage between thing and thing signified is arbitrary: no physical correlation exists between the color red and the action associated with "Stop!" Vakoch argues that the use of icons, or signs that visually resemble the signified, may help to resolve the problem of the arbitrary linkage between sign and symbol, even while there remains the fundamental problem that the interpreter may still not understand the physical correlation between the icon and the thing it signifies.[20] Indeed, if an extraterrestrial has different sensory organs from humans, the idea of what constitutes iconic symbols may not be useful. Would an image of Abraham Lincoln on a five-dollar bill "look" like the actual Abraham Lincoln to a creature that uses echolocation to sense its surroundings?

Perhaps one way to deal with this problem is to recognize that the point of contact will represent a context in which not only is the intended message interpretable, but the methods of communicating and representing information are also interpretable, perhaps more so than the intended meaning. I would like to suggest that should we encounter evidence of extraterrestrial intelligence in the form of a signal (directed at us or not), we should be concerned with deciphering the meaning of the signal not only in terms of its intended content but also in terms of what it tells us about the being who sent it. A signal conveys both explicit and implicit information about the sender. The fact, for example, that humans have been sending television images out into the galaxy for several decades could tell extraterrestrials much about us, if they are able to recognize those signals as containing information that can be represented in a visual medium. The simple fact that we send out electromagnetic signals that can be interpreted visually and aurally indicates

---

19. Although this is certainly a worthy endeavor, it is best reserved for another paper.

20. Douglas A. Vakoch, "The View from a Distant Star: Challenges of Interstellar Message-Making," posted online March/April 1999 and available at *http://www.astrosociety.org/pubs/mercury/9902/vakoch.html* (accessed 12 June 2013). This article originally appeared in *SETIQuest* 4, nos. 1–2 (1998): 8–10 and 15–17.

a great deal about how we process the world: that we have sense organs which translate sound and light into information we can use, as well as the types of limitations (in terms of the light spectrum, for example) of human senses. An alien intelligence that recognizes this fact would have a basis upon which to create a message we might be able to understand.

The messages sent out to date, such as Drake's broadcast pictures and binary information, which were assumed to require no prior understanding of our technology, are attempts to anticipate the capacities of another civilization of intelligent beings. Drake's message, for example, provides some basic information about us and our knowledge, including numbers from 1 to 10 plus images representing the human form, DNA structure, hydrogen and carbon atoms, and information about our solar system. Drake himself has noted that when he presented his prototype message to different scientists, they had trouble interpreting all of the content—with most being able to understand only the sections immediately relevant to their own areas of expertise—leaving us to wonder how well extraterrestrials would do if they stumbled across the message.[21]

Indeed, the difficulty in interpreting the intended meaning of the message suggests that another approach might well be taken. Instead of being concerned primarily with the content of a message, we might want to consider focusing on what the message tells us about who sent it. In Drake's message there are several subtexts that convey information about us that are not part of the intended meaning. For example, the manner in which the message is constructed would suggest that we think in terms of binary relationships—we encode information in terms of 1s and 0s—and understand two-dimensional images. Extraterrestrials might assume that this is how our language works or that this structure represents how humans organize thought in general, an assumption that would be misleading at best. However, the fact that the message represents information in a visual manner, like our television signals, would imply correctly that we are visually oriented beings. If the message were to be interpreted as having been sent by "an alien civilization" for the purpose of making contact, then it would quite inaccurately indicate that we are a unified society or culture interested in communication with civilizations in other parts of the universe.

These thoughts suggest that future research on interstellar message construction should involve not only study of the explicit message intended but

---

21. Leslie Mullen, "The Man to Contact," interview with Frank Drake, *Astrobiology Magazine*, 27 August 2007, available at *http://astrobio.net/news/modules.php?op=modload&name=News& file=article&sid=2441&mode=thread&order=0&thold=0* (accessed 12 June 2013).

also direct consideration of the implicit information that is being conveyed along with the explicit message. Rather than just asking "What does ET mean in a message?" or "What information do we want to convey in a message from us to ET?" we should also be asking "What are the implicit indicators and forms of information about ET and ourselves that are contained in any message sent or received?" These questions should lead to consideration of how we might develop useful tools to interpret such implicit information, should we encounter a signal, and also of how to encode that type of information in any signal we might send. In many respects, knowing how to interpret implicit information may prove more important than being able to interpret the explicit message, given the cultural and biological differences that might exist between humans and extraterrestrial others as well as the inevitable differences in personal intentions and interpretations on both sides that will be fundamental parts of contact.

CHAPTER ELEVEN

Speaking for Earth
Projecting Cultural Values Across Deep Space and Time

Albert A. Harrison

Ample evidence suggests that people seek to inform future generations about their lives, times, and accomplishments. Earth is sprinkled liberally with time capsules, monuments, tombstones, and other tributes to ego, achievement, and in some cases folly. Of such commemoratives Carl Sagan wrote, "For those who have something they consider worthwhile, communication to the future is an almost irresistible temptation.... In the best of cases it is an optimistic and far-seeing act; it expresses great hope for the future; it time-binds the human community; it gives us a perspective on the significance of our own actions at this moment in the long historical journey of our species."[1] Converging factors—including recognition that we may not be alone in the universe, realization that a major Near-Earth Object (NEO) impact or other terrestrial or cosmic catastrophe could spell the end of humankind, and emerging interstellar communication technologies—encourage us to reach out to new, unseen audiences.

In this chapter I consider Active SETI, that is, attempts to make extraterrestrial civilizations aware of our own. (This pursuit is also known as METI, or messaging extraterrestrial intelligence.[2]) Although a simple continuous-wave beacon might suffice, actual attempts have been more elaborate: encoding information in grids, plaques showing Earth's location in the Milky Way, recordings of sights and sounds of Earth, eerie electronic music, representations of human DNA, and personal letters. In his definitive history of time

---

1. Carl Sagan, *Murmurs of Earth* (New York: Random House, 1978), quoted here from Douglas A. Vakoch, "Across Generations: SETI Looks to the Future," *Space.com*, 10 April 2003, *http://archive.seti.org/seti/projects/imc/articles/xc_generations.php* (accessed 29 April 2012).

2. Alexander Zaitsev, "METI: Messaging to Extraterrestrial Intelligence," in *Searching for Extraterrestrial Intelligence: Past, Present, and Future*, ed. H. Paul Shuch (Berlin and Heidelberg: Springer-Praxis, 2010), pp. 399–428.

capsules, William E. Jarvis defines *space-time capsules* as slices of culture, frozen in time and sent beyond Earth.[3] These include spacecraft that bear greetings from humankind and microwave transmissions that transcend physical containers and carry time capsule–like messages at the speed of light to distant stars. As in the great time capsules of the 20th century, space-time capsules are deliberate efforts to communicate with audiences that differ, perhaps in radical ways, from the people who assembled the contents. As is true for even the most ambitious terrestrial time capsules, we really do not know if and when a space-time capsule will be retrieved. If the recipient is many light-years away, discovery may occur long after our society has ground to a halt. Whether they receive one of our space-time capsules—or we receive one of theirs—it could be a message from ancient history.

Developing Interstellar Messages

Thoughtfully done, Active SETI requires more than developing powerful communications technology. Political, legal, and moral issues must be addressed. Douglas Vakoch proposes that when we make the decision to communicate (and frame our message to ET), we should look out for our own security and welfare, tell the truth, and include information likely to educate and benefit the receiving civilization.[4] The International Academy of Astronautics' SETI Committee urges that any attempt to communicate with extraterrestrial intelligence should be on behalf of all humankind. The goal is for Earth-dwellers to speak in a unified voice for the planet as a whole without favoring one group or set of interests over another. Consequently, the SETI Committee's desire has been to work through the UN, consult broadly, and involve diverse groups of people from around the world.[5]

Message development is a useful exercise because it may help us to understand a transmission that we receive and because it could reduce the lag time if we choose to frame a response. Early efforts included developing formal languages based on logic and mathematics, such as Hans Freudenthal's

---

3. William E. Jarvis, *Time Capsules: A Cultural History* (Jefferson, NC: McFarland, 2003).

4. Douglas A. Vakoch, "Responsibility, Capability and Active SETI: Policy, Law, Ethics and Communication with Extraterrestrial Intelligence," *Acta Astronautica* 68, nos. 3–4 (2011): 512–519.

5. Michael A. G. Michaud, "Ten Decisions That Could Shake The World," *Space Policy* 19, no. 2 (2003): 131–136.

Lingua Cosmica, or *Lincos*.[6] Science provides the building blocks for a language proposed by Carl DeVito and Richard Oehrle.[7] Formal languages could lead eventually to discussions of topics such as philosophy, history, and politics, but for these topics Vakoch (who seeks to communicate culture in all of its richness and diversity) proposes a more direct approach, based on icons.[8] His work includes three-dimensional pictures (grids give two-dimensional cues of depth) that are presented sequentially to tell a story—something like a storyboard or flip art. Through conveying the concept of pain, he hopes to further explain what it means to be human.[9] Vakoch also seeks to communicate "maxims," or the principles that people live by.[10] These maxims have to do with gratitude, forgiveness, and other principles shared by many world religions. To promote interstellar cooperation, he has developed pictorial narratives intended to express altruism and reciprocity.[11]

An early Space Age attempt to communicate with life beyond Earth consisted of affixing plaques to Pioneer 10 and Pioneer 11. Launched in the early 1970s, these NASA spacecraft have now completed their exploration of our solar system and are proceeding on a million-year journey to other stars. They were followed in the late 1970s by two Voyager spacecraft carrying plaques and recordings of terrestrial sights and sounds, along with instructions and playback equipment. The Voyager disks include 100 images (carefully chosen to reflect diversity and minimize confusion on the part of observers unfamiliar with our ways), greetings in 55 languages, and brief excerpts of music from around the world. Arguably the richest portrayal of life on Earth thus far sent into space, themes within the images and sequences of music help to tell the

6. Hans Freudenthal, *Lincos: Design of a Language for Cosmic Intercourse* (Amsterdam: North-Holland Publishing, 1960).

7. Carl L. DeVito and Richard T. Oehrle, "A Language Based on the Fundamental Facts of Science," *Journal of the British Interplanetary Society* 43, no. 12 (1990): 561–568.

8. Douglas A. Vakoch, "An Iconic Approach to Communicating Musical Concepts in Interstellar Messages," *Acta Astronautica* 67, nos. 11–12 (2011): 1406–1409; and Douglas A. Vakoch, "Representing Culture in Interstellar Messages," *Acta Astronautica* 63, nos. 5–6 (2008): 657–664.

9. Douglas A. Vakoch, "What Does It Mean to Be Human? Reflections on the Portrayal of Pain in Interstellar Messages," *Acta Astronautica* 68, nos. 3–4 (2010): 445–450.

10. Douglas A. Vakoch, "A Taxonomic Approach to Communicating Maxims in Interstellar Messages," *Acta Astronautica* 68, nos. 3–4 (2011): 500–511.

11. Vakoch, "A Taxonomic Approach to Communicating Maxims in Interstellar Messages," passim.

story of human evolution.[12] Commenting on the improbability that any of these spacecraft would be discovered, SETI pioneer Barney Oliver said: "There is only an infinitesimal chance that the plaque will be seen by even a single extraterrestrial, but it will certainly be seen by billions of terrestrials. Its real function, therefore, is to appeal to and expand the human spirit and to make contact with extraterrestrial intelligence a welcome expectation of mankind."[13]

Maybe someday in the spirit of Voyager, an international group will produce a major compendium describing life, mind, and society on Earth. Partly a historical document, partly an expression of contemporary culture and values, this *Encyclopedia Terrestria* would convey the essence or "feel" of our time. It could contain hundreds of thousands of images, sound bites, and video clips, all woven into a rich and detailed overview of our past, present, and projected future. In the course of preparing this multimedia compendium, humanity would step back and look at the big picture. Deciding what might be important to another civilization would force us to move beyond our characteristically short time span and develop a long-term perspective. Determining what we should say and how to say it could be a useful self-study that fosters self-contemplation and encourages consensus. These deliberations could clarify how we see our place in the universe, what makes us human, and where we are going. In the meantime, Earth is already speaking with many voices, reflecting multiple values and interests.

Reaching Interstellar Audiences

Experience gained with terrestrial time capsules suggests certain rules of thumb for announcing our presence in the universe. Earth's message should be conspicuous so that it will be easy to find—a powerful transmission that cuts through the static the way a foghorn drowns out the chatter of seagulls, a spacecraft that appears large and bright to the eye. Redundancy, or multiple copies, is another way to increase the chances of discovery. A transmission could be continuously repeated, perhaps from multiple sites. Messages that are capable of renewing themselves would offer particular advantages. Gregory Benford gives oral traditions, passed from generation to generation

---

12. Douglas A Vakoch, "What's Past Is Prologue: Future Messages of Cosmic Evolution," in Shuch, ed., *Searching for Extraterrestrial Intelligence*, pp. 373–398.

13. Barney Oliver, quoted here from Carl Sagan, *Murmurs of Earth* (New York: Random House, 1978), p. 11.

by word of mouth, high marks for reliability and accuracy.[14] The longevity of many narratives derives from their adaptability to the needs of successive generations. The Bible, for example, is reviewed and revised periodically. Such revisions have produced the King James version, which remains dominant today, and a modern English version that was released in the 1950s. Unlike terrestrial time capsules, space-time capsules cannot be opened periodically, have their contents inspected, and then be repacked with updated materials. However, early space-time capsules can be followed by later updates, much as the great printed encyclopedias of the past were supplemented with annual yearbooks between editions.

SETI (or at least its precursor) began as an active process in the mid- to late 1800s. Florence Raulin-Cerceau has recently discussed plans developed during that era to make ourselves known to possible neighbors within our solar system.[15] At that time, scientists could still hypothesize that the Moon, Mars, and Venus were inhabited. Despite the occasional flash of light or other mysterious phenomenon, no unambiguous signals were sent our way, and so it was up to us to take the lead. In the absence of spacecraft or radio, this meant creating visual displays that were large enough to draw the attention of their hypothetical recipients. By composing messages in such a way as to illustrate our virtuosity in math or science, it was supposed, we would demonstrate our intelligence. Through the clever use of mirrors (and, later on, powerful electric lights), we could communicate telegraphically. These plans did not reach fruition because of the tremendous costs of constructing giant mirrors, igniting miles of kerosene-topped trench systems, and planting huge forests to grow in geometric patterns.

Raulin-Cerceau points out that certain ideas from that time have persisted into the modern era. First and foremost is the notion that it is possible to conduct an empirical test of the hypothesis that we are not alone in the universe. Second, the assumption that since we all live in the same universe governed by the same laws of nature, science provides a good starting point for interstellar discussions. Finally, there is the assumption that just as we have astronomers who study their planet, their astronomers will study our planet and recognize that we are intelligent.

During the early part of the 20th century, Guglielmo Marconi and other radio pioneers sought to intercept extraterrestrial transmissions but either

---

14. Gregory Benford, *Deep Time: How Humanity Communicates Across the Millennia* (New York: Perennial, 1999).

15. Florence Raulin-Cerceau, "The Pioneers of Interplanetary Communication: From Gauss to Tesla," *Acta Astronautica* 67, nos. 11–12 (2010): 1391–1398.

found nothing unusual or stumbled across something that was interesting at the time but which could not be attributed to extraterrestrial intelligence. Shortly after the 20th century's midpoint, computations demonstrating the feasibility of interstellar communication coupled with the first radio-telescope search further pushed the search from an active to the passive process. The early acronym for Communicating with Extraterrestrial Intelligence, CETI, gave way to SETI, which did not imply transmissions from Earth. The names for searches during the years of NASA sponsorship (1969–1994) were the Microwave Observing Project and later the High-Resolution Microwave Survey. As John Billingham points out, during those years attention was focused on increasing the sensitivity of antennas and receivers, increasing the number of frequencies that could be monitored simultaneously, and developing sufficient computer power to process the massive amounts of data being collected.[16]

Interstellar Transmissions

As methods for propagating human legacy, microwave radios and lasers offer low-cost, off-the-shelf technology and the ability to cover all but unimaginable distances at the speed of light. Interception by extraterrestrials requires that distant civilizations have advanced to—but not entirely beyond—these technologies. The first deliberate interstellar microwave broadcast took place at the dedication of the Arecibo radio telescope on 14 November 1974.[17] The pixels of this digital message, arranged into 73 lines of 23 characters each, form graphic representations of hydrogen, carbon, oxygen, phosphorous atoms, and DNA; chemical formulae for sugars and nucleic acids; and line drawings of both a human figure and a radio-telescope dish antenna. The message was aimed in the direction of the Hercules star cluster Messier 13 (M13), tens of thousands of light-years away.

Alexander Zaitsev, a vigorous proponent and practitioner of Active SETI, has reviewed at least 20 major transmissions launched between the late 1990s and 2008.[18] One of these powerful transmissions was sent from Zaitsev's

---

16. John Billingham, "SETI: The NASA Years," in Shuch, ed., *Searching for Extraterrestrial Intelligence*, pp. 65–86; and chapter 1 of this volume.

17. Frank Drake and Dava Sobel, *Is Anyone Out There? The Scientific Search for Extraterrestrial Intelligence* (New York: Delacorte Press, 1992), pp. 180–185.

18. Alexander Zaitsev, "METI: Messaging to Extraterrestrial Intelligence," in Shuch, ed., *Searching for Extraterrestrial Intelligence*, pp. 399–428.

Evpatoria Planetary Radar (EPR) in Ukraine in May 1999. Yvan Dutil and Stephane Dumas of the Defence Research Establishment Valcartier (DREV) in Quebec, Canada, designed the message.[19] Intended to be an "Interstellar Rosetta Stone," it built on previous attempts, including *Lincos*, to develop an interstellar language and depended heavily on science and mathematics. Packed full of scientific notation, the message was put together like a textbook, starting with very simple ideas, such as the hydrogen atom, and then moving on to increasingly difficult topics. This transmission was beamed to four carefully selected stars, well within the transmitter's range of 100 light-years. Recipients are encouraged to respond.

In August and September 2001, Zaitsev transmitted a "Concert for ET" from Evpatoria to six nearby Sun-like stars; the music included Gershwin's "Summertime," the finale of Beethoven's Ninth Symphony, and the melody of the Russian folksong "Kalinka-Malinka" performed on a solo instrument known as a theremin.[20] By waving his or her hands over two sensors that control the theremin's volume and tone, the performer produces swoopy, tremulous sounds ranging from a deep staccato buzz to a high-pitched whine. Zaitsev considered the instrument a good technical choice because it provides a sharp and clear signal that stands out against background noise and should carry with reasonable fidelity across interstellar distances.[21]

Since the theremin is regarded differently in Russia and the United States, I wonder what ET might make of it. The instrument's Russian inventor, Leon Theremin, saw it as one more solo instrument—comparable to a violin or cello.[22] In the early years of the 20th century his invention, which debuted at an electrical workers' convention, delighted Lenin and drew large audiences. It was considered an instrument of culture and refinement. Highly regarded performers played classical music to upscale audiences and received rave reviews from critics who shared Lenin's and then Stalin's enthusiasm. Apart from providing the focal point for a few experimental, avant-garde concerts in the 1930s, the theremin never made it big with U.S. music lovers. But in the 1940s the instrument made it to Hollywood, where

19. Alexander Zaitsev, Charles M. Chafer, and Richard Braastad, "Making a Case for METI," SETI League Guest Editorial, March 2005, *http://www.setileague.org/editor/meti/htm*.

20. Zaitsev, Chafer, and Braastad, "Making a Case for METI."

21. Alexander L. Zaitsev, "Design and Implementation of the 1st Theremin Concert for Aliens," Sixth International Space Arts Workshop, Paris, 17 March 2002, p. 3.

22. James Wierzbicki, "Weird Vibrations: How the Theremin Gave Musical Voice to Hollywood's Extraterrestrial 'Others': Electronic Music from 1950s Science Fiction Films," *Journal of Popular Film and Television* 30, no. 4 (2002): 125–135.

it replaced conventional ensembles in certain movie genres—suspense and horror. By the 1950s the theremin had become tied, irrevocably, to classic science-fiction films such as *The Day the Earth Stood Still*. How ET might react to this kind of music is anyone's guess, but these East-West differences remind us that technical considerations alone are unlikely to determine reactions to interstellar messages.

Zaitsev, Charles M. Chafer, and Richard Braastad teamed up to send scientific and personal messages to five Sun-like stars in "Cosmic Call II" in 2003.[23] Chafer was the president of "Team Encounter," which sought to reach out to our galactic neighbors through microwave transmissions and automated spacecraft. Whereas an earlier broadcast included the names of and brief messages from people who were directly involved in the project, this transmission included photos, drawings, and audio and video files submitted by "Team Encounter" members worldwide. Customers signed up, mostly on the Internet, and paid a fee to support a "people's space program," which Chafer saw as the wave of the future. The materials were digitized and then transmitted at full power to stars between 32.8 and 45.9 light-years away from Earth. This broadcast began with the phrase "Greetings from Earth," a segment presented by noted news broadcaster, journalist, and television personality Hugh Downs.

Each of the five transmissions (aimed at one star) included the Interstellar Rosetta Stone, a brief description of the spacecraft that Team Encounter had under development, a copy of the Arecibo message, and a Bilingual Image Glossary (BIG). Other contents included 282 flags of the world, pictures of Ukrainian school children, music and images of KFT (a Hungarian rock band), the song "Starman" by musician David Bowie, and, as a gesture of peace and friendship, the text of a resolution passed by the New Mexico state legislature in 2003 designating the second Tuesday in February as Extraterrestrial Culture Day in New Mexico.

Team Encounter has also offered the opportunity to send personal messages on extrasolar missions based on solar-sail technology. They hoped that millions of people will pay to carry messages—sheets of paper containing text or pictures and strands of hair carrying DNA—to the aliens. Author and inventor Arthur C. Clarke signed up for the project and contributed a sample of his DNA. Concluding his interview with Team Encounter leader Chafer, Graham Phillips reported, "According to this marketing

---

23. Richard Braastad and Alexander Zaitsev, "Synthesis and Transmission of Cosmic Call 2003 Interstellar Radio Message," 2003, *http://www.cplire.ru/html/ra&sr/irm/CosmicCall-2003/* (accessed 10 October 2004).

man, projects like this are the real beginnings of the Space Age—when the public can become involved. Deadmen in orbit and Arthur C Clarke's hair space odyssey. They're not crazy ideas—they are the first steps to our cosmic destiny."[24]

In 2005 the Deep Space Communications Network transmitted more than 130,000 electronic messages and enticed customers with the offer of 5-minute voice transmissions for $99. Messages were not to be profane, offensive, or lewd (by human standards). *TalktoAliens.com* posted a 900 (toll) telephone number where, for $3.99 a minute, clients could record a message to be beamed to the stars.[25]

In 2008 "A Message from Earth" set forth on a 20-year voyage from Evpatoria to Gliese 581c, a large extrasolar planet believed to have Earth-like characteristics.[26] Project organizers hoped to capture young people's imaginations and prompt them to think about humanity, our home planet, and our place in the universe. This effort was a partnership of Bebo, a social networking Web site, and RDF Digital, a subsidiary of a media group that sponsors such popular UK reality-television shows as *Shipwrecked*, *Location Location Location*, and *Wifeswap*. The public submitted text, drawings, and photographs for posting on a Web site. Then viewers voted, and on the basis of popularity, the 500 best were broadcast in a 4½-hour transmission in October of that year. This space-time capsule contained descriptions of people's lives and ambitions, images of famous landmarks and notable figures, and thoughts about world peace. One actress submitted pictures of opposing political candidates (one to epitomize good and the other evil), and a male rock singer obsessed on a songstress's bodily perfection. The media company was said to be contemplating a television series based on this project and tentatively entitled "A Message from Earth."

That same year the UK public competed to come up with the best idea for a 30-second commercial for the snack food Doritos, to be beamed from the EISCAT Space Center in Svalbard, Norway, to the habitable zone around one of the stars in the Ursa Major constellation. Concerned about the first impression we might make, Jason Palmer asked, "Couldn't we advertise something

24. Graham Phillips, "Space Encounter," *ABC Catalyst*, 11 October 2001, *http://www.abc.net.au/catalyst/stories/s386244.htm* (accessed 29 June 2013).

25. Alan Boyle, "Would You Pay to Send Messages Into Space?," *Cosmic Log*, 18 March 2005, *http://www.msnbc.com/id/7180932* (accessed 30 January 2006).

26. "A Message From Earth (2008)," Wikipedia, *http://en.wikipedia.org/woko/A_Message_From-Earth* (accessed 19 July 2009).

more representative of our cultures, our hopes and dreams and interplanetary worthiness? Like Spam? Corn dogs?"[27]

In 2010, to publicize the debut of Paul Davies's *The Eerie Silence: Are We Alone in the Universe?*,[28] the book's publisher, Penguin UK, solicited 5,000 personal messages (each limited to 40 words) to transmit in the direction of Orion. The top 50 messages, as determined by a panel of judges, received copies of Davies's new book. Among the winning comments were these: "Did you think YOU were alone in the universe?" "We don't bite, do you?" "Please send pictures of your celebrities," and a binary number that translates as *You are not alone.*[29] Approximately 1,000 messages were received and all were transmitted.

After this type of commercialization, could religious spokespersons be far behind? Methodist missionary Tom Hoffman, who served in Russia, has expressed keen interest in SETI.[30] A mission is a ministry commissioned by a church or some other organization for the purpose of propagating its faith or carrying on humanitarian work. Theology and discipleship are central themes. Missionary work encourages church members to rethink their theology (for example, to accommodate newly found cultures) and inspires people at home as well as at the site of the mission. Compared to earlier missionaries who helped European explorers claim new territories, today's missionaries are heavily invested in humanitarian efforts and tend to soft-pedal dogma and prophecy. Exomissionaries would focus instead on the histories, theologies, and futures of Christian missions as they relate to issues of space exploration and SETI. Exomissionaries could help scientists by speaking with an independent voice in cross-cultural exchanges and working as cultural brokers who incorporate perspectives from behavioral science and social work. It may be difficult for exomissionaries to win favor from scientists (many of whom are agnostic or atheist), but training missionaries in fields such as space medicine or linguistics would increase their practical value to a space crew or SETI team.

---

27. Jason Palmer, "Are We Sending the Right Message to ET?," New Scientist Space Blog, 2008, *http://www.newscientist.com/blog/space/2008/is-nowhere-safe-from_advertising* (accessed 19 July 2009).

28. Paul Davies, *The Eerie Silence: Are We Alone in the Universe?* (London: Penguin, 2010).

29. Graham Southorn, "The Eerie Silence – Winning Messages," *Sky at Night Magazine, http:// www.skyatnightmagazine.com/forum/the-eerie-silence-winning-messages-t110073.html* (accessed 21 May 2010).

30. Thomas Hoffman, *A Brief Handbook of Protestant Exomissiology*, MS Thesis, Department of Futures Studies, University of Houston–Clear Lake (2004); Thomas Hoffman, "Exomissiology: The Launching of Exotheology," *Dialog: A Journal of Theology* 43, no. 4 (2004): 324–336.

Satellites

Perhaps a bit closer to the SETI Committee's ideal of speaking for Earth as a whole was the KEO satellite—a project planned but not completed, due to the death of its originator. This was an international venture conceptualized by the late artist Jean-Marc Philippe, led by Europeans, and strongly supported by non-Western countries such as India.[31] This orbiting space-time capsule was intended for future generations on Earth but under doomsday scenarios could survive the species that launched it. (Perhaps we should think of it as a tomb for history.) KEO was planned with enough storage capacity to allow every man, woman, and child on Earth to contribute up to a four-page essay, and organizers solicited widely for messages. People could record voice messages or send letters as well as enter their thoughts on the KEO Web site. Contributions could be in any language, were uncensored, and would be available to the public after KEO launched. The millions of messages were to be encoded on special tough glass CDs that would not deteriorate over time, and the satellite would include a user's manual, complete with information on how to build a CD player. In addition to the "Fresco of Messages," KEO was to include the "Library of Alexandria," a description of life in our time, an astronomical clock, portraits of human beings as they appear today, and samples of air, water, soil, and human blood encased in diamond.

KEO was designed to be bright and conspicuous, serving as a shining reminder of the 21st century and easy to spot when falling back to Earth 50,000 years after its launch. If humanity fails to survive an asteroid impact or other major calamity, and extraterrestrial explorers in our solar system spot a satellite like KEO, then it may be such a satellite that perpetuates the human legacy.

How Dangerous?

As Michael Michaud points out, there is always the possibility that our broadcasts or probes will attract the attention of a civilization that chooses to exploit Earth or eliminate us as a possible threat.[32] Michaud is among the many

---

31. Jean-Marc Philippe, "The KEO Satellite," paper presented at the 1999 meeting of the International Astronautical Federation, Amsterdam, IAF-99-P.3.10, October 1999.

32. Michael A. G. Michaud, "Ten Decisions That Could Shake The World," *Space Policy* 19, no. 2 (2003): 131–136; Michael A. G. Michaud, *Contact with Alien Civilizations* (New York: Copernicus Books, 2007), pp. 368–374.

microwave SETI supporters who prefer passive SETI—simply listening and watching. If we detect an extraterrestrial civilization, he hopes that we will fight the temptation to respond immediately and will instead perform as much reconnaissance as possible before taking a potentially fatal next step. For such reasons, Michaud has described the decision to actively broadcast as one of the great decisions that could shake the world. Radio astronomer Dan Werthimer points out that we are, in the cosmic scheme of things, a relatively primitive civilization, having had radio for only about a century.[33] He recommends that we keep listening for the next few hundred years, see what we learn, and only then consider broadcasting. Scientist and science-fiction author David Brin also urges caution, noting widespread aggression and violence on Earth.[34] Elsewhere, building on data from political science, I have argued that long-lived societies are democratic, peaceful, and enduring, and that self-serving, authoritarian, and aggressive societies inevitably collapse due to internal flaws and external opposition.[35] Convergent evidence strongly suggests that societies that endure over appreciable periods of time are likely to be peaceful and benign. But even if an optimistic analysis is correct, it is probabilistic; and we cannot be assured that first contact will be with a group that wants to make friends.

Proponents such as Alexander Zaitsev portray Active SETI as continuous with science.[36] Just as a biologist might try to stimulate a response from an organism, Active SETI tries to stimulate a response from an extraterrestrial civilization. SETI, proponents note, operates on the assumption that other civilizations are not afraid to reveal themselves. Why should not we, too, be willing to do this? If everyone is only listening, how could anyone find anyone else? If a distant civilization is willing to provide us with scientific insights and information useful for solving our practical problems, then there is a certain risk in *not* attracting their attention. Apart from the fate of our space-time capsules, we might get "caught" anyway, since Earth's radio signature expands outward in all directions at the rate of one light-year per year. Very high power

---

33. Adrian Hon, "Interview: SETI with Professor Dan Werthimer," *Astrobiology: The Living Universe*, 12 December 2001, available at *http://library.thinkquest.org/C003763/pdf/interview03.pdf* (accessed 3 September 2013).

34. David Brin, "A Contrarian Perspective on Altruism," in Shuch, ed., *Searching for Extraterrestrial Intelligence*, pp. 429–450.

35. Albert A. Harrison, "The Relative Stability of Belligerent and Peaceful Societies: Implications for SETI," *Acta Astronautica* 46, nos. 10–12 (2000): 707–712; Albert A Harrison, "The ETI Myth: Idolatrous Fantasy or Plausible Inference?," *Theology and Science* 8, no. 1 (2010): 51–67.

36. Zaitsev et al., "Making a Case for METI."

broadcasts began around World War II, so we may be identifiable out to approximately 60 light-years. Powerful military radar signals should be easily detected at great distances, as should the radar pulses used to study distant planets. Hypothetically, we could have been detected beyond the boundary of our radio signature if alien astrobiologists have found means to identify life-bearing planets such as ours.

Certainly nobody worries too much about, say, someone flashing a laser pointer at a distant star. Nor does Frank Drake's three-minute transmission from Arecibo raise many hackles. To detect this brief broadcast, listeners in the vicinity of M13 will have to be lucky indeed. But suppose the transmission continued for decades. Concerns arise in the case of transmissions that are both powerful and sustained. Despite some agreement within the SETI community that international consultation should occur before communicating with ET, controlling broadcasters is all but impossible. SETI is (correctly) presented to the public as a harmless activity. Arguing in favor of international consultation before a message is dispatched from Earth implies that there is something to worry about.

In actuality there is no real way to control efforts to speak for humankind. As more and more people gain access to powerful computing and broadcasting equipment, there are few if any practical ways to keep free-lancers off the air. Any government, scientist, theologian, entrepreneur, or hobbyist who has access to a powerful radio transmitter, laser, or spacecraft could send an irretrievable message into the void. In the final analysis, many people may speak for Earth. Michaud cautions: "Having Humankind speak with many voices may be representative of diversity, but it also may be bad policy. Imagine yourself in the place of an ETI that receives a barrage of messages from the Earth. How could you conduct a rational dialogue, and whom will you believe?"[37]

Donald Tarter discusses what might occur if ET were bombarded with many conflicting messages.[38] He envisions a scenario in which we receive a microwave broadcast from another civilization. Even in the case of a "dial tone" devoid of superimposed information, we would be able to identify the direction and distance of the alien transmitter. SETI post-detection protocols require composing a response from all humankind, but preparing one would take a long time. In the interim, many different parties would take it upon themselves to beam messages to ET, creating exactly the kind of situ-

---

37. Michaud, "Ten Decisions That Could Shake The World," p. 131.
38. Donald E. Tarter, "Reply Policy and Signal Type: Assumptions Drawn from Minimal Source Information," *Acta Astronautica* 42, nos. 10–12 (1998): 685–689.

ation that Michaud hopes to avoid. To circumvent this, Tarter recommends a preemptive strike. As soon as we detect ET, we send a powerful response. This response should consist of an acknowledgment that we have received the transmission plus a secret code. ET is instructed to ignore all future messages from Earth except those that include the secret code. Tarter presumes that the "good guys" will send the first reply and that its recipients will accept it because it is prompt and transmitted at high power. We will then hope that ET ignores the subsequent welter of incoming messages while Earth's designated spokespersons prepare a more detailed response on behalf of our entire planet. Later, this response will be sent along with the secret code that proves the message's legitimacy. Tarter adds that a failure to reply (especially if the message was deliberately beamed to Earth) could be interpreted as an interstellar insult.

Decades and even centuries could pass between our transmission and their response. The fastest possible reply would take twice the time that it took for the message to reach its destination: it would take a minimum of 100 years to receive a reply to a message sent to a star 50 light-years away. This would be a blink of the eye in comparison to the hundreds or thousands of years of turnaround time for some of our messages that are wending their way across the galaxy. In the absence of a central registry, nobody on Earth could remember the date and contents of the original transmission. The reply from ET could be analogous to having a large unwanted pizza, ordered by some previous tenant, arrive at your residence. Furthermore, their response could be poorly timed, for instance, hitting the news when the world is teetering on the brink of war. In this case people might fear that an extraterrestrial civilization would align with one side or the other.

There are ways to send space-time capsules with minimal risks to our safety. Orbiting satellites such as KEO or markers placed on the Moon or Mars are relatively low risk. The reason is that any extraterrestrials capable of interstellar travel who might arrive there will already have plenty of other evidence of human existence. If we took steps to ensure that deliberate microwave broadcasts were no more powerful than earlier transmissions, they would extend no further beyond our current radio signature and hence could not attract audiences that otherwise would not have discovered us. Also, we might learn from movie villains who elude capture by using post-office boxes rather than residence addresses, or who pay intermediaries to resend their letters from an out-of-town location. A patient and security-minded civilization could locate their transmitters a few light-years away from their local sun. Communications between the home planet and the remote transmitter are focused as much as possible (thereby making them difficult for others to detect), while the remote transmitter blasts the skies in other directions as a diversionary tactic.

Kathryn Denning observes that the debate over Active SETI is difficult if not impossible to resolve because participants approach it from different perspectives.[39] The scientist hopes to test a scientific hypothesis; the political scientist is concerned about the ramifications of entering into a relationship with an unknown adversary; the artist strives to celebrate life in the universe; and other people want to make money or have fun. Denning urges us to "see interstellar transmissions not as unregulated scientific experiments, or unauthorized diplomatic initiatives, or public relations stunts, but instead as something bigger and deeper which encompasses all of those: a technologically mediated manifestation of our drive to represent ourselves and connect with the unseen."[40] The question becomes: "What is the right way to balance the desires of some people against the concerns of others, and who is entitled to make decisions about the future of the world that we all share?"[41] She suggests that we look at how such multifaceted issues have been addressed successfully in the past.

Donald Tarter suspects that as long as SETI remains little more than an exercise, the government can afford to treat the activity with benign neglect.[42] As soon as detection occurs, however, no government is likely to be willing to leave matters in the hands of the scientific community. When ET becomes real, governments will seek to control outgoing messages or to sponsor its own messages, intended to win converts, promote commerce, forge alliances, and prevent wars.

Conclusion

Planned efforts to communicate with extraterrestrial audiences should force us to step back, look at the big picture, and formulate an approach that is in the interests of humankind. KEO's leading exponent, Jean-Marc Philippe, certainly believed this, noting that his project gives us the opportunity to share each individual's hopes, dreams, fears, doubts, and deepest convictions

---

39. Kathryn Denning, "Unpacking the Great Transmission Debate," *Acta Astronautica* 67, nos. 11–12 (2010): 1399–1405.

40. Denning, "Unpacking the Great Transmission Debate," p. 1342.

41. Denning, "Unpacking the Great Transmission Debate," p. 1344.

42. Donald E. Tarter, "Security Considerations in Signal Detection," *Acta Astronautica* 46, nos. 10–12 (2000): 725–728.

and, in doing so, to discover our common humanity.[43] Right now, microwave broadcasts intended for other worlds are racing through the galaxy, while probes such as Pioneer and Voyager are lumbering along further and further behind. Some broadcasters use low-power (500 watt) transmitters, while some attempts to communicate are more reminiscent of science fiction than science. Over time, however, we can expect our technology and techniques to improve. More people will gain access to radio telescopes and powerful lasers, and, as the costs of spaceflight decrease, an increasing number of organizations will even launch spacecraft. Slowly, these broadcasts will make the transition from the symbolic to the functional, and, as the number of space-time capsules increases, so will the chances that one or more of these will be found. Perhaps the great radio silence that envelops our part of the galaxy will someday be replaced by a great cacophony, with Earth itself responsible for most of the noise.

43. Philippe, "The KEO Satellite."

CHAPTER TWELVE

The Evolution of Extraterrestrials

The Evolutionary Synthesis and Estimates of the Prevalence of Intelligence Beyond Earth

Douglas A. Vakoch

Introduction

The notion of extraterrestrial beings as bizarre yet somewhat humanoid life-forms existed well before science-fiction movies became popular. In Christiaan Huygens's *The Celestial Worlds Discover'd, Or, Conjectures Concerning the Inhabitants, Plants and Productions of the Worlds in the Planets*, we can see two poles of thought about life beyond Earth that are reflected in more recent works. That monograph, published posthumously in 1698, depicts possible denizens of other planets as very similar to humans in some respects yet radically distinct from us in others. After explaining why "Planetarians" would be upright beings with hands, feet, and eyes, Huygens claims that their form could still be quite alien:

> Nor does it follow from hence that they must be of the same shape with us. For there is such an infinite possible variety of Figures to be imagined, that both the Oeconomy of the whole Bodies, and every part of them, may be quite distinct and different from ours.[1]

Huygens was neither the first nor the last astronomer to speculate on extraterrestrial morphology. But his position *is* representative of his profession. For many astronomers, the progressive development of life has been seen as an ineluctable occurrence given proper environmental conditions on a planet. And even though Huygens and his scientific heirs did not expect

---

1. Christiaan Huygens, *The Celestial Worlds Discover'd: Or, Conjectures Concerning the Inhabitants, Plants and Productions of the Worlds in the Planets* (London: Frank Cass and Co., 1968), p. 74 (facsimile reproduction of 1698 edition).

such beings to be identical to humans, they did predict significant parallels between terrestrial and extraterrestrial life-forms. A striking contrast is seen in the writings of nonphysical scientists. Members of this latter group hold more widely differing views. But within this diversity, reasons for their variation become more apparent when we understand how views about extraterrestrials can be related to the differential emphasis placed on modern evolutionary theory by scientists of various disciplines.

Understanding the disparities among the biologists, paleontologists, and anthropologists who have speculated on extraterrestrials becomes easier when we pay attention to who was doing the speculating. Given the relatively small number of commentators on the topic, it seems more than coincidental that four of the major contributors to the modern evolutionary synthesis of the 1930s and 1940s are among them. The exobiological arguments of Theodosius Dobzhansky and George Gaylord Simpson and, less directly, of H. J. Muller and Ernst Mayr are all related to their earlier work on synthetic evolution. By examining the variety of views held by nonphysical scientists, we can see substantial disagreements between them about evolution as late as the 1960s. By the close of the next decade, however, many but by no means all believed that "higher" life, particularly intelligent life, probably occurs quite infrequently in the universe. Their reasons for these various beliefs suggest a cause for the shift: an increasing acceptance of the evolutionary synthesis.

Early Critiques of Darwin's Theory of Evolution

To understand the modern evolutionary synthesis, it is useful to recall the main features of Darwin's theory as expressed in the first edition of *The Origin of Species*, published in 1859. His basic position can be summarized in two concepts: variation and natural selection. Darwin limited himself to minute differences between organisms that could be passed on to subsequent generations. Each organism would be uniquely equipped for the "struggle for existence," and those best suited to their environments would have the greatest chance of surviving to reproduce offspring that shared some of their characteristics. Darwin succinctly stated the relationship between this process of natural selection and variation: "This preservation of favorable variations and the rejection of injurious variations, I call Natural Selection."[2]

---

2. Charles Darwin, *The Origin of Species by Means of Natural Selection: Or, the Preservation of Favoured Races in the Struggle for Life*, with an introduction by J. W. Burrow (1859; Harmondsworth: Penguin Books, 1968), p. 131.

In subsequent years, the efficacy of natural selection was challenged and refuted by many. Fleeming Jenkin, for example, contended that any small, beneficial variations would be diluted quickly in a population that included many other organisms not similarly adapted.[3] In later editions of *The Origin*, Darwin relied more heavily on "sports," individual offspring varying markedly from their forebears. This caused some critics to charge that Darwin had shifted to a position very similar to an earlier view that periodically new species abruptly appear.

Ironically, the mathematical analysis of heredity that was to central to formulating the modern evolutionary synthesis began as an argument against the transmission of small variations from one generation to the next. When Francis Galton examined the "swamping effect" that Jenkin described, he concluded that any variations from the mean type of a species would be lost in following generations. Thus, in the long run organisms would tend to have common characteristics. Deviations from the norm were, by Galton's analysis, transient. His protégé, Karl Pearson, came to the opposite conclusion. Pearson argued against the assumption that the fate of variations should be measured against a fixed ancestral type. Rather, he said that variations from an organism's ancestors could result in lasting changes in future generations.

In contrast to Pearson, others argued that evolution could be accounted for only through large-scale mutations. Supporting their views with Gregor Mendel's newly discovered paper, William Bateson, Hugo de Vries, and Wilhelm Johannsen proposed salutatory accounts of evolution. Mendel's early work focused on the inheritance of discontinuous characteristics. For example, for some of his experiments he used pea plants that had either pure yellow or pure green peas. When these plants were crossed, he did not obtain peas of an intermediate hue but only of the same pure yellow of one of the parents. This emphasis on inheritance of discrete characteristics supported the views of those who explained evolution in terms of gross mutations. Moreover, many were skeptical of the existence of natural selection. For example, as late as 1915, Johannsen saw no reason to assume that natural selection played a role in evolution: "Selection of differing individuals creates nothing new; a shift of the 'biological type' in the direction of selection has never been substantiated."[4]

---

3. Fleeming Jenkin, "Review of The Origin of Species," *The North British Review* 46 (June 1867): 277–318, reprinted in David L. Hull, *Darwin and His Critics: The Receptions of Darwin's Theory of Evolution by the Scientific Community* (Cambridge, MA: Harvard University Press, 1973), pp. 303–344.

4. W. L. Johannsen, "Experimentelle Grundlagen der Deszendenslehre. Variabilität, Vererbung, Kreuzung, Mutation," in Carl Chun and Wilhelm Johannsen, *Allgemeine Biologie*, Part III of *Kultur Der Gegenwort*, gen. ed. Paul Hinneberg (Leipzig: B. G. Teubner, 1915), vol. 1, ch. 4, p. 609;

The Evolutionary Synthesis

The second and third decades of the century saw a return to the theory of gradualistic evolution. The inadequacies of Darwin's original formulation were overcome by reconceptualizing variation and natural selection. From the combination of experimental and theoretical approaches to understanding these processes, the evolutionary synthesis was born.

A major emphasis of the evolutionary synthesis was to explain natural selection in mathematical terms. Especially in the work of R. A. Fisher, J. B. S. Haldane, and Sewall Wright, inheritance at the level of populations was explained through statistical models. Despite the highly theoretical nature of their contributions, their work was not divorced from experimentation. Fisher's work in quantifying variation and natural selection typified this synthesis of mathematics and empirical research. Using Muller's experiments, he showed how variation by micromutation could be estimated. The result was an indication of the rate at which variations entered populations. Next, he was able to specify the degree of selection by environmental factors. Either by comparing the differential rate of increase of two or more populations or by measuring changes of gene frequency within single populations, he was able to propose a statistical model of natural selection.

For all of Fisher's interest in natural populations, he was still a mathematician with little training in biology. At the other end of the mathematical/experimental continuum was H. J. Muller. By exposing genes to mutation-inducing x rays, Muller was able to show the influence of environment on variation. But before the various strands of the evolutionary synthesis could be braided together, populations had to be understood both statistically and as they occur in nature. Dobzhansky, Simpson, and Mayr were particularly adept at this task.

When we consider Dobzhansky's background, it is easy to see why he made such an important contribution to the evolutionary synthesis. His early training with Sergei Chetverikov emphasized population genetics. In 1927 he traveled to the United States to work with Muller's mentor, T. H. Morgan. By combining Morgan's stress on experimentation with the Russian statistical approach, Dobzhansky broke new ground in the genetics of free-living populations. This is evident even in his early research on variations of

---

quoted here from Ernst Mayr, "Prologue: Some Thoughts on the History of the Evolutionary Synthesis," in *The Evolutionary Synthesis: Perspectives on the Unification of Biology*, ed. Ernst Mayr and William B. Provine (Cambridge, MA: Harvard University Press, 1980), pp. 1–8, esp. p. 7.

Drosophila in isolated mountain ranges.[5] More influential, however, was his *Genetics and the Origin of Species*, published in 1937.[6]

Among those stimulated by this book was George Gaylord Simpson. As a paleontologist, his contacts with colleagues within his profession contributed little to his training in evolutionary theory. Paleontologists in the 1930s were more concerned with descriptive systematics than with the foundations of evolution. Consequently, Simpson relied on studies by people outside his discipline, including works by Fisher, Haldane, Wright, and Dobzhansky.[7] After the 1930s, he also had personal contacts with Dobzhansky and Mayr.[8] The high degree to which he assimilated populational approaches is evident in his *Tempo and Mode in Evolution*, published in 1944. His conclusions were in marked contrast to those of the Mendelians, whose position had been dominant a few years earlier. Simpson acknowledged the importance of variation but rejected macromutations:

> Single mutations with large, fully discrete, localized phenotypic effects are most easily studied; but paleontological and other evidence suggests that these are relatively unimportant at any level of evolution.[9]

His view of natural selection was diametrically opposed to that of Johannsen. According to Simpson, "Selection is a truly creative force and not solely negative in action. It is one of the crucial determinants of evolution."[10]

A third major figure in the history of the modern evolutionary synthesis began by studying neither bones nor fruit flies but birds. Unlike most other ornithologists of his day, however, Ernst Mayr worked in population genetics. Though Fisher, Haldane, and Wright had little influence on his early work, he was quickly attracted to the Russian school because of its emphasis on

---

5. R. C. Lewontin, John A. Moore, William B. Provine, and Bruce Wallace, eds., *Dobzhansky's Genetics of Natural Populations I–XLIII* (New York: Columbia University Press, 1981).

6. Theodosius Dobzhansky, *Genetics and the Origin of Species*, 3rd ed. (New York: Columbia University Press, 1951).

7. George Gaylord Simpson, *Concession to the Improbable: An Unconventional Autobiography* (New Haven, CT: Yale University Press, 1978), pp. 114–115.

8. Ernst Mayr, "George Gaylord Simpson," in Mayr and Provine, eds., *The Evolutionary Synthesis*, pp. 452–463, esp. p. 455.

9. George Gaylord Simpson, *Tempo and Mode in Evolution* (New York: Columbia University Press, 1944), p. 94.

10. Simpson, *Tempo and Mode in Evolution*, p. 96.

naturally occurring populations and taxonomy.[11] Mayr's central concern was speciation, which he thought could be discussed without recourse to large-scale mutations: "Speciation is explained by the geneticist on the assumption that through the gradual accumulation of mutational steps a threshold is finally crossed which signifies the evolution of a new species."[12] Similarly, natural selection played a key role for Mayr: "Even genes with a small selective advantage will eventually spread over entire populations."[13]

The Evolutionary Synthesis and Extraterrestrial Life

Simpson on the Nonprevalence of Humanoids

Now that we have seen how Darwin's notions of variation and selection were reformulated in the 1930s and 1940s by synthetic evolutionists, we are prepared to see the extent to which these ideas influenced later speculations on the possibility of extraterrestrial life. An appropriate starting point is Simpson's 1964 article "The Nonprevalence of Humanoids." In addition to drawing on evolutionary factors already mentioned above, Simpson discussed other considerations affecting the probability of life beyond Earth. He agreed with those who held that rudimentary macromolecules probably form from chemical processes, which should occur throughout the universe. But, Simpson said, this view did not commit him to the conclusion reached by many others, particularly physical scientists: that therefore more complex forms of life will also evolve.

To transition from chemical to biological activity, Simpson said three processes were required: "mutation, recombination, and selection."[14] (While two of these three are familiar from earlier discussions, recombination did not play as significant a role in the evolutionary synthesis.) The critical question for Simpson was whether or not these three factors interact in such a way as to make advanced

---

11. Ernst Mayr, "How I Became a Darwinian," in Mayr and Provine, eds., *The Evolutionary Synthesis*, pp. 413–423, esp. pp. 421–422.

12. Ernst Mayr, *Systematics and the Origin of Species: From the Viewpoint of a Zoologist* (New York: Columbia University Press, 1942), p. 67.

13. Mayr, *Systematics*, p. 293.

14. George Gaylord Simpson, "The Nonprevalence of Humanoids," *Science* 143, no. 3608 (1964): 769–775, esp. p. 772; reprinted in George Gaylord Simpson, *This View of Life* (New York: Harcourt, Brace, and World, 1964), pp. 253–271. For a related article see George Gaylord Simpson, "Some Cosmic Aspects of Organic Evolution," in *Evolution und Hominisation*, ed. Gottfried Kurth (Stuttgart: Gustav Fischer, 1962), pp. 6–20; also reprinted in Simpson, *This View of Life*, pp. 237–252.

forms of life a likely outcome of pre-biotic molecules. He argued that there are two ways to approach this issue: through the actual history of life on Earth and from theoretical considerations. In either case Simpson was not optimistic that the development of extraterrestrial life would be a common occurrence.

According to Simpson, paleontological evidence gave no indication of the inevitability of higher forms of life: "The fossil record shows very clearly that there is no central line leading steadily, in a goal-directed way, from a protozoan to man."[15] Variations are introduced through mutation, and individual differences are increased even more through recombination. Through interactions between the organisms and their environments, however, only a fraction of these variations will become established in the population. Given the combination of the numerous factors responsible for the evolution of any particular species, Simpson argued that terrestrial life is almost certainly unique:

> The existing species would surely have been different if the start had been different and if any stage of the histories of organisms and their environments had been different. . . . Man cannot be an exception to this rule. If the causal chain had been different, *Homo sapiens* would not exist.[16]

Dobzhansky Against the Convergent Evolution of Extraterrestrial Life

Though the thrust and conclusion of Dobzhansky's argument paralleled Simpson's line of reasoning, Dobzhansky discussed explicitly two issues that Simpson dealt with only in passing: chance and convergence in evolution. Dobzhansky isolated the same three factors of mutation, sexual recombination, and natural selection as central to evolution. But only the first two, he said, operate randomly; selection works against chance. While acknowledging that selection is probabilistic, he maintained that because it relates the individual and its environment through a feedback mechanism, it is an antichance process.

Dobzhansky's speculations about extraterrestrial life were consistent with the emphasis on mutation and selection in the early days of the evolutionary synthesis. While recognizing recombination as a factor in terrestrial evolution, when he committed himself to determining the characteristics that all life should possess, Dobzhansky mentioned only selection and mutation:

---

15. Simpson, "Nonprevalence," p. 773.
16. Simpson, "Nonprevalence," p. 773.

Despite all the uncertainties inevitable in dealing with a topic so speculative as extraterrestrial life, two inferences can be made. First, the genetic materials will be subject to mutation. Accurate self-copying is the prime function of any genetic materials, but it is hardly conceivable that no copy erors [sic] will ever be made. If such errors do occur, the second inference can be drawn: the variants that arise will set the stage for natural selection. This much must be a common denominator of terrestrial and extra-terrestrial life.[17]

Dobzhansky also addressed the issue of convergent versus divergent evolution. He pointed out that in many instances, organisms of disparate ancestries can have similar characteristics. As an example, he noted that fish and whales have similar forms because they both adapted to an aqueous environment. Some have held that because this sort of convergent evolution is so common on Earth, the process may be universal; therefore, the argument goes, extra-terrestrials may well resemble life-forms on Earth. Dobzhansky rejects this belief on the grounds that similar environments have frequently resulted in not *con*vergent but *di*vergent evolution.[18]

Dobzhansky concluded that, given the number of discrete interactions between organism and environment in the evolutionary history of the human species, the probability of humans evolving on another Earth-like planet is virtually zero. Even assuming the existence of another planet equipped with all of the life-forms that occurred in the Eocene period, the re-evolution of humankind would require the same mutations and the same selection on the roughly 50,000 genes that would have changed in *Homo sapiens* since then.[19]

Muller, Mutation, and Intelligence

When H. J. Muller addressed the question of life beyond Earth, it is not surprising that he emphasized mutation. What may seem more remarkable is that someone who played such an important role in the evolutionary synthesis still allowed for interplanetary convergence of intelligence. He agreed with Simpson and Dobzhansky about the importance of chance:

---

17. Theodosius Dobzhansky, "Darwinian Evolution and the Problem of Extraterrestrial Life," *Perspectives in Biology and Medicine* 15, no. 2 (1972): 157–175, esp. p. 170. For an earlier formulation of Dobzhansky's view, see Sol Tax, ed., *Evolution after Darwin*, vol. 1 (Chicago: University of Chicago Press, 1960).

18. Dobzhansky, "Darwinian Evolution," pp. 168–169.

19. Dobzhansky, "Darwinian Evolution," p. 173.

Just what steps will be taken at a particular point is sometimes a matter of accident: of what mutation manages to take hold, and then what combination of mutations, until some novel structure o[r] manner of functioning is thereby brought into being that acts as a key to open up an important new way of living.[20]

Though Muller believed a wide range of morphologies was possible, he regarded intelligence as the natural product of evolution.[21] This conviction may reflect the influence of one of his students, Carl Sagan.[22] Though Sagan worked with him for only one summer, Sagan said Muller "always kept in touch with him."[23] By the time Muller wrote the above article, the young Sagan had also published about life beyond Earth.

Mayr and the Importance of Chance

Though Mayr claimed his analysis was very similar to Simpson's, there were significant differences. Most obvious is Mayr's lesser emphasis on mechanisms of evolution. Instead, he provided an extended summary of the history of the human species. This choice may simply be a reflection of the time in which Mayr was writing. Dobzhansky, Simpson, and Muller all wrote first about extraterrestrials in the early 1960s. Mayr's article was written two decades later. By then the evolutionary synthesis may have been so widely accepted that a detailed justification of its basic tenets would have seemed superfluous. Nevertheless, throughout the piece, his discussion was guided by a belief in the importance of chance. Though his primary concern was to assess the likelihood of extraterrestrial intelligence, not merely multicellular life, he reached the same conclusions as Simpson.

Mayr amplified Dobzhansky's argument against the convergent evolution of intelligence by addressing the multiple emergence of vision on Earth. Many scholars have argued that evidence for the widespread occurrences of convergent evolution can be seen in the independent evolution of eyes in numerous species. Mayr's own studies led him to conclude that eyes have developed at

---

20. H. J. Muller, "Life Forms To Be Expected Elsewhere than on Earth," *Spaceflight* 5, no. 3 (1963): 74–85, esp. p. 80; reprinted from *The American Biology Teacher* 23, no. 6 (1961): 331–346.

21. Muller, "Life Forms To Be Expected Elsewhere than on Earth," p. 83.

22. Elof Axel Carlson, *Genes, Radiation, and Society: The Life and Work of H. J. Muller* (Ithaca, NY: Cornell University Press, 1981), p. 389.

23. Henry S. F. Cooper, Jr., *The Search for Life on Mars: Evolution of an Idea* (New York: Holt, Rinehart and Winston, 1980), pp. 42–43.

least 40 different times in unrelated lineages. By contrast, intelligence has evolved only once on Earth.[24]

Divergent Views of Extraterrestrial Life:
Outside and Within the Evolutionary Synthesis

Speculations prior to the 1970s by those not intimately involved with the evolutionary synthesis were less homogeneous than the views we have seen thus far. For example, in 1953 the anthropologist Loren Eiseley focused on the uniqueness of humankind. After examining mimicry among terrestrial organisms, he concluded that mimicry could not be used to argue for extraterrestrials' resembling life on Earth: "No animal is likely to be forced by the process of evolution to imitate, even superficially, a creature upon which it has never set eyes and with which it is in no form of competition."[25]

Even more fascinating is Eiseley's description of the opinion of cytologist Cyril D. Darlington. In Eiseley's words, Darlington "dwells enthusiastically on the advantages of two legs, a brain in one's head and the position of surveying the world from the splendid height of six feet."[26] Why would a contributor to the evolutionary synthesis hold a view so different from those of the other four key figures we have discussed? First, because Darlington was writing several years before the others, the evolutionary synthesis may not yet have solidified. Second, he favored Henry Fairfield Osborn's orthogenesis and Rensch's directed evolution, which held that evolution is teleological.[27]

Another anthropologist, William Howells, concluded in 1961 that extraterrestrial intelligence probably exists. He repeatedly contradicted mainstream views of the evolutionary synthesis, even suggesting on several occasions that evolution is a volitional process. For example, Howells said, "Intelligent creatures will have made a choice, early in evolution, of a nervous system which is more open to fresh impressions: a brain which can learn."[28] He thought such "choices" would likely lead to intelligence very human in appearance.

---

24. Ernst Mayr, "The Probability of Extraterrestrial Intelligent Life," in *Extraterrestrials: Science and Alien Intelligence*, ed. Edward Regis Jr. (Cambridge: Cambridge University Press, 1985), pp. 23–30. For a summary of Mayr's debate with Carl Sagan about the likelihood of extraterrestrial intelligence, see Stephen J. Garber, "A Political History of NASA's SETI Program," chapter 2 in this volume.

25. Loren C. Eiseley, "Is Man Alone in Space?," *Scientific American* 189, no. 7 (1953): 80–86, esp. p. 84.

26. Eiseley, "Is Man Alone in Space?," p. 81.

27. C. D. Darlington, *The Evolution of Man and Society* (New York: Simon and Schuster, 1969), p. 22.

28. William Howells, "The Evolution of 'Humans' on Other Planets," *Discovery* 22 (June 1961): 237–241, esp. p. 239.

Oceanographer and ecologist Robert Bieri's conclusions were similar to those of Howells, but the basis for Bieri's belief was more explicit. Bieri opened his 1964 article "Humanoids on Other Planets?" with a quotation from geneticist G. W. Beadle, against whom he proceeded to argue. In opposition to Beadle's assertion that there are an extraordinary number of evolutionary pathways open to life, Bieri stressed the limitations imposed by the properties of chemical elements and by the available "forms of energy."[29] Such constraints, Bieri wrote, are evident in the finite range of variability of terrestrial organisms. Because of these restrictions, organisms beyond Earth will conform to the same patterns imposed on life as we know it. After considering a number of characteristics that he thought would be universal, Bieri concluded with this prediction: "If we ever succeed in communicating with conceptualizing beings in outer space, they won't be spheres, pyramids, cubes, or pancakes. In all probability they will look an awful lot like us."[30]

Bacteriologist Francis Jackson and co-author astronomer Patrick Moore seemed less certain. At one point in their 1962 book, they declared it absurd to imagine that humans are constructed on an ideal model that would be followed on other planets.[31] Yet a few pages later, they stated: "It is by no means impossible that, on planets closely similar to the Earth, chemical and biological evolution might have followed a strikingly similar course, even occasionally to the production of men."[32] There is no absolute contradiction between these two views. However, it is noteworthy that Jackson and Moore were open to both possibilities.

As we examine later works, we see a variety of perspectives. Dale Russell, a paleontologist, was reluctant to generalize from evolution on Earth to extraterrestrial conditions. In only one sentence did he suggest that the existence of extraterrestrial life is by no means a foregone conclusion. Within the context of astrophysical considerations, he concluded, "It would seem that the origin of life is intrinsically a much more probable event than the origin of higher intelligence," a view recently echoed by paleontologist Peter Ward and astronomer

---

29. Robert Bieri, "Humanoids on Other Planets?," *American Scientist* 52, no. 4 (1964): 425–458, esp. pp. 452 and 457; see also G. W. Beadle, "The Place of Genetics in Modern Biology," Eleventh Annual Arthur Dehon Little Memorial Lecture (Cambridge: The Massachusetts Institute of Technology, 1959).

30. Bieri, "Humanoids on Other Planets?," p. 457.

31. Francis Jackson and Patrick Moore, *Life in the Universe* (London: Routledge and Kegan Paul, 1962), p. 115.

32. Jackson and Moore, *Life in the Universe*, p. 124.

Donald Brownlee in their *Rare Earth*.[33] Another paleontologist, C. Owen Lovejoy, was more definitive than Russell. Lovejoy believed that extraterrestrial intelligence could be quite common, but he distinguished this from cognition, which he reckoned would be much rarer beyond Earth. Because cognition as exemplified in humans is the result of our specific evolutionary path, said Lovejoy, the combination of events making cognition possible is highly unlikely to occur on most planets where intelligent life is present.[34]

In spite of the increasing trend to view the possibility of extraterrestrials in light of synthetic evolutionary theory, concerns remained about some of its founders' principles. Gerald Feinberg and Robert Shapiro, a physicist and a biochemist, rejected the assertion by space scientists Roger MacGowan and Frederick Ordway that "the majority of intelligent extrasolar land animals will be of the two legged and two armed variety."[35] Instead they pointed out, citing Simpson, that great divergences from terrestrial forms are possible through the joint action of mutation and natural selection. Yet they also maintained that "we will undoubtedly encounter [convergent evolution] on other worlds."[36] Paleontologist David Raup certainly understood the force of arguments against convergence toward humanoid forms elsewhere, but he countered that too little is known about the process of convergence to make any definitive claims. The evolution of other humanoids may be highly improbable, he wrote, but not necessarily impossible.[37]

Evolutionary paleobiologist Simon Conway Morris is certainly conversant with the evolutionary synthesis, but he emphasizes the ubiquity of convergence, contesting the view that historical contingencies makes it impossible to predict the likely forms of life on other worlds:

> Rerun the tape of the history of life, as S. J. Gould would have us believe, and the end result will be an utterly different biosphere.

---

33. Dale A. Russell, "Speculations on the Evolution of Intelligence in Multicellular Organisms," in *Life in the Universe*, ed. John Billingham (Cambridge: The MIT Press, 1981), pp. 259–275, esp. p. 270; Peter Ward and Donald Brownlee, *Rare Earth: Why Complex Life Is Uncommon in the Universe* (New York: Springer, 2000).

34. C. Owen Lovejoy, "Evolution of Man and Its Implications for General Principles of the Evolution of Intelligent Life," in Billingham, ed., *Life in the Universe*, pp. 317–329, esp. p. 327.

35. Roger A. MacGowan and Frederick I. Ordway III, *Intelligence in the Universe* (Englewood Cliffs, NJ: Prentice Hall, 1966), p. 240.

36. Gerald Feinberg and Robert Shapiro, *Life Beyond Earth: The Intelligent Earthling's Guide to Life in the Universe* (New York: William Morrow and Company, Inc. 1980), p. 411.

37. David M. Raup, "ETI without Intelligence," in Regis, ed., *Extraterrestrials*, pp. 31–42, esp. p. 36.

Most notably there will be nothing remotely like a human, so reinforcing the notion that any other biosphere, across the galaxy and beyond, must be as different as any other: perhaps things slithering across crepuscular mudflats, but certainly never the prospect of music, no sounds of laughter. Yet, what we know of evolution suggests the exact reverse: convergence is ubiquitous and the constraints of life make the emergence of the various biological properties very probable, if not inevitable. Arguments that the equivalent of *Homo sapiens* cannot appear on some distant planet miss the point: what is at issue is not the precise pathway by which we evolved, but the various and successive likelihoods of the evolutionary steps that culminated in our humanness.[38]

Among those supporting Conway Morris's emphasis on convergence are anthropologists Kathryn Coe, Craig T. Palmer, and Christina Pomianek, who note, "It is now time to take the implications of evolutionary theory a little more seriously, and convergence is the norm."[39] They also maintain that "evolutionary theory, theoretically, should apply anywhere to anything that is living," in a line of reasoning similar to that adopted by biologist Richard Dawkins in his argument for "Universal Darwinism."[40]

Two other tendencies have also emerged among nonphysical scientists: hardheaded theorizing and more free-form speculation. In a manner somewhat reminiscent of the earlier evolutionary systematists, James Valentine approached the question by distinguishing between microevolution, involving selection within a population, and macroevolution, dealing with evolution above the species level. He concluded that the microevolutionary details of life on another planet—e.g., their genetic materials—would probably be very different from those of their terrestrial counterparts. But macroevolution,

---

38. Simon Conway Morris, *Life's Solution: Inevitable Humans in a Lonely Universe* (Cambridge: Cambridge University Press, 2003), pp. 283–284.

39. Kathryn Coe, Craig T. Palmer, and Christina Pomianek, "ET Phone Darwin: What Can an Evolutionary Understanding of Animal Communication and Art Contribute to Our Understanding of Methods for Interstellar Communication?," in *Civilizations Beyond Earth: Extraterrestrial Life and Society*, ed. Douglas A. Vakoch and Albert A. Harrison (New York: Berghahn Books, 2011), pp. 214–225, esp. p. 219.

40. Coe, Palmer, and Pomianek, "ET Phone Darwin," p. 215; Richard Dawkins, "Universal Darwinism," in *Evolution from Microbes to Men*, ed. D. S. Bendall (Cambridge: Cambridge University Press, 1983), pp. 403–425.

he thought, should yield extraterrestrial patterns of "multicellular diversification" similar to the patterns seen on Earth.[41]

Imagination reigned in Bonnie Dalzell's 1974 exhibit of possible alien creatures for the Smithsonian, which drew upon her artistic talent as well as her background in paleontology.[42] By hypothesizing planets that vary from Earth in gravity and temperature, she imagined environments that would foster a wide variety of land-bound, aquatic, and aerial life. Anthropologist Doris Jonas and psychiatrist David Jonas, by contrast, considered not only the morphology but also the possible perceptual worlds of extraterrestrials. Though their work was not as informed by theory as that of some of the contributors to the evolutionary synthesis, their basic tenet was the same:

> One thing is for certain: we have no reason to assume that evolutionary forces on other planets will produce forms or intelligences that are the same as ours even though the basic raw materials must be similar. Whatever chance factors combine to produce any form of life, infinitely more must combine to produce an advanced form.[43]

Conclusion

Some of the most incisive arguments for and against the possibility of extraterrestrial life have come from scientists who have only a passing interest in the question. Their views typically were more influenced by their professional work in their own disciplines than by more extended contacts with others interested in life beyond Earth. Thus, when trying to evaluate their positions, it is vital to understand the conceptual frameworks within which their speculations arose. One theoretical framework that played a major role in the 20th and 21st centuries is modern evolutionary theory. By examining the extent to which this paradigm has impacted various fields over the past few decades, we can better understand the diversity of views about extraterrestrial life held by scientists from a variety of disciplines.

---

41. James W. Valentine, "Emergence and Radiation of Multicellular Organisms," in Billingham, ed., *Life in the Universe*, pp. 229–257, esp. p. 253.

42. Bonnie Dalzell, "Exotic Bestiary for Vicarious Space Voyagers," *Smithsonian Magazine* 5 (October 1974): 84–91.

43. Doris Jonas and David Jonas, *Other Senses, Other Worlds* (New York: Stein and Day, 1976), p. 9.

CHAPTER THIRTEEN

Biocultural Prerequisites for the Development of Interstellar Communication

Garry Chick

In 1961, astronomer Frank Drake developed a formula for estimating the number of extraterrestrial civilizations in our galaxy via the quantification of what he felt to be seven relevant factors. The Drake Equation contains two terms, f_i and f_c, that refer, respectively, to the fraction of planets that harbor intelligent life and the fraction of those with intelligent life capable of developing a technology that would allow communication with other worlds. These terms are two of the most difficult in the equation for which to estimate values, and, not surprisingly, a wide range of values has been offered for each. Estimates of these values depend on a number of conjectures and assumptions about the nature of intelligence; aspects of embodiment, such as sensory modalities and faculties to manipulate the environment; and aspects of culture that seem to be crucial for the development of advanced technology. The only data we have on the technological development necessary for interstellar communication come from our own experience here on Earth. While numerous Earthly species use technologies, only the technologies created by humans qualify as complex. Similarly, many species show various forms of intelligence and even some nonhuman species are also said to have culture, depending on how that word is defined. My purpose is to examine how intelligence, embodiment, culture, and their interactions, based on what we know of their Earthly manifestations, might affect the values of Drake's two most contested terms.

The Drake Equation

In an attempt to quantify the number of civilizations capable of interstellar communication in the Milky Way galaxy, Frank Drake proposed the following equation:

$$N = R^* \cdot f_p \cdot n_e \cdot f_l \cdot f_i \cdot f_c \cdot L,$$

where

N is the number of civilizations in our galaxy capable of interstellar communication

R^* is the rate of star formation per year in the galaxy

f_p is the fraction of stars with planets

n_e is average number of habitable planets per star with planets

f_l is the fraction of habitable planets that develop life

f_i is the fraction of planets with life that develop intelligent life

f_c is the fraction of intelligent civilizations able (and willing) to communicate

and L is the expected lifetime of such civilizations.

There are several excellent online calculators for the Drake Equation, but the one provided by the *NOVA* "Origins" series is especially attractive and user-friendly.[1] These calculators permit interested parties to plug in their own estimates for the parameter values described above, but they simultaneously raise troubling questions: Are the parameter values in the Drake Equation any more than just guesses? Are they even "'informed guesses'"? In a 2003 address at the California Institute of Technology, author Michael Crichton discussed this aspect of the Drake Equation:

> This serious-looking equation gave SETI a serious footing as a legitimate intellectual inquiry. The problem, of course, is that none of the terms can be known, and most cannot even be estimated. The only way to work the equation is to fill in with guesses. And guesses—just so we're clear—are merely expressions of prejudice. Nor can there be "informed guesses." If you need to state how many planets with life choose to communicate, there is simply no way to make an informed guess. It is simply prejudice.[2]

Crichton went on to claim that since the Drake Equation cannot be tested, SETI is therefore based not on science but on faith. It is possible, however, to bring relevant data to bear on the issue of extraterrestrial intelligence, as I hope to demonstrate here.

---

1. Public Broadcasting System, "The Drake Equation," 2004, available at *http://www.pbs.org/wgbh/nova/space/drake-equation.html*.

2. Michael Crichton, "Aliens Cause Global Warming," Caltech Michelin Lecture, 17 January 2003, available at *http://www.michaelcrichton.net*.

Drake Parameter Estimates

The parameters of the Drake Equation have been estimated numerous times using methods that range from pure guessing to various sorts of statistical analyses. The initial values assigned by Drake and his colleagues to each parameter are as follows:

$$R^* = 10.0/\text{year}$$
$$f_p = 0.5$$
$$n_e = 2.0$$
$$f_l = 1.0$$
$$f_i = 0.01$$
$$f_c = 0.01$$
$$L = 10,000 \text{ years}$$

These estimates produce a value of 0.01 for N.

Using redefined variables, Carl Sagan generated a different set of values:[3]

$$R^* = 4.0 \times 10^{11}$$
$$f_p = 0.33$$
$$n_e = 2.0$$
$$f_l = 0.33$$
$$f_i = 0.1$$
$$f_c = 0.1$$
$$L = 0.01$$

These values result in a value of approximately 10^7 for N, an estimate wildly different from the one proposed 19 years earlier by Drake and his colleagues. According to the PBS *NOVA* "Origins" series,[4] Drake's current estimated values are:

$$R^* = 5.0/\text{year}$$
$$f_p = 0.5$$
$$n_e = 2.0$$
$$f_l = 1.0$$
$$f_i = 0.2$$
$$f_c = 1.0$$
$$L = 10,000 \text{ years}$$

---

3. Carl Sagan, *Cosmos* (New York: Random House, 1980), p. 301. Sagan also redefined R^* as "the number of stars in the Milky Way Galaxy" and L as "the fraction of a planetary lifetime graced by a technical civilization" (p. 299). These changes obviously lead to a very different estimate of N.
4. Public Broadcasting System, "The Drake Equation."

These values give an N of 10,000 communicating civilizations in the Milky Way.

The difficulty with these values is that they are merely estimates. I believe there are empirical means by which these estimates can be enhanced. To do so, we must reevaluate some known facts in order to narrow our estimates of the two most intractable terms in Drake's formula, f_i and f_c. First, however, we will look at how the other parameters have been estimated.

Over the past half century, R^* has generally been defined as the rate of star formation per year in the galaxy. However, it has also been defined as the rate of formation of *suitable* stars, meaning Sun-like stars rather than, for example, red giants. Thus, estimates range from about 20 stars of all sorts to 1 Sun-like star per year. Carl Sagan defined R^* simply as "the number of stars in the Milky Way Galaxy," without referring to their rate of formation.[5] The huge difference between the rate of star formation and the number of stars in the galaxy is a discrepancy that profoundly influences the results of the equation.

When R^* is defined as the rate of star formation per year in the galaxy or as the rate of suitable star formation in the galaxy, its approximate value can be roughly calculated on the basis of observed data; and most estimates that use one of these definitions generate values between about 5 and 20. There is, however, much less data to inform our estimates of Drake's other parameters. What do we know about f_p, the fraction of stars with planets? The first confirmed exoplanet was discovered orbiting the star 51 Pegasi in October 1995. As of 27 February 2012, a total of 1,790 host stars with 2,321 extrasolar planet candidates had been detected.[6] NASA's Kepler mission team recently located the first confirmed rocky planet orbiting a star other than the Sun. Named Kepler-10b and approximately 1.4 times the size of Earth, this planet was found on the basis of data gathered by the Kepler space telescope between May 2009 and January 2010.[7] Kepler-10b's orbit takes less than a day, indicating that it is more than 20 times closer to its star than Mercury is to the Sun and must therefore be blazing hot and uninhabitable.[8]

In June 2002, Geoffrey Marcy of the University of California at Berkeley and Paul Butler of the Carnegie Institution in Washington announced their

---

5. Sagan, *Cosmos*, p. 299.

6. NASA, "Planet Candidates," *http://kepler.nasa.gov/Mission/discoveries/candidates/* (accessed 26 March 2012); see also *http://exoplanets.newscientistapps.com/*.

7. NASA, "NASA's Kepler Mission Discovers Its First Rocky Planet," *http://www.nasa.gov/topics/universe/features/rocky_planet.html* (accessed 30 January 2011).

8. NASA, "Kepler Discoveries," *http://kepler.nasa.gov/Mission/discoveries/* (accessed 21 July 2013). As of 21 July 2013, NASA's Kepler team had a confirmed planet count of 135.

discovery of a planet approximately 4 times as massive as Jupiter orbiting the star 55 Cancri at a distance of about 500 million miles; 55 Cancri is about the same mass and age as the Sun and is located about 41 light-years from Earth in the constellation Cancer. This massive planet takes 14 years to complete a single orbit, and its enormous gravity may draw cosmic debris away from other planets orbiting closer to 55 Cancri, thus protecting them from comet and asteroid impacts just as Jupiter protects Earth.

Four additional planets have since been found closer to 55 Cancri. The planet closest to the star is about the size of Neptune and orbits in about three days. The second planet is slightly smaller than Jupiter and orbits in 14.7 days, while the third is similar in size to Saturn and completes its orbit every 44 days. The fourth planet, the most recently discovered, is about 45 times as large as Earth and appears to be similar to Saturn in composition. It completes its orbit in 260 days. While no Earth-like planets have been discovered orbiting 55 Cancri, all of the gas-giant in our solar system are orbited by large, rocky moons. It appears that some of these, such as Enceladus, a moon of Saturn, and Europa and Callisto, two of Jupiter's moons, may have underground liquid water and, potentially, the ingredients necessary for life.[9]

In addition to gas-giant planets, "super-Earth" planets may orbit up to a third of stars.[10] These planets are only slightly larger than Earth and may be rocky rather than gaseous. At least 45 super-Earth planets are known, but nearly all orbit so close to their stars as to render them incapable of supporting life. The Sun-like star HD 40307, about 42 light-years from Earth, appears to be orbited by at least three super-Earth planets.[11] Discovery of the smallest super-Earth planet, Gliese 581 e (only 1.9 Earth masses), was announced on 21 April 2009. Its orbit is much too close to its star to be habitable, but another super-Earth planet, Gliese 581 d, found on 24 April 2007, appears to be about 8 Earth masses and far enough from its star so that liquid water could be present. The star Gliese 581 is in the constellation Libra and is about 20 light-years from Earth. It is a red dwarf approximately one-third the size of the Sun, and it appears to have at least four planets.[12] Kepler-22b is the first confirmed extra-solar planet known to orbit in the "habitable zone"—that is, where liquid water

---

9. NASA, "Callisto Makes a Big Splash," 2009, available at *http://science.nasa.gov/newhome/headlines/ast22oct98_2.htm* (accessed 17 July 2009).

10. D. Vergano, "'Super-Earth' Planets Discovered," *USA Today*, available at *http://www.usatoday.com/tech/science/space/2008-06-16-super-Earth-planets_N.htm* (accessed 17 July 2009).

11. Vergano, "'Super-Earth' Planets Discovered."

12. M. Mayor et al., "The HARPS Search for Southern Extra-solar Planets. XVII. An Earth-Mass Planet in the GJ 581 Planetary System," *Astronomy & Astrophysics*, ms. no. GJ 581 (2009).

could exist on its surface—of a Sun-like star. It is approximately 2.4 times the radius of Earth, and its surface composition is unknown.[13]

The Sun, although often misleadingly referred to in the popular press as an "average star," is classified on the Hertzsprung-Russell (H-R) Diagram as a Type G2V star. The H-R Diagram plots star color (an indicator of surface temperature) in relation to luminosity (an indicator of intrinsic brightness) and shows star color, temperature, luminosity, spectral type, and evolutionary stage, although it does not indicate the frequency of the types. A G2V star such as the Sun is a main-sequence yellow dwarf, which is, in our own galaxy, a relatively uncommon type. Up to 90 percent of the approximately 400 billion stars in the Milky Way are (Type M) red dwarfs, while Sun-like stars constitute only about 5 percent.[14] Red dwarfs, both smaller and cooler than the Sun, emit large x-ray bursts but not much ultraviolet radiation. The former is not favorable for life as we know it, while the latter may be essential. Nevertheless, Todd Henry suggests that more attention be paid to M-type stars because, while their habitable zones are very narrow, there are so many more of them than G-type stars that the odds of M-type stars having planets in the habitable zone is fairly high.[15]

In 2003, Charles Lineweaver and Daniel Grether suggested that at least 20 percent of Sun-like stars have planets, but recent estimates are much higher.[16] Alan Boss, for example, proposes that every Sun-like star may, on average, have one Earth-like planet, meaning that there could be as many as 100 billion Earth-like planets in the Milky Way galaxy alone.[17]

The value of f_l, the fraction of hospitable planets that actually develop life, has generally been thought to be very high, usually 1.0. Given that life developed on Earth soon after it cooled enough to permit liquid water, and that life on Earth inhabits a very wide range of ecologies, this estimate seems reasonable. The estimates of f_i and f_c, however, are far more uncertain than those for any of the previous terms in the equation.

---

13. NASA, "NASA's Kepler Mission Confirms Its First Planet in Habitable Zone of Sun-like Star," available at *http://www.nasa.gov/mission_pages/kepler/news/kepscicon-briefing.html* (accessed 26 March 2012).

14. Maggie Turnbull, "SETI and the Smallest Stars," 2004, available at *http://donate.seti.org/page.aspx?pid=1012* (accessed 31 August 2013).

15. "M Dwarfs: The Search for Life Is On: Interview with Todd Henry," *Astrobiology Magazine*, available at *http://www.astrobio.net/interview/1694/m-dwarfs-the-search-for-life-is-on* (accessed 21 July 2013).

16. C. H. Lineweaver and D. Grether, "What Fraction of Sun-like Stars Have Planets?," *The Astrophysical Journal* 598, no. 2 (2003): 1350–1360.

17. Alan Boss, *The Crowded Universe: The Search for Living Planets* (New York: Basic Books, 2009).

Estimating f_i

According to the Principle of Mediocrity, Earth, the solar system, our location in the Milky Way, the Milky Way galaxy, and its location in the universe are not special in any sense.[18] Hence, Earth is representative of other Earth-like planets in other Sun-like solar systems. So, while any data we can bring to bear on f_i—the fraction of planets with life that develop intelligent life—is based on a sample size of only 1, those data are nevertheless valid and reliable. But what evidence do we actually have? How many "intelligent" species have existed on Earth?

Intelligence

Like many, if not most, constructs in the social and behavioral sciences, the nature of intelligence has been under scrutiny for more than a century, but no single, universally accepted definition presently exists. In a general sense, however, two definitions seem to cover the territory. The first definition, proposed in a letter signed by 52 scholars with expertise in intelligence and related fields, appeared in the 13 December 1994 issue of *The Wall Street Journal* in response to exchanges over Charles Murray and Richard Herrnstein's book *The Bell Curve*:

> Intelligence is a very general mental capability that, among other things, involves the ability to reason, plan, solve problems, think abstractly, comprehend complex ideas, learn quickly and learn from experience. It is not merely book learning, a narrow academic skill, or test-taking smarts. Rather, it reflects a broader and deeper capability for comprehending our surroundings—"catching on," "making sense" of things, or "figuring out" what to do.[19]

The second was offered by the American Psychological Association in 1995:

---

18. David J. Darling, "Mediocrity, Principle of," *Encyclopedia of Astrobiology, Astronomy and Spaceflight,* 2005, *http://www.daviddarling.info/encyclopedia/M/mediocrity.html* (accessed 29 June 2013).

19. Linda S. Gottfredson, "Mainstream Science on Intelligence," available at *http://www.udel.edu/educ/gottfredson/reprints/1994WSJmainstream.pdf* (accessed 1 July 2013) and *http://www.udel.edu/educ/gottfredson/reprints/1997mainstream.pdf* (accessed 1 July 2013). See also C. Murray and R. J. Herrnstein, *The Bell Curve: Intelligence and Class Structure in American Life* (New York: Free Press, 1994).

Individuals differ from one another in their ability to understand complex ideas, to adapt effectively to the environment, to learn from experience, to engage in various forms of reasoning, to overcome obstacles by taking thought. Although these individual differences can be substantial, they are never entirely consistent: a given person's intellectual performance will vary on different occasions, in different domains, as judged by different criteria. Concepts of "intelligence" are attempts to clarify and organize this complex set of phenomena.[20]

Intelligence is very commonly addressed from a psychometric perspective; that is, intelligence is effectively what is measured by tests such as the Stanford-Binet, the Wechsler Adult Intelligence Test, and others. Scores on such tests, recorded as *IQ* (Intelligence Quotient) or *g* (General Intelligence) numbers, are considered reliable even though their validity has often been challenged. Critics question whether they can accurately measure the range of what should be thought of as intelligence. Largely in response to this issue, psychologists such as Howard Gardiner and Robert J. Sternberg have proposed theories of multiple intelligences, each of which may be possessed in greater or lesser quantities.[21] Sternberg offers a triarchic theory wherein intelligence involves the degree to which individuals successfully adapt to environmental changes throughout their life-span.[22] He identifies three aspects of intelligence—analytic, creative, and practical—only one of which, the analytic, is usually addressed by intelligence tests. Analytic questions typically have one "right" answer, while practical questions may have several correct responses. Gardiner included verbal-linguistic and mathematical-logical intelligences, mirroring the categories used by traditional intelligence tests. He also included visual-spatial, body-kinesthetic, auditory-musical, and inter- and intra-personal communication, for a total of seven "intelligences" ("naturalism" is sometimes included as an eighth). Gardiner argues that psychometric tests ignore aspects of intelligence beyond the verbal, logical, and

---

20. "Intelligence: Knowns and Unknowns," Report of a Task Force established by the Board of Scientific Affairs of the American Psychological Association, 7 August 1995, available at *http://www.lrainc.com/swtaboo/taboos/apa_01.html*.

21. Howard Gardiner, *Frames of Mind: The Theory of Multiple Intelligence* (New York: Basic Books, 1985); R. J. Sternberg, *Beyond IQ: A Triarchic Theory of Intelligence* (Cambridge: Cambridge University Press, 1985).

22. Sternberg, *Beyond IQ.*

some aspects of spatial both in the types of questions asked and in how the tests are administered (i.e., pencil and paper or by computer).

There is an enormous amount of literature on the nature of intelligence and its measurement. The question that concerns me here, however, is this: What sort of intelligence do we have in mind when we talk of extraterrestrial intelligence? While Gardiner's theory of multiple intelligences lacks wide support, Sternberg and others feel that intelligence cannot be reduced to a single number such as *IQ* or *g*. What sort of intelligence might an extraterrestrial require in order to develop a technological civilization capable of interstellar communication?

Which of Earth's Animals Are "Intelligent"?

Given the two definitions of intelligence quoted above and setting aside for the moment the possibility of various sorts of multiple intelligences, which animals can be considered the most intelligent? Often we judge the animals that behave most like humans to be the most intelligent. We therefore regard great apes (chimpanzees, bonobos, gorillas, orangutans) as quite intelligent. Since the use of tools signals intelligence, and since each of these species uses tools, they are pretty smart in our book. Although tool use among Cetaceans (specifically, the bottlenose dolphin) has been observed only recently, dolphins, whales, and porpoises are generally deemed very bright, as well. All mammals appear to engage in at least some pre-adult learning from parents and others. Some birds, such as crows and parrots, appear to be precocious. The African gray parrot, for example, seems to be remarkably adept at both linguistic and cognitive activities. Cephalopods (octopus, squid, cuttlefish, nautilus) are thought the most intelligent of nonvertebrates. Indeed, researchers claim to have observed play behavior, a strong correlate of cortical development, in the octopus.[23]

The nature of chimpanzee and gorilla intelligence is undoubtedly similar to our own, but what of dolphin intelligence or octopus intelligence? Does the notion of a dolphin *IQ* or *g* in an octopus make any sense? If we were to apply Gardiner's criteria for intelligence to dolphins or octopi, we might make a case for both having very high body-kinesthetic and visual-spatial intelligence. Dolphins might also rate highly in terms of intra- and interpersonal communication as well as auditory-musical intelligence. They could even demonstrate mathematical-logical intelligence. Since we have been unable

---

23. Garry Chick, "What Is Play For? Sexual Selection and the Evolution of Play," *Play and Culture Studies* 3 (2001): 3–25; Robert F. Service, "Random Samples: Suckers for Fun," *Science* 281, no. 5379 (1998): 909.

to decipher their "language" of whistles, clicks, and so on, no meaningful assessment of their verbal-linguistic intelligence can be made.

What Good Is Intelligence?

Why and how did humans end up being as intelligent as we are? While the exact course of human evolution is open to debate, one distinctive feature of hominids from the earliest period to the present is increasing brain size and complexity. Why this happens is not clear, although theories abound. Intelligence is not required for evolutionary success as measured either in terms of the number of individual organisms or in biomass. The biomass of Antarctic krill (*Euphausia superba*), for example, is estimated to be between 125 million and 6 billion metric tons.[24] Oceanic bacteria comprise perhaps 150 times the cumulative biomass of humans and, given their size, are many orders of magnitude greater in number.

Nevertheless, intelligence surely helped our evolutionary ancestors in the struggle to survive since humans have few other natural weapons. There is now only one human species despite evidence that two or more may have existed simultaneously at one or more times in the past. Perhaps our direct ancestors contributed to the demise of our less-well-adapted relatives. Over the past few decades, we have all but exterminated our hominoid relatives (along with numerous other species). However, the crucial adaptation after the ancestors of both humans and chimpanzees diverged seems to have been not intelligence but an upright stance. Indeed, some estimates place an upright stance some 2 million years prior to encephalization and 500,000 years prior to tool manufacture and use.[25] The key here, by the way, is *manufacture* and use, as all other extant hominoids use tools but do not necessarily manufacture them.

---

24. "Krill (*Euphausiacea*)," *National Geographic*, 2009, available at *http://animals. nationalgeographic.com/animals/invertebrates/krill.html* (accessed 17 July 2009); Stephen Nicol and Yoshinari Endo, *Krill Fisheries of the World*, FAO Fisheries Technical Paper 367 (Rome: Food and Agriculture Organization of the United Nations, 1997), available at *http:// www.fao.org/docrep/003/w5911e/w5911e00.HTM* (accessed 17 July 2009); "Who's Eating Who?," Classroom Antarctica, 2005, available at *http://www.antarctica.gov.au/__data/assets/ pdf_file/0003/20793/ml_394205001041667_2_whoseatingwho_lowlife.pdf* (accessed 30 August 2013).

25. Tim D. White, Gen Suwa, and Berhane Asfaw, "*Australopithecus ramidus*, A New Species of Early Hominid from Aramis, Ethiopia," *Nature* 371 (1994):306–312; Sileshi Semaw et al., "2.6-Million-Year-Old Stone Tools and Associated Bones from OGS-6 and OGS-7, Gona, Afar, Ethiopia," *Journal of Human Evolution* 45, no. 2 (2003): 169–177.

In 2005, Mark Flinn, David Geary, and Carol Ward reviewed theories of why hominids developed high intelligence and found little evidence for the majority of them.[26] Environmentally based theories failed to explain why other animals that faced ecological problems similar to those likely confronting early humans did not evolve similar cognitive abilities. Explanations that posited intelligence as a social tool explanations ran into like problems. Social group size and brain size correlate across many taxa, and hominid group size appears to have been about the same as that of other extant hominoids.[27] So why did other social species not develop high intelligence?

Richard Alexander's ecological dominance-social competition hypothesis offers an answer to this question.[28] Briefly, Alexander theorizes that hominids became the "ecologically dominant" species, meaning that selection pressure on them gradually shifted from external causes (e.g., predators, climate, resources) to internal ones (that is, interactions with members of their own species). Flinn et al. present evidence that supports the ecological-dominance hypothesis and that indicates "significant increases of ecological dominance roughly coincided with the appearance of *H. erectus*."[29] They do not, however, speculate on how pre-*Homo* human ancestors established ecological dominance while other hominids did not.

Intelligence and the Ability To Manipulate the Environment

Cetaceans and cephalopods have yet another problem. Even if they are deemed intelligent according to one or more of Gardiner's criteria, they fail in terms

---

26. Mark V. Flinn, David C. Geary, and Carol V. Ward, "Ecological Dominance, Social Competition, and Coalitionary Arms Races: Why Humans Developed Extraordinary Intelligence," *Evolution and Human Behavior* 26, no. 1 (2005): 10–46.

27. H. Kudo, and R. I. M. Dunbar, "Neocortex Size and Social Network Size in Primates," *Animal Behaviour* 62, no. 4 (2001): 711–722; Carel P. van Schaik and Robert O. Deaner, "Life History and Cognitive Evolution in Primates," in *Animal Social Complexity: Intelligence, Culture, and Individualized Societies*, ed. Frans B. M. de Waal and Peter L. Tyack (Cambridge, MA: Harvard University Press, 2003), pp. 5–25.

28. Flinn et al., "Ecological Dominance," passim; Richard D. Alexander, "Evolution of the Human Psyche," in *The Human Revolution: Behavioural and Biological Perspectives on the Origins of Modern Humans*, ed. Paul Mellars and Chris Stringer (Princeton, NJ: Princeton University Press, 1989), pp. 455–513. Animals such as lions, elephants, dolphins, and orcas seem to be ecologically dominant, and their reproductive success appears to be influenced heavily by interactions with conspecifics.

29. Flinn et al., "Ecological Dominance," p. 22.

of J. L. Casti's requirements for the emergence of intelligence.[30] Casti points out that interstellar communication requires tool-making, and he identifies the conditions necessary for developing such technology:

1. Development of an atmosphere containing free oxygen
2. Migration of life from the sea to land
3. Emergence of hands and eyes
4. Use of tools
5. Appearance of social structures[31]

Leaving aside the issue of an oxygen-rich atmosphere, what about the other criteria? First, if movement from sea to land is required, the cetaceans have it backwards, as their ancestors were land-dwellers. Cephalopod tentacles, while apparently handy in the water, are all but useless out of it. Second, some sort of hand-like appendages are essential for making and using tools. Various creatures grasp and manipulate food or objects by means of claws (e.g., crabs, lobsters, scorpions, praying mantises), their bodies (e.g., snakes), their mouths (e.g., dogs), mouthparts (e.g., ants), or beaks (e.g., birds). None of these means seem to be as effective as hands, however. Many animals also have eyes or some type of light-sensing organ, and eyes come in many designs. Whether sight evolved independently in insects, vertebrates, and mollusks, for example, or whether the same genetic structure underlies all eyes remains in dispute.[32] Moreover, some species whose ancestors had eyes have lost them (e.g., cave-dwelling fish and insects), while others augment eyesight with other sensory or signaling apparatus such as echolocation (e.g., bats and cetaceans), electric fields (e.g., eels), or light-producing organs (e.g., fireflies and many species of deep-sea animals). Still, complex eyes dominate. Tomarev et al. note that while only 6 of 30 animal phyla have complex eyes, these 6 are the dominant animals on the planet.[33] They estimate that 95 percent of all animal species have complex eyes based on about a dozen different designs.

Intelligence and Technological Development

So how do Casti's criteria apply to f_i? If Casti is right, aquatic species will never develop substantial technologies. So we can eliminate cephalopods and cetaceans, however "intelligent," from our list of potential communicators

---

30. J. L. Casti, *Paradigms Lost: Tackling the Unanswered Mysteries of Modern Science* (New York: Avon Books, 1989).

31. Casti, *Paradigms Lost*, pp. 357–359.

32. Stanislav I. Tomarev et al., "Squid Pax-6 and Eye Development," *Proceedings of the National Academy of Sciences U.S.A.* 94, no. 6 (1997): 2421–2426.

33. Tomarev et al., "Squid Pax-6 and Eye Development," p. 2421.

via technology and, therefore, any similar species that might exist on extra-solar planets. Somewhere between 1.5 and 2 million living species have been cataloged on Earth, and estimates for the actual number of species run much higher (generally between 2 and 50 million but some up to 100 million). Of these, there are about 800 known living species of cephalopods and about 80 living species of cetaceans. Hence, cetaceans constitute less than 0.05 percent (0.0005) of extant species even when using only 2 million as an estimate for the total number of living species. There are currently approximately 18 to 20 species in the superfamily *Hominoidea* (apes and humans). These include 12 species divided among 4 genera of the family *Hylobatidae* and 6, or possibly 7, species in the family *Hominidae*, which comprises humans, gorillas (1 or 2 species), chimpanzees (2 species), and orangutans (2 species).[34] When 20 species of hominoids are included in that total of 2 million extant species, primates constitute only 0.001 percent (0.00001) of the living species on Earth. Moreover, only 1 of these 20 species has developed a technology capable of interstellar communication. In sum, the development of high intelligence on Earth has been extremely rare, and there is little evidence to support the idea that its development is inevitable. Even if some forms of intelligence do evolve on other planets, there is no good reason to believe that at least one of them must be human-like. Hence, high estimates of f_i may be not only anthropocentric but also highly optimistic.

At least three significant unanswered questions remain:

1. Why is high intelligence worth having?
2. Why, if it is worth having, did it develop only once in more than 3.5 billion years of biological evolution on Earth?
3. How did it evolve at all?

The answers to these questions, assuming we ever discover them, will allow much more precise estimates of f_i than we are presently capable of producing.

Estimating f_c

Drake defined f_c as the fraction of intelligent civilizations both able and willing to communicate. The concept of *civilization* seemingly eliminates the

---

34. Gibbon Conservation Center, *http://www.gibboncenter.org/about_gibbons.htm*; "Animal Info—Gorilla," AnimalInfo.org, *http://www.animalinfo.org/species/primate/gorigori.htm*; P. Myers et al., The Animal Diversity Web, *http://animaldiversity.org* (accessed 25 October 2005); "All about Orangutans!" Orangutan Foundation International, *http://www.orangutan.org/facts/orangutanfacts.php*.

possibility that intelligence could appear in forms other than collectives of organisms. So Fred Hoyle's fictional *Black Cloud*, an intelligent entity composed of a network of disparate molecules that arrives at our solar system, discovers intelligent life on Earth, and proceeds to communicate, is ruled out.[35] Hive intelligence—exhibited by social animals such as ants, termites, and many bees and portrayed, always negatively, in science fiction (in films such as *Invasion of the Body Snatchers*, on television with *Star Trek*'s Borg, and in novels such as Arthur C. Clarke's *Childhood's End*)—also appears to be out.[36] So what must a collective of individually intelligent organisms have in order to develop a means of interstellar communication? Minimally, they must be able to develop information, share it, and work cooperatively. That means they must have a culture and some sort of social organization.

What Is Culture?

Definitions of culture abound; in their 1952 book, A. L. Kroeber and Clyde Kluckhohn identified more than 160 definitions, and many more have been developed since then.[37] Edward Burnett Tylor offered the first definition of culture from an anthropological perspective in 1871, describing it as "that complex whole which includes knowledge, belief, art, law, morals, custom, and any other capabilities and habits acquired by man as a member of society."[38] While Tylor's gloss is still useful, a more cognitively oriented definition may have greater value in the present context.[39] Ward Goodenough's highly influential definition of culture is a step in the right direction:

> A society's culture consists of whatever it is one has to know or believe in order to operate in a manner acceptable to its members. Culture is not a material phenomenon; it does not consist of things, behavior, or emotions. It is rather an organization of these things. It is the form of things that people have

---

35. F. Hoyle, *The Black Cloud* (New York: Signet, 1959).

36. *Invasion of the Body Snatchers* (dir. Don Siegel, prod. Walter Wanger; Allied Artists, 1956); Arthur C. Clarke, *Childhood's End* (New York: Ballantine Books, 1953).

37. A. L. Kroeber and Clyde Kluckhohn, *Culture: A Critical Review of Concepts and Definitions* (Cambridge, MA: Peabody Museum, 1952).

38. Edward Burnett Tylor, *Primitive Culture: Researches into the Development of Mythology, Philosophy, Religion, Language, Art, and Custom,* 2 vols., 7th ed. (1871; New York: Brentano's, 1924).

39. For a categorization of types of definitions of culture, see Garry Chick, "Cultural Complexity: The Concept and Its Measurement," *Cross-Cultural Research* 31, no. 4 (1997): 275–307.

in mind, their models for perceiving, relating, and otherwise interpreting them.[40]

Goodenough thus holds culture to be information. John M. Roberts developed a related definition of culture in 1964 that augments Goodenough's:

> It is possible to regard all culture as information and to view any single culture as an "information economy" in which information is received or created, retrieved, transmitted, utilized, and even lost.[41]

The "information economy" of which the developed world is a part dates to antiquity. While significant information attributable to ancient civilizations has already been lost, such as the engineering of the Egyptian pyramids or the rules for the Aztecs' famed Mesoamerican ballgame), cultural knowledge stored in the heads of members of extinct or vanishing indigenous peoples may represent a far greater loss. Nonetheless, diffusion of cultural information has surely occurred over the millennia. The question, of course, is how much of our present cultural information—what we need to know to operate in a way acceptable to our fellows—can be traced to antiquity. Since we lack a means to measure culture content as well as comprehensive knowledge of that content between then and now, this determination is not presently possible.

Culture and the Development of Technology

Being intelligent, having hands and eyes, and living in a favorable environment, while necessary conditions, do not appear to be sufficient in themselves for the development of advanced technology. Casti's final prerequisite for the development of advanced technologies, including interstellar communication, was social organization.[42] The problem is that all human groups have social organization of one form or another but not all are technologically complex. Nor does complexity in one area of human life predict complexity

---

40. W. H. Goodenough, "Cultural Anthropology and Linguistics," in *Report of the Seventh Annual Round Table Meeting on Linguistics and Language Study,* Monograph Series on Languages and Linguistics 9, ed. Paul L. Garvin (Washington, DC: Georgetown University Press, 1957), pp. 167–173.

41. J. M. Roberts, "The Self Management of Cultures," in *Explorations in Cultural Anthropology*, ed. W. H. Goodenough (New York: McGraw-Hill, 1964), pp. 433–454, esp. p. 438.

42. Casti, *Paradigms Lost*, p. 359.

in others. The Kayapó, for example, a native Amazonian tribe, are similar to many other small-scale societies in having a rich ceremonial life and a complex cosmology without ever having developed a complex technology.[43] However, the development of complex technologies is commonly seen as an extension of the development of complex cultures. Ways of assessing cultural complexity exist that do not include technological complexity as a defining factor but that nevertheless accurately predict technological complexity. The most common, and probably most promising, relates to aspects of population size and density.

In a prescient 1956 paper, Raoul Naroll linked the complexity of social organization to population size.[44] Specifically, he showed that the size of the largest community in a society correlates with measures of cultural complexity, such as the number of craft specializations and what he termed "organizational ramification," that is, the number of control officials, such as police or military, in a society. About 10 years later, Robert Carneiro found that population size of societies correlates with organizational complexity, designated as involving "the coordinated activity of two or more persons."[45] Edgar Bowden determined that his own Index of Sociocultural Development, based on earlier work by Carneiro using Guttman Scaling of the presence or absence of 354 cultural traits to measure cultural complexity, correlated at .97 with the base-10 logarithm of the maximum settlement size of a community.[46] Most recently, Michelle Kline and Robert Boyd, using data from a cross-cultural sample of 10 societies in Oceania from around the time of Western contact (c. 1770), examined the relationship between population size and the number and complexity of tools used in marine foraging. They found that islands with larger populations had "more kinds of marine foraging

43. J. Bamberger-Turner, "Environment and Cultural Classification: A Study of the Northern Kayapó" (Ph.D. dissertation, Department of Anthropology, Harvard University, Cambridge, MA, 1967); Vanessa Lea, "Mebengokre (Kayapó) Onomastics: A Facet of Houses as Total Social Facts in Central Brazil," *Man*, n.s., 27, no. 1 (1992): 129–153.

44. Raoul Naroll, "A Preliminary Index of Social Development," *American Anthropologist* 58, no. 4 (1956): 687–715.

45. Robert L. Carneiro, "On the Relationship Between Size of Population and Complexity of Social Organization," *Southwestern Journal of Anthropology* 23, no. 3 (1967): 234–243.

46. Edgar Bowden, "An Index of Sociocultural Development Applicable to Precivilized Societies," *American Anthropologist* 71, no. 3 (1969): 454–461. Robert L. Carneiro, "Scale Analysis as an Instrument for the Study of Cultural Evolution," *Southwestern Journal of Anthropology* 18, no. 2 (1962): 149–169.

tools and more complex tools than smaller, isolated populations."[47] Hence, at least on Earth, the development of complex technology requires intelligence, the physical ability to manipulate the environment, culture, and minimum limits for population size and density. And these factors must interact with the environment, since population size alone is not enough. It has been estimated, for example, that Tenochtitlán was one of the world's largest cities at the time of the Spanish conquest in 1521. Nevertheless, the superiority of Spanish technology, especially in terms of metallurgy, assured their defeat of the Aztecs, who lacked the raw materials for the production of iron or bronze, as I will discuss in more detail below.

Many estimates of f_c are also in the 1 in 10 (0.1) range. Is this reasonable, given the data we have available from Earth? Applying the Principle of Mediocrity, we can ask what percent of known societies/cultures achieved, or would have achieved, the technological sophistication to make interstellar contact possible? No database covers all known societies/cultures from the beginning of such groups until now, and how does one determine where one society/culture ends and another begins? The Roman Empire, for example, never developed the means for interstellar communication, but Western cultures of the 20th century were able to do so in part because they retain cultural knowledge developed by the citizens and subjects of Imperial Rome, who utilized cultural knowledge developed even earlier by the Greeks (and many others). So, while the political entity known now as the Roman Empire has long since disappeared, much of the culture associated with it has not.

How can knowledge of human societies be used to estimate f_c? One way would be to choose a sample of historical civilizations from around the world (such as those of the ancient Egyptians, Harappa–Mohenjo-daro, the Inca, the Natchez, the Greeks, and so on) and to speculate on their potential for becoming technologically sophisticated enough to engage in interstellar communication. Jared Diamond, in his Pulitzer Prize–winning book *Guns, Germs, and Steel*, offered environmental reasons why some societies progressed technologically while others did not.[48] The West had access to the raw materials (including plant and animal species capable of being domesticated) that were necessary to support technical culture, as well as lines of communication and migration that did not cross inhospitable territory. In his next book, *Collapse*, Diamond provided case studies of several societies that failed due to various

---

47. Michelle A. Kline and Robert Boyd, "Population Size Predicts Technological Complexity in Oceania," *Proceedings of the Royal Society B* 277, no. 1693 (2010): 2559–2564.

48. Jared Diamond, *Guns, Germs, and Steel: The Fates of Human Societies* (New York: W. W. Norton, 1997), passim.

combinations of environmental degradation, climate change, hostile neighbors, lack of friendly trading partners, and inept responses to environmental problems.[49] While his data and methods have been criticized, Diamond raised important issues and provided answers that may have some validity. It may be that the Inca and the Aztecs, for example, if left on their own, would never have developed advanced technology because they lacked the raw materials in their respective environments that would have enabled them to do so. The ancient Chinese were extremely inventive and great engineers, but many of their inventions (e.g., gunpowder and moveable type) never had the impact in ancient Asia that was later seen in the West. But cherry-picking past civilizations and then forecasting their possible technological evolutions had they not collapsed or been conquered involves speculations better reserved for science fiction.[50]

An alternative is to take a sample of societies from the recent anthropological record and then calculate what percentage of them ultimately developed advanced technology. For this task, I chose the Standard Cross-Cultural Sample (SCCS), developed by George Murdock and Douglas White in 1969.[51] The SCCS is composed of 186 societies chosen specifically to represent a global distribution of cultures and languages in order to minimize Galton's Problem. The SCCS is widely used in cross-cultural comparative research, and codes for approximately 2,000 variables are currently available for it, including one for "cultural complexity." In 1973, Murdock and Caterina Provost coded the SCCS for cultural complexity based on "ten groups of comparable traits, each ordered according to a five-point scale of relative complexity."[52] These traits are 1) Writing and Records, 2) Fixity of Residence, 3) Agriculture, 4) Urbanization, 5) Technological Specialization, 6) Land Transport, 7) Money, 8) Density of Population, 9) Level of Political Integration, and 10) Social Stratification. A major weakness of the SCCS is that it lacks any modern, industrial societies.

Murdock and Provost assumed that their index is unidimensional, an assumption demonstrated by the fact that they added the 10 individual scales to provide a single, overall index of cultural complexity. However,

---

49. Jared Diamond, *Collapse: How Societies Choose to Fail or Succeed* (New York: Viking, 2004).

50. See, e.g., "Bread and Circuses," *Star Trek*, Episode 43 (dir. D. McDougall and R. Gist, 1966), in which the Enterprise discovers an Earth-like planet on which the Roman Empire never fell.

51. G. P. Murdock and D. R. White, "Standard Cross-cultural Sample," *Ethnology* 8 (1969): 329–369.

52. G. P. Murdock and C. Provost, "Measurement of Cultural Complexity," *Ethnology* 11 (1973): 254–295.

Table 14.1: Principal-Components Analysis of the SCCS Index of Cultural Complexity[a]

Complexity Scales	Factor 1	Factor 2	Communality
Writing and Records	**0.848**[b]	0.150	0.741
Land Transport	**0.846**	0.047	0.719
Social Stratification	**0.716**	0.402	0.675
Level of Political Integration	**0.669**	0.466	0.665
Technological Specialization	**0.606**	0.442	0.563
Money	**0.578**	0.401	0.495
Fixity of Residence	0.068	**0.918**	0.847
Agriculture	0.213	**0.849**	0.766
Density of Population	0.284	**0.824**	0.759
Urbanization	0.454	**0.542**	0.500
Percentage of Total Variance Explained by Unrotated Factors	52.77	14.53	

a. N of Cases = 186.

b. The variables that define each factor are set in **bold type**.

a principal-components analysis (with varimax rotation, factors extracted where the eigenvalue is ≤ 1) of the 10 individual scales indicates two factors, not one, as assumed by Murdock and Provost. Factor 1 appears to be related to social and technological complexity, while Factor 2 contains variables related to the complexity of the human ecology of societies. These variables are shown in Table 14.1.

Whether or not this index is an appropriate measure of cultural complexity is debatable, depending on how one defines both *culture* and *complexity*.[53] Nevertheless, it is the most widely used measure of the construct and may be of some value for estimating f_c. It is also important because Factor 2 is closely related to alternative measures of cultural complexity, discussed below.

How many of the societies in the SCCS either did or would have been likely to develop technology that would permit interstellar contact? Of the 186 societies in the sample, 7 have the maximum possible score of 30 when the six variables making up the social and technological complexity factor are summed, while 7 more have a score of 29. These 14 societies therefore constitute about 7.5 percent of the SCCS. Only one society has a score of 28, while three score 27 and two score 26; so a score of 29 is something of

---

53. For a discussion of these issues, see Chick, "Cultural Complexity," passim.

a natural breakpoint. The 14 most complex societies, and the year at which their culture was pinpointed, are:

Burmese	1965
Koreans	1947
Babylonians	1750 BCE
Romans	110
Balinese	1958
Irish	1932
Basques	1934
Javanese	1954
Uttar Pradeshi	1945
Siamese	1955
Chinese	1936
Japanese	1950
Turks	1950
Russians	1955

Would any or all of these societies, left to their own devices, have developed the means for interstellar communication? Despite Murdock and White's efforts to ensure the independence of the societies in the SCCS, it is clear that this condition does not apply to these 14. Babylonian culture surely had some influence on the Romans via the Greeks and some knowledge of it passed through the Romans to us. All of the other societies had at least some contact with each other and contact with Western (and therefore Roman) culture by the date of Murdock and Provost's study. So is it most appropriate to regard these societies as having only 1 technical tradition, 14 different ones, or something in between?

Karl Jansky discovered radio waves emanating from the Milky Way in 1932, and Grote Reber constructed the first dish radio telescope at his home in Wheaton, Illinois, in 1937. So human society has had the capability of receiving extraterrestrial signals for approximately 75 years while sending them (from commercial radio stations, at least) for approximately a dozen years longer. Of the 14 societies in the sample, major radio telescopes are currently located in 5 (Korea, India, China, Japan, and Russia).[54] Optimistically then, out of a sample of 186 human cultures only 5 (2.7 percent) might have developed the means to communicate with extraterrestrials. Less optimistically, since there is really only one cultural tradition of radio-telescope devel-

---

54. Gallery of Radio Telescopes, *http://www.nro.nao.ac.jp/~kotaro/RTs/rts.html.*

opment and use—a tradition passing though the Roman Empire—only 0.5 percent of human civilizations would ultimately have developed the means to communicate with extraterrestrials.[55] Hence, one finding from this exercise is that the value for f_c may lie between 0.005 and 0.027.

One Culture or Many?

A more important finding, however, may be that looking at a sample of human cultures studied pretty much across a slice of time and then attempting to extrapolate from them proves that this method is highly questionable due to the problem of cultural diffusion. Indeed, in the early history of anthropology, several schools of thought claimed that humans were basically uninventive and that important technological advances had occurred only once and thereafter moved to other areas of the world either through cultural diffusion or migration. These include the German *Kulturkreis* school, which held that inventions spread via migration; the American "cultural area" school, which emphasized diffusion; and, the most extreme, the pan-Egyptian or heliolithic theory, which asserted that all cultural advances, especially modern inventions, came from Egypt, a perspective championed by G. Eliot Smith and, later, his student William James Perry.[56] These schools emerged, in part, as a reaction to early cultural evolutionism that emphasized fixed stages through which all cultures must develop. So, while these schools of thought have largely faded away, the ideas they promoted continue to influence American anthropology, in particular, through attention to individual cultural histories and through lingering notions of culture areas, as manifested, for example, in the sampling for the SCCS.

While there is little evidence to suggest that the Aztec or Inca civilizations were influenced by Egyptian, Chinese, or Roman civilization (excepting a few contested theories about the lost tribes of Israel), the question remains whether we can reasonably trace modern radio astronomy back to the ancient Greeks or perhaps even to earlier civilizations of the Middle East. Does SETI result from one cultural tradition or many?

---

55. A search of the eHRAF (electronic Human Relations Area Files), an online database of 230 (as of 13 May 2011) societies, yielded results similar to those with the SCCS. None of the societies in the eHRAF had independently developed radio astronomy, and radio telescopes were associated with only three of the societies in the sample.

56. For reviews of these perspectives, see, H. R. Hays, *From Ape to Angel: An Informal History of Social Anthropology* (New York: Alfred A. Knopf, 1958); A. de Waal Malefijt, *Images of Man: A History of Anthropological Thought* (New York: Alfred A. Knopf, 1974); M. Harris, *The Rise of Anthropological Theory* (New York: Thomas Crowell Company, 1968).

Political scientist David Wilkinson has argued that an economic and military integration of Egypt and Mesopotamia around 3500 BP resulted in what he terms the "Central Civilization."[57] According to Wilkinson, this civilization expanded over the next several millennia to include the entire Middle East and Europe. Finally, via European expansion, Central Civilization came to include the Americas, much of Africa, China, and Japan. Hence, our advanced technology, including that used in SETI, developed originally in this polycultural Central Civilization rather than in later cultures, societies, or empires.

Summary and Conclusions

Estimating any of the values for variables in the Drake Equation involves a lot of guesswork, although our knowledge of R^* and, especially, f_p has increased dramatically in recent years. We may soon be able to estimate n_e on a more empirical and less speculative basis. There is general agreement that the fraction of habitable planets that develop life should be very high. However, the fraction of planets that develop intelligent life and the fraction of those that develop both the means and the will to communicate across space may remain unknown and unknowable by humans. In the meantime, however, we can determine exactly what we are talking about and looking for. The question "what is life?" has been extensively discussed.[58] Numerous authors have also discussed what we mean by *intelligence*.[59] As noted above, the general mode of thought when considering extraterrestrial intelligence is anthropomorphism—we imagine that aliens will be like us. Additionally, the evolution of intelligence is often seen as inevitable or, at least, as the endpoint of progressive evolution. In other words, once multicellular life evolves, intelligence is on its way. Discussion of intelligent dinosaurs—who might still be here except for a random asteroid or comet hitting Earth some 65 million years ago—reflects this progressive notion of evolution. However, as Richard Byrne points out, "the assumption that our descent was linear and progressive," that "when we studied a lemur or monkey we were seeing in a

---

57. D. Wilkinson, "Central Civilization," *Comparative Civilizations Review* 17 (1987): 31–59.

58. David J. Darling, *Life Everywhere: The Maverick Science of Astrobiology* (New York, NY: Basic Books, 2001).

59. Casti, *Paradigms Lost;* Darling, *Life Everywhere;* Iosif S. Shklovskii and Carl Sagan, *Intelligent Life in the Universe* (San Francisco: Holden-Day, Inc., 1966).

direct way what our ancestors were like," "is just plain wrong."[60] All other "modern animals have evolved for exactly as long as we have," and yet, after all this evolution, only one species has developed the sort of intelligence that has led to the technology and the interest to seek communications with other species in the universe.[61] These conclusions do not lend much support to the proposition that the development of our kind of intelligence is inevitable, let alone common, once life appears.

As for f_c, the fraction of intelligent civilizations able and willing to communicate, the exercise reported above using a sample of human societies culled from the anthropological record also does not support high estimates. Robin Dunbar reported a strong relationship in primates between the neocortex ratio (defined as the volume of the neocortex divided by that of the remainder of the brain) and group size.[62] A regression equation, using a ratio of group size to neocortex, permits estimation of group size for species for which we know only the former. In the case of humans, the estimate is about 150.[63] As Dunbar points out, group size refers to the network of individuals who know each other and have strong affiliative relationships, who interact with one another frequently, and who maintain some type of spatial coherence over time. The ethnographic record supports group sizes of 125–200 in recent and contemporary human societies. Finally, Dunbar notes that there are two main determinants of group size. First, living in groups provides two important benefits: defense against predators and enhanced ability to defend resources. These benefits act in opposition to the costs of group living, which include the need for greater food resources, sometimes involving energetically costly travel (and possible predation), and the need to devote more time and energy to social interaction in the prevention of group conflicts. Models of maximum group size based on only three variables (mean annual temperature, mean annual rainfall, and rainfall seasonality) among chimpanzees, geladas, and baboons are "surprisingly robust."[64] Dunbar notes that "mean group size is, of course, a rough measure of social complexity."[65] As it turns out, an

---

60. R. W. Byrne, "Social and Technical Forms of Primate Intelligence," in *Tree of Origin: What Primate Behavior Can Tell Us about Human Social Evolution*, ed. Frans B. M. de Waal (Cambridge, MA: Harvard University Press, 2001), pp. 145–172, esp. pp. 147–148.

61. Byrne, "Social and Technical Forms of Primate Intelligence," p. 148.

62. Robin I. M. Dunbar, "Brains on Two Legs: Group Size and the Evolution of Intelligence," in de Waal, ed., *Tree of Origin*, pp. 173–191.

63. Dunbar, "Brains on Two Legs," in de Waal, ed., *Tree of Origin*, p. 181.

64. Dunbar, "Brains on Two Legs," in de Waal, ed., *Tree of Origin*, p. 186.

65. Dunbar, "Brains on Two Legs," in de Waal, ed., *Tree of Origin*, p. 179.

excellent way to measure cultural complexity in human societies is simply to use the size of the largest settlement in the society, rather than to scale societies in terms of several parameters, such as in the Murdock and Provost index discussed above.[66]

So even if intelligent and technologically capable life develops, environmental parameters constrain the likelihood that societies composed of such beings will become sufficiently complex to support advanced technologies. We do not presently know if other Earth-like planets exist or, if they do, what sort of limiting environmental conditions may exist on them. If we apply the Principle of Mediocrity, analyses such as those by Diamond suggest that such societies will develop only rarely.[67] I have argued here that such a culture developed on Earth only once.

---

66. Murdock and Provost, "Measurement of Cultural Complexity," passim. To be precise, the base-10 logarithm of the size of the largest settlement is used rather than the population number itself. This serves to reduce excessive variance caused by curvilinearity, thus increasing correlations with other linear variables. See also E. Bowden, "Standardization of an Index of Sociocultural Development for Precivilized Societies," *American Anthropologist* 74 (1972): 1122–1132; R. Naroll and W. T. Divale, "Natural Selection in Cultural Evolution: Warfare Versus Peaceful Diffusion," *American Ethnologist* 4 (1976): 97–128; and Chick, "Cultural Complexity," passim.

67. Diamond, *Guns, Germs, and Steel*, passim.

CHAPTER FOURTEEN

Ethology, Ethnology, and Communication with Extraterrestrial Intelligence

Dominique Lestel

The Search for Extraterrestrial Intelligence (SETI) raises profound philosophical questions that demand serious discussion. Our attempts to establish contact with alien civilizations compel us, for example, to define exactly what we mean by *communication*. In the past, anthropologists have categorized contacts with new cultures as either ethnological or ethological. In this chapter I will argue that interactions with ETIs will constitute a third type of contact since they will be located at the intersection of ethnology on the one hand and ethology on the other. Because humans have had no experience with this type of contact, communicating with extraterrestrials will pose complex new challenges.

Communicating with Extraterrestrial Civilizations

Two major errors must be avoided when one thinks about extraterrestrial civilizations. The first error, representing a solely *ethological* approach, is to consider such a task as either *purely physical* (the search for and analysis of extraterrestrial signals) or *purely biological* (the identification of a non-human species and the establishment of communication with it). The second error is to consider such a task as exclusively *ethnological*, requiring only that two cultures (a human culture and an extraterrestrial culture) be allowed to establish meaningful contact in the ways we usually observe between two human cultures.

Indeed, to identify and meet an extraterrestrial civilization is a particularly difficult task precisely because it is both ethological *and* ethnological. We already know how to establish contact with nonhuman animals on Earth, but we have never communicated with agents with whom we share no history at all, not even a phylogenetic one. How can communication be established between two groups of living beings who 1) have had independent biological

229

evolutions, 2) have had independent cultural histories, and 3) have never previously interacted with one another? To accomplish this task—one without any precedent in the history of humankind—we can take inspiration from *ethology* to conceptualize contact between different *biological species* and inspiration from *ethnology* to conceptualize contact between different *cultures*.

Ethology of Communicating with Extraterrestrials

On Earth, humans share genes with *all* other living beings. Human history intertwines with that of every other living being, including plants. Humans are also genetically similar to some other animals. For example, they share around 99 percent of their genes with chimpanzees.[1] Humans also share more than 50 percent of their genes with some plants, such as carrots. With an extraterrestrial civilization, the situation would undoubtedly be different. One thing is nevertheless (almost) sure: if extraterrestrials are living beings, they will have undergone a process of natural evolution. Up to now, all living beings we know of have been designed in such a way. The "almost" is, however, not at all trivial. Indeed, the extraterrestrials that humans may come into contact with could be *artificial creatures* that have become (or have not become) autonomous agents. Artificial agents, even though built by other living beings, could differ radically from creatures that resulted only or mainly from natural evolution.[2]

Even in that situation, where contact is made with artificial intelligence created by a naturally evolved alien species, the central features of the extraterrestrial mind that have been shaped by an evolutionary process will be reflected in the design or the uses of these artifacts. It seems likely that extraterrestrial natural evolution has occurred through selection involving *prey/predator relationships, social deception,* and *instrumental manipulation of the environment.*[3] That last point—that intelligent extraterrestrials will be capable of manipulating their environment—can be assumed for the purposes of this discussion, because if we are able to communicate with extraterrestrials, it

---

1. M. C. King and A. C. Wilson, "Evolution at Two Levels in Humans and Chimpanzees," *Science* 188, no. 4184 (1975): 107–116.

2. D. Lestel, "Metaphors of Complexity: Language and Cognitive Resources of Artificial Life," *Social Science Information* 35, no. 3 (1996): 511–540.

3. For a detailed discussion of nonhuman social abilities from an evolutionary perspective, see N. Emery and N. Clayton, "Comparative Social Cognition," *Annual Review of Psychology* 60 (2009): 87–113.

will be precisely because they already have a sophisticated technology. In any case, humans need to be cautious. They need to be perceived neither as naïve prey nor as threatening predators—especially if they try to portray themselves as altruistic creatures.

A species that goes beyond a certain point of social complexity necessarily develops a political society. For example, such a process has been observed in species as biologically diverse as chimpanzees, dolphins, and ravens.[4] In other words, extraterrestrials will certainly be divided about numerous problems, including the kind of relationships they should have with creatures living on Earth.

This evolutionary background helps to explain why communication with extraterrestrials will be likely to take a special form. Paradoxically, it could be equally important *not* to make contact with extraterrestrials. All communication with them will necessarily involve a dual message, and we need to take that into account in order to appreciate it: any contact conveys both *what* we tell (which is not necessarily what we wish to tell) *and* that we *exist* to tell it. In other words, every first communication with extraterrestrials is both a *semantic* and an *existential* exchange. This is why we should think about designing a message that gives no clues to Earth's location. Similarly, an extraterrestrial message could have such a structure.

Ethnology and Ethology of Communicating with Extraterrestrials

We can be sure that contacts with extraterrestrial cultures will be entirely different from everything we already know and maybe from everything we have anticipated to date. Thus, an ethological model must be adopted with caution. It will help to illuminate only one dimension of what might occur. Indeed, we can reasonably assume that such a contact will need to be thought of as occurring at the intersection of ethnology and ethology, a location with which humans have thus far had no experience. Basically, three kinds of contact can be distinguished:

---

4. Christopher Boehm, "Segmentary 'Warfare' and the Management of Conflict: Comparison of East African Chimpanzees and Patrilineal-Patrilocal Humans," in *Coalitions and Alliances in Humans and Other Animals*, ed. A. Harcourt and Frans B. M. de Waal (Oxford: Oxford University Press, 1992), pp. 137–173; Janet Mann et al., eds., *Cetacean Societies: Field Studies of Dolphins and Whales* (Chicago: University of Chicago Press, 2000); and Bernd Heinrich, *Mind of the Raven: Investigations and Adventures with Wolf-Birds* (New York: Cliff Street Books, 1999).

Table 15.1. Three Possible Types of Contact with Extraterrestrial Intelligence

Types of Contact	Types of Groups Making Contact	Examples
I. Ethnological	Contact between cultures that are different from one another but are homogeneous together (both were human cultures)	Contact between human culture and human culture (e.g., Spanish and Aztec cultures)
II. Ethological	Contact between human cultures and animal societies	Contacts between a human culture and a noncultural society (e.g., an ant colony) or a primitively cultural society (e.g., a community of chimpanzees)
III. Etho-ethnological	Contact between two heterogeneous advanced cultural societies	Contact between human cultures and extraterrestrial cultures

The terrestrial history of contacts with foreign cultures shows that the major problem during contact between two human cultures is frequently a problem of perception rather than one of communication, strictly speaking. One can *translate* discourses from one language into another, but *understanding* what is really being said is always a much more difficult task.

One of the main challenges of human/extraterrestrial contact could occur at the interface between culture, meaning, and physiological senses. To understand what is at stake, it is useful to refer back to Jakob von Uexküll's approach to animal *Umwelten*. At the beginning of the 20th century, von Uexküll showed that animals of different species relate differently to the same environment because of the radical variations among the physiological senses with which they perceive their own world.[5] Bees, for example, are sensitive to infrared wavelengths of light that humans cannot perceive and will therefore not inhabit the same environment in the way that humans would. A similar problem could arise with extraterrestrials, whose physiological senses might turn out to be quite different from those of humans.

Paradoxically, communication with such extraterrestrials might be easier precisely because it would be not a *proximal* communication but a *distal*

---

5. Jakob von Uexküll, "A Stroll Through the Worlds of Animals and Men: A Picture Book of Invisible Worlds," in *Instinctive Behavior: The Development of a Modern Concept*, ed. and trans. Claire H. Schiller (New York: International Universities Press, 1957), pp. 5–80. For a full bibliography and a critical contemporary discussion of von Uexküll, see Kaveli Kull, "Jakob von Uexküll: An Introduction," *Semiotica* 134, nos. 1–4 (2001): 1–59.

one. Communication between humans and extraterrestrials (whatever they are) will necessarily need an abstract artificial mediation, such as a highly elaborated code.[6] Even if it requires a code that will be a very complex one for us, such a communication would be much less complex than if it were a multimodal, contiguous, proximal, physical exchange.

Basically, we must remain open to *all* possibilities. The challenge is not to anticipate the most likely possibility but rather to describe exhaustively all of the potential situations that could occur and to find ways to address each one. In particular, humans must be ready to face very disturbing situations. For example, humans may face a scenario in which they will be unable to conclude whether or not extraterrestrials exist, being unable to make a rational decision about such a weighty issue.

This prospect raises a truly fundamental question: do humans have the cognitive, epistemic, technological, and cultural abilities that will enable them to establish communication with extraterrestrials? From an evolutionary point of view, there is no reason that we should be capable of dealing with such a circumstance. We have had no need to develop such a useless ability! Therefore, the more pertinent question may be this: in the attempt to communicate with extraterrestrials, could *Homo sapiens* use technological and cultural capabilities to compensate for a lack of innate power?

Universal Interlocutors? Language as a Metaphor for Communication with Extraterrestrials

Are we really justified in saying that humans are universal interlocutors? This is precisely what numerous contemporary linguists do when they assert the existence of a great divide between human language, which can describe everything, and animal communications, which are at best able to refer only to very particular aspects of the world, such as the so-called bee dance language.[7] But is this distinction true? First of all, one could wonder whether language is actually able to describe everything. This first problem is simply a logical one, not even an empirical problem. What could be the meaning

---

6. For a discussion about the Turing Test in this perspective, see D. Lestel, "Metaphors of Complexity," *Social Sciences Information* 35, no. 3 (1996): 511–540.

7. See, for example, the debate between French linguist Emile Benveniste and Austrian ethologist Karl von Frisch during the 1950s: Emile Benveniste, "Animal Communication and Human Language: The Language of the Bees," *Diogenes* 1, no. 1 (1953): 1–7; and Karl von Frisch and Emile Benveniste, "Letters to the Editor," *Diogenes* 2, no. 7 (1954): 106–109.

of such a statement? How could language demonstrate that it is capable of representing everything? In other words, if language cannot describe some topic, would language be able to show that failure? This seems doubtful. On the contrary, language users may firmly believe that language allows them to talk about everything because they have no access to what language cannot talk about.[8] We are justified in doubting the ability of language to display its limits and weaknesses. Our belief that language is able to talk about everything could in reality reflect an epistemic and logical weakness of language, and not one of its major strengths. Perhaps the main characteristic of language is not that it can describe *everything*, but rather that it possesses the bizarre ability to describe *anything*. Such an ability could seriously handicap any attempt to communicate with living beings whom we assume to be very different not only from every other living being we have known so far but also from *everything* that humans have encountered up to now. The point is not that language production itself is insane but that human language has the surprising ability to talk convincingly about anything (including the most absurd things) without meeting any serious objections to its referential credentials, either from the speakers or from the hearers.

In contrast to the above line of reasoning, which raises concerns about easy communication with extraterrestrials on theoretical grounds, there are also empirical reasons to be skeptical about easy communication. Humans struggle to decipher nonhuman animal communications, although these are supposed to be very primitive in comparison with human languages. On this point, the field of ethology can offer a major lesson: even with creatures that are regarded as much less complex than humans, we cannot accurately say whether we could know when we finally have a good description of a non-human animal communication system.

Human scientists are very bad at making sense of nonhuman communicative systems, even when these are considered primitive. Primatologists have shown how easy it is to deceive ourselves about that point.[9] They say that humans miss the true complexity of great ape communication systems because we refuse *a priori* to attribute to these systems the complexity required for them to be fully understood, and not because great apes are epistemically or cognitively beyond our power of understanding. This idea is deeply trou-

---

8. But keep in mind that the extreme difficulty could be as challenging to deal with as the impossibility would be. Remember that even some human scripts still wait to be deciphered.

9. E. S. Savage-Rumbaugh et al., "Language Perceived: Paniscus Branches Out," in *Great Ape Societies*, ed. W. McGrew, L. Marchant, and T. Nishida (Cambridge: Cambridge University Press, 1996), pp. 173–184.

bling because it shows that an epistemic step is also always an ethical one. It also shows that, from an ethical or moral point of view, we could have good reasons *not* to communicate with extraterrestrials.

Our materialist concerns are likely to be as difficult as our epistemic concerns: in which ways are we really ready to invest resources (of money, time, energy, education, research, etc.) into methods for deciphering the meaning of messages that we may or may not receive? This is a serious question. The *material* and *psychological cost* of such an investigation could be so high that it might dissuade anyone from being involved in it. A question as seemingly simple as how long a message should be could lead to very deep difficulties. Charles Hartshorne, for example, has already shown that the time scale of communication is a big issue when comparing human communication with bird communication.[10] Humans may need to send extraterrestrials fractal messages, repeated at multiple time scales ranging from the nanosecond to the century; similarly, humans may need to write programs that could read messages received from extraterrestrials in this way.

Philosophical Openness

Up to now, there has been no attempt at *purely abstract cultural contact* with another intelligent species or even with an isolated group of humans. When two humans communicate by means of a device such as e-mail, they always already have had a physical contact with another human. All ethnological and ethological contacts have been conducted through actual rather than virtual meetings. The difference between communicating *only* via e-mail and communicating *occasionally* via e-mail is enormous.

The central issue in extraterrestrial/human communication concerns the nature of communication itself. In other words, should communication with extraterrestrials be considered a *true communication*, or should it be taken as a metaphor? The metaphor of communication may not help us to understand what is actually at stake. Every contact with extraterrestrials will be, for example, an existential experience. One of the reasons, as has already been explained, is that such a contact will establish the existence of the other. No matter how prepared we may be to believe that extraterrestrial civilizations do exist, to be in contact with one of them will be a genuine shock—and the word is far too weak to express what will happen.

---

10. Charles Hartshorne, *Born to Sing: An Interpretation and World Survey of Bird Song* (Bloomington: Indiana University Press, 1992).

It is likely that the contact with extraterrestrials will lead to a very deep existential crisis for humans. Humans could be confronted with their inability to answer questions of enormous importance to them. First, to *become aware* of such cognitive and epistemic limits, and second, to *accept* these limits may seriously test humans. Indeed, up to now, every epistemological crisis humans have faced has led them to alter their conception of the world. The next epistemological crisis, a crisis precipitated by contact with extraterrestrials, could be very different. Humans may come to understand that there exists in the universe a set of phenomena that they will never be able to know because they are not clever enough.

Conclusion

Communication with extraterrestrials through the SETI project will not look like any known communications, either with other humans or with nonhuman animals. Such a communication will be not only ethological *and* ethnological; it will also be uniquely abstract. How could such a communication be possible? The question remains open. Western linguists have proposed that language is a universal medium, able to tell everything and to be effectively used in all situations; but they have neither empirical facts nor sound theoretical arguments to support that belief. On the other hand, humans also could have very good reasons—political, psychological, and metaphysical reasons—to avoid all possibilities of establishing contact with an extraterrestrial civilization.

CHAPTER FIFTEEN

Constraints on Message Construction for Communication with Extraterrestrial Intelligence

William H. Edmondson

Introduction

Communication with Extraterrestrial Intelligence (CETI) must address four issues: detectability; communications protocols; message design—my focus here; and long-term social context, stability, and resourcing.[1] I will here contextualize CETI within efforts focused more generally on the Search for Extraterrestrial Intelligence (SETI), as envisaged by Earthlings. All of this is done in the context set by the preceding chapters as they investigate the theme of this volume.

Anthropologists and archaeologists necessarily make assumptions in relation to essential properties of human beings—e.g., some physical/biological processes are taken for granted. Setting aside any general doubts about the pitfalls of anthropomorphism, I will note two areas of concern. One, discussed by other contributors to this volume, is the risk of "getting it wrong."[2] The other is the difficulty we humans have in studying nonhuman terrestrial species, such as dolphins or bonobos, that are significant to our enquiry by virtue of their demonstrated intelligence, communicative ability, and social

---

1. On detectability, see W. H. Edmondson and I. R. Stevens, "The Utilization of Pulsars as SETI Beacons," *International Journal of Astrobiology* 2, no. 4 (2003): 231–271; on communications protocols, see G. Seth Shostak, ed., *Progress in the Search for Extraterrestrial Life*, ASP Conference Series, vol. 74 (San Francisco: Astronomical Society of the Pacific, 1995).

2. John W. Traphagan, "Anthropology at a Distance: SETI and the Production of Knowledge in the Encounter with an Extraterrestrial Other," chapter 8 in this volume; Paul K. Wason, "Inferring Intelligence: Prehistoric and Extraterrestrial," chapter 7 in this volume.

organization, or perhaps as philosophical challenges.[3] All of which is to say that while we can attempt some discussion, or even analysis, of what an ETI might be like, we must remain aware of our fundamental constraints. We can explore those constraints, but we must recognize them—we cannot do anthropology here on Earth "over the telephone," so why should we expect to do it well over the ether and with another species in an environment we cannot experience?[4] These issues can be addressed in relation to some specifics, the sort of concerns any anthropologist or archaeologist has with respect to assumptions about the objects of a study. So we must begin by considering these assumptions.

What is *necessary* in any communication scenario involving ETI, and what limits must be put on our conceptions of possible messages? When answering these questions, we will consider work in cognitive science along with archaeological and historical examples that include rock art, tool-making, and a 15th-century codex. It is *not* assumed that systems of explanation are the same as ours, merely that what is explained or known must be about the same universe—and the term *universe* covers physical aspects of the universe as well as cognitive and behavioral aspects of beings. It is assumed that any ETI will be an embodied intelligence—a being with a brain to control its actuators and to monitor its environment using sensors to record external stimuli such as atmospheric pressure, acoustic pressure, and electromagnetic radiation.

Assumptions—I

Physics and Biophysics: We can assume that the physics of the universe is knowable locally. We monitor our local environment and interact with it to make remote observations of other parts of the universe. Plausibly, beings on other planets can do the same. Further, we can assume that the sensory biophysics of any ETI is *functionally* equivalent to ours. Beings will be able to sense the world—or portions of the spectral data available—because the physics and chemistry of the universe are uniform. But it is not claimed, for example, that

---

3. For related discussions, see Dominique Lestel, "Ethology, Ethnology, and Communication with Extraterrestrial Intelligence," chapter 14 in this volume; and John W. Traphagan, "Culture and Communication with Extraterrestrial Intelligence," chapter 10 in this volume.

4. Ben Finney and Jerry Bentley, "A Tale of Two Analogues: Learning at a Distance from the Ancient Greeks and Maya and the Problem of Deciphering Extraterrestrial Radio Transmissions," chapter 4 in this volume.

the visual system of an ETI would map in detail onto ours in terms of, say, comparable spectral sensitivities of retinal cells or flicker/fusion performance or acuity and likewise, *mutatis mutandis*, for audition, touch, taste, or smell. All this, in my view, can be taken uncontroversially as established. More obscurely, perhaps, but still working with notions of universality in the physical world, it is plausible to assume that the biochemistry we know about on Earth is essentially universal (alternatives have been explored theoretically).[5] So-called weird life is best left to science fiction.

The significance of these observations for CETI is considerable, and in particular it is arguable that what we call audition will not be shared in any interesting sense by an ETI. The speed of sound on any planet will be determined by its atmospheric density, geologic composition, temperature, and other local factors. The range of acoustic frequencies to which an organism is sensitive is not predictable on physical grounds. Consider the range exploited on Earth: human audition has a restricted range; other organisms are sensitive to frequencies "outside" our hearing range and it took some time for this to be recognized. Further, creatures dwelling in the oceans use acoustic information and signaling, but the medium is very different and so, we must imagine, is their sound world. By contrast the electromagnetic spectrum has relatively unambiguous ranges for *heat, vision,* and so forth because the physics of the world (and our Sun) determines what is *heat* and what is *light* (in terms of, say, photochemical reactions, vibrational motion of atoms, liquid/solid/vapor transitions, or the disruption of and damage to complex cellular assemblages of materials and molecules). *Vision* as we know it terrestrially covers a broader range of the spectrum than is covered by human vision, but not much broader. We might reflect on the fact that eyes tend to be recognizable as such in a huge range of species, and they work in much the same way. Of course, the assumption here is that our local experience of stellar radiation is more or less universal in the sense that the primary source of electromagnetic radiation is our star, and it makes sense to assume sensory evolution in the context of that source, and such sources are widely encountered in the universe. To be sure, atmospheric filtering is required—if too much ultraviolet reaches Earth's surface, the biochemical balance is seriously disrupted.

---

5. Alternative theories are explored by J. A Baross et al. in National Research Council, *The Limits of Organic Life in Planetary Systems* (Washington, DC: National Academies Press, 2007), available at *http://www.nap.edu/openbook.php?record_id=11919.*

Implications—I

If the reader accepts these assumptions, then our first constraint on possible messages is simple: don't think of "sound worlds" or music or speech as the domains, vehicles, or contents of ETI messages. Regardless of semiotic concerns (see below), the accessibility of acoustic messaging must remain doubtful. Furthermore, there will be intended and unintended aspects of performance, which elaborate the difficulties of using sound. In my view avoidance of the sound world need not be controversial.

On the other hand, vision and the use of images would appear to be at least plausible. Although spectral details cannot be considered universal, the physical arrangement of objects on a habitable planet's surface will be shaped in part by gravity (the notion of a horizon might well be universal) and thus multispectral images might plausibly be considered worthwhile for messages. More generally, the implications for considering SETI/CETI as some sort of anthropological challenge need teasing out. We will return to this below.

Assumptions—II

In this section we will consider four factors—cognition, distributed cognition, symbols, and intentions—before looking in detail at some of their implications.

Cognition: I assume that some general cognitive principles have universal applicability, and also that some aspects of cognitive functioning (e.g., intentionality, distributed cognition, and contextualization) are necessary and thus universal corollaries of intelligent behavior. This view is not widely shared and may be considered controversial. Such cognitive principles are not species-specific and express a broad notion of the functionality of the brain (any brain—note that we understand how the heart works and what the heart is for in just such a general way).[6] The main idea is simply that the brain provides the means whereby the temporal dimension of experience and behavior is mapped into and out of cognitive entities (memories, plans, thoughts, intentions, desires, beliefs, etc.) that may be about such temporal structures without being temporal in the same sense. My notion of boiling an egg does not itself bubble along for four minutes; it is about

---

6. W. H. Edmondson, "General Cognitive Principles: The Structure of Behaviour and the Sequential Imperative," *International Journal of Mind, Brain and Cognition* 1, no. 1 (2010): 7–40, available at *http://www.cs.bham.ac.uk/~whe/GCPSOBSI.pdf*.

duration without having duration (it endures, which is different). Likewise, my notion of the structure of a sentence, with subject and predicate arranged as in English, does not itself have that same sequential structure; it is about that structure. Sequentiality is required psychophysically to penetrate the corporeal boundary: atemporal cognitive entities must be sequenced to be externalized; perception requires "desequencing" in order to internalize. (The visual system of organisms imposes sequentiality through saccades and/or head movements.) I refer to this psychophysical requirement as the "sequential imperative," and it is at the core of any functional specification of any brain, including, I believe, the brains of ETIs. We will consider the implications of this requirement later in this chapter.

Distributed cognition: While cognitive activity is often represented as isolated and occurring exclusively "within the head," the core concept of distributed cognition as set out by Edwin Hutchins is that brains are not completely isolated cognizers processing concepts in relation to sensory data; rather, it is more accurate to think of cognition as spread out in space and time and among other cognizers.[7] Humans are good at distributing cognition over *space*: we leave Post-it notes all over our offices, and we use diaries and address books as cognitive extensions. We also distribute cognition over *people*: in power-station control rooms or when performing discrete tasks in different locations during the operation of complex equipment, such as a naval vessel, humans rely on situational awareness in order to coordinate cognition within the group. Cognition can also be distributed over *time*, both within individuals (which Hutchins does not discuss) and across individuals. It has recently been argued that affect is similarly distributed[8] and that cognition and affect can be projected (an act reflecting intentionality).[9]

Solving a problem or developing a specific tool can take time and repeated cognitive application. Sometimes success depends on "interaction" between sequential cognizers, who recognize the cognitive activity of a predecessor and engage it at a "temporal distance." David de Léon offers an interesting illustration of this phenomenon.[10] The development of the firing mechanism for a rifle can be tracked through various instantiations, each of which is assumed

---

7. E. Hutchins, *Cognition in the Wild* (Cambridge, MA: The MIT Press, 1996).

8. W. H. Edmondson, "General Cognitive Principles," pp. 7–40.

9. W. H. Edmondson and R. Beale, "Projected Cognition—Extending Distributed Cognition for the Study of Human Interaction with Computers," *Interacting with Computers* 20 (2008): 128–140.

10. D. de Léon, "Building Thought into Things," in *Third European Conference on Cognitive Science*, ed. S. Bagnara (Rome: Istituto di Psicologia del Consiglio Nazionale della Ricerche, 1999), pp. 37–47.

to have been "read" by appropriately skilled craftsmen producing the "next" iteration/interpretation of the solution to the problem. The craftsmen in each generation are, in a sense, doing some very local cognitive archaeology, but they respond to their interpretation of what they find by producing a new interpretation that they then cast in the form of a new solution—built on, or extending, the previous solution in a process that may cover a couple of hundred years. This aspect of cognition is likely to be familiar to anthropologists and archaeologists, and some of its implications are addressed below.

Symbols: When sequence is not constrained by physical events, tool use, or deployment of physiology, it is semiotically free and thus available to carry symbolic meaning as desired. The arbitrariness of meaning associated with physical behavior is problematic for CETI because the behavior alone is simply not informative. Also, the use of *symbol systems* requires both cultural and situational contextualization; we must be able to consider the symbol usage alongside other behavior, the situations in which all these behaviors take place, and the circumstances of both learning and cultural transmission. The background knowledge and situational context are not part of the symbol system in any narrow sense, however, and thus are unavailable to an ETI. As a consequence, the conditions for ETI to learn a human language are not in place. So symbol systems and languages look implausible as components or goals in any CETI attempt. The fact that on Earth we can currently find approximately 7,000 spoken and signed languages suggests that the arbitrariness is not a trivial obstacle—especially when we recognize why that arbitrariness exists.[11] The approach taken here is at odds with more widely accepted message models. We can suppose that an ETI might well be aware of the issues and principles involved, and it's possible that alien semioticians and cognitive scientists will have reached similar conclusions.

Intentions: In human discourse the existence and comprehensibility of intentionality are presumed—communication fails if intentions are not clear. It is reasonable to assume that an ETI interested in communication with other ETIs will endeavor to behave with some communicative intentions, paying explicit attention to the conditions that inform the communication. Once detected, ETI may attempt to specify the means for a response, to commence

---

11. C. F. Hockett, "The Problem of Universals in Language," in *Universals of Language*, ed. Joseph H. Greenberg, 2nd ed. (Cambridge, MA: The MIT Press, 1965). See also C. F. Hockett, "Linguistic Elements and Their Relations," *Language* 37 (1961): 29–53. The approach taken here is at odds with more widely accepted message models. For a study that exemplifies the message model approach, see M. D. Hauser, *The Evolution of Communication* (Cambridge, MA: The MIT Press, 1997).

a dialogue rather than merely post a notice, to display situational awareness, and so on. This does not mean that ETI will presume a drive to linguistic communication or the posing/solving of interstellar sudoku puzzles.

Implications—II

The sequential imperative will be universal, and behaviors dependent on culturally determined serial organization of behavior will therefore be so arbitrary as to be incomprehensible—there will be no basis for contextualization. By contrast, where sequentialization is determined physically, it is recognizable and its lack of arbitrariness is readable as such. This observation may prove useful in the design of messages.

Semiosis—the attribution of meaning to artifacts and the systematic organization of artifacts (language)—is culturally constrained, as semioticians have often demonstrated. While the fact of semiosis is plausibly universal, the means of expression and much of the "content" are irrevocably parochial. Systems through which humans explain the universe (e.g., our theories in mathematics and physics) are local, although the phenomena to be explained (e.g., properties in the light of distant stars observed in our local star that can be reproduced in our laboratories) are universal. We might therefore assume that an ETI's understanding of cognition and semiosis means that they won't attempt linguistic communication but will choose other ways to contact us.

I believe that cognition can be distributed over species as well.[12] If the physics of the universe determines certain properties of tools and artifacts on our planet, then surely our deliberations about such items might match those of other species on other planets. The deployment of levers would be a clear example, as would the design of wheels for particular terrains. In order to apprehend or interpret the shapes of such items in the world of an ETI, we should exploit the sense of sharing that is fundamental to distributed cognition. This is not a hard constraint but goes beyond mere possibility. We might also ponder that an ETI, as much as we Earthlings, will reflect on the fact that we both know that we both know we share a problem—how to communicate.

Consider again, therefore, the desirability of establishing symbolic/linguistic communication with ETI. It is helpful to review some parallels from human existence that pose problems for us today. One of these is "rock art," which consists of patterns or shapes cut into rock many thousands of years

---

12. W. H. Edmondson, "General Cognitive Principles," pp. 7–40.

Figure 15.1. An example of Northumbrian Rock Art. Three-dimensional scan produced by M. Lobb and H. Moulden *(IBM VISTA/University of Birmingham)*, used by permission and provided courtesy of V. Gaffney.

ago. Such ancient stone carvings can be found in many countries, and the example in Figure 15.1 is from Doddington Moor, Northumbria, England. We can say little, if anything, about what these patterns signify, why they were cut into rocks, or who created them. For all intents and purposes, they might have been made by aliens.[13] Unless we find a readable exegesis of them produced at the time they were made, we will never be able to say with certainty what the patterns mean.

The Voynich manuscript offers another parallel that may be helpful in understanding the difficulties with symbolic CETI. This 240-page vellum codex probably dates from the early 15th century and remains undeciphered despite many efforts to identify the script.[14] Whether or not the "writing" (see Figure 15.2) is in fact genuinely linguistic is still unclear; there are no convincing reasons to suppose the document is not a hoax. Intriguingly, one is under the impression that one can say some things about its context and possible content—the proposed date and format of the manuscript suggest the ravings of a secretive alchemist, but even the illustrations are not readily interpretable.

The Voynich manuscript illustrates how linguistic, or serial, organization of symbols can present an intractable problem for interpretation because of their arbitrariness and semiotic opacity. It would be unfortunate

---

13. One need only think of books by Immanuel Velikovsky or Erich von Däniken to see where that line of thinking can end up.

14. The Voynich manuscript (Beinecke MS 408) is held in the General Collection of the Beinecke Rare Book and Manuscript Library at Yale University. A digital facsimile of the entire manuscript is available online at *http://brbl-dl.library.yale.edu/vufind/Record/3519597*. For just two of many articles on this baffling artifact, see Betya Ungar-Sargon, "Cracking the Voynich Code," *Tablet*, 15 April 2013, available at *http://www.tabletmag.com/jewish-arts-and-culture/books/129131/cracking-the-voynich-code*; and Reed Johnson, "The Unread: The Mystery of the Voynich Manuscript," *The New Yorker*, 9 July 2013, available at *http://www.newyorker.com/online/blogs/books/2013/07/the-unread-the-mystery-of-the-voynich-manuscript.html*.

Figure 15.2. The Voynich Manuscript *(Beinecke MS 408)*, fol. 9ʳ, General Collection, Beinecke Rare Book and Manuscript Library, Yale University, New Haven, Connecticut.

and counterproductive if CETI were to become some sort of galactic encryption/decipherment exercise or challenge (or even game? how would we ever know?). Indeed, the situation might be even worse—a signaling system devoted to conveying arbitrary symbols could confuse would-be interlocutors by making it difficult for them to know whether they had accurately sorted out the protocol (content cannot be obviously distinguished from medium when both are essentially arbitrary). Furthermore, ETI's intention in sending messages must be understood for messaging to work. ETI and Earthlings both know this, and that the intention cannot successfully be communicated.

These considerations lead to another constraint: CETI can be neither linguistic nor based on any sort of symbol system. The requirements for successful decipherment cannot be established—there is no shared experience, location, or behavior, and there is no parallel text. So what are we left with?

Message Design

We have ruled out symbols, language, and systems based on sounds. The significance of the sequential imperative is that sequentially organized material is generally unsuitable because processing sequentially organized material will be a species-specific activity. Additionally, a focus on concepts shared through problem-solving endeavors (levers, wheels, etc.) exploits what we understand from distributed cognition, and similar concerns oblige us to think carefully about the intentions of any ETI communicating with us. In order to better understand the content of any extraterrestrial signal sent to us, we need to think about how we would construct a message.

I believe we should seek to transmit/receive images that contain task or conceptual material that does not *require* sequential interpretation (but which could be informative about sequencing). Furthermore, the intentionality must take us way beyond a cosmic "Hi there." We must craft a message along the following lines: "We, who look like this, are here, which looks like this, and we know about this sort of thing, which we think is the minimum you should be able to recognize and build on if we are to establish a dialogue of some sort." In other words, we should expect intelligences to think altruistically, in the sense of putting themselves in the situation of the intelligence who receives their messages. Altruism is not to be encoded *in* any message; it is the frame of mind that makes communication possible at all and is thus expressed by whatever system/message is deployed.

I propose that we transmit a three-color image—or rather several images— of our planet and its inhabitants, properties, and so on, arranged in a grid, rather like one of those postcards that offers several different images from the city or region one is visiting. Call this component of the transmission "Postcard Earth"; perhaps an ETI is sending out such postcard images. As a separate component, a monochrome diagram or diagrams that depict our galaxy and that require no sequential interpretation could be sent in tandem with the postcard signal.[15] This proposal is, of course, fanciful, but arguably less so than sending audio files or coded information about prime numbers.

Importantly, the selection and arrangement of the images is in part an aesthetic matter and known to be so because there is no comprehensive rational basis for such a selection. To be sure, one can rationally decide to show humans at different ages or to show some gross differences between species (swimmers, fliers, walkers, climbers, etc.); but subjective value judgments will ultimately have to be made, and this fact will be known to both parties.

"Postcard Earth" seems an attractive concept—to focus our minds as much as to encourage youngsters to study science in schools. Should we take it seriously? That we have not yet detected any signals from ETI may mean that we are not approaching the search in the right frame of mind. Or maybe they, like us, have yet to start systematic transmissions. Perhaps we have misunderstood the context for CETI?

Recontextualizing CETI

The foregoing discussion of constraints on what could constitute message construction (form and content) says little about message protocols or other relevant factors. Leaving those issues for others to explore, I will focus here on the context of CETI. It can be argued that SETI should proceed on principles unrelated to message construction.[16] Indeed, more recently it has been argued that SETI is probably most efficiently accomplished using extremely large optical telescopes, in an extension of the search for exoplanets.[17] An optical telescope of diameter 1,000 km could resolve an object of diameter 1 km at a distance of 100 light-years. Such a telescopic instrument (or its equivalent—for example, a device using aperture synthesis) is just about

---

15. The message/signal protocols are assumed to be unproblematic (e.g., scanning as in TV transmission or facsimile transmission is an obvious solution to sequencing the content, pixel by pixel, of an image).

16. Edmondson and Stevens, "The Utilization of Pulsars as SETI Beacons," pp. 231–271.

17. W. H. Edmondson, "Targets and SETI: Shared Motivations, Life Signatures and Asymmetric SETI," *Acta Astronautica* 67, nos. 11–12 (2010): 1410–1418.

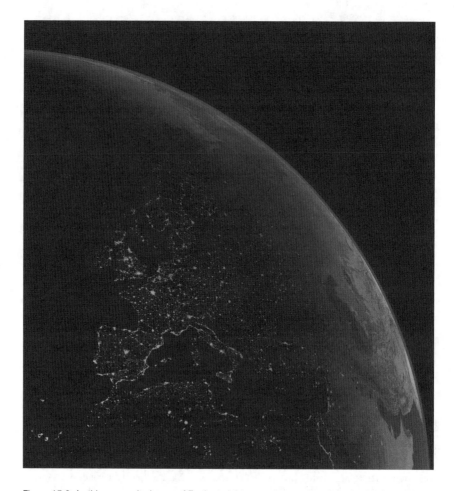

Figure 15.3. As this composite image of Earth at night suggests, our planet's emitted light could serve as a biomarker for extraterrestrial intelligence. The image was assembled from data collected by the Suomi National Polar-orbiting Partnership satellite in April 2012 and October 2012. *(NASA)*

feasible with today's technology—although it will be technically challenging and extremely costly. Figure 15.3 illustrates what such a telescope might be able to accomplish from perhaps as far as 100 parsecs away from us, assuming good weather on Earth.

The point of including this image here is simply to show that the presence of intelligent life-forms on such a planet is readily determined passively and from a considerable distance. The user (human or extraterrestrial) of such a telescope doesn't *need* to send or receive messages to know that it is not alone. In other words, CETI does not need to be predicated on the assumption that it is being used for discovery, for SETI itself.

CETI in the Context of a SETI Solution—I

An ETI, viewing the image opposite on its computer screens and knowing it is not alone, would still face all the CETI design problems discussed earlier. To be sure, spectroscopic analysis of the light sources on the landmasses in this figure would tell ETI something about our vision system and our technologies but not enough to resolve major issues in CETI.

We can put ourselves in ETI's position and imagine what we might do after having observed a planet with occupied landmasses. In such a situation the "Postcard Earth" approach is readily appreciated as having some merit. One small "scene" on the postcard could be an image such as that shown in Figure 15.3, and another could of course be our view of ETI's planet. The successful decoding of the postcard would be demonstrated by their recognition of a known image—a view of their planet from Earth's perspective. And, *mutatis mutandis*, we would be well placed to feel confident of message processing if we detected and processed an image that looked like Figure 15.3.

CETI in the Context of a SETI Solution—II

The last two issues addressed here will be the targets to be used for SETI and the time scale of effort. Both issues serve to flesh out CETI in its new context.

Targets: The debate within the SETI community on whether to look everywhere for anything or to target searches for specific reasons is ongoing, with strongly held views on both sides. My own endeavors focus on targeted searching.[18] However, if we assume an expanding exoplanet inventory, with increasing resources devoted to the "hunt" for Earth-like planets, then the refinement of a list of targets for SETI simply becomes a by-product of other science. Indeed, discovery of ETI may be accidental in this scenario.

Time scale: Both message transmission and signal searching (for a message or a beacon or a *we-are-here* signal of some sort) presume a considerable sociotechnical resolve—especially if conducted for SETI and without certainty of ETI's existence. Commitment of significant resources over extended periods of time for no immediately apparent benefit presents significant problems. On Earth we have evidence from large artifacts, such as Stonehenge and the Egyptian pyramids, that resource commitment is possible, although the benefits to the communities that created such monuments are still debated. In passing we might note, revisiting our earlier theme, that

---

18. Edmondson and Stevens, "The Utilization of Pulsars as SETI Beacons," pp. 231–271.

these artifacts still present considerable problems for modern science. While Stonehenge does demonstrate celestial alignments, its functionality is problematic. The construction of the pyramids presents challenges that today's engineers would struggle with even using current technologies—we simply don't know how they were built. These colossal constructions defy archaeology and anthropology—and they are in our backyards, so to speak, not a hundred light-years away!

But if we conjecture that CETI becomes interesting to society (ours or ETI's) only when we detect ETI through observation of exoplanets, then it becomes plausible to speculate that long-term human commitment can be made to sustaining technologies for both transmission and reception (Arecibo-scale equipment, for example, or powerful lasers coupled with optical telescopes). The design challenge remains, and "Postcard Earth" is just one of many possible solutions.

Conclusions

The lessons from archaeology and anthropology as filtered through modern work in cognitive science are simple. Communicating with intelligent terrestrial beings removed from us in time is deeply problematic. Understanding artifacts without any social context is deeply problematic—even when we have a good general understanding of the role of artifacts in society and in cognition. The recovery of the originators' intentions is deeply problematic, and without that information the interpretation of ancient artifacts is also deeply problematic.

The arguments presented above illustrate the theme of constraining message design for CETI. Perhaps the biggest constraint of all is a sociotechnical one: "Wait until you find ETI." The semiotic issues, the physical and biophysical uncertainties, the transmission protocol—all these problems remain after ETI is found. But motivation will increase immeasurably, and the constraints that humans now contend with will be refined, removed, or simply accepted as CETI is engaged.

Mirrors of Our Assumptions
Lessons from an Arthritic Neanderthal

Douglas A. Vakoch

Astrobiologists—those scientists studying the origins, prevalence, and distribution of life in the universe—share a common challenge with SETI scientists. They are both limited in the amount of observational data they can gather to test their theories. SETI researchers are separated from potential interlocutors by the vast distances between stars. Geologists studying other planets and moons within our solar system face a similar challenge, exploring other worlds through the proxy of spacecraft.

Even when we can go to other worlds, the amount of information we can gather continues to be severely restricted. The pair of Mars Exploration Rovers that landed on the red planet in 2004 were limited to exploring the vicinity of their landing sites. The rover Spirit traveled less than 5 miles before it went silent, and Opportunity traversed just over 20 miles in its first eight years on Mars. Though these distances far surpassed expectations for the vehicles, the total area covered nevertheless amounted to a tiny fraction of the planet's surface. Consequently, conclusions built on observations at these locations should be extrapolated to other regions only with the greatest caution.

A vivid reminder of the limitations of such "local knowledge" comes from NASA's Phoenix Mars Lander, a fixed craft that in 2008 explored the North Plains of Mars, an arctic region with unique conditions not previously examined by other landers. During the five months that Phoenix made observations from the surface of Mars, scientists encountered unexpected challenges in analyzing soil samples at its polar landing site, where soil clumped so readily it was difficult to get into the ovens designed to analyze the soil's chemical composition. Based on previously available observations, there was no hint that arctic soil on Mars would be "clingy."

As we move from understanding extraterrestrial geology to comprehending extraterrestrial cultures, additional challenges will undoubtedly arise, as noted in earlier chapters. By the nature of the instrumentation we use to process signals during SETI, we may well be able to detect distinctly artificial signals without being able to extract any information-rich messages

Figure Epilogue.1. NASA's Phoenix Mars Lander poised to deposit a soil sample into one of its ovens, where samples were heated to determine their chemical composition. *(NASA)*

embedded within those signals. We could know that extraterrestrials are out there but have no direct way of knowing much about them.

In a sense, we are faced with challenges akin to those of anthropologists who reconstruct extinct species from fragmentary evidence. Like SETI scientists, anthropologists are looking for evidence of other forms of intelligence; and in the best case scenario, they have only a fraction of the observational data they would like to have. What lessons might SETI scientists learn from them?

Reconstructing Neanderthals

Consider for a moment the challenges anthropologists faced in reconstructing *Homo neanderthalensis*, first discovered near Düsseldorf, Germany, in 1856. By the early 20th century, it was widely held that these now-extinct hominids were brutish in form. In 1924, for example, G. Elliot Smith described an "uncouth and repellent Neanderthal man" in his book *The Evolution of Man*: "His short, thick-set, and coarsely built body was carried in a half-stooping slouch upon short, powerful, and half-flexed legs of peculiarly ungraceful form."[1]

A few years earlier, Henry Fairfield Osborn had included illustrations of stooped Neanderthals in various editions of his book *Men of the Old Stone Age*, in which he portrayed Neanderthals as having "knees habitually bent forward without the power of straightening the joint or of standing fully erect" and hands deficient in fine motor control, lacking "the delicate play between the thumb and fingers characteristic of modern races."[2] Similarly, William L. Straus Jr. and A. J. E. Cave, in their 1957 article "Pathology and Posture of Neanderthal Man," described the stereotype of Neanderthals in the mid-20th century as follows:

> Neanderthal man is commonly pictured as but incompletely erect; as an almost hunchbacked creature with head thrust forward, knees habitually bent.... According to this view, he was a thoroughly unattractive fellow who was but imperfectly adapted to the upright, bipedal posture and locomotion characteristics of the modern type of man.[3]

But there is one critical problem with this account: anthropologists now believe Neanderthals walked upright. The turning point came with the article by Straus and Cave just quoted. After citing all of the same passages mentioned above that characterize Neanderthals as stooped, they argued convincingly that this portrait, accepted as typical of the entire species, in fact represented an individual Neanderthal who just happened to suffer from arthritis.

Central to this image of Neanderthal as brutish savage was the reconstruction of one especially complete skeleton, found in La Chapelle-aux-Saints, by French anatomist Marcellin Boule. Why did this particular skeleton play such a dominant role in determining our image of Neanderthals, when there were many other remains discovered elsewhere? The skeleton from

---

1. G. Elliot Smith, *The Evolution of Man* (London: Oxford University Press, 1924), as cited in William L. Straus, Jr., and A. J. E. Cave, "Pathology and Posture of Neanderthal Man," *Quarterly Review of Biology* 32, no. 4 (1957): 348–363, esp. p. 349.
2. Henry Fairfield Osborn, *Men of the Old Stone Age*, 3rd ed. (New York: Charles Scribner's Sons), as cited in Straus and Cave, "Pathology and Posture of Neanderthal Man," p. 349.
3. Straus and Cave, "Pathology and Posture of Neanderthal Man," p. 348.

La Chapelle-aux-Saints, it turns out, included a good sampling of vertebrae—bones essential to reconstructing a hominid's posture, and Boule's specimen provided a logical starting point for studying the gait of early hominids.

While the Neanderthal from La Chapelle-aux-Saints *may* have had the stooped posture characteristic of a modern-day human with arthritis, other Neanderthals did not. Moreover, the La Chapelle-aux-Saints Neanderthal did not resemble the illustrated figures in Osborn's book. Rather, Straus and Cave argued, "if he could be reincarnated and placed in a New York subway—provided that he were bathed, shaved, and dressed in modern clothing—it is doubtful whether he would attract any more attention than some of its other denizens."[4]

Compounding the fact that this particular Neanderthal had arthritis, Straus and Cave contended, was the widespread presupposition that Neanderthals were ancestral to all later hominids, rather than an independent line. Consequently, it would be natural to attribute to them more ape-like characteristics—a trap that many anthropologists fell into.

What lessons can SETI researchers learn from the reconstruction of Neanderthal posture?[5] Whether sampling Martian soil or analyzing Neanderthal bones, the conclusions we draw will depend on the observational data we have available. If we find a civilization on a planet circling a Sun-like star, we should be wary of assuming that it represents a typical extraterrestrial civilization. Rather, we should anticipate that this particular observation—this particular civilization—is influenced by a panoply of biological, cultural, and historical factors that we will be able to sort out only after many years, if ever.

Finally, recall that early anthropologists were influenced in their reconstructions of Neanderthals by their presupposition that Neanderthals represented a phase of development in the evolution of *Homo sapiens*. So, too, should we guard against imposing our own presuppositions on extraterrestrial civilizations, making our images of extraterrestrials not so much reflections of *their* true nature but rather mirrors of *our* assumptions.

---

4. Straus and Cave, "Pathology and Posture of Neanderthal Man," p. 359.

5. The reconstruction of Neanderthals based on the remains from La Chapelle-aux-Saints also gives us an important lesson on the role of the popular press in communicating scientific discoveries, providing an analogy for the journalistic response to the discovery of extraterrestrial intelligence. For more on the conflicting desires and images generated by the "Old Man from La Chapelle-aux-Saints," see Marianne Sommer, "Mirror, Mirror on the Wall: Neanderthal as Image and 'Distortion' in Early 20th-Century French Science and Press," *Social Studies of Science* 36, no. 2 (2006): 207–240.

ABOUT THE AUTHORS

Jerry Bentley, Ph.D., is Professor in the Department of History at the University of Hawai'i and editor of the *Journal of World History*. He has written extensively on the cultural history of early modern Europe and on cross-cultural interactions in world history. His research on the religious, moral, and political writings of the Renaissance led to the publication of *Humanists and Holy Writ: New Testament Scholarship in the Renaissance* (1983) and *Politics and Culture in Renaissance Naples* (1987). Bentley's more recent research has concentrated on global history and particularly on processes of cross-cultural interaction. His book *Old World Encounters: Cross-Cultural Contacts and Exchanges in Pre-Modern Times* (1993) studies processes of cultural exchange and religious conversion before modern times. His current interests include processes of cross-cultural interaction and cultural exchange in modern times.

John Billingham, B.M., B.Ch., was Senior Scientist and Trustee of the SETI Institute. He passed away on 3 August 2013, at the age of 83. From 1991 to 1994 he served as Chief of the NASA SETI Office at the Ames Research Center (ARC). Prior to that, he was Chief of the NASA ARC Life Sciences Division, Chief of the NASA ARC Extraterrestrial Research Division, Chief of the NASA ARC Biotechnology Division, and Chief of the NASA Johnson Space Center Environmental Physiology Branch. He also served as a Medical Officer in the Royal Air Force. Billingham was also the co-editor of *The Search for Extraterrestrial Intelligence: SETI* (1977) and *Social Implications of the Detection of an Extraterrestrial Civilization* (1999). In recognition of his contributions to the field of SETI research, the International Academy of Astronautics' SETI Permanent Committee established the annual Billingham Cutting-Edge Lecture in 2005.

Garry Chick, Ph.D., is Department Head and Professor of Recreation, Park, and Tourism Management, as well as Professor of Anthropology, at the Pennsylvania State University. His scholarly interests include cross-cultural research, research methods, and the relationship between culture and behavior, and his geographical specializations include Mesoamerica, China, and western Pennsylvania. Chick has co-edited *The Many Faces of Play* (1986) and *Diversions and Divergences in Fields of Play* (1998) and is a contributor to *A Handbook of Leisure Studies* (2006). He is a former president of the Society for Cross-Cultural Research, as well as a past president of the Association for the Study of Play. Chick has served as editor-in-chief of the journal *Leisure Sciences*, and he was founding editor of *Play & Culture* (now *Play and Culture Studies*).

Kathryn E. Denning, Ph.D., is Associate Professor in the Department of Anthropology at York University. Her research examines scholarly and popular ideas about Others, their relationships to us, and how we can know them. The Others she studies include the ancient (in archaeology), the animal (in zoos), and the alien (in SETI). In SETI, Denning studies scientists' reasoning processes, the technology and sites used to search the sky for signals, and ideas about how one might communicate with a radically different intelligence. She is a member of the International Academy of Astronautics' SETI Committee and has research projects with the NASA Astrobiology Institute.

Steven J. Dick, Ph.D., is currently serving a one-year appointment as the Baruch S. Blumberg NASA/Library of Congress Chair in Astrobiology at the Library of Congress's John W. Kluge Center. From 2011 to 2012 he held the Charles A. Lindbergh Chair in Aerospace History at the National Air and Space Museum. Dick served as the NASA Chief Historian and Director of the NASA History Office from 2003 to 2009 and, prior to that, as an astronomer and historian of science at the U.S. Naval Observatory for more than two decades. Among his books are *Plurality of Worlds: The Origins of the Extraterrestrial Life Debate from Democritus to Kant* (1982), *The Biological Universe: The Twentieth-Century Extraterrestrial Life Debate and the Limits of Science* (1996), *Life on Other Worlds* (1998), *Many Worlds: The New Universe, Extraterrestrial Life, and the Theological Implications* (2000), and *The Living Universe: NASA and the Development of Astrobiology* (2004). In 2006, Dick received the LeRoy E. Doggett Prize from the American Astronomical Society for a career that has significantly influenced the field of the history of astronomy. In 2009, minor planet 6544 Stevendick was named in his honor.

William H. Edmondson, Ph.D., is Honorary Senior Research Fellow at the University of Birmingham. His research interests include topics in linguistics, human-computer interaction, ubiquitous computing, and novel SETI search strategies and methods of data analysis. At the University of Birmingham he has been actively involved in the Artificial Intelligence and Cognitive Science Group, the Advanced Interaction Group, the Natural Language Processing Group, and the Linguistics Group. As former Admissions Tutor for Computer Science at the University of Birmingham, Edmondson was responsible for undergraduate admissions for one of the leading programs in computer science in the United Kingdom.

Ben Finney, Ph.D., is Professor Emeritus in the Department of Anthropology at the University of Hawai'i. His fieldwork has taken him throughout Polynesia and to Papua New Guinea, as well as to NASA's Johnson Space Center and Russia's Star City. His research involves testing reconstructed Polynesian voyaging canoes and methods of navigation on long ocean crossings to resolve issues concerning island discovery, settlement, and subsequent inter-island voyaging, as well as applying anthropological perspectives to SETI and to human exploration of and expansion into space. Finney's books include *Pacific Navigation and Voyaging* (1976), *Hokule'a: The Way to Tahiti* (1979), and *Interstellar Migration and the Human Experience* (1985), *From Sea to Space* (1992), and *Voyage of Rediscovery: A Cultural Odyssey Through Polynesia* (1994).

Stephen J. Garber, M.P.I.A., M.S., works in the NASA History Program Office, where he is responsible for editing multiple book projects, running the office's intern program, and maintaining its Web sites. He began his career at NASA in 1993 as a Presidential Management Intern in the Office of Space Science. He served as the acting head of the NASA History Office from 2002 to 2003 and again from 2009 to 2010. He has written on NASA's organizational culture, President Kennedy's attitudes toward space, the design of the Space Shuttle, and the Soviet Buran Space Shuttle and is currently finishing a policy history of NASA's Decadal Planning Team and President George W. Bush's Vision for Space Exploration. He also has written on intelligence history, international affairs, and defense policy He holds a bachelor's degree in politics from Brandeis University, a master's degree in public and international affairs from the University of Pittsburgh, and a master's degree in science and technology studies from the Virginia Polytechnic Institute and State University.

Albert A. Harrison, Ph.D., is Professor Emeritus in the Department of Psychology at the University of California, Davis. In addition to researching the societal dimensions of astrobiology and SETI, he studies human adaptation to spaceflight and spaceflight-analogous environments. Harrison's books include *Living Aloft: Human Requirements for Extended Spaceflight* (1985), and *From Antarctica to Outer Space: Life in Isolation and Confinement* (1991), *After Contact: The Human Response to Extraterrestrial Life* (1997), *Spacefaring: The Human Dimension* (2001), and *Starstruck: Cosmic Visions in Science, Religion, and Folklore* (2007).

Dominique Lestel, Ph.D., is Associate Professor at the École normale supérieure (ENS). A founding member of the Department of Cognitive Science at

ENS, Lestel is also a member of its Department of Philosophy. Since 1998, he also has been a researcher at the Muséum National d'Histoire Naturelle, where he became the Director of the Ethoecology and Cognitive Ethology Research Group of the Laboratory of Eco-anthropology and Ethnobiology. Lestel is developing a philosophical anthropology that maintains, first, that to be human is to establish particularly strong connections to other animals and, second, that new technologies could significantly improve these connections. His books include *L'animal singulier* (2004), and *Les grandes singes: L'humanité au fond des yeux* (2005), *Les animaux sont-ils intelligents?* (2006), *Les origines animales de la culture* (2009), *L'animal est l'avenir de l'homme* (2010), and *Apologie du carnivore* (2011).

Douglas Raybeck, Ph.D., is Professor Emeritus in the Department of Anthropology at Hamilton College as well as Visiting Lecturer in Anthropology at Amherst College. His research addresses topics ranging from nonverbal communication and psycholinguistics to physiological correlates of behavioral dispositions. He is an expert in future studies and has written a book titled *Looking Down the Road: A Systems Approach to Future Studies* (2000) on the topic. He has studied Malaysian culture and in 1996 published *Mad Dogs, Englishmen, and the Errant Anthropologist*, a book summarizing his fieldwork in Kelantan, Malaysia. Raybeck is co-editor of *Deviance: Anthropological Perspectives* (1991) and *Improving College Education of Veterans* (2010), as well as co-author of *Improving Student Memory* (1993) and *Improving Memory and Study Skills: Advances in Theory and Practice* (2002). He has been a Fellow at the National Institutes of Health and is past president of the Society for Cross-Cultural Research.

Richard Saint-Gelais, Ph.D., is Professor in the Department of Literature at the Université Laval, where his research and teaching focus on literary theory, 20th-century literature, and paraliterature. Following his work on the *Nouveau Roman*, Saint-Gelais examined the relationship between science fiction and modern fiction; more recently, he has explored the concept of transfictionality. Saint-Gelais is a member of the Interuniversity Research Center on Quebec Literature and Culture, and his books include *L'empire du pseudo: Modernités de la science-fiction* (1999), *Nouvelles tendances en théorie des genres* (1998), and *Fictions transfugés: La transfictionnalité et ses enjeux* (2011).

John W. Traphagan, Ph.D., is Professor of Religious Studies and a faculty affiliate of the Population Research Center at the University of Texas, Austin, where he also serves as Centennial Commission in the Liberal Arts Fellow. His research interests revolve around three primary areas: religion and society in Japan, medical ethics and medical anthropology, and anthropological approaches to religion. He is the author of *Rethinking Autonomy: A Critique of Principlism in Biomedical Ethics* (2013), *Taming Oblivion: Aging Bodies and the Fear of Senility in Japan* (2000), and *The Practice of Concern: Ritual, Well-Being, and Aging in Rural Japan* (2004). In addition, Traphagan has edited and co-edited a number of books on similar topics. In support of his research, Traphagan has received grants from the National Institutes of Health, the Wenner-Gren Foundation for Anthropological Research, the Social Science Research Council, the Association for Asian Studies, and the American Philosophical Society. In 2010 he was elected Secretary General of the Japan Anthropology Workshop.

Douglas A. Vakoch, Ph.D., is Director of Interstellar Message Composition at the SETI Institute, as well as Professor in the Department of Clinical Psychology at the California Institute of Integral Studies. He serves as chair of both the International Academy of Astronautics (IAA) Study Group on Interstellar Message Construction and the IAA Study Group on Active SETI: Scientific, Technical, Societal, and Legal Dimensions. Vakoch's books include *Communication with Extraterrestrial Intelligence* (2011), *Psychology of Space Exploration: Contemporary Research in Historical Perspective* (2011), *Ecofeminism and Rhetoric: Critical Perspectives on Sex, Technology, and Discourse* (2011), *Feminist Ecocriticism: Environment, Women, and Literature* (2012), *Astrobiology, History, and Society: Life Beyond Earth and the Impact of Discovery* (2013), *Altruism in Cross-Cultural Perspective* (2013), and *Extraterrestrial Altruism: Evolution and Ethics in the Cosmos* (2014).

Paul K. Wason, Ph.D., is Vice President of Life Sciences and Genetics at the John Templeton Foundation, where he develops new research initiatives on the fundamental nature and evolution of life and mind, especially as they intersect with meaning and purpose. Prior to joining the Templeton Foundation, he was Director of Foundations and Corporations at Bates College. In *The Archaeology of Rank* (1994), Wason examines social evolution, inequality, and archaeological theory.

THE NASA HISTORY SERIES

Reference Works, NASA SP-4000:

Grimwood, James M. *Project Mercury: A Chronology*. NASA SP-4001, 1963.

Grimwood, James M., and Barton C. Hacker, with Peter J. Vorzimmer. *Project Gemini Technology and Operations: A Chronology*. NASA SP-4002, 1969.

Link, Mae Mills. *Space Medicine in Project Mercury*. NASA SP-4003, 1965.

Astronautics and Aeronautics, 1963: Chronology of Science, Technology, and Policy. NASA SP-4004, 1964.

Astronautics and Aeronautics, 1964: Chronology of Science, Technology, and Policy. NASA SP-4005, 1965.

Astronautics and Aeronautics, 1965: Chronology of Science, Technology, and Policy. NASA SP-4006, 1966.

Astronautics and Aeronautics, 1966: Chronology of Science, Technology, and Policy. NASA SP-4007, 1967.

Astronautics and Aeronautics, 1967: Chronology of Science, Technology, and Policy. NASA SP-4008, 1968.

Ertel, Ivan D., and Mary Louise Morse. *The Apollo Spacecraft: A Chronology, Volume I, Through November 7, 1962*. NASA SP-4009, 1969.

Morse, Mary Louise, and Jean Kernahan Bays. *The Apollo Spacecraft: A Chronology, Volume II, November 8, 1962–September 30, 1964*. NASA SP-4009, 1973.

Brooks, Courtney G., and Ivan D. Ertel. *The Apollo Spacecraft: A Chronology, Volume III, October 1, 1964–January 20, 1966*. NASA SP-4009, 1973.

Ertel, Ivan D., and Roland W. Newkirk, with Courtney G. Brooks. *The Apollo Spacecraft: A Chronology, Volume IV, January 21, 1966–July 13, 1974*. NASA SP-4009, 1978.

Astronautics and Aeronautics, 1968: Chronology of Science, Technology, and Policy. NASA SP-4010, 1969.

Newkirk, Roland W., and Ivan D. Ertel, with Courtney G. Brooks. *Skylab: A Chronology*. NASA SP-4011, 1977.

Van Nimmen, Jane, and Leonard C. Bruno, with Robert L. Rosholt. *NASA Historical Data Book, Volume I: NASA Resources, 1958–1968*. NASA SP-4012, 1976; rep. ed. 1988.

Ezell, Linda Neuman. *NASA Historical Data Book, Volume II: Programs and Projects, 1958–1968*. NASA SP-4012, 1988.

Ezell, Linda Neuman. *NASA Historical Data Book, Volume III: Programs and Projects, 1969–1978*. NASA SP-4012, 1988.

Gawdiak, Ihor, with Helen Fedor. *NASA Historical Data Book, Volume IV: NASA Resources, 1969–1978*. NASA SP-4012, 1994.

Rumerman, Judy A. *NASA Historical Data Book, Volume V: NASA Launch Systems, Space Transportation, Human Spaceflight, and Space Science, 1979–1988*. NASA SP-4012, 1999.

Rumerman, Judy A. *NASA Historical Data Book, Volume VI: NASA Space Applications, Aeronautics and Space Research and Technology, Tracking and Data Acquisition/Support Operations, Commercial Programs, and Resources, 1979–1988*. NASA SP-4012, 1999.

Rumerman, Judy A. *NASA Historical Data Book, Volume VII: NASA Launch Systems, Space Transportation, Human Spaceflight, and Space Science, 1989–1998*. NASA SP-2009-4012, 2009.

Rumerman, Judy A. *NASA Historical Data Book, Volume VIII: NASA Earth Science and Space Applications, Aeronautics, Technology, and Exploration, Tracking and Data Acquisition/Space Operations, Facilities and Resources, 1989–1998*. NASA SP-2012-4012, 2012.

No SP-4013.

Astronautics and Aeronautics, 1969: Chronology of Science, Technology, and Policy. NASA SP-4014, 1970.

Astronautics and Aeronautics, 1970: Chronology of Science, Technology, and Policy. NASA SP-4015, 1972.

Astronautics and Aeronautics, 1971: Chronology of Science, Technology, and Policy. NASA SP-4016, 1972.

Astronautics and Aeronautics, 1972: Chronology of Science, Technology, and Policy. NASA SP-4017, 1974.

Astronautics and Aeronautics, 1973: Chronology of Science, Technology, and Policy. NASA SP-4018, 1975.

Astronautics and Aeronautics, 1974: Chronology of Science, Technology, and Policy. NASA SP-4019, 1977.

Astronautics and Aeronautics, 1975: Chronology of Science, Technology, and Policy. NASA SP-4020, 1979.

Astronautics and Aeronautics, 1976: Chronology of Science, Technology, and Policy. NASA SP-4021, 1984.

Astronautics and Aeronautics, 1977: Chronology of Science, Technology, and Policy. NASA SP-4022, 1986.

Astronautics and Aeronautics, 1978: Chronology of Science, Technology, and Policy. NASA SP-4023, 1986.

Astronautics and Aeronautics, 1979–1984: Chronology of Science, Technology, and Policy. NASA SP-4024, 1988.

Astronautics and Aeronautics, 1985: Chronology of Science, Technology, and Policy. NASA SP-4025, 1990.

Noordung, Hermann. *The Problem of Space Travel: The Rocket Motor.* Edited by Ernst Stuhlinger and J. D. Hunley, with Jennifer Garland. NASA SP-4026, 1995.

Gawdiak, Ihor Y., Ramon J. Miro, and Sam Stueland. *Astronautics and Aeronautics, 1986–1990: A Chronology.* NASA SP-4027, 1997.

Gawdiak, Ihor Y., and Charles Shetland. *Astronautics and Aeronautics, 1991–1995: A Chronology.* NASA SP-2000-4028, 2000.

Orloff, Richard W. *Apollo by the Numbers: A Statistical Reference.* NASA SP-2000-4029, 2000.

Lewis, Marieke, and Ryan Swanson. *Astronautics and Aeronautics: A Chronology, 1996–2000.* NASA SP-2009-4030, 2009.

Ivey, William Noel, and Marieke Lewis. *Astronautics and Aeronautics: A Chronology, 2001–2005.* NASA SP-2010-4031, 2010.

Buchalter, Alice R., and William Noel Ivey. *Astronautics and Aeronautics: A Chronology, 2006.* NASA SP-2011-4032, 2010.

Lewis, Marieke. *Astronautics and Aeronautics: A Chronology, 2007.* NASA SP-2011-4033, 2011.

Lewis, Marieke. *Astronautics and Aeronautics: A Chronology, 2008.* NASA SP-2012-4034, 2012.

Lewis, Marieke. *Astronautics and Aeronautics: A Chronology, 2009.* NASA SP-2012-4035, 2012.

Management Histories, NASA SP-4100:
Rosholt, Robert L. *An Administrative History of NASA, 1958–1963.* NASA SP-4101, 1966.

Levine, Arnold S. *Managing NASA in the Apollo Era.* NASA SP-4102, 1982.

Roland, Alex. *Model Research: The National Advisory Committee for Aeronautics, 1915–1958.* NASA SP-4103, 1985.

Fries, Sylvia D. *NASA Engineers and the Age of Apollo.* NASA SP-4104, 1992.

Glennan, T. Keith. *The Birth of NASA: The Diary of T. Keith Glennan.* Edited by J. D. Hunley. NASA SP-4105, 1993.

Seamans, Robert C. *Aiming at Targets: The Autobiography of Robert C. Seamans.* NASA SP-4106, 1996.

Garber, Stephen J., ed. *Looking Backward, Looking Forward: Forty Years of Human Spaceflight Symposium.* NASA SP-2002-4107, 2002.

Mallick, Donald L., with Peter W. Merlin. *The Smell of Kerosene: A Test Pilot's Odyssey.* NASA SP-4108, 2003.

Iliff, Kenneth W., and Curtis L. Peebles. *From Runway to Orbit: Reflections of a NASA Engineer.* NASA SP-2004-4109, 2004.

Chertok, Boris. *Rockets and People, Volume I.* NASA SP-2005-4110, 2005.

Chertok, Boris. *Rockets and People: Creating a Rocket Industry, Volume II.* NASA SP-2006-4110, 2006.

Chertok, Boris. *Rockets and People: Hot Days of the Cold War, Volume III.* NASA SP-2009-4110, 2009.

Chertok, Boris. *Rockets and People: The Moon Race, Volume IV.* NASA SP-2011-4110, 2011.

Laufer, Alexander, Todd Post, and Edward Hoffman. *Shared Voyage: Learning and Unlearning from Remarkable Projects.* NASA SP-2005-4111, 2005.

Dawson, Virginia P., and Mark D. Bowles. *Realizing the Dream of Flight: Biographical Essays in Honor of the Centennial of Flight, 1903–2003.* NASA SP-2005-4112, 2005.

Mudgway, Douglas J. *William H. Pickering: America's Deep Space Pioneer.* NASA SP-2008-4113, 2008.

Wright, Rebecca, Sandra Johnson, and Steven J. Dick. *NASA at 50: Interviews with NASA's Senior Leadership.* NASA SP-2012-4114, 2012.

Project Histories, NASA SP-4200:

Swenson, Loyd S., Jr., James M. Grimwood, and Charles C. Alexander. *This New Ocean: A History of Project Mercury*. NASA SP-4201, 1966; rep. ed. 1999.

Green, Constance McLaughlin, and Milton Lomask. *Vanguard: A History*. NASA SP-4202, 1970; rep. ed. Smithsonian Institution Press, 1971.

Hacker, Barton C., and James M. Grimwood. *On the Shoulders of Titans: A History of Project Gemini*. NASA SP-4203, 1977; rep. ed. 2002.

Benson, Charles D., and William Barnaby Faherty. *Moonport: A History of Apollo Launch Facilities and Operations*. NASA SP-4204, 1978.

Brooks, Courtney G., James M. Grimwood, and Loyd S. Swenson, Jr. *Chariots for Apollo: A History of Manned Lunar Spacecraft*. NASA SP-4205, 1979.

Bilstein, Roger E. *Stages to Saturn: A Technological History of the Apollo/Saturn Launch Vehicles*. NASA SP-4206, 1980 and 1996.

No SP-4207.

Compton, W. David, and Charles D. Benson. *Living and Working in Space: A History of Skylab*. NASA SP-4208, 1983.

Ezell, Edward Clinton, and Linda Neuman Ezell. *The Partnership: A History of the Apollo-Soyuz Test Project*. NASA SP-4209, 1978.

Hall, R. Cargill. *Lunar Impact: A History of Project Ranger*. NASA SP-4210, 1977.

Newell, Homer E. *Beyond the Atmosphere: Early Years of Space Science*. NASA SP-4211, 1980.

Ezell, Edward Clinton, and Linda Neuman Ezell. *On Mars: Exploration of the Red Planet, 1958–1978*. NASA SP-4212, 1984.

Pitts, John A. *The Human Factor: Biomedicine in the Manned Space Program to 1980*. NASA SP-4213, 1985.

Compton, W. David. *Where No Man Has Gone Before: A History of Apollo Lunar Exploration Missions*. NASA SP-4214, 1989.

Naugle, John E. *First Among Equals: The Selection of NASA Space Science Experiments*. NASA SP-4215, 1991.

Wallace, Lane E. *Airborne Trailblazer: Two Decades with NASA Langley's 737 Flying Laboratory*. NASA SP-4216, 1994.

Butrica, Andrew J., ed. *Beyond the Ionosphere: Fifty Years of Satellite Communications*. NASA SP-4217, 1997.

Butrica, Andrew J. *To See the Unseen: A History of Planetary Radar Astronomy*. NASA SP-4218, 1996.

Mack, Pamela E., ed. *From Engineering Science to Big Science: The NACA and NASA Collier Trophy Research Project Winners*. NASA SP-4219, 1998.

Reed, R. Dale. *Wingless Flight: The Lifting Body Story*. NASA SP-4220, 1998.

Heppenheimer, T. A. *The Space Shuttle Decision: NASA's Search for a Reusable Space Vehicle*. NASA SP-4221, 1999.

Hunley, J. D., ed. *Toward Mach 2: The Douglas D-558 Program*. NASA SP-4222, 1999.

Swanson, Glen E., ed. *"Before This Decade Is Out…" Personal Reflections on the Apollo Program*. NASA SP-4223, 1999.

Tomayko, James E. *Computers Take Flight: A History of NASA's Pioneering Digital Fly-By-Wire Project*. NASA SP-4224, 2000.

Morgan, Clay. *Shuttle-Mir: The United States and Russia Share History's Highest Stage*. NASA SP-2001-4225, 2001.

Leary, William M. *"We Freeze to Please": A History of NASA's Icing Research Tunnel and the Quest for Safety*. NASA SP-2002-4226, 2002.

Mudgway, Douglas J. *Uplink-Downlink: A History of the Deep Space Network, 1957–1997*. NASA SP-2001-4227, 2001.

No SP-4228 or SP-4229.

Dawson, Virginia P., and Mark D. Bowles. *Taming Liquid Hydrogen: The Centaur Upper Stage Rocket, 1958–2002*. NASA SP-2004-4230, 2004.

Meltzer, Michael. *Mission to Jupiter: A History of the Galileo Project*. NASA SP-2007-4231, 2007.

Heppenheimer, T. A. *Facing the Heat Barrier: A History of Hypersonics*. NASA SP-2007-4232, 2007.

Tsiao, Sunny. *"Read You Loud and Clear!" The Story of NASA's Spaceflight Tracking and Data Network*. NASA SP-2007-4233, 2007.

Meltzer, Michael. *When Biospheres Collide: A History of NASA's Planetary Protection Programs*. NASA SP-2011-4234, 2011.

Center Histories, NASA SP-4300:
Rosenthal, Alfred. *Venture into Space: Early Years of Goddard Space Flight Center*. NASA SP-4301, 1985.

Hartman, Edwin P. *Adventures in Research: A History of Ames Research Center, 1940–1965*. NASA SP-4302, 1970.

Hallion, Richard P. *On the Frontier: Flight Research at Dryden, 1946–1981*. NASA SP-4303, 1984.

Muenger, Elizabeth A. *Searching the Horizon: A History of Ames Research Center, 1940–1976*. NASA SP-4304, 1985.

Hansen, James R. *Engineer in Charge: A History of the Langley Aeronautical Laboratory, 1917–1958*. NASA SP-4305, 1987.

Dawson, Virginia P. *Engines and Innovation: Lewis Laboratory and American Propulsion Technology*. NASA SP-4306, 1991.

Dethloff, Henry C. *"Suddenly Tomorrow Came…": A History of the Johnson Space Center, 1957–1990*. NASA SP-4307, 1993.

Hansen, James R. *Spaceflight Revolution: NASA Langley Research Center from Sputnik to Apollo.* NASA SP-4308, 1995.

Wallace, Lane E. *Flights of Discovery: An Illustrated History of the Dryden Flight Research Center.* NASA SP-4309, 1996.

Herring, Mack R. *Way Station to Space: A History of the John C. Stennis Space Center.* NASA SP-4310, 1997.

Wallace, Harold D., Jr. *Wallops Station and the Creation of an American Space Program.* NASA SP-4311, 1997.

Wallace, Lane E. *Dreams, Hopes, Realities. NASA's Goddard Space Flight Center: The First Forty Years.* NASA SP-4312, 1999.

Dunar, Andrew J., and Stephen P. Waring. *Power to Explore: A History of Marshall Space Flight Center, 1960–1990.* NASA SP-4313, 1999.

Bugos, Glenn E. *Atmosphere of Freedom: Sixty Years at the NASA Ames Research Center.* NASA SP-2000-4314, 2000.

No SP-4315.

Schultz, James. *Crafting Flight: Aircraft Pioneers and the Contributions of the Men and Women of NASA Langley Research Center.* NASA SP-2003-4316, 2003.

Bowles, Mark D. *Science in Flux: NASA's Nuclear Program at Plum Brook Station, 1955–2005.* NASA SP-2006-4317, 2006.

Wallace, Lane E. *Flights of Discovery: An Illustrated History of the Dryden Flight Research Center.* NASA SP-2007-4318, 2007. Revised version of NASA SP-4309.

Arrighi, Robert S. *Revolutionary Atmosphere: The Story of the Altitude Wind Tunnel and the Space Power Chambers.* NASA SP-2010-4319, 2010.

Bugos, Glenn E. *Atmosphere of Freedom: Seventy Years at the NASA Ames Research Center.* NASA SP-2010-4314, 2010. Revised Version of NASA SP-2000-4314.

General Histories, NASA SP-4400:

Corliss, William R. *NASA Sounding Rockets, 1958–1968: A Historical Summary.* NASA SP-4401, 1971.

Wells, Helen T., Susan H. Whiteley, and Carrie Karegeannes. *Origins of NASA Names.* NASA SP-4402, 1976.

Anderson, Frank W., Jr. *Orders of Magnitude: A History of NACA and NASA, 1915–1980.* NASA SP-4403, 1981.

Sloop, John L. *Liquid Hydrogen as a Propulsion Fuel, 1945–1959.* NASA SP-4404, 1978.

Roland, Alex. *A Spacefaring People: Perspectives on Early Spaceflight.* NASA SP-4405, 1985.

Bilstein, Roger E. *Orders of Magnitude: A History of the NACA and NASA, 1915–1990.* NASA SP-4406, 1989.

Logsdon, John M., ed., with Linda J. Lear, Jannelle Warren Findley, Ray A. Williamson, and Dwayne A. Day. *Exploring the Unknown: Selected Documents in the History of the U.S. Civil Space Program, Volume I: Organizing for Exploration.* NASA SP-4407, 1995.

Logsdon, John M., ed., with Dwayne A. Day and Roger D. Launius. *Exploring the Unknown: Selected Documents in the History of the U.S. Civil Space Program, Volume II: External Relationships.* NASA SP-4407, 1996.

Logsdon, John M., ed., with Roger D. Launius, David H. Onkst, and Stephen J. Garber. *Exploring the Unknown: Selected Documents in the History of the U.S. Civil Space Program, Volume III: Using Space.* NASA SP-4407, 1998.

Logsdon, John M., ed., with Ray A. Williamson, Roger D. Launius, Russell J. Acker, Stephen J. Garber, and Jonathan L. Friedman. *Exploring the Unknown: Selected Documents in the History of the U.S. Civil Space Program, Volume IV: Accessing Space.* NASA SP-4407, 1999.

Logsdon, John M., ed., with Amy Paige Snyder, Roger D. Launius, Stephen J. Garber, and Regan Anne Newport. *Exploring the Unknown:*

Selected Documents in the History of the U.S. Civil Space Program, Volume V: Exploring the Cosmos. NASA SP-2001-4407, 2001.

Logsdon, John M., ed., with Stephen J. Garber, Roger D. Launius, and Ray A. Williamson. *Exploring the Unknown: Selected Documents in the History of the U.S. Civil Space Program, Volume VI: Space and Earth Science.* NASA SP-2004-4407, 2004.

Logsdon, John M., ed., with Roger D. Launius. *Exploring the Unknown: Selected Documents in the History of the U.S. Civil Space Program, Volume VII: Human Spaceflight: Projects Mercury, Gemini, and Apollo.* NASA SP-2008-4407, 2008.

Siddiqi, Asif A., *Challenge to Apollo: The Soviet Union and the Space Race, 1945–1974.* NASA SP-2000-4408, 2000.

Hansen, James R., ed. *The Wind and Beyond: Journey into the History of Aerodynamics in America, Volume 1: The Ascent of the Airplane.* NASA SP-2003-4409, 2003.

Hansen, James R., ed. *The Wind and Beyond: Journey into the History of Aerodynamics in America, Volume 2: Reinventing the Airplane.* NASA SP-2007-4409, 2007.

Hogan, Thor. *Mars Wars: The Rise and Fall of the Space Exploration Initiative.* NASA SP-2007-4410, 2007.

Vakoch, Douglas A., ed. *Psychology of Space Exploration: Contemporary Research in Historical Perspective.* NASA SP-2011-4411, 2011.

Monographs in Aerospace History, NASA SP-4500:

Launius, Roger D., and Aaron K. Gillette, comps. *Toward a History of the Space Shuttle: An Annotated Bibliography.* Monographs in Aerospace History, No. 1, 1992.

Launius, Roger D., and J. D. Hunley, comps. *An Annotated Bibliography of the Apollo Program.* Monographs in Aerospace History, No. 2, 1994.

Launius, Roger D. *Apollo: A Retrospective Analysis.* Monographs in Aerospace History, No. 3, 1994.

Hansen, James R. *Enchanted Rendezvous: John C. Houbolt and the Genesis of the Lunar-Orbit Rendezvous Concept*. Monographs in Aerospace History, No. 4, 1995.

Gorn, Michael H. *Hugh L. Dryden's Career in Aviation and Space*. Monographs in Aerospace History, No. 5, 1996.

Powers, Sheryll Goecke. *Women in Flight Research at NASA Dryden Flight Research Center from 1946 to 1995*. Monographs in Aerospace History, No. 6, 1997.

Portree, David S. F., and Robert C. Trevino. *Walking to Olympus: An EVA Chronology*. Monographs in Aerospace History, No. 7, 1997.

Logsdon, John M., moderator. *Legislative Origins of the National Aeronautics and Space Act of 1958: Proceedings of an Oral History Workshop*. Monographs in Aerospace History, No. 8, 1998.

Rumerman, Judy A., comp. *U.S. Human Spaceflight: A Record of Achievement, 1961–1998*. Monographs in Aerospace History, No. 9, 1998.

Portree, David S. F. *NASA's Origins and the Dawn of the Space Age*. Monographs in Aerospace History, No. 10, 1998.

Logsdon, John M. *Together in Orbit: The Origins of International Cooperation in the Space Station*. Monographs in Aerospace History, No. 11, 1998.

Phillips, W. Hewitt. *Journey in Aeronautical Research: A Career at NASA Langley Research Center*. Monographs in Aerospace History, No. 12, 1998.

Braslow, Albert L. *A History of Suction-Type Laminar-Flow Control with Emphasis on Flight Research*. Monographs in Aerospace History, No. 13, 1999.

Logsdon, John M., moderator. *Managing the Moon Program: Lessons Learned from Apollo*. Monographs in Aerospace History, No. 14, 1999.

Perminov, V. G. *The Difficult Road to Mars: A Brief History of Mars Exploration in the Soviet Union.* Monographs in Aerospace History, No. 15, 1999.

Tucker, Tom. *Touchdown: The Development of Propulsion Controlled Aircraft at NASA Dryden.* Monographs in Aerospace History, No. 16, 1999.

Maisel, Martin, Demo J. Giulanetti, and Daniel C. Dugan. *The History of the XV-15 Tilt Rotor Research Aircraft: From Concept to Flight.* Monographs in Aerospace History, No. 17, 2000. NASA SP-2000-4517.

Jenkins, Dennis R. *Hypersonics Before the Shuttle: A Concise History of the X-15 Research Airplane.* Monographs in Aerospace History, No. 18, 2000. NASA SP-2000-4518.

Chambers, Joseph R. *Partners in Freedom: Contributions of the Langley Research Center to U.S. Military Aircraft of the 1990s.* Monographs in Aerospace History, No. 19, 2000. NASA SP-2000-4519.

Waltman, Gene L. *Black Magic and Gremlins: Analog Flight Simulations at NASA's Flight Research Center.* Monographs in Aerospace History, No. 20, 2000. NASA SP-2000-4520.

Portree, David S. F. *Humans to Mars: Fifty Years of Mission Planning, 1950–2000.* Monographs in Aerospace History, No. 21, 2001. NASA SP-2001-4521.

Thompson, Milton O., with J. D. Hunley. *Flight Research: Problems Encountered and What They Should Teach Us.* Monographs in Aerospace History, No. 22, 2001. NASA SP-2001-4522.

Tucker, Tom. *The Eclipse Project.* Monographs in Aerospace History, No. 23, 2001. NASA SP-2001-4523.

Siddiqi, Asif A. *Deep Space Chronicle: A Chronology of Deep Space and Planetary Probes, 1958–2000.* Monographs in Aerospace History, No. 24, 2002. NASA SP-2002-4524.

Merlin, Peter W. *Mach 3+: NASA/USAF YF-12 Flight Research, 1969–1979.* Monographs in Aerospace History, No. 25, 2001. NASA SP-2001-4525.

Anderson, Seth B. *Memoirs of an Aeronautical Engineer: Flight Tests at Ames Research Center: 1940–1970.* Monographs in Aerospace History, No. 26, 2002. NASA SP-2002-4526.

Renstrom, Arthur G. *Wilbur and Orville Wright: A Bibliography Commemorating the One-Hundredth Anniversary of the First Powered Flight on December 17, 1903.* Monographs in Aerospace History, No. 27, 2002. NASA SP-2002-4527.

No monograph 28.

Chambers, Joseph R. *Concept to Reality: Contributions of the NASA Langley Research Center to U.S. Civil Aircraft of the 1990s.* Monographs in Aerospace History, No. 29, 2003. NASA SP-2003-4529.

Peebles, Curtis, ed. *The Spoken Word: Recollections of Dryden History, The Early Years.* Monographs in Aerospace History, No. 30, 2003. NASA SP-2003-4530.

Jenkins, Dennis R., Tony Landis, and Jay Miller. *American X-Vehicles: An Inventory—X-1 to X-50.* Monographs in Aerospace History, No. 31, 2003. NASA SP-2003-4531.

Renstrom, Arthur G. *Wilbur and Orville Wright: A Chronology Commemorating the One-Hundredth Anniversary of the First Powered Flight on December 17, 1903.* Monographs in Aerospace History, No. 32, 2003. NASA SP-2003-4532.

Bowles, Mark D., and Robert S. Arrighi. *NASA's Nuclear Frontier: The Plum Brook Research Reactor.* Monographs in Aerospace History, No. 33, 2004. NASA SP-2004-4533.

Wallace, Lane, and Christian Gelzer. *Nose Up: High Angle-of-Attack and Thrust Vectoring Research at NASA Dryden, 1979–2001.* Monographs in Aerospace History, No. 34, 2009. NASA SP-2009-4534.

Matranga, Gene J., C. Wayne Ottinger, Calvin R. Jarvis, and D. Christian Gelzer. *Unconventional, Contrary, and Ugly: The Lunar Landing Research Vehicle*. Monographs in Aerospace History, No. 35, 2006. NASA SP-2004-4535.

McCurdy, Howard E. *Low-Cost Innovation in Spaceflight: The History of the Near Earth Asteroid Rendezvous (NEAR) Mission*. Monographs in Aerospace History, No. 36, 2005. NASA SP-2005-4536.

Seamans, Robert C., Jr. *Project Apollo: The Tough Decisions*. Monographs in Aerospace History, No. 37, 2005. NASA SP-2005-4537.

Lambright, W. Henry. *NASA and the Environment: The Case of Ozone Depletion*. Monographs in Aerospace History, No. 38, 2005. NASA SP-2005-4538.

Chambers, Joseph R. *Innovation in Flight: Research of the NASA Langley Research Center on Revolutionary Advanced Concepts for Aeronautics*. Monographs in Aerospace History, No. 39, 2005. NASA SP-2005-4539.

Phillips, W. Hewitt. *Journey into Space Research: Continuation of a Career at NASA Langley Research Center*. Monographs in Aerospace History, No. 40, 2005. NASA SP-2005-4540.

Rumerman, Judy A., Chris Gamble, and Gabriel Okolski, comps. *U.S. Human Spaceflight: A Record of Achievement, 1961–2006*. Monographs in Aerospace History, No. 41, 2007. NASA SP-2007-4541.

Peebles, Curtis. *The Spoken Word: Recollections of Dryden History Beyond the Sky*. Monographs in Aerospace History, No. 42, 2011. NASA SP-2011-4542.

Dick, Steven J., Stephen J. Garber, and Jane H. Odom. *Research in NASA History*. Monographs in Aerospace History, No. 43, 2009. NASA SP-2009-4543.

Merlin, Peter W. *Ikhana: Unmanned Aircraft System Western States Fire Missions*. Monographs in Aerospace History, No. 44, 2009. NASA SP-2009-4544.

Fisher, Steven C., and Shamim A. Rahman. *Remembering the Giants: Apollo Rocket Propulsion Development*. Monographs in Aerospace History, No. 45, 2009. NASA SP-2009-4545.

Gelzer, Christian. *Fairing Well: From Shoebox to Bat Truck and Beyond, Aerodynamic Truck Research at NASA's Dryden Flight Research Center*. Monographs in Aerospace History, No. 46, 2011. NASA SP-2011-4546.

Arrighi, Robert. *Pursuit of Power: NASA's Propulsion Systems Laboratory No. 1 and 2*. Monographs in Aerospace History, No. 48, 2012. NASA SP-2012-4548.

Goodrich, Malinda K., Alice R. Buchalter, and Patrick M. Miller, comps. *Toward a History of the Space Shuttle: An Annotated Bibliography, Part 2 (1992–2011)*. Monographs in Aerospace History, No. 49, 2012. NASA SP-2012-4549.

Electronic Media, NASA SP-4600:
Remembering Apollo 11: The 30th Anniversary Data Archive CD-ROM. NASA SP-4601, 1999.

Remembering Apollo 11: The 35th Anniversary Data Archive CD-ROM. NASA SP-2004-4601, 2004. This is an update of the 1999 edition.

The Mission Transcript Collection: U.S. Human Spaceflight Missions from Mercury Redstone 3 to Apollo 17. NASA SP-2000-4602, 2001.

Shuttle-Mir: The United States and Russia Share History's Highest Stage. NASA SP-2001-4603, 2002.

U.S. Centennial of Flight Commission Presents Born of Dreams—Inspired by Freedom. NASA SP-2004-4604, 2004.

Of Ashes and Atoms: A Documentary on the NASA Plum Brook Reactor Facility. NASA SP-2005-4605, 2005.

Taming Liquid Hydrogen: The Centaur Upper Stage Rocket Interactive CD-ROM. NASA SP-2004-4606, 2004.

Fueling Space Exploration: The History of NASA's Rocket Engine Test Facility DVD. NASA SP-2005-4607, 2005.

Altitude Wind Tunnel at NASA Glenn Research Center: An Interactive History CD-ROM. NASA SP-2008-4608, 2008.

A Tunnel Through Time: The History of NASA's Altitude Wind Tunnel. NASA SP-2010-4609, 2010.

Conference Proceedings, NASA SP-4700:
Dick, Steven J., and Keith Cowing, eds. *Risk and Exploration: Earth, Sea and the Stars*. NASA SP-2005-4701, 2005.

Dick, Steven J., and Roger D. Launius. *Critical Issues in the History of Spaceflight*. NASA SP-2006-4702, 2006.

Dick, Steven J., ed. *Remembering the Space Age: Proceedings of the 50th Anniversary Conference*. NASA SP-2008-4703, 2008.

Dick, Steven J., ed. *NASA's First 50 Years: Historical Perspectives*. NASA SP-2010-4704, 2010.

Societal Impact, NASA SP-4800:
Dick, Steven J., and Roger D. Launius. *Societal Impact of Spaceflight*. NASA SP-2007-4801, 2007.

Dick, Steven J., and Mark L. Lupisella. *Cosmos and Culture: Cultural Evolution in a Cosmic Context*. NASA SP-2009-4802, 2009.

INDEX

Numbers in **bold** indicate pages with photos and tables.

A

Abduction, 84–85, 85n8, 94

Acta Astronautica, 16, 59, 69

Active SETI: control over messages sent, 187–88; definition and concept of, xxv, 101, 175–76; design and subject of messages, 140, 176–185; KEO satellite project, xxvi, 185, 188, 189–190; opinions and concerns about, 185–89. *See also* Messaging extraterrestrial intelligence (METI).

Adams, Jim, 4

Adovasio, James, 122

Advanced Solid Rocket Motor program, 38

Aesthetics, 161–62

Africa, 226

After Contact (Harrison), 60

Agency: human agency detection device, 128; inferring agency and archaeology, 113–14; recognition of intentional and purposeful, 117–18, 127–29

Air Force, U.S., Allen Telescope Array use by, 43, 43n66, 47

Alberts, Bruce, 45n74

Aldrovandi, Ulisse, 117

Alexander, Richard, 215

Allen, Paul, 41–42

Allen Telescope Array (ATA), 6, 42–43, 43n66, 47

Alphabets, 85

Altruism, 82, 170, 246

Ambartsumian, Viktor, 2–3

American Anthropological Association (AAA) conferences, xiv–xv, xv n2, 55, 61

American Society of Engineering Education, 4

Americas: Central Civilization, 226; Columbus's arrival in, 100; dating of archaeological sites in, 121–22

Ames Research Center: Biotechnology Division, 3; Committee on Interstellar Communications, 6; Engineering Systems Design, Summer Faculty Fellowship Program, 4–5; Exobiology Division, 3, 8, 8n15, 13; funding for SETI, 6, 9, 10–11, 12; interstellar communication lecture series, 4; as lead Center for SETI, 12, 26, 53–54; Life Sciences Division, 4, 14; Mark role at, 4; mission of, 3–4; NASA Astrobiology Institute, 46, 46n77; Science Workshops on SETI, 6–8, 54; SETI Science Working Group, 9–10. *See also* NASA SETI Program.

Animals: communication of, xxviii, 213–14, 237–38; ecological dominance, 215n28; evolution of, 54, 214–15, 226–27; genetic similarities between humans and, 230; hive intelligence, 218; intelligence of, 213–14, 237–38; physiological senses, 232; study of communication of, xxviii

Anthropology: analogy to SETI research, xiv, xxii–xxv, 51, 60–61, 99, 131–33, 144, 252; armchair and distant research, 131, 132, 134, 136–141;

O

Z

G**P**O ☆ U.S. GOVERNMENT PRINTING OFFICE : 2014 – 383-439/00030